image ® COMICS PRESENTS

BY SCOTT R. KURTZ

Collecting issues 1-6 of PvP, Vol. 2
Originally published by Image Comics

FOR IMAGE COMICS

Erik Larsen - Publisher
Todd McFarlane - President
Marc Silvestri - CEO
Jim Valentino - Vice President
Eric Stephenson - Executive Director
Jim Demonakos - PR & Marketing Coordinator
Mia MacHatton - Accounts Manager
Laurenn McCubbin - Art Director
Allen Hui - Production Artist
Joe Keatinge - Traffic Manager
Jonathan Chan - Production Assistant
Drew Gill - Production Assistant
Traci Hui - Administrative Assistant

www.imagecomics.com

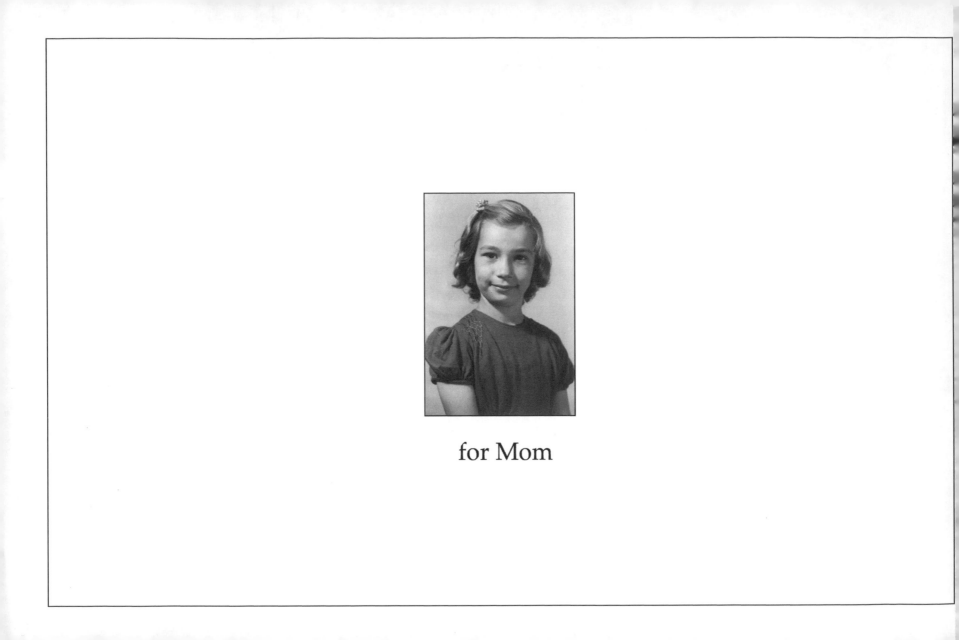

for Mom

· I N T R O D U C T I O N ·

I'm not a gamer. I tried to be a gamer once. You know, bought a system and 20 games for it as well as another 30 for my computer —- I was multi-platform, baby. I even bought a multi-user license for one of the first networked games on the Macintosh. We'd sneak into work and play after hours on the "performance" systems of the day. In my early thirties, a buddy and I were once branded nerds by teenage girls at a Blockbuster for renting "Nofriendo" games. It all feels so quaint now. But you know what? It was all so quaint then.

You see, I didn't inhale. I was, as Skull says, a poser.

So why do I like a comic strip about gamers and gaming so much? It's simple. PVP is funny and it has great characters. Cole is like a surrogate parent for the employees of Player vs. Player Magazine. Brent is the everyman (well, okay the Macintosh-using version) and Jade is, um, well, Jade is smart.*

Scott Kurtz's PVP is a well-crafted endeavor. He is as good a writer as he is a fine artist. You'll quickly find that out for yourself. And this is the kind of book that you want to keep reading. The characters really are that much fun.

*Smart is french for "hot."

But let's not forget that this is daily online comic strip that's now published in comic book form. Being free of the Orwellian rules of taste (aka daily newspaper syndication), Scott can tread where the rest of us can't -- in the real world. The tone of PVP reflects our current culture better than most strips in syndication. As the creator of a syndicated daily comic strip, I envy Scott's position.

So take the time to read the manual for Scott Kurtz's PVP comic strip (that would be this book, stay with me here). Whether you're a gamer or not, you're going to love it.

Michael Jantze
Creator, The Norm

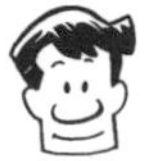

· THE HISTORY OF PVP ·

It all started back in 1997. I had all but given up on my dream of becoming a nationally syndicated cartoonist and let the dust start to gather on my drawing table. I turned my attention to other time-wasting activities; namely....video games.

I got hooked on a new addiction called MASSIVELY MULTIPLAYER ONLINE GAMES (or Massmogs for short). Huge communities grew around these games with dedicated websites and message boards. We would gather in real life to meet in person those whom we had been slaying dragons with in the virtual world.

It wasn't long before the requests came in for me to draw cartoons about our online exploits. The cartoons would be circulated around the internet and slowly but surely a demand for more grew.

I made my first website in late 1997 featuring my video game cartoons. The site was linked by all the major communities. It was a hit and the best part was, I was cartooning again.

One of the larger sites dedicated to these games offered me a chance to get paid for my work. They were actually willing to pay for the privilege of having my cartoons appear on their website. I leapt at the opportunity to finally be a paid, professional cartoonist.

PvP first appeared on the web on May 4th, 1998. We only had a couple hundred readers, but that number grew fast. By 2000, PvP had over 3 million monthly pageviews and I was earning enough money to quit my day job and make cartooning my full time gig.

As this book goes to print, PvP is viewed on the web daily by over 100,000 people at **www.pvponline.com**. We receive over 12 million pageviews a month and have a monthly comic book published by Image Comics.

I hope you enjoy this book and join us on the web every day for more fun with the PvP gang.

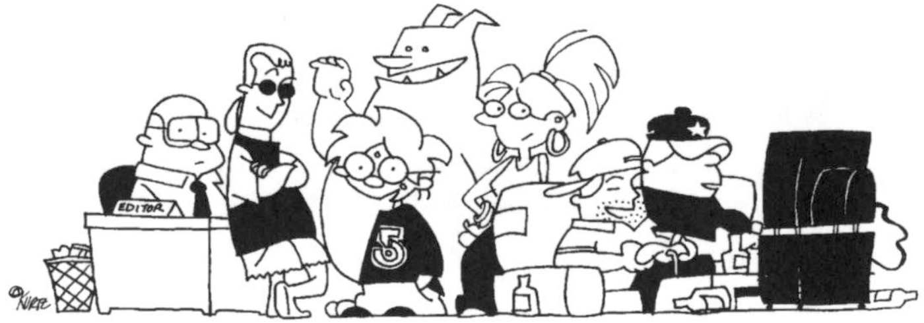
EDITOR
5

The first drawing I did of the PvP staff.

CHOOSE YOUR PLAYER

COLE RICHARDS
Editor in Chief

SPECIAL MOVE:
Assign Overtime.

The glue that holds PvP together, Cole tries to retain a small semblance of sanity amidst the chaos of his employees. This makes him an obvious target. Confused and disturbed by the latest computer game releases, Cole is happiest playing classic 80's arcade game emulators on his computer.

BRENT SIENNA
Creative Director

SPECIAL MOVE:
Caffeine Rage

Brent has little time to play computer games, however he always finds time to mock those who do. Pretentious and pompous, Brent is the master of the inappropriate comment. Despite his rough exterior, he's managed to show Jade his softer side and the two have become romantically involved.

JADE FONTAINE
Lead Staff Writer

SPECIAL MOVE:
"The Stare"

"Women play games too." That's what Jade Fontaine wants to tell the world. Jade can compete with the best of the boys but prefers the escape of a good online RPG and is hopelessly addicted to chat and email. Despite herself, Jade has fallen for Brent Sienna, the Magazine's Creative Director.

FRANCIS OTTOMAN
Tech Support

SPECIAL MOVE:
Spinning Cobra Clutch

If you have ever wanted to kill someone you've met online, then you know Francis Ray Ottoman. That's not to say that Francis is all bad, he does call in sick every once in a while. Francis knows everything there is to know about gaming, mostly because his life revolves around it.

CHOOSE YOUR PLAYER

PREPARE FOR HUMOR BATTLE!

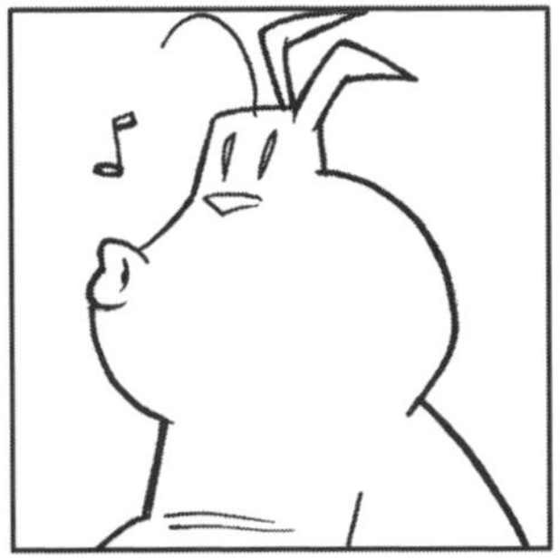

SKULL
The Troll

SPECIAL MOVE:
Stand Dumbfounded

The heart of PvP Magazine lies deep within the chest of this gentle giant. Skull was living in the janitor's closet when the staff moved in. Being a creature of Myth Skull's only need is attention; something the staff is more than willing to provide. Skull holds the position of intern, a title he's quite proud of.

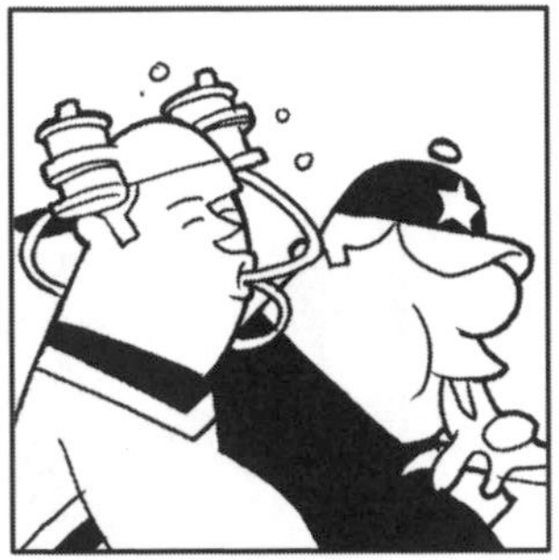

ROBBIE & JASE
Charity Cases.

SPECIAL MOVE:
Convert beer to pee

P

Their asses firmly attached to their old couch, these two ex-jocks spend all day playing sports games, drinking beer and eating junk food. Despite his better judgment, Cole can't bring himself to fire Robbie and Jase, who he used to dorm with back in college. The two serve no practical function whatsoever.

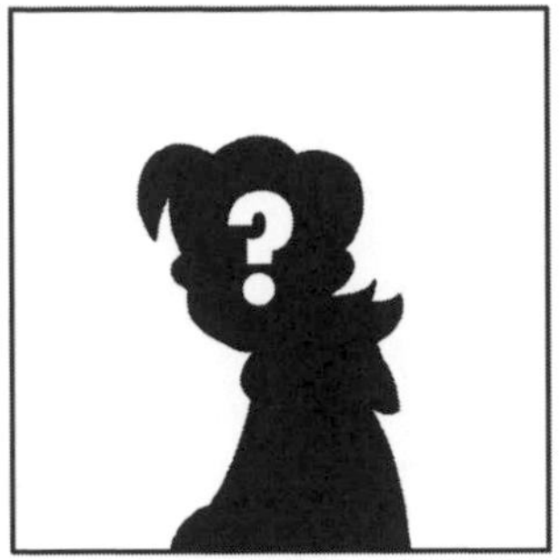

UNKNOWN
You have not unlocked this character yet. Keep playing!

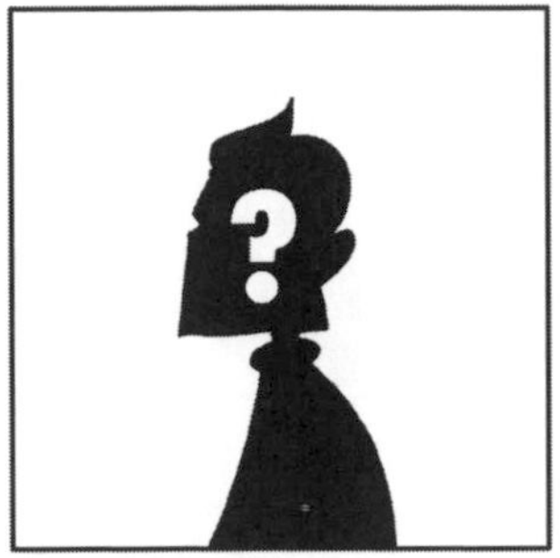

UNKNOWN
You have not unlocked this character yet. Keep playing!

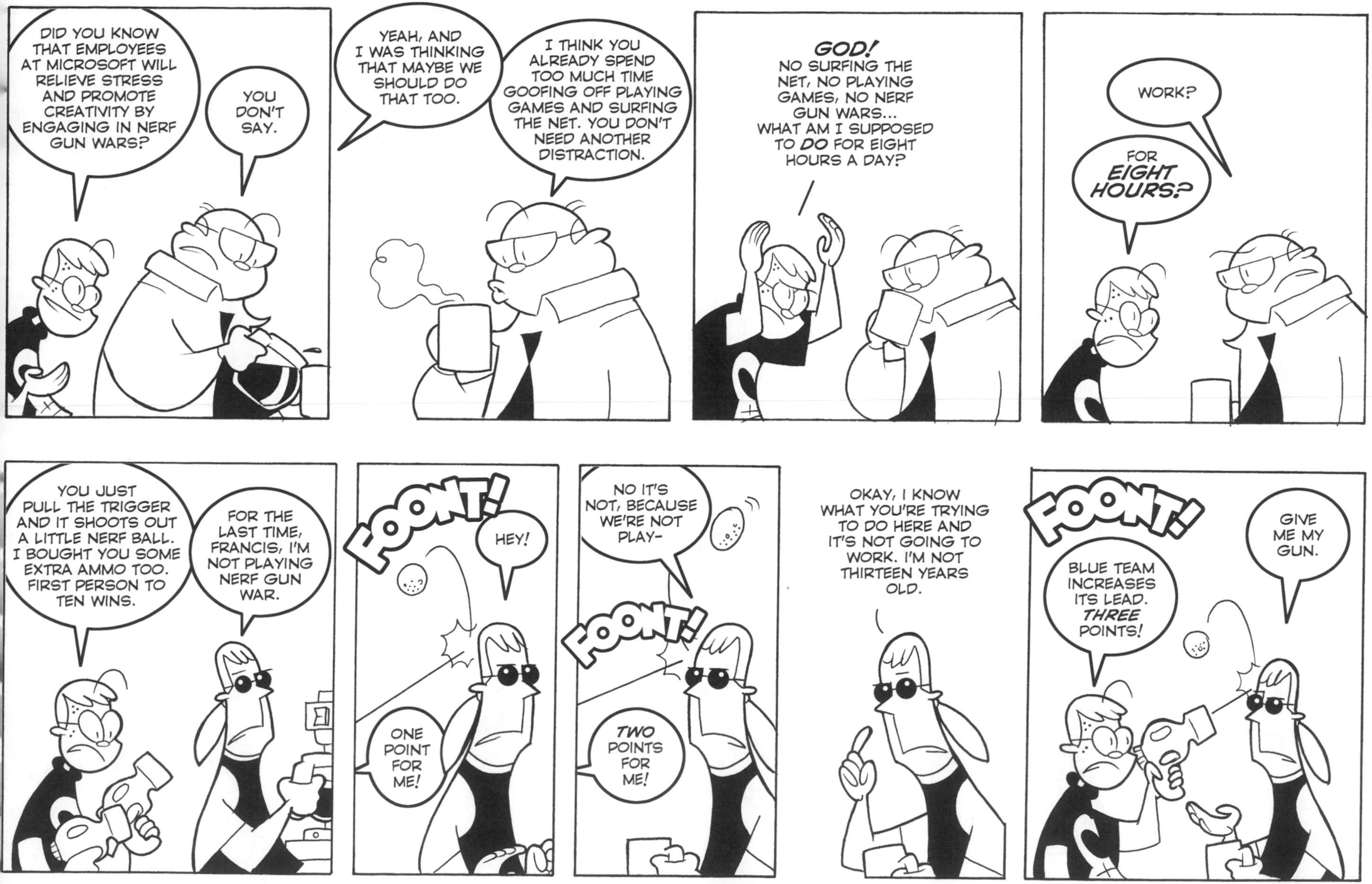
DID YOU KNOW THAT EMPLOYEES AT MICROSOFT WILL RELIEVE STRESS AND PROMOTE CREATIVITY BY ENGAGING IN NERF GUN WARS?
YOU DON'T SAY.
YEAH, AND I WAS THINKING THAT MAYBE WE SHOULD DO THAT TOO.
I THINK YOU ALREADY SPEND TOO MUCH TIME GOOFING OFF PLAYING GAMES AND SURFING THE NET. YOU DON'T NEED ANOTHER DISTRACTION.
GOD! NO SURFING THE NET, NO PLAYING GAMES, NO NERF GUN WARS... WHAT AM I SUPPOSED TO DO FOR EIGHT HOURS A DAY?
WORK?
FOR EIGHT HOURS?
YOU JUST PULL THE TRIGGER AND IT SHOOTS OUT A LITTLE NERF BALL. I BOUGHT YOU SOME EXTRA AMMO TOO. FIRST PERSON TO TEN WINS.
FOR THE LAST TIME, FRANCIS, I'M NOT PLAYING NERF GUN WAR.
FOONT!
HEY!
ONE POINT FOR ME!
NO IT'S NOT, BECAUSE WE'RE NOT PLAY-
FOONT!
TWO POINTS FOR ME!
OKAY, I KNOW WHAT YOU'RE TRYING TO DO HERE AND IT'S NOT GOING TO WORK. I'M NOT THIRTEEN YEARS OLD.
FOONT!
BLUE TEAM INCREASES ITS LEAD. THREE POINTS!
GIVE ME MY GUN.

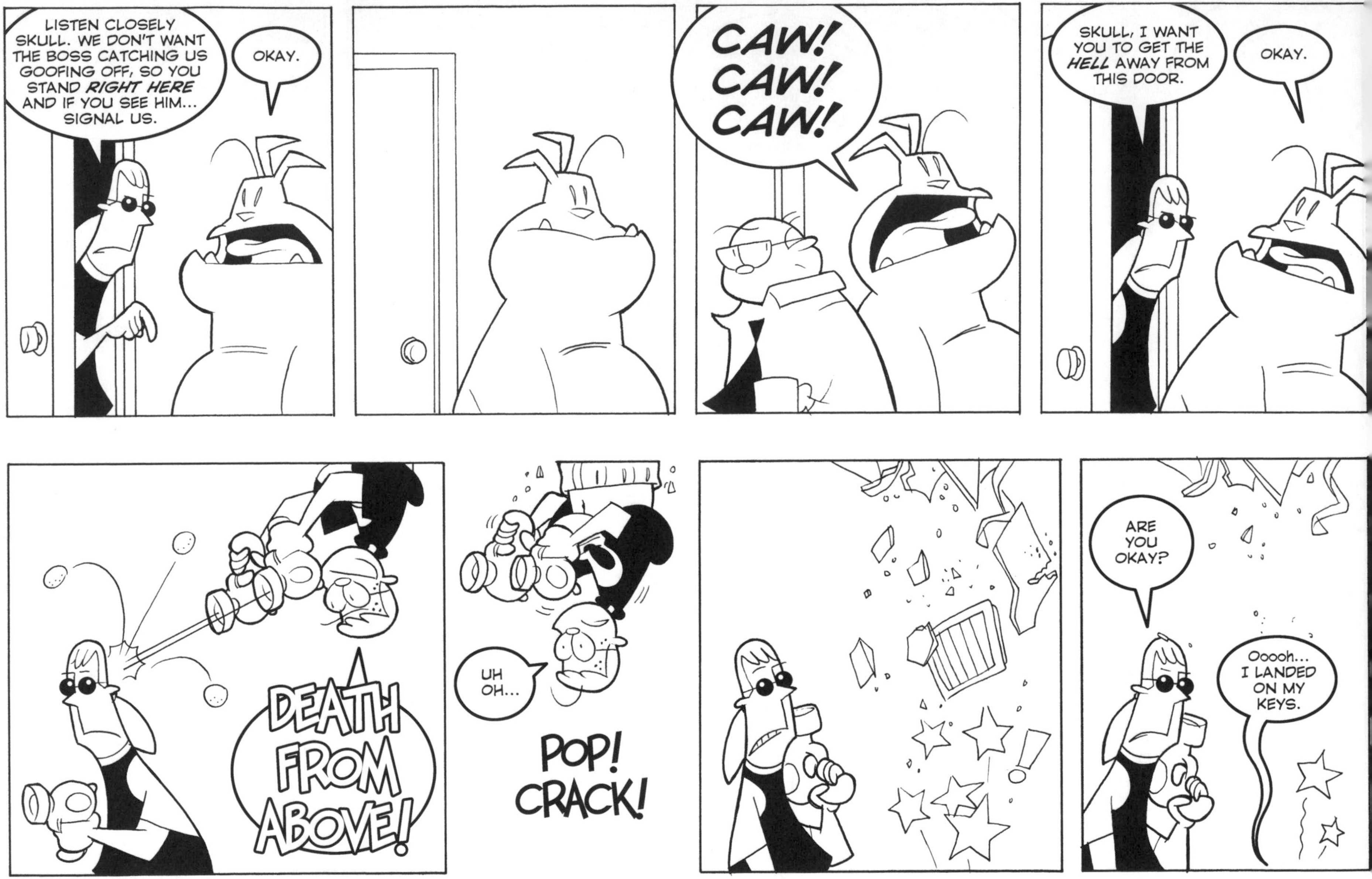
LISTEN CLOSELY SKULL. WE DON'T WANT THE BOSS CATCHING US GOOFING OFF, SO YOU STAND *RIGHT HERE* AND IF YOU SEE HIM... SIGNAL US.
OKAY.
CAW! CAW! CAW!
SKULL, I WANT YOU TO GET THE *HELL* AWAY FROM THIS DOOR.
OKAY.
DEATH FROM ABOVE!
UH OH...
POP! CRACK!
!
ARE YOU OKAY?
Ooooh... I LANDED ON MY KEYS.

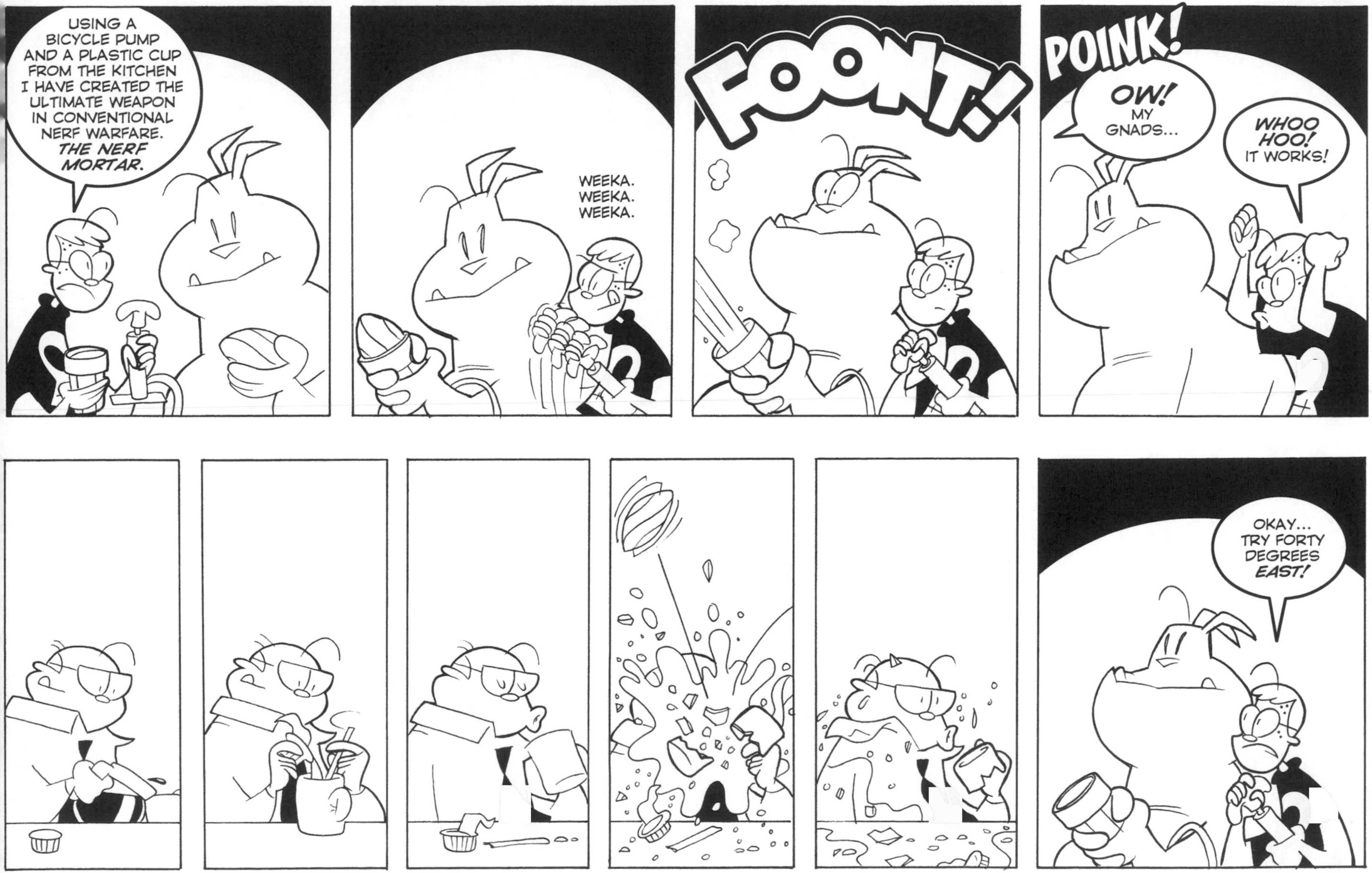

USING A BICYCLE PUMP AND A PLASTIC CUP FROM THE KITCHEN I HAVE CREATED THE ULTIMATE WEAPON IN CONVENTIONAL NERF WARFARE. THE NERF MORTAR.
WEEKA. WEEKA. WEEKA.
FOONT!
POINK!
OW! MY GNADS...
WHOO HOO! IT WORKS!
OKAY... TRY FORTY DEGREES EAST!

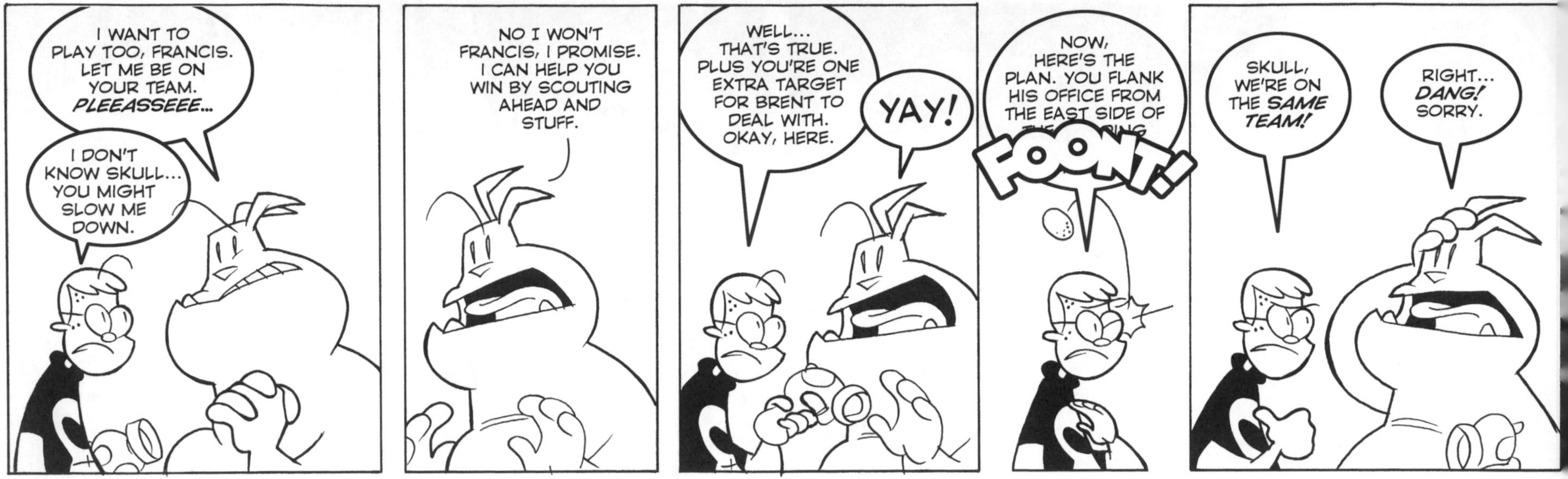

I WANT TO PLAY TOO, FRANCIS. LET ME BE ON YOUR TEAM. *PLEEASSEEE...*
I DON'T KNOW SKULL... YOU MIGHT SLOW ME DOWN.
NO I WON'T FRANCIS, I PROMISE. I CAN HELP YOU WIN BY SCOUTING AHEAD AND STUFF.
WELL... THAT'S TRUE. PLUS YOU'RE ONE EXTRA TARGET FOR BRENT TO DEAL WITH. OKAY, HERE.
YAY!
NOW, HERE'S THE PLAN. YOU FLANK HIS OFFICE FROM THE EAST SIDE OF
FOONT!
SKULL, WE'RE ON THE *SAME TEAM!*
RIGHT... *DANG!* SORRY.

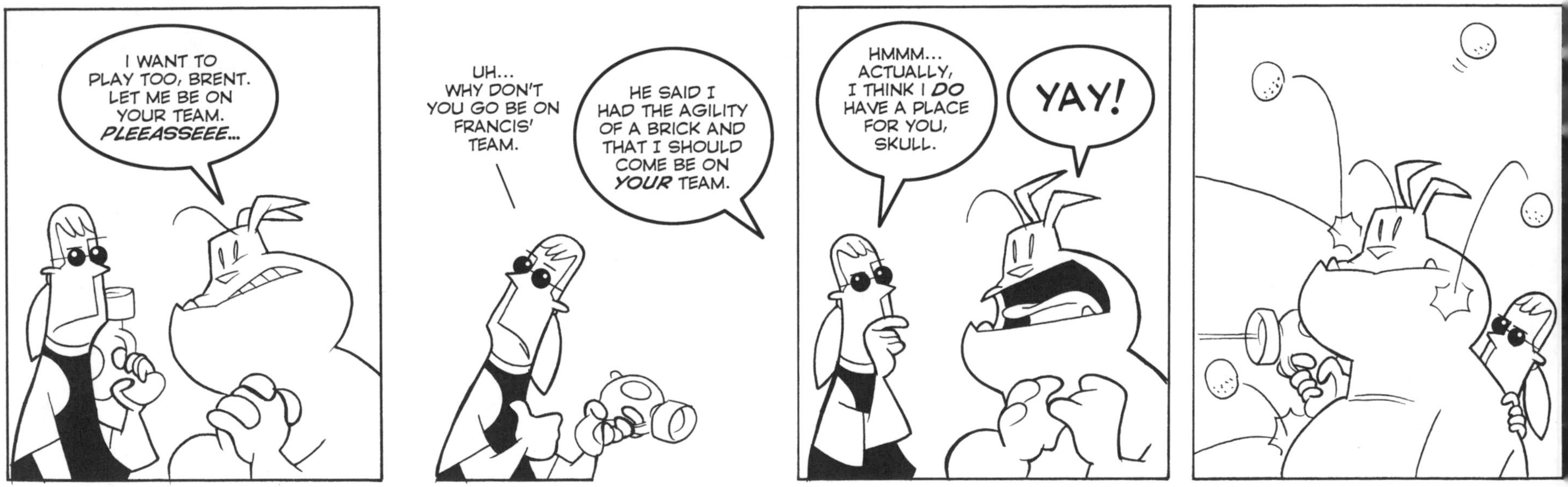

I WANT TO PLAY TOO, BRENT. LET ME BE ON YOUR TEAM. *PLEEASSEEE...*
UH... WHY DON'T YOU GO BE ON FRANCIS' TEAM.
HE SAID I HAD THE AGILITY OF A BRICK AND THAT I SHOULD COME BE ON *YOUR* TEAM.
HMMM... ACTUALLY, I THINK I *DO* HAVE A PLACE FOR YOU, SKULL.
YAY!

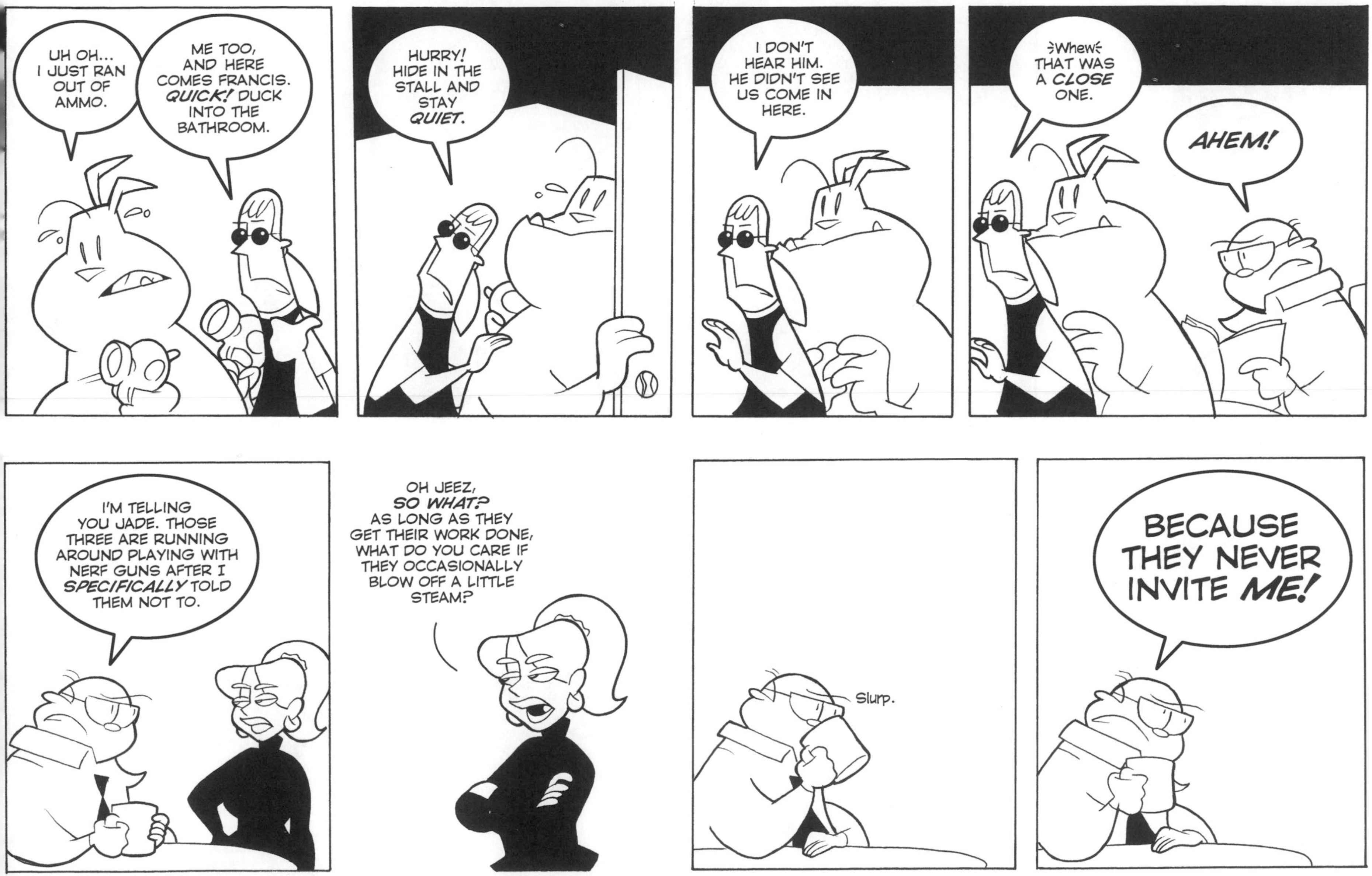
UH OH... I JUST RAN OUT OF AMMO.
ME TOO, AND HERE COMES FRANCIS. QUICK! DUCK INTO THE BATHROOM.
HURRY! HIDE IN THE STALL AND STAY QUIET.
I DON'T HEAR HIM. HE DIDN'T SEE US COME IN HERE.
Whew THAT WAS A CLOSE ONE.
AHEM!
I'M TELLING YOU JADE. THOSE THREE ARE RUNNING AROUND PLAYING WITH NERF GUNS AFTER I SPECIFICALLY TOLD THEM NOT TO.
OH JEEZ, SO WHAT? AS LONG AS THEY GET THEIR WORK DONE, WHAT DO YOU CARE IF THEY OCCASIONALLY BLOW OFF A LITTLE STEAM?
Slurp.
BECAUSE THEY NEVER INVITE ME!

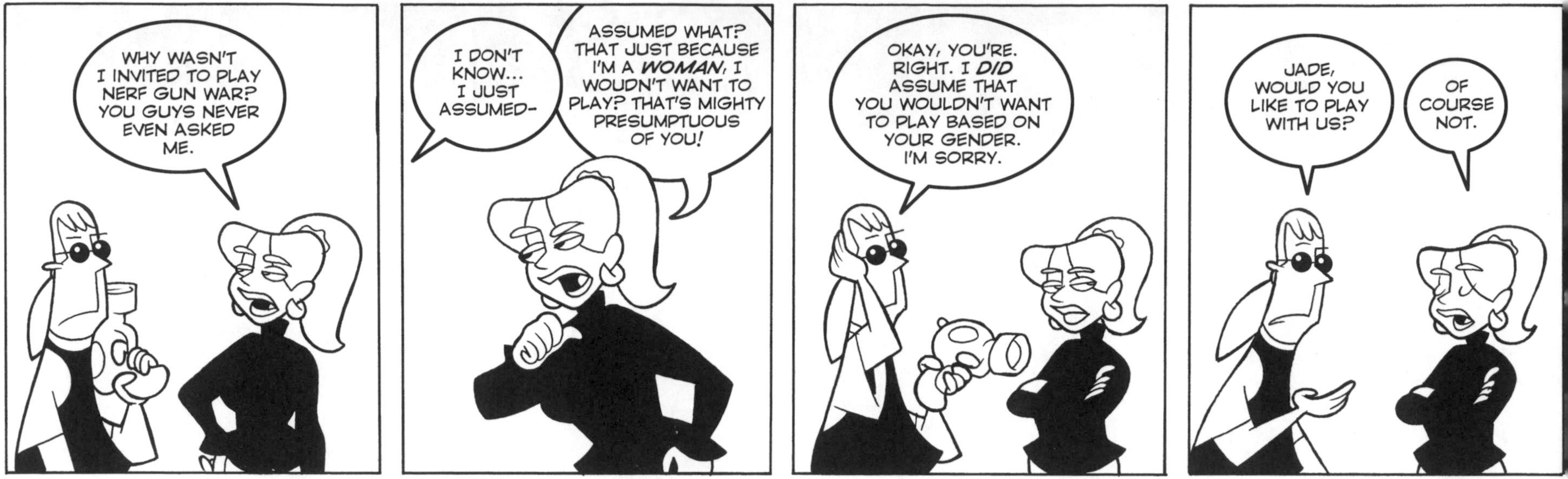
WHY WASN'T I INVITED TO PLAY NERF GUN WAR? YOU GUYS NEVER EVEN ASKED ME.
I DON'T KNOW... I JUST ASSUMED-
ASSUMED WHAT? THAT JUST BECAUSE I'M A *WOMAN*, I WOUDN'T WANT TO PLAY? THAT'S MIGHTY PRESUMPTUOUS OF YOU!
OKAY, YOU'RE. RIGHT. I *DID* ASSUME THAT YOU WOULDN'T WANT TO PLAY BASED ON YOUR GENDER. I'M SORRY.
JADE, WOULD YOU LIKE TO PLAY WITH US?
OF COURSE NOT.

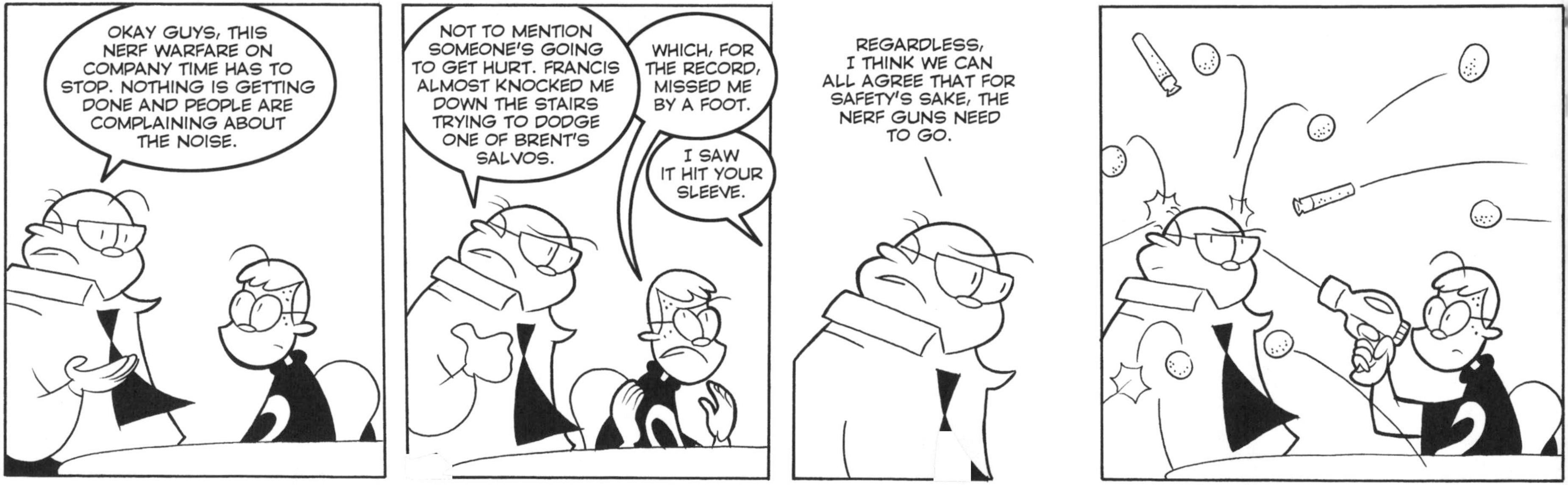
OKAY GUYS, THIS NERF WARFARE ON COMPANY TIME HAS TO STOP. NOTHING IS GETTING DONE AND PEOPLE ARE COMPLAINING ABOUT THE NOISE.
NOT TO MENTION SOMEONE'S GOING TO GET HURT. FRANCIS ALMOST KNOCKED ME DOWN THE STAIRS TRYING TO DODGE ONE OF BRENT'S SALVOS.
WHICH, FOR THE RECORD, MISSED ME BY A FOOT.
I SAW IT HIT YOUR SLEEVE.
REGARDLESS, I THINK WE CAN ALL AGREE THAT FOR SAFETY'S SAKE, THE NERF GUNS NEED TO GO.

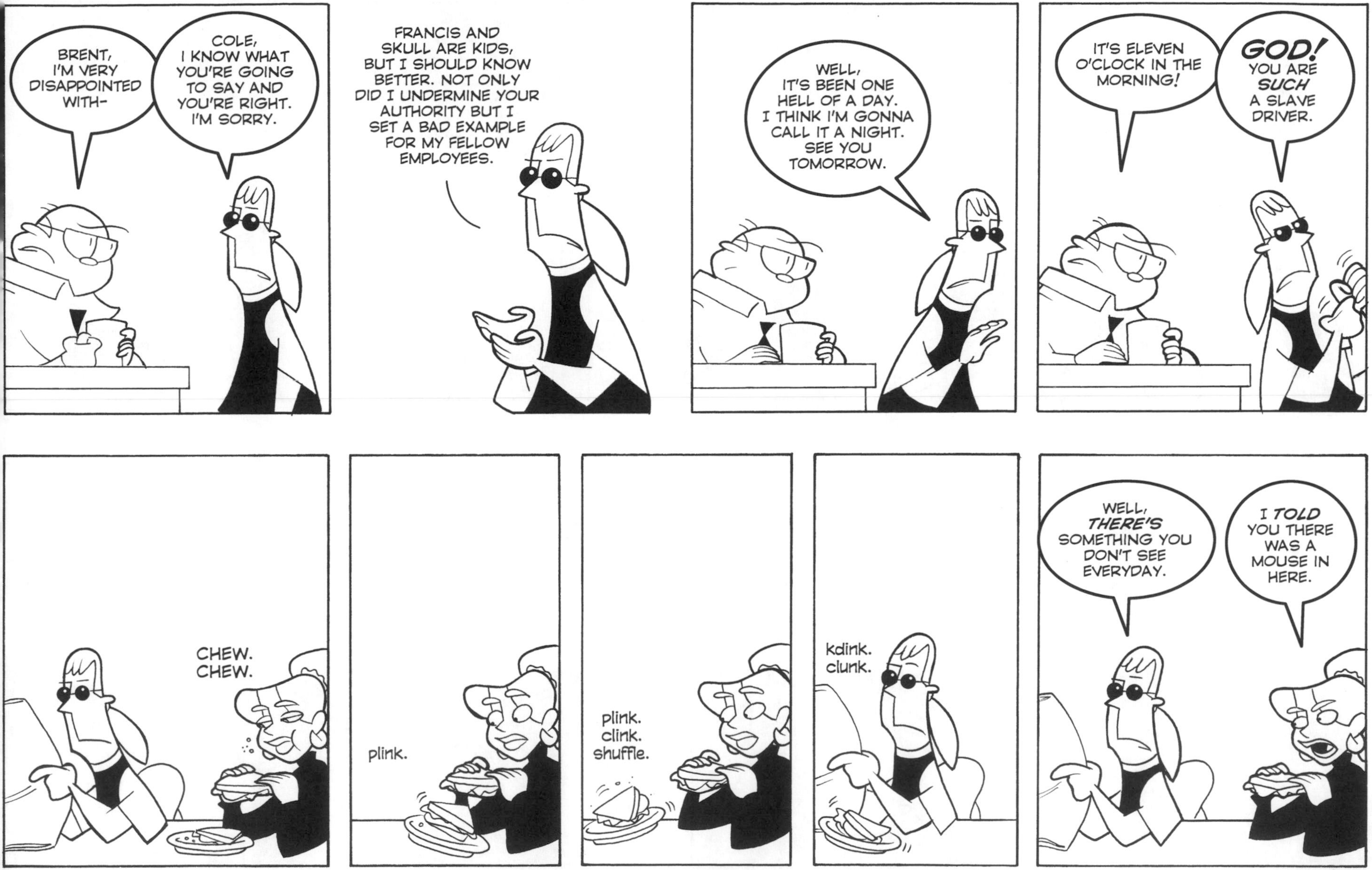
BRENT, I'M VERY DISAPPOINTED WITH-
COLE, I KNOW WHAT YOU'RE GOING TO SAY AND YOU'RE RIGHT. I'M SORRY.
FRANCIS AND SKULL ARE KIDS, BUT I SHOULD KNOW BETTER. NOT ONLY DID I UNDERMINE YOUR AUTHORITY BUT I SET A BAD EXAMPLE FOR MY FELLOW EMPLOYEES.
WELL, IT'S BEEN ONE HELL OF A DAY. I THINK I'M GONNA CALL IT A NIGHT. SEE YOU TOMORROW.
IT'S ELEVEN O'CLOCK IN THE MORNING!
GOD! YOU ARE SUCH A SLAVE DRIVER.
CHEW. CHEW.
plink.
plink. clink. shuffle.
kdink. clunk.
WELL, THERE'S SOMETHING YOU DON'T SEE EVERYDAY.
I TOLD YOU THERE WAS A MOUSE IN HERE.

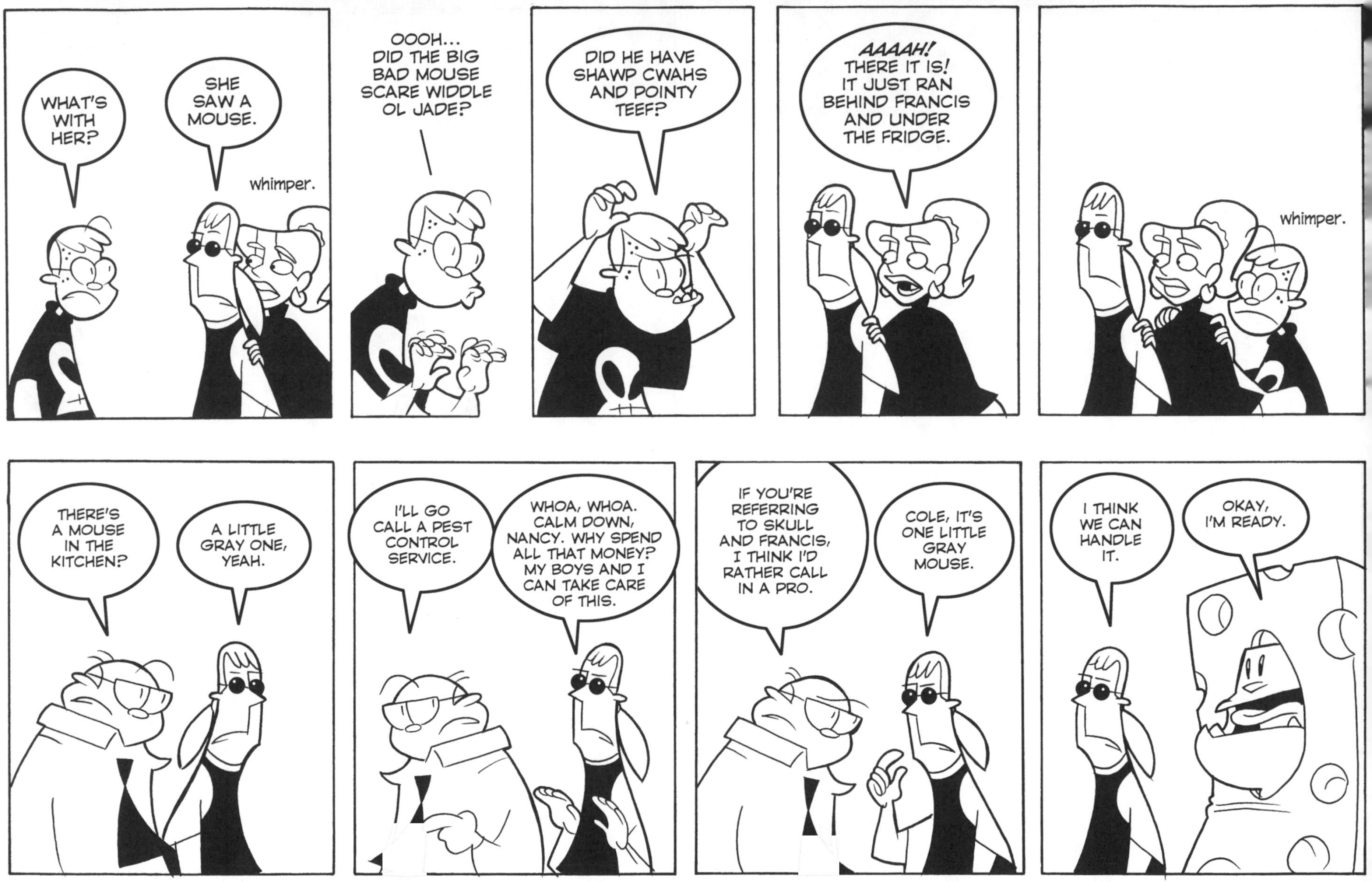
WHAT'S WITH HER?
SHE SAW A MOUSE.
whimper.
OOOH... DID THE BIG BAD MOUSE SCARE WIDDLE OL JADE?
DID HE HAVE SHAWP CWAHS AND POINTY TEEF?
AAAAH! THERE IT IS! IT JUST RAN BEHIND FRANCIS AND UNDER THE FRIDGE.
whimper.
THERE'S A MOUSE IN THE KITCHEN?
A LITTLE GRAY ONE, YEAH.
I'LL GO CALL A PEST CONTROL SERVICE.
WHOA, WHOA. CALM DOWN, NANCY. WHY SPEND ALL THAT MONEY? MY BOYS AND I CAN TAKE CARE OF THIS.
IF YOU'RE REFERRING TO SKULL AND FRANCIS, I THINK I'D RATHER CALL IN A PRO.
COLE, IT'S ONE LITTLE GRAY MOUSE.
I THINK WE CAN HANDLE IT.
OKAY, I'M READY.

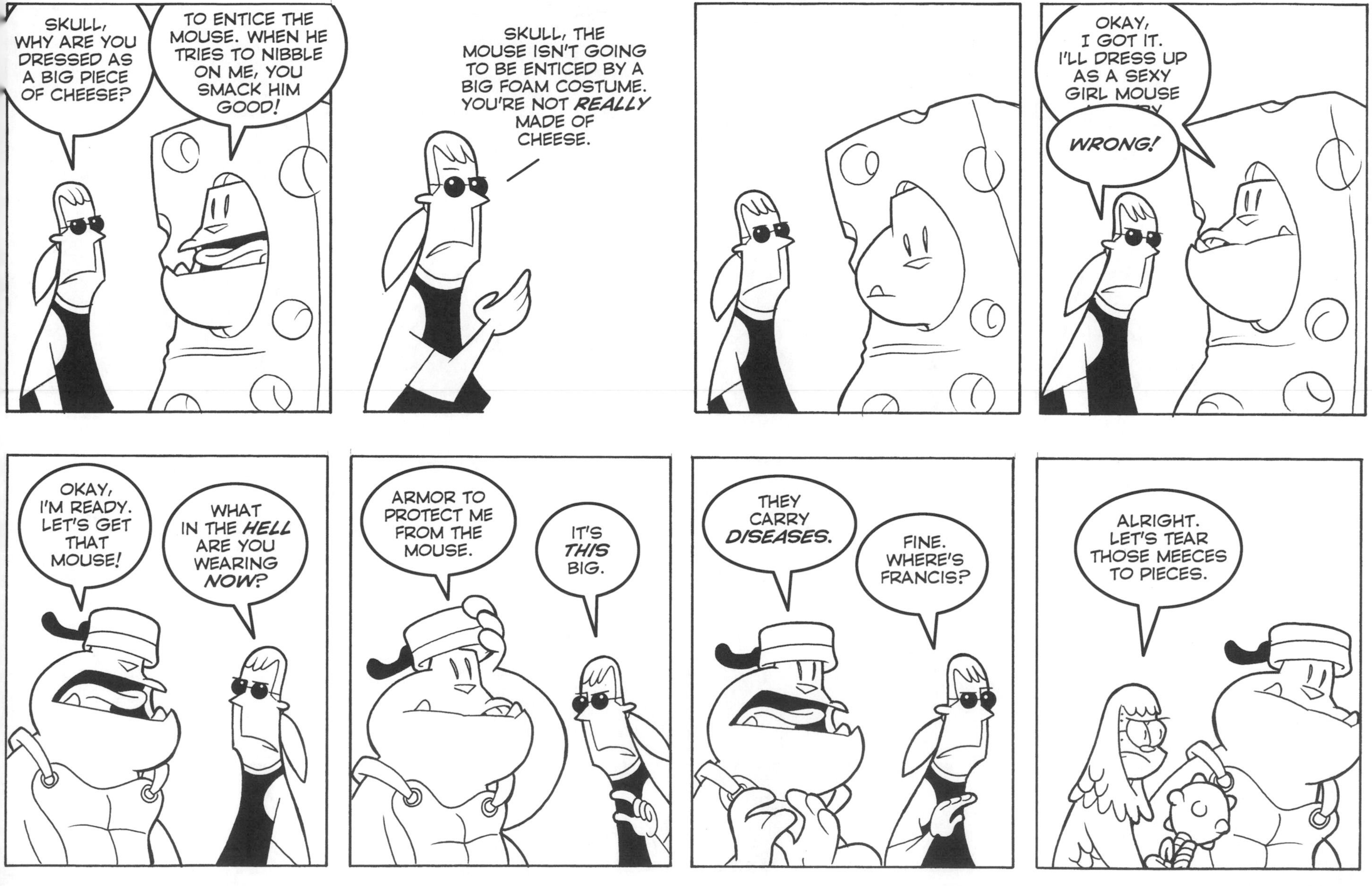
SKULL, WHY ARE YOU DRESSED AS A BIG PIECE OF CHEESE?
TO ENTICE THE MOUSE. WHEN HE TRIES TO NIBBLE ON ME, YOU SMACK HIM GOOD!
SKULL, THE MOUSE ISN'T GOING TO BE ENTICED BY A BIG FOAM COSTUME. YOU'RE NOT *REALLY* MADE OF CHEESE.
OKAY, I GOT IT. I'LL DRESS UP AS A SEXY GIRL MOUSE
WRONG!
OKAY, I'M READY. LET'S GET THAT MOUSE!
WHAT IN THE *HELL* ARE YOU WEARING *NOW?*
ARMOR TO PROTECT ME FROM THE MOUSE.
IT'S *THIS* BIG.
THEY CARRY *DISEASES.*
FINE. WHERE'S FRANCIS?
ALRIGHT. LET'S TEAR THOSE MEECES TO PIECES.

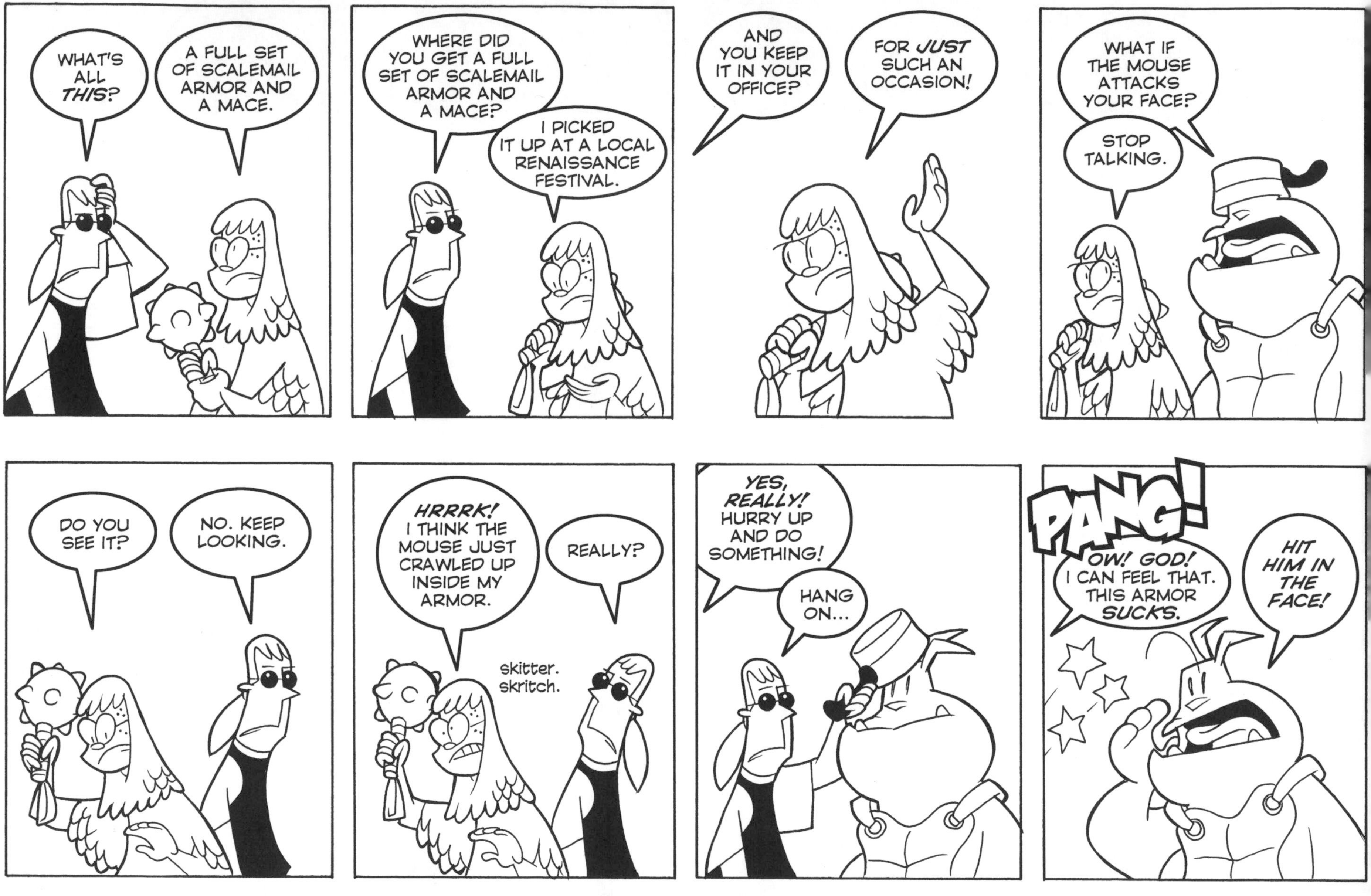
WHAT'S ALL *THIS*?
A FULL SET OF SCALEMAIL ARMOR AND A MACE.
WHERE DID YOU GET A FULL SET OF SCALEMAIL ARMOR AND A MACE?
I PICKED IT UP AT A LOCAL RENAISSANCE FESTIVAL.
AND YOU KEEP IT IN YOUR OFFICE?
FOR *JUST* SUCH AN OCCASION!
WHAT IF THE MOUSE ATTACKS YOUR FACE?
STOP TALKING.
DO YOU SEE IT?
NO. KEEP LOOKING.
HRRRK! I THINK THE MOUSE JUST CRAWLED UP INSIDE MY ARMOR.
REALLY?
skitter. skritch.
YES, REALLY! HURRY UP AND DO SOMETHING!
HANG ON...
PANG!
OW! GOD! I CAN FEEL THAT. THIS ARMOR *SUCKS*.
HIT HIM IN THE FACE!

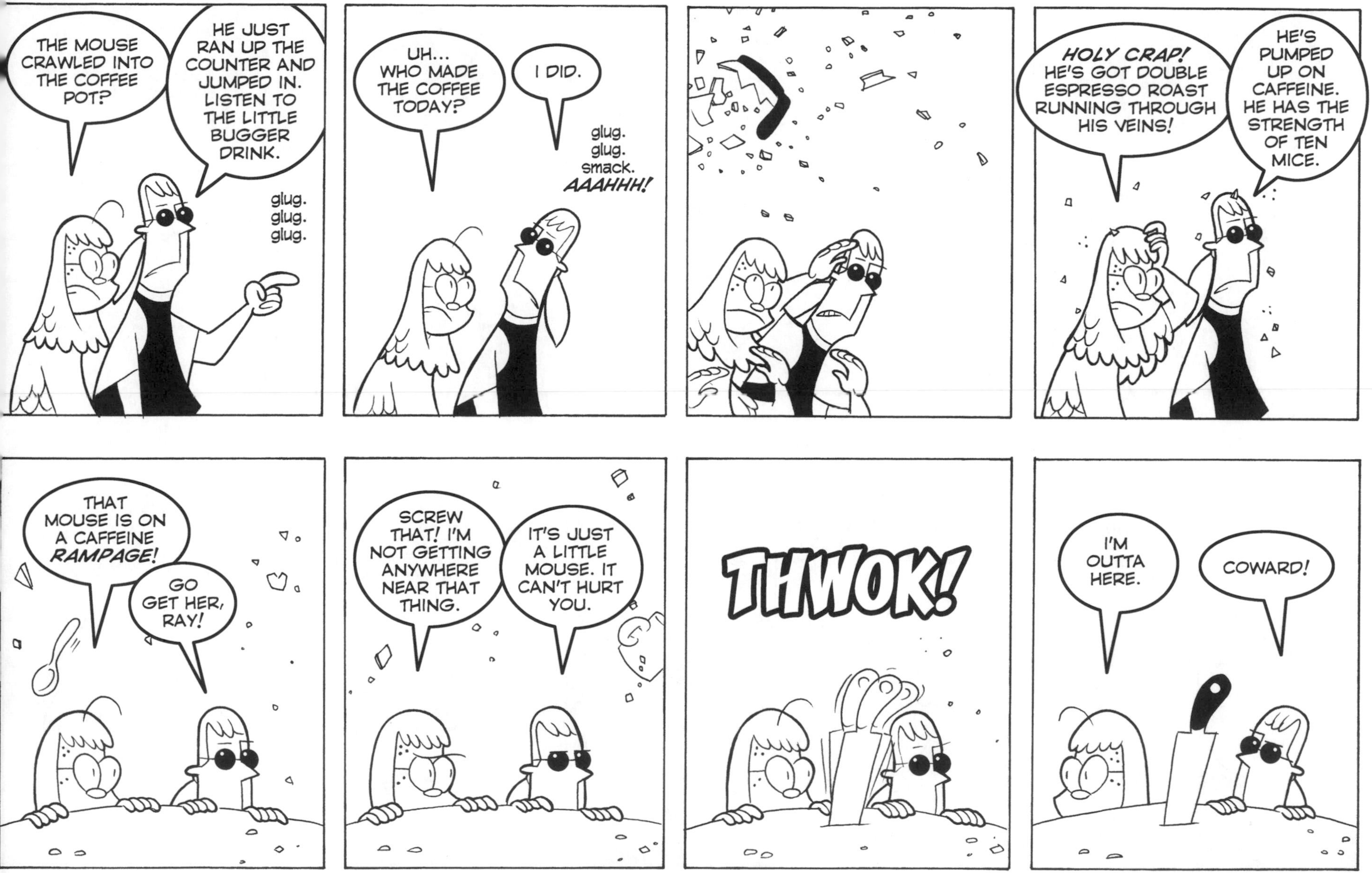

THE MOUSE CRAWLED INTO THE COFFEE POT?
HE JUST RAN UP THE COUNTER AND JUMPED IN. LISTEN TO THE LITTLE BUGGER DRINK.
glug. glug. glug.
UH... WHO MADE THE COFFEE TODAY?
I DID.
glug. glug. smack. AAAHHH!
HOLY CRAP! HE'S GOT DOUBLE ESPRESSO ROAST RUNNING THROUGH HIS VEINS!
HE'S PUMPED UP ON CAFFEINE. HE HAS THE STRENGTH OF TEN MICE.
THAT MOUSE IS ON A CAFFEINE RAMPAGE!
GO GET HER, RAY!
SCREW THAT! I'M NOT GETTING ANYWHERE NEAR THAT THING.
IT'S JUST A LITTLE MOUSE. IT CAN'T HURT YOU.
THWOK!
I'M OUTTA HERE.
COWARD!

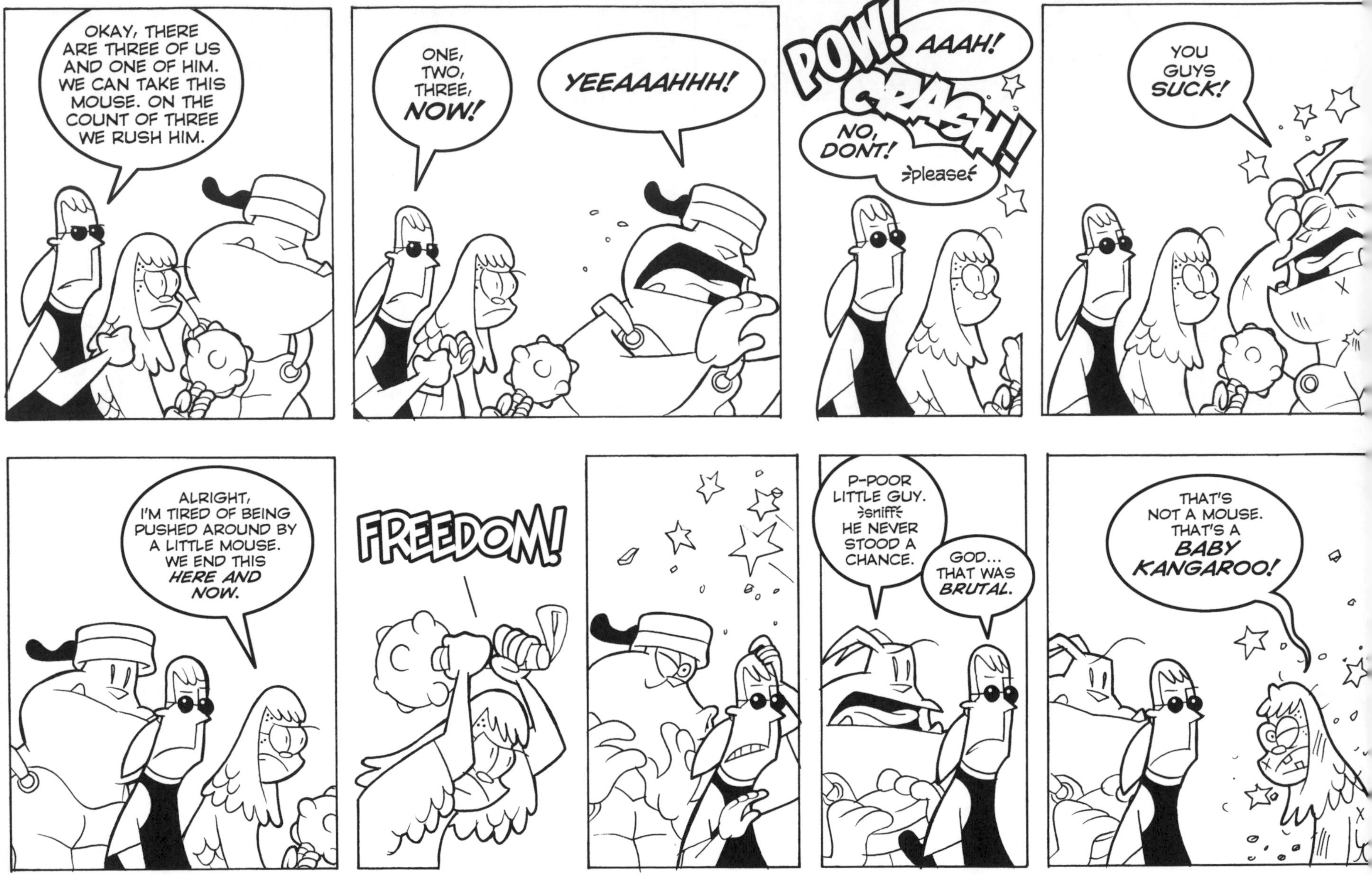

OKAY, THERE ARE THREE OF US AND ONE OF HIM. WE CAN TAKE THIS MOUSE. ON THE COUNT OF THREE WE RUSH HIM.
ONE, TWO, THREE, NOW!
YEEAAAHHH!
POW!
AAAH!
CRASH!
NO, DONT!
please
YOU GUYS SUCK!
ALRIGHT, I'M TIRED OF BEING PUSHED AROUND BY A LITTLE MOUSE. WE END THIS HERE AND NOW.
FREEDOM!
P-POOR LITTLE GUY. sniff HE NEVER STOOD A CHANCE.
GOD... THAT WAS BRUTAL.
THAT'S NOT A MOUSE. THAT'S A BABY KANGAROO!

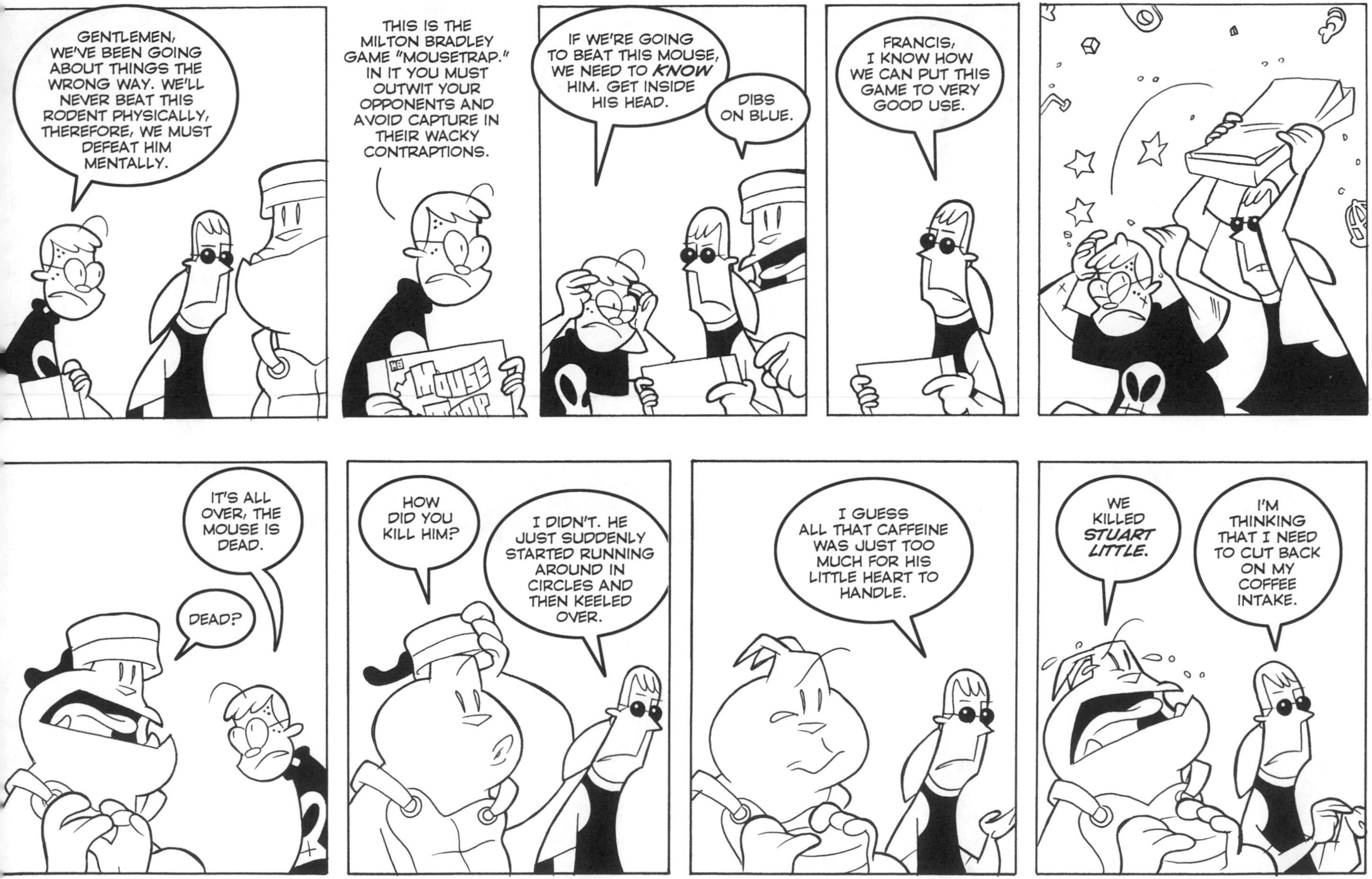
GENTLEMEN, WE'VE BEEN GOING ABOUT THINGS THE WRONG WAY. WE'LL NEVER BEAT THIS RODENT PHYSICALLY, THEREFORE, WE MUST DEFEAT HIM MENTALLY.
THIS IS THE MILTON BRADLEY GAME "MOUSETRAP." IN IT YOU MUST OUTWIT YOUR OPPONENTS AND AVOID CAPTURE IN THEIR WACKY CONTRAPTIONS.
MOUSE
IF WE'RE GOING TO BEAT THIS MOUSE, WE NEED TO *KNOW* HIM. GET INSIDE HIS HEAD.
DIBS ON BLUE.
FRANCIS, I KNOW HOW WE CAN PUT THIS GAME TO VERY GOOD USE.
IT'S ALL OVER, THE MOUSE IS DEAD.
DEAD?
HOW DID YOU KILL HIM?
I DIDN'T. HE JUST SUDDENLY STARTED RUNNING AROUND IN CIRCLES AND THEN KEELED OVER.
I GUESS ALL THAT CAFFEINE WAS JUST TOO MUCH FOR HIS LITTLE HEART TO HANDLE.
WE KILLED *STUART LITTLE*.
I'M THINKING THAT I NEED TO CUT BACK ON MY COFFEE INTAKE.

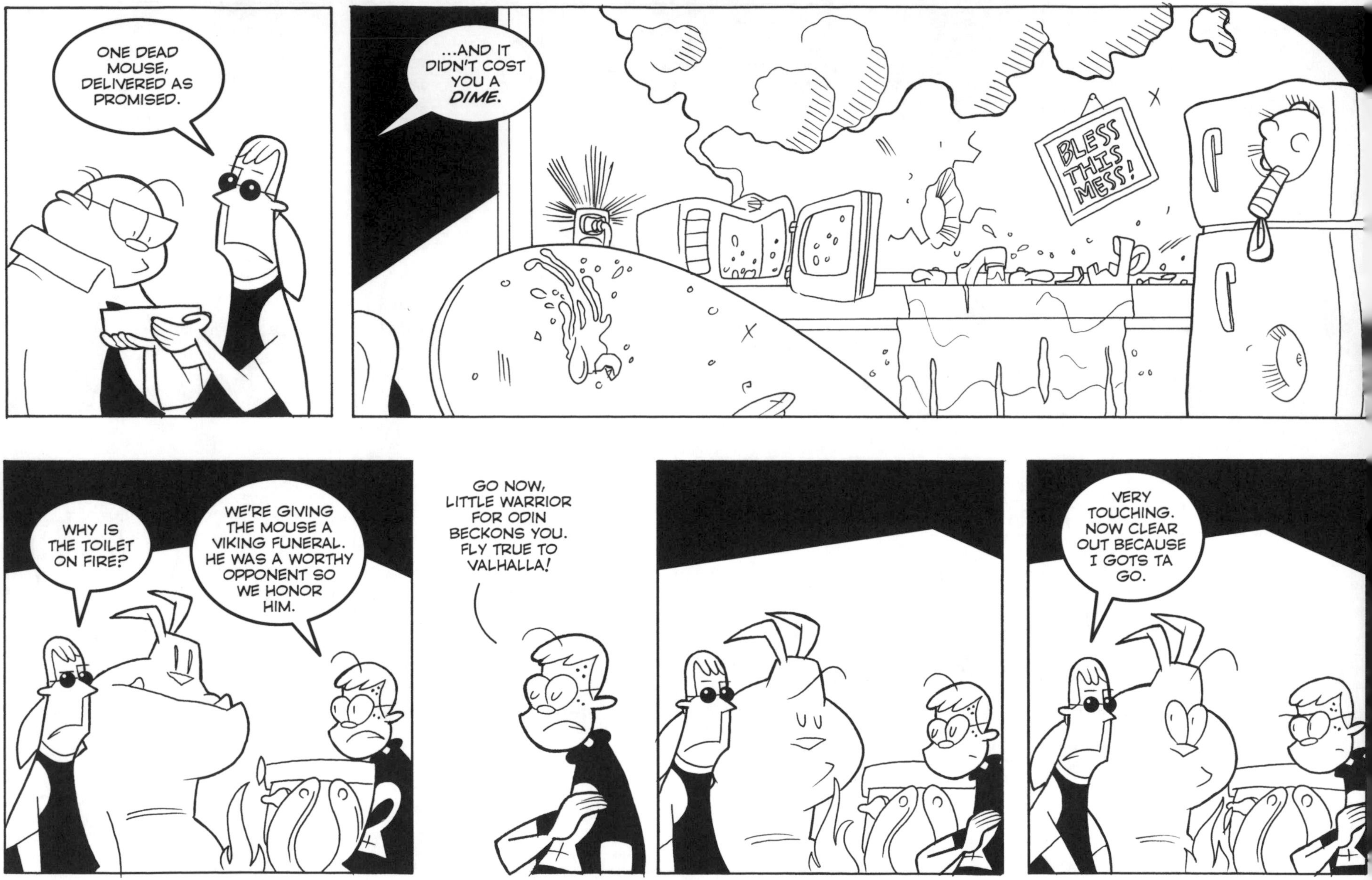
ONE DEAD MOUSE, DELIVERED AS PROMISED.
...AND IT DIDN'T COST YOU A *DIME.*
BLESS THIS MESS!
WHY IS THE TOILET ON FIRE?
WE'RE GIVING THE MOUSE A VIKING FUNERAL. HE WAS A WORTHY OPPONENT SO WE HONOR HIM.
GO NOW, LITTLE WARRIOR FOR ODIN BECKONS YOU. FLY TRUE TO VALHALLA!
VERY TOUCHING. NOW CLEAR OUT BECAUSE I GOTS TA GO.

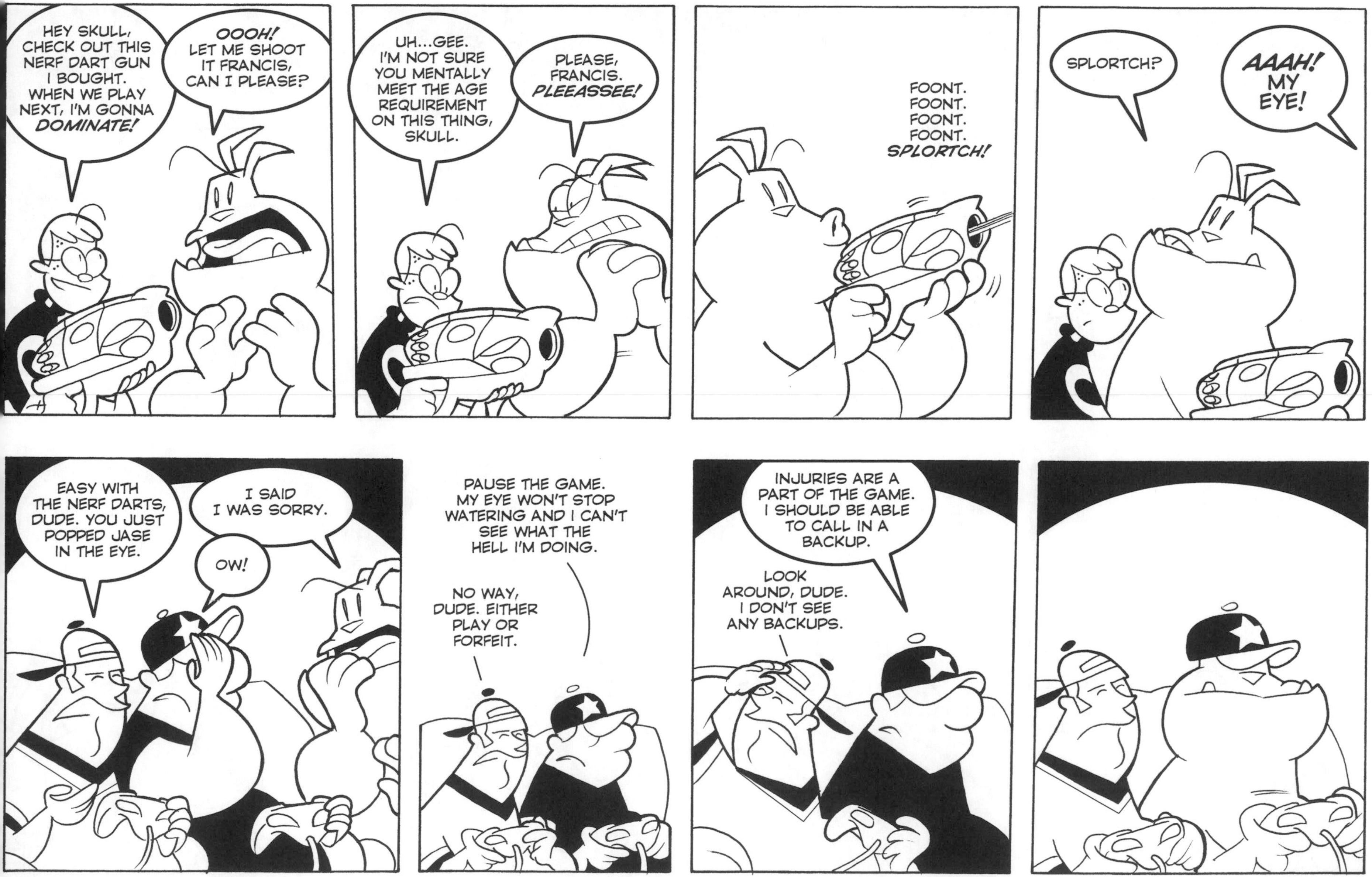
HEY SKULL, CHECK OUT THIS NERF DART GUN I BOUGHT. WHEN WE PLAY NEXT, I'M GONNA DOMINATE!
OOOH! LET ME SHOOT IT FRANCIS, CAN I PLEASE?
UH...GEE. I'M NOT SURE YOU MENTALLY MEET THE AGE REQUIREMENT ON THIS THING, SKULL.
PLEASE, FRANCIS. PLEEASSEE!
FOONT. FOONT. FOONT. FOONT. SPLORTCH!
SPLORTCH?
AAAH! MY EYE!
EASY WITH THE NERF DARTS, DUDE. YOU JUST POPPED JASE IN THE EYE.
I SAID I WAS SORRY.
OW!
PAUSE THE GAME. MY EYE WON'T STOP WATERING AND I CAN'T SEE WHAT THE HELL I'M DOING.
NO WAY, DUDE. EITHER PLAY OR FORFEIT.
INJURIES ARE A PART OF THE GAME. I SHOULD BE ABLE TO CALL IN A BACKUP.
LOOK AROUND, DUDE. I DON'T SEE ANY BACKUPS.

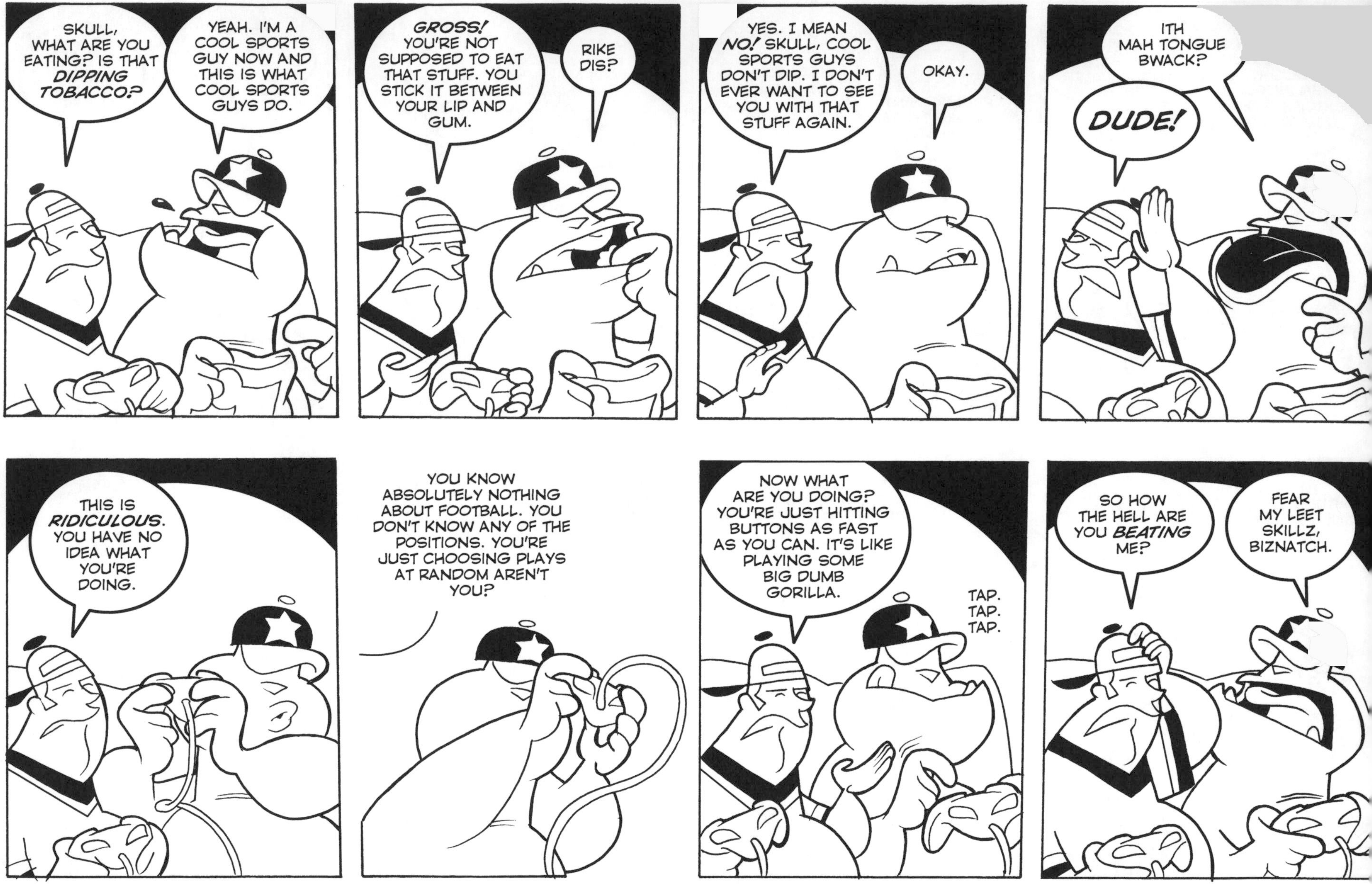
SKULL, WHAT ARE YOU EATING? IS THAT *DIPPING TOBACCO?*
YEAH. I'M A COOL SPORTS GUY NOW AND THIS IS WHAT COOL SPORTS GUYS DO.
GROSS! YOU'RE NOT SUPPOSED TO EAT THAT STUFF. YOU STICK IT BETWEEN YOUR LIP AND GUM.
RIKE DIS?
YES. I MEAN *NO!* SKULL, COOL SPORTS GUYS DON'T DIP. I DON'T EVER WANT TO SEE YOU WITH THAT STUFF AGAIN.
OKAY.
ITH MAH TONGUE BWACK?
DUDE!
THIS IS *RIDICULOUS*. YOU HAVE NO IDEA WHAT YOU'RE DOING.
YOU KNOW ABSOLUTELY NOTHING ABOUT FOOTBALL. YOU DON'T KNOW ANY OF THE POSITIONS. YOU'RE JUST CHOOSING PLAYS AT RANDOM AREN'T YOU?
NOW WHAT ARE YOU DOING? YOU'RE JUST HITTING BUTTONS AS FAST AS YOU CAN. IT'S LIKE PLAYING SOME BIG DUMB GORILLA.
TAP. TAP. TAP.
SO HOW THE HELL ARE YOU *BEATING* ME?
FEAR MY LEET SKILLZ, BIZNATCH.

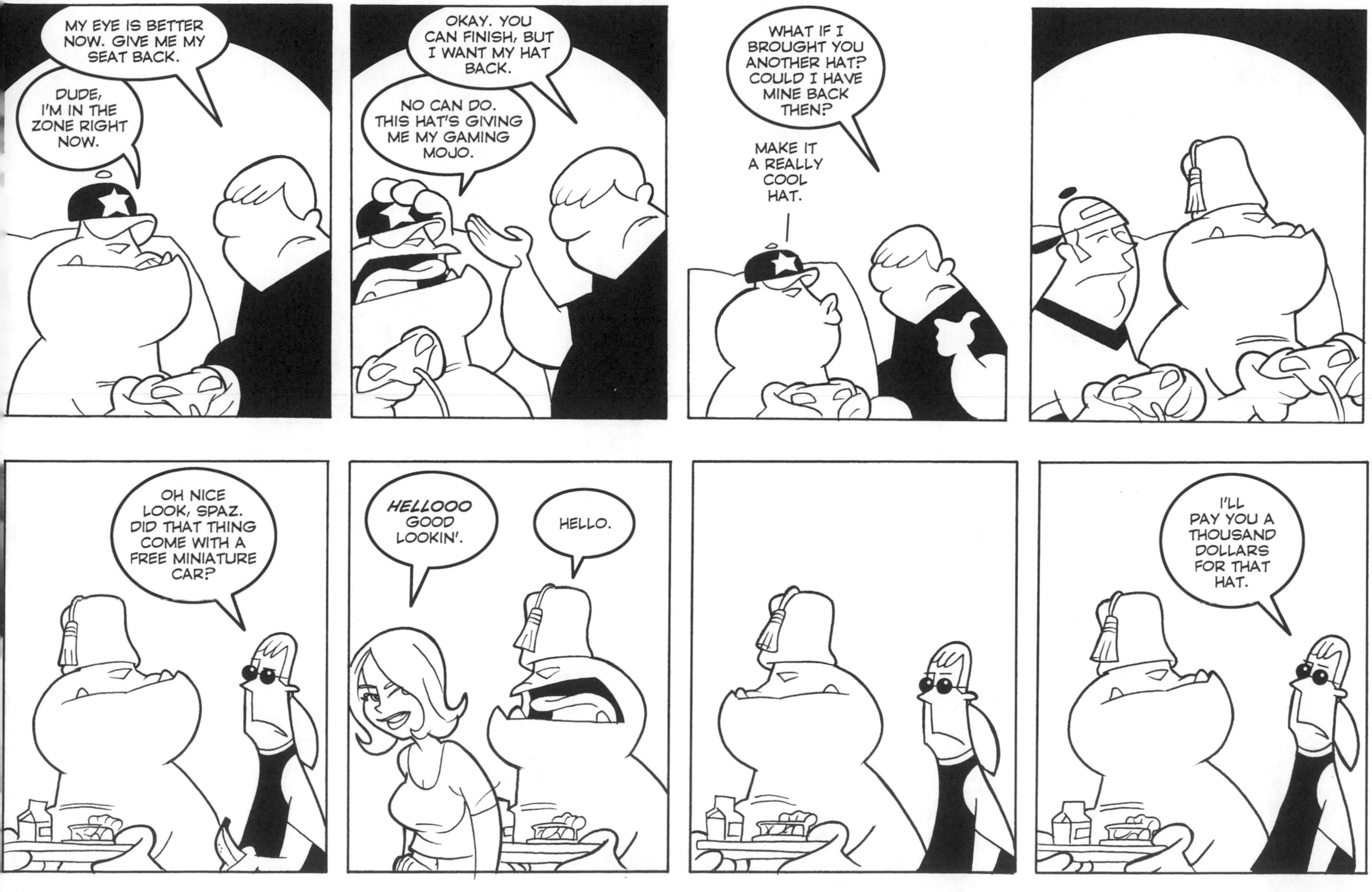
MY EYE IS BETTER NOW. GIVE ME MY SEAT BACK.
DUDE, I'M IN THE ZONE RIGHT NOW.
OKAY. YOU CAN FINISH, BUT I WANT MY HAT BACK.
NO CAN DO. THIS HAT'S GIVING ME MY GAMING MOJO.
WHAT IF I BROUGHT YOU ANOTHER HAT? COULD I HAVE MINE BACK THEN?
MAKE IT A REALLY COOL HAT.
OH NICE LOOK, SPAZ. DID THAT THING COME WITH A FREE MINIATURE CAR?
HELLOOO GOOD LOOKIN'.
HELLO.
I'LL PAY YOU A THOUSAND DOLLARS FOR THAT HAT.

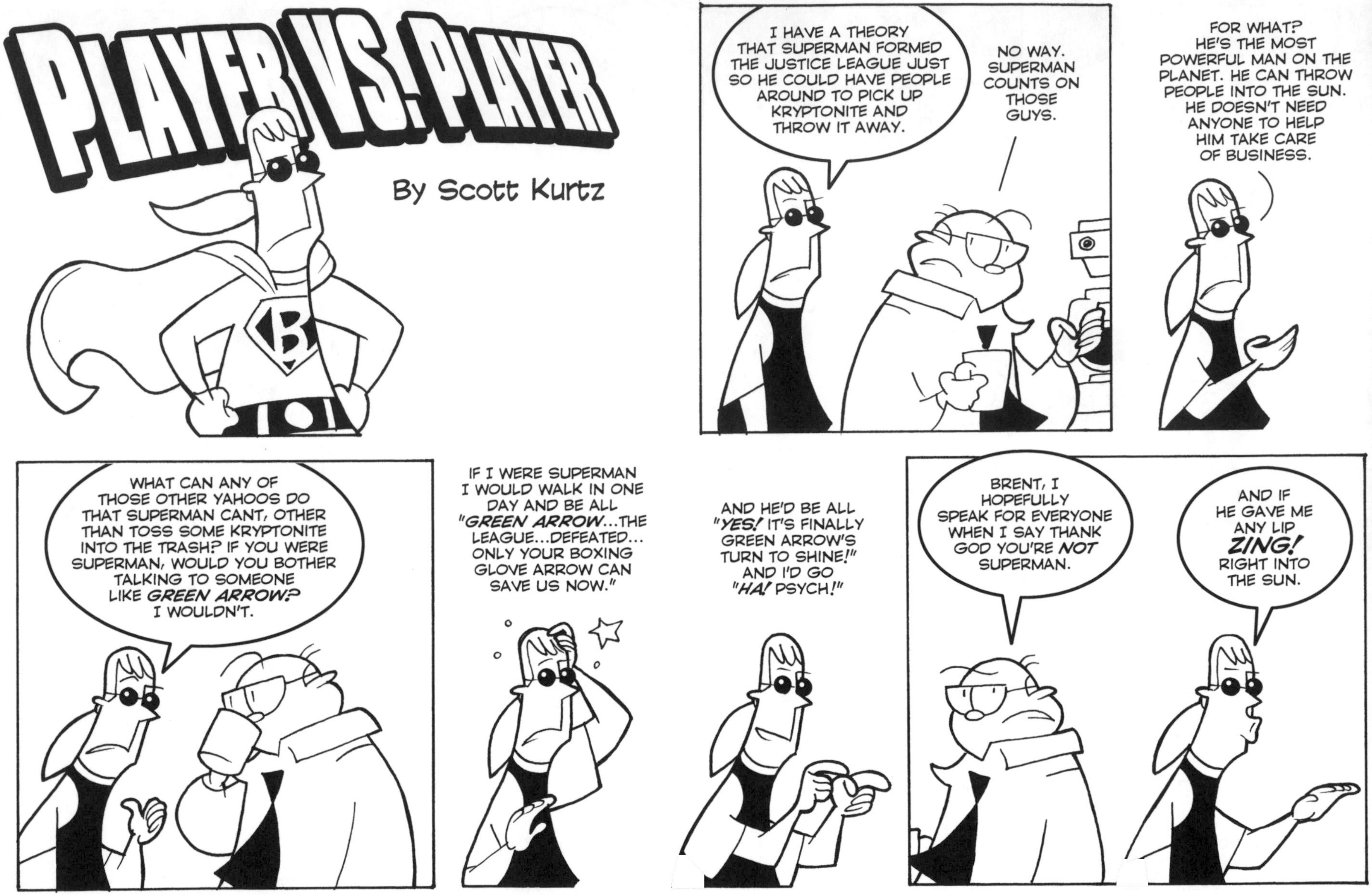
PLAYER VS. PLAYER
By Scott Kurtz
I HAVE A THEORY THAT SUPERMAN FORMED THE JUSTICE LEAGUE JUST SO HE COULD HAVE PEOPLE AROUND TO PICK UP KRYPTONITE AND THROW IT AWAY.
NO WAY. SUPERMAN COUNTS ON THOSE GUYS.
FOR WHAT? HE'S THE MOST POWERFUL MAN ON THE PLANET. HE CAN THROW PEOPLE INTO THE SUN. HE DOESN'T NEED ANYONE TO HELP HIM TAKE CARE OF BUSINESS.
WHAT CAN ANY OF THOSE OTHER YAHOOS DO THAT SUPERMAN CANT, OTHER THAN TOSS SOME KRYPTONITE INTO THE TRASH? IF YOU WERE SUPERMAN, WOULD YOU BOTHER TALKING TO SOMEONE LIKE *GREEN ARROW?* I WOULDN'T.
IF I WERE SUPERMAN I WOULD WALK IN ONE DAY AND BE ALL "*GREEN ARROW*...THE LEAGUE...DEFEATED... ONLY YOUR BOXING GLOVE ARROW CAN SAVE US NOW."
AND HE'D BE ALL "*YES!* IT'S FINALLY GREEN ARROW'S TURN TO SHINE!" AND I'D GO "*HA!* PSYCH!"
BRENT, I HOPEFULLY SPEAK FOR EVERYONE WHEN I SAY THANK GOD YOU'RE *NOT* SUPERMAN.
AND IF HE GAVE ME ANY LIP *ZING!* RIGHT INTO THE SUN.

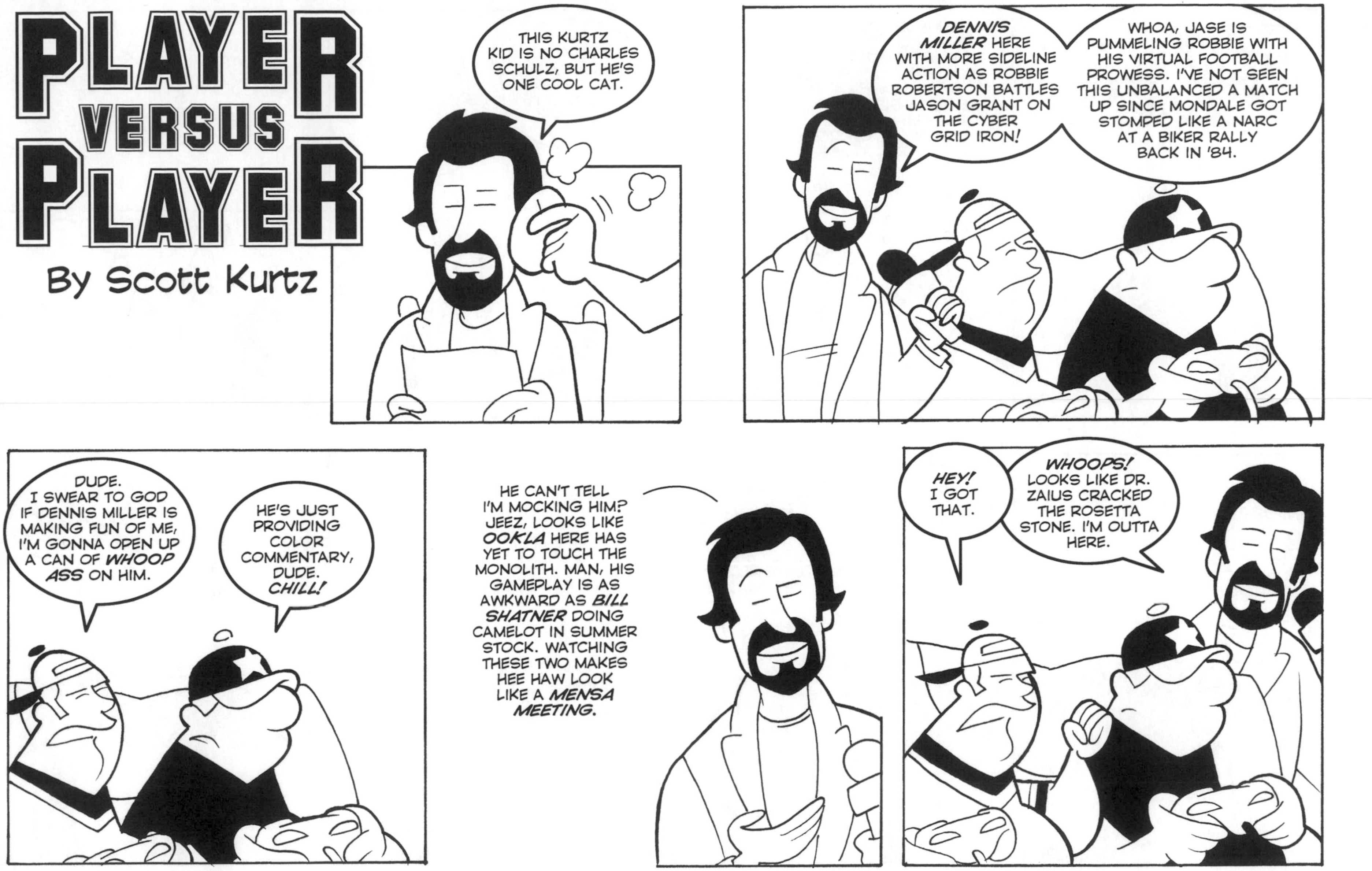
PLAYER VERSUS PLAYER
By Scott Kurtz
THIS KURTZ KID IS NO CHARLES SCHULZ, BUT HE'S ONE COOL CAT.
DENNIS MILLER HERE WITH MORE SIDELINE ACTION AS ROBBIE ROBERTSON BATTLES JASON GRANT ON THE CYBER GRID IRON!
WHOA, JASE IS PUMMELING ROBBIE WITH HIS VIRTUAL FOOTBALL PROWESS. I'VE NOT SEEN THIS UNBALANCED A MATCH UP SINCE MONDALE GOT STOMPED LIKE A NARC AT A BIKER RALLY BACK IN '84.
DUDE. I SWEAR TO GOD IF DENNIS MILLER IS MAKING FUN OF ME, I'M GONNA OPEN UP A CAN OF WHOOP ASS ON HIM.
HE'S JUST PROVIDING COLOR COMMENTARY, DUDE. CHILL!
HE CAN'T TELL I'M MOCKING HIM? JEEZ, LOOKS LIKE OOKLA HERE HAS YET TO TOUCH THE MONOLITH. MAN, HIS GAMEPLAY IS AS AWKWARD AS BILL SHATNER DOING CAMELOT IN SUMMER STOCK. WATCHING THESE TWO MAKES HEE HAW LOOK LIKE A MENSA MEETING.
HEY! I GOT THAT.
WHOOPS! LOOKS LIKE DR. ZAIUS CRACKED THE ROSETTA STONE. I'M OUTTA HERE.

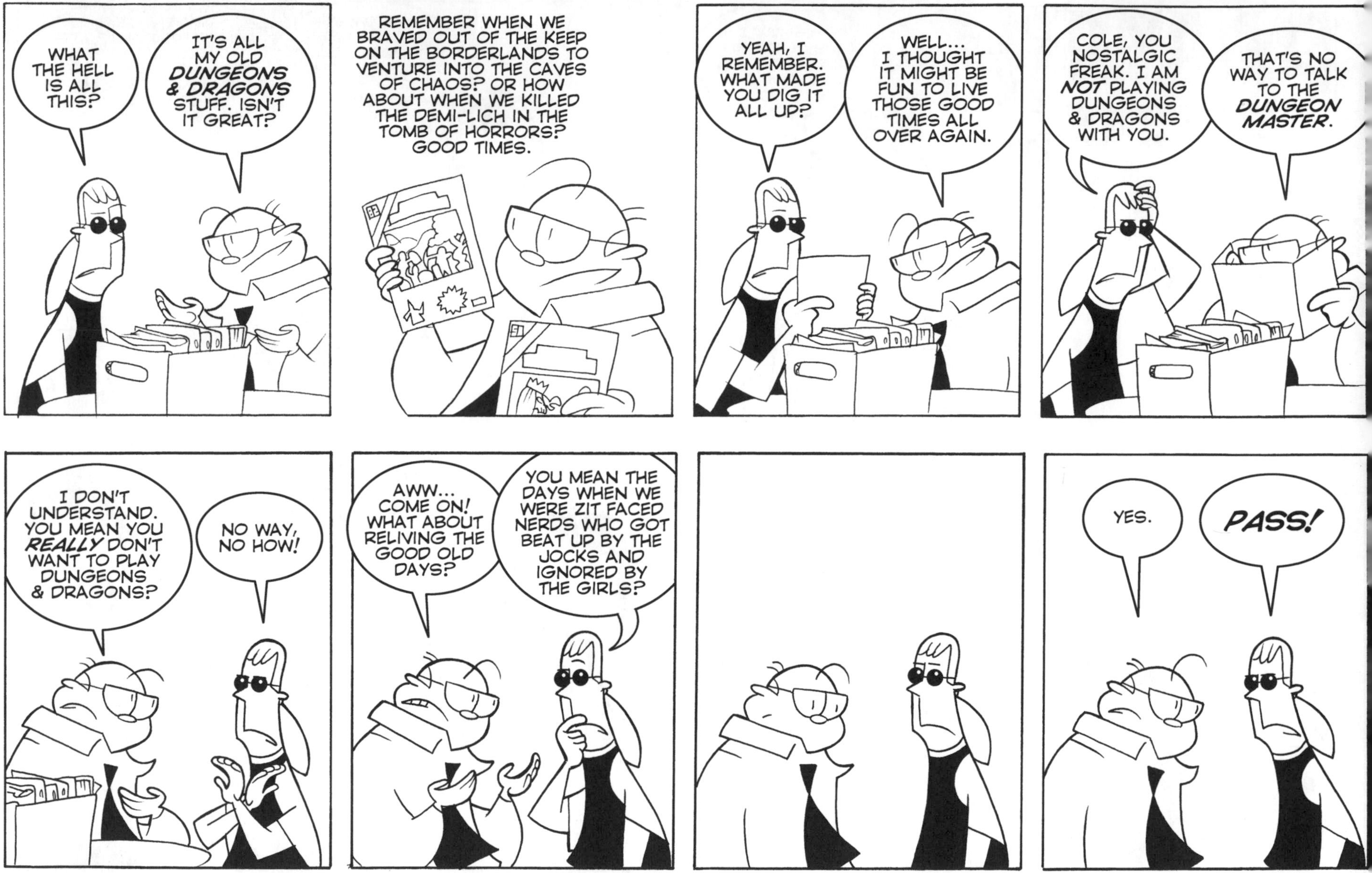
WHAT THE HELL IS ALL THIS?
IT'S ALL MY OLD ***DUNGEONS & DRAGONS*** STUFF. ISN'T IT GREAT?
REMEMBER WHEN WE BRAVED OUT OF THE KEEP ON THE BORDERLANDS TO VENTURE INTO THE CAVES OF CHAOS? OR HOW ABOUT WHEN WE KILLED THE DEMI-LICH IN THE TOMB OF HORRORS? GOOD TIMES.
YEAH, I REMEMBER. WHAT MADE YOU DIG IT ALL UP?
WELL... I THOUGHT IT MIGHT BE FUN TO LIVE THOSE GOOD TIMES ALL OVER AGAIN.
COLE, YOU NOSTALGIC FREAK. I AM ***NOT*** PLAYING DUNGEONS & DRAGONS WITH YOU.
THAT'S NO WAY TO TALK TO THE ***DUNGEON MASTER***.
I DON'T UNDERSTAND. YOU MEAN YOU ***REALLY*** DON'T WANT TO PLAY DUNGEONS & DRAGONS?
NO WAY, NO HOW!
AWW... COME ON! WHAT ABOUT RELIVING THE GOOD OLD DAYS?
YOU MEAN THE DAYS WHEN WE WERE ZIT FACED NERDS WHO GOT BEAT UP BY THE JOCKS AND IGNORED BY THE GIRLS?
YES.
PASS!

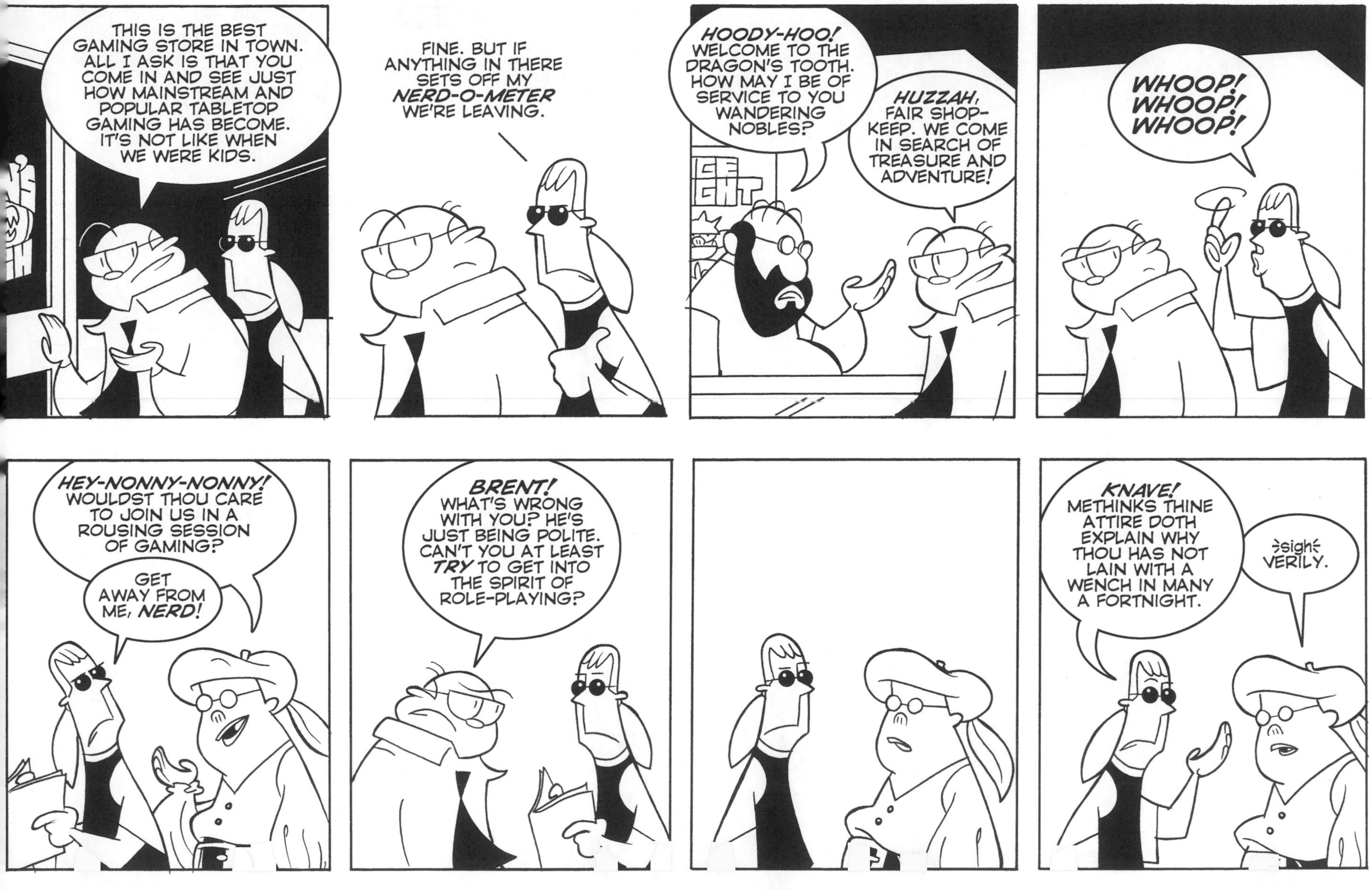
THIS IS THE BEST GAMING STORE IN TOWN. ALL I ASK IS THAT YOU COME IN AND SEE JUST HOW MAINSTREAM AND POPULAR TABLETOP GAMING HAS BECOME. IT'S NOT LIKE WHEN WE WERE KIDS.
FINE. BUT IF ANYTHING IN THERE SETS OFF MY NERD-O-METER WE'RE LEAVING.
HOODY-HOO! WELCOME TO THE DRAGON'S TOOTH. HOW MAY I BE OF SERVICE TO YOU WANDERING NOBLES?
HUZZAH, FAIR SHOP-KEEP. WE COME IN SEARCH OF TREASURE AND ADVENTURE!
WHOOP! WHOOP! WHOOP!
HEY-NONNY-NONNY! WOULDST THOU CARE TO JOIN US IN A ROUSING SESSION OF GAMING?
GET AWAY FROM ME, NERD!
BRENT! WHAT'S WRONG WITH YOU? HE'S JUST BEING POLITE. CAN'T YOU AT LEAST TRY TO GET INTO THE SPIRIT OF ROLE-PLAYING?
KNAVE! METHINKS THINE ATTIRE DOTH EXPLAIN WHY THOU HAS NOT LAIN WITH A WENCH IN MANY A FORTNIGHT.
sigh VERILY.

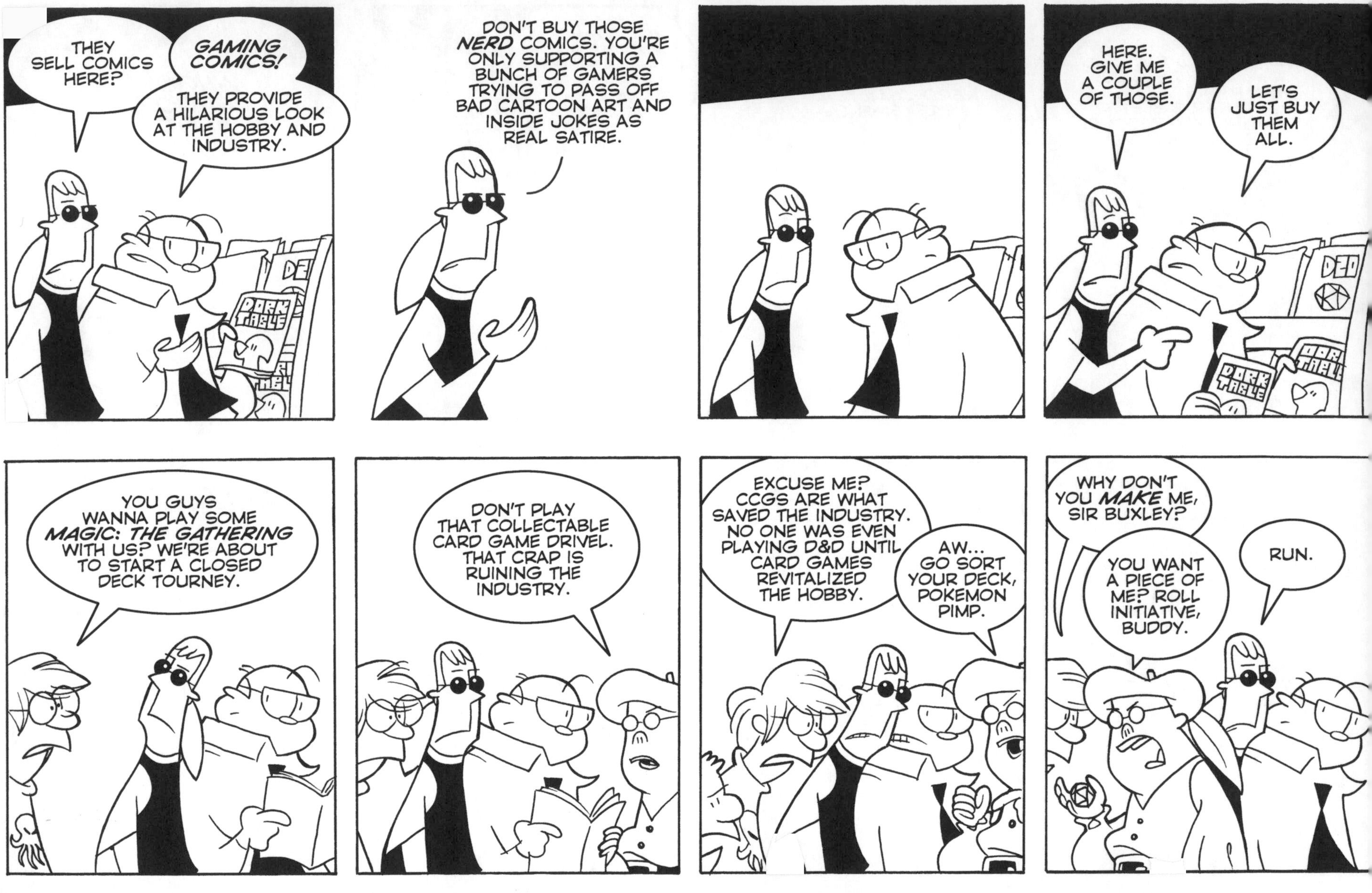
THEY SELL COMICS HERE?
GAMING COMICS!
THEY PROVIDE A HILARIOUS LOOK AT THE HOBBY AND INDUSTRY.
DORK TABLE
DON'T BUY THOSE NERD COMICS. YOU'RE ONLY SUPPORTING A BUNCH OF GAMERS TRYING TO PASS OFF BAD CARTOON ART AND INSIDE JOKES AS REAL SATIRE.
HERE. GIVE ME A COUPLE OF THOSE.
LET'S JUST BUY THEM ALL.
D&D
DORK TABLE
YOU GUYS WANNA PLAY SOME MAGIC: THE GATHERING WITH US? WE'RE ABOUT TO START A CLOSED DECK TOURNEY.
DON'T PLAY THAT COLLECTABLE CARD GAME DRIVEL. THAT CRAP IS RUINING THE INDUSTRY.
EXCUSE ME? CCGS ARE WHAT SAVED THE INDUSTRY. NO ONE WAS EVEN PLAYING D&D UNTIL CARD GAMES REVITALIZED THE HOBBY.
AW... GO SORT YOUR DECK, POKEMON PIMP.
WHY DON'T YOU MAKE ME, SIR BUXLEY?
YOU WANT A PIECE OF ME? ROLL INITIATIVE, BUDDY.
RUN.

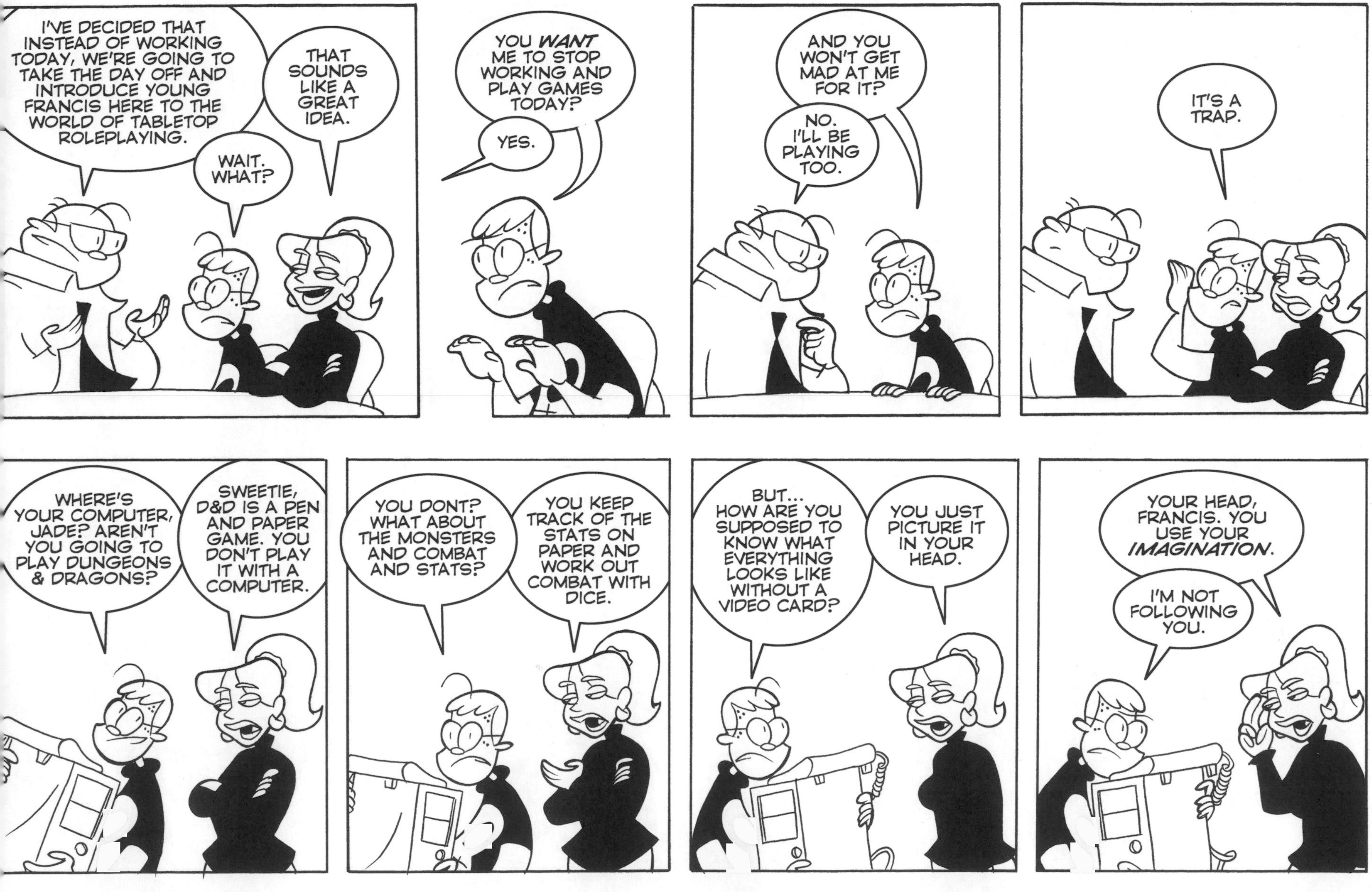
I'VE DECIDED THAT INSTEAD OF WORKING TODAY, WE'RE GOING TO TAKE THE DAY OFF AND INTRODUCE YOUNG FRANCIS HERE TO THE WORLD OF TABLETOP ROLEPLAYING.
WAIT. WHAT?
THAT SOUNDS LIKE A GREAT IDEA.
YOU *WANT* ME TO STOP WORKING AND PLAY GAMES TODAY?
YES.
AND YOU WON'T GET MAD AT ME FOR IT?
NO. I'LL BE PLAYING TOO.
IT'S A TRAP.
WHERE'S YOUR COMPUTER, JADE? AREN'T YOU GOING TO PLAY DUNGEONS & DRAGONS?
SWEETIE, D&D IS A PEN AND PAPER GAME. YOU DON'T PLAY IT WITH A COMPUTER.
YOU DONT? WHAT ABOUT THE MONSTERS AND COMBAT AND STATS?
YOU KEEP TRACK OF THE STATS ON PAPER AND WORK OUT COMBAT WITH DICE.
BUT... HOW ARE YOU SUPPOSED TO KNOW WHAT EVERYTHING LOOKS LIKE WITHOUT A VIDEO CARD?
YOU JUST PICTURE IT IN YOUR HEAD.
YOUR HEAD, FRANCIS. YOU USE YOUR *IMAGINATION*.
I'M NOT FOLLOWING YOU.

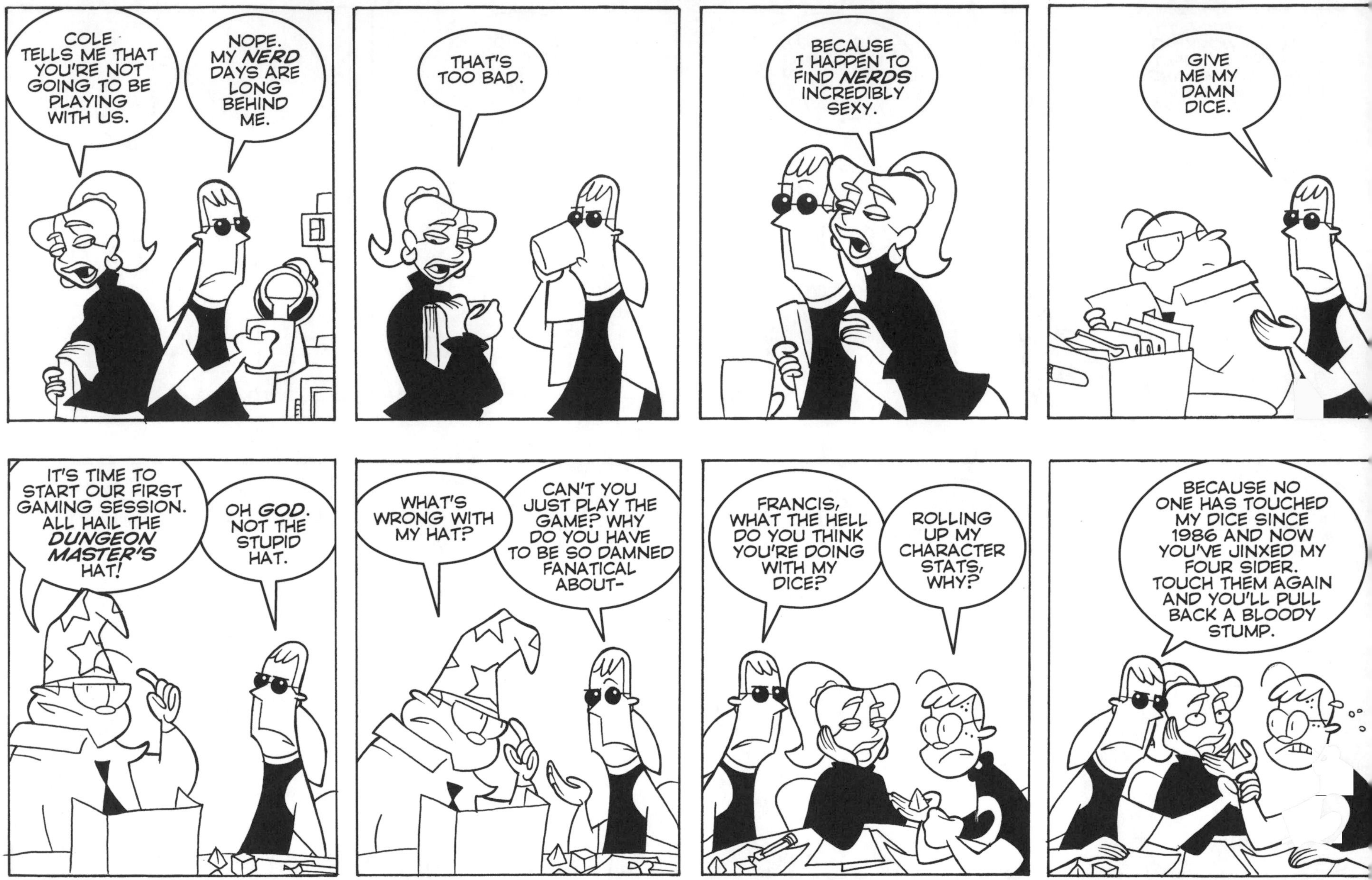
COLE TELLS ME THAT YOU'RE NOT GOING TO BE PLAYING WITH US.
NOPE. MY NERD DAYS ARE LONG BEHIND ME.
THAT'S TOO BAD.
BECAUSE I HAPPEN TO FIND NERDS INCREDIBLY SEXY.
GIVE ME MY DAMN DICE.
IT'S TIME TO START OUR FIRST GAMING SESSION. ALL HAIL THE DUNGEON MASTER'S HAT!
OH GOD. NOT THE STUPID HAT.
WHAT'S WRONG WITH MY HAT?
CAN'T YOU JUST PLAY THE GAME? WHY DO YOU HAVE TO BE SO DAMNED FANATICAL ABOUT-
FRANCIS, WHAT THE HELL DO YOU THINK YOU'RE DOING WITH MY DICE?
ROLLING UP MY CHARACTER STATS, WHY?
BECAUSE NO ONE HAS TOUCHED MY DICE SINCE 1986 AND NOW YOU'VE JINXED MY FOUR SIDER. TOUCH THEM AGAIN AND YOU'LL PULL BACK A BLOODY STUMP.

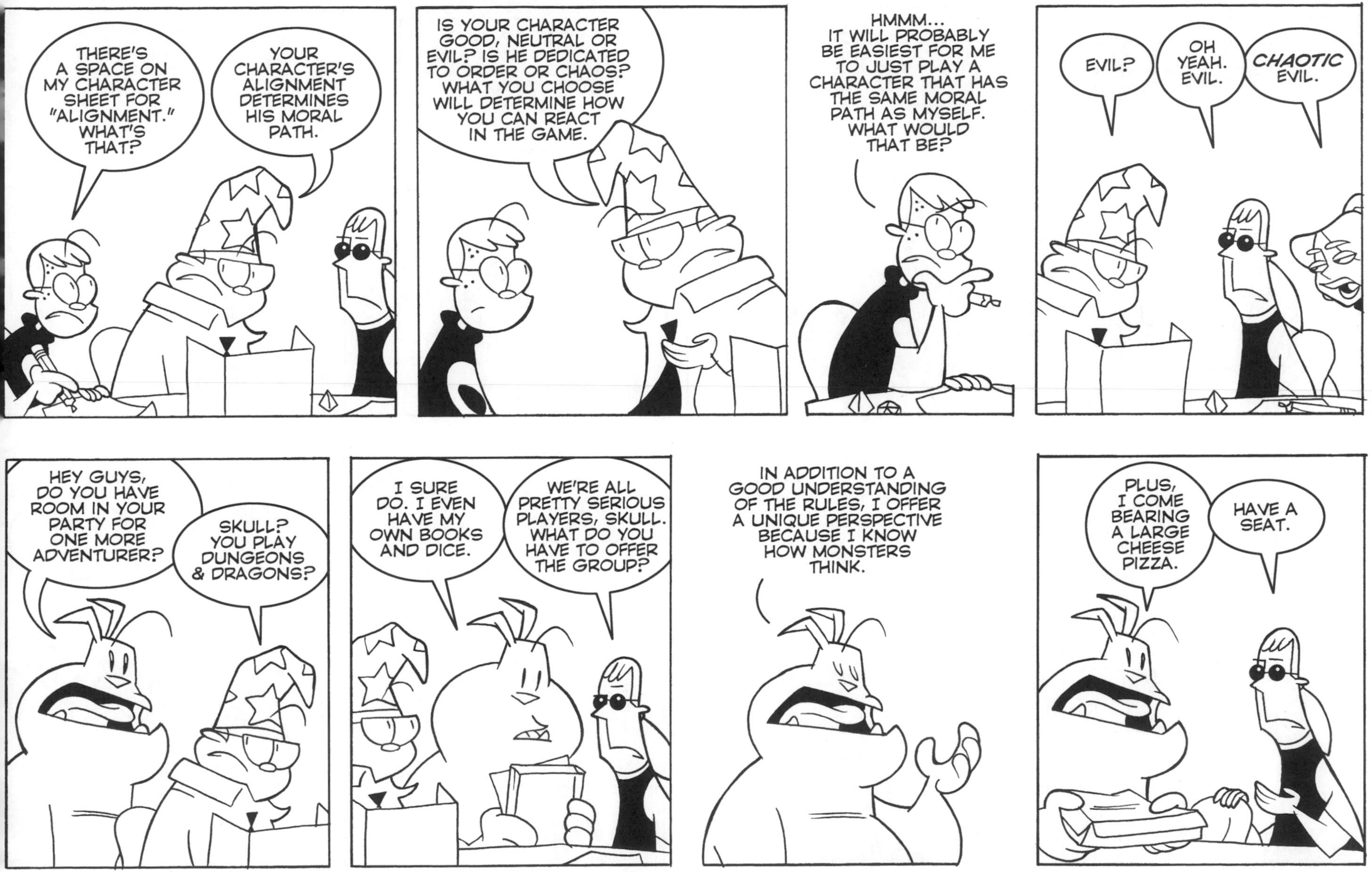
THERE'S A SPACE ON MY CHARACTER SHEET FOR "ALIGNMENT." WHAT'S THAT?
YOUR CHARACTER'S ALIGNMENT DETERMINES HIS MORAL PATH.
IS YOUR CHARACTER GOOD, NEUTRAL OR EVIL? IS HE DEDICATED TO ORDER OR CHAOS? WHAT YOU CHOOSE WILL DETERMINE HOW YOU CAN REACT IN THE GAME.
HMMM... IT WILL PROBABLY BE EASIEST FOR ME TO JUST PLAY A CHARACTER THAT HAS THE SAME MORAL PATH AS MYSELF. WHAT WOULD THAT BE?
EVIL?
OH YEAH. EVIL.
CHAOTIC EVIL.
HEY GUYS, DO YOU HAVE ROOM IN YOUR PARTY FOR ONE MORE ADVENTURER?
SKULL? YOU PLAY DUNGEONS & DRAGONS?
I SURE DO. I EVEN HAVE MY OWN BOOKS AND DICE.
WE'RE ALL PRETTY SERIOUS PLAYERS, SKULL. WHAT DO YOU HAVE TO OFFER THE GROUP?
IN ADDITION TO A GOOD UNDERSTANDING OF THE RULES, I OFFER A UNIQUE PERSPECTIVE BECAUSE I KNOW HOW MONSTERS THINK.
PLUS, I COME BEARING A LARGE CHEESE PIZZA.
HAVE A SEAT.

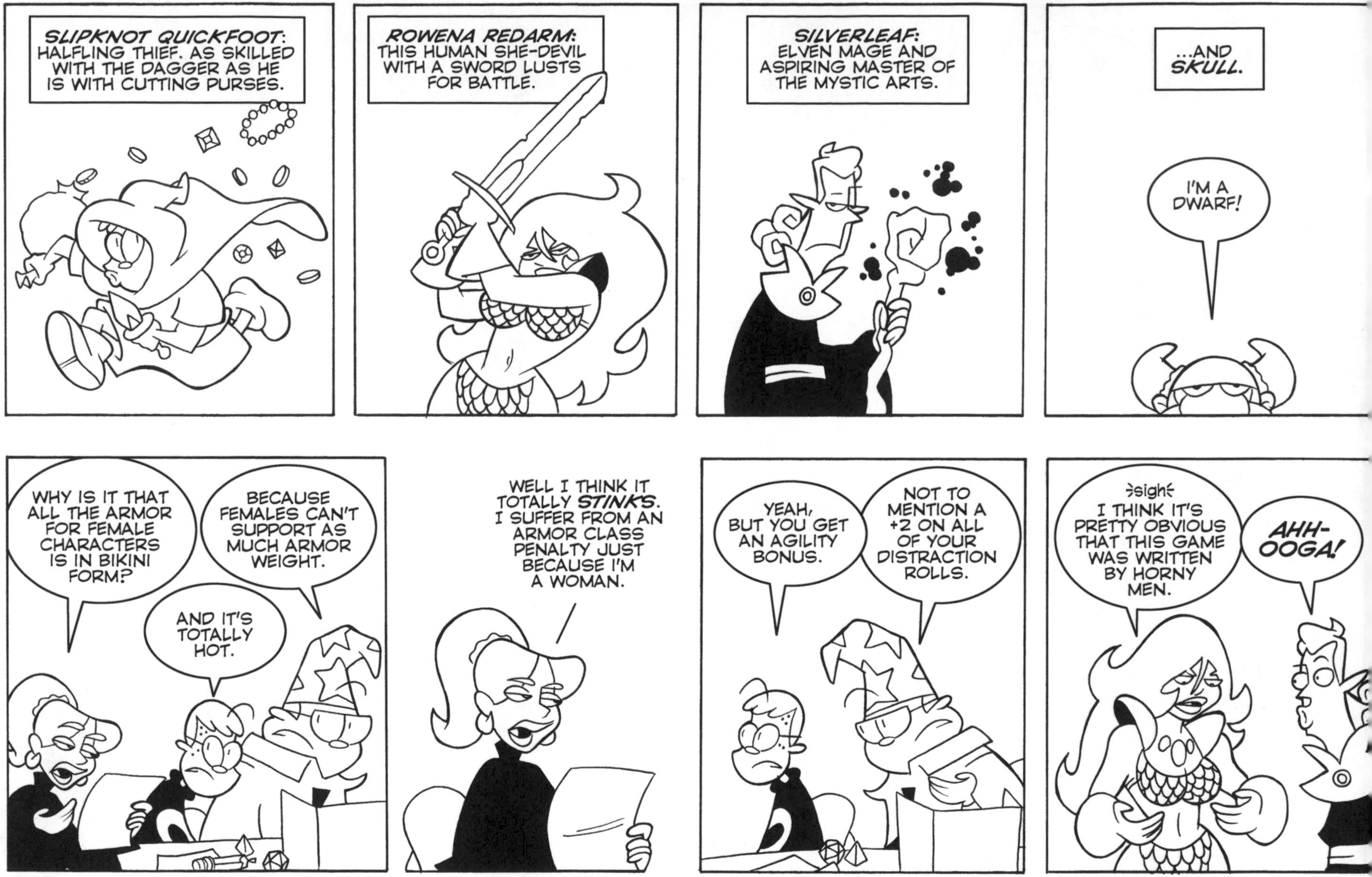

SLIPKNOT QUICKFOOT: HALFLING THIEF. AS SKILLED WITH THE DAGGER AS HE IS WITH CUTTING PURSES.
ROWENA REDARM: THIS HUMAN SHE-DEVIL WITH A SWORD LUSTS FOR BATTLE.
SILVERLEAF: ELVEN MAGE AND ASPIRING MASTER OF THE MYSTIC ARTS.
...AND SKULL.
I'M A DWARF!
WHY IS IT THAT ALL THE ARMOR FOR FEMALE CHARACTERS IS IN BIKINI FORM?
BECAUSE FEMALES CAN'T SUPPORT AS MUCH ARMOR WEIGHT.
AND IT'S TOTALLY HOT.
WELL I THINK IT TOTALLY STINKS. I SUFFER FROM AN ARMOR CLASS PENALTY JUST BECAUSE I'M A WOMAN.
YEAH, BUT YOU GET AN AGILITY BONUS.
NOT TO MENTION A +2 ON ALL OF YOUR DISTRACTION ROLLS.
sigh I THINK IT'S PRETTY OBVIOUS THAT THIS GAME WAS WRITTEN BY HORNY MEN.
AHH-OOGA!

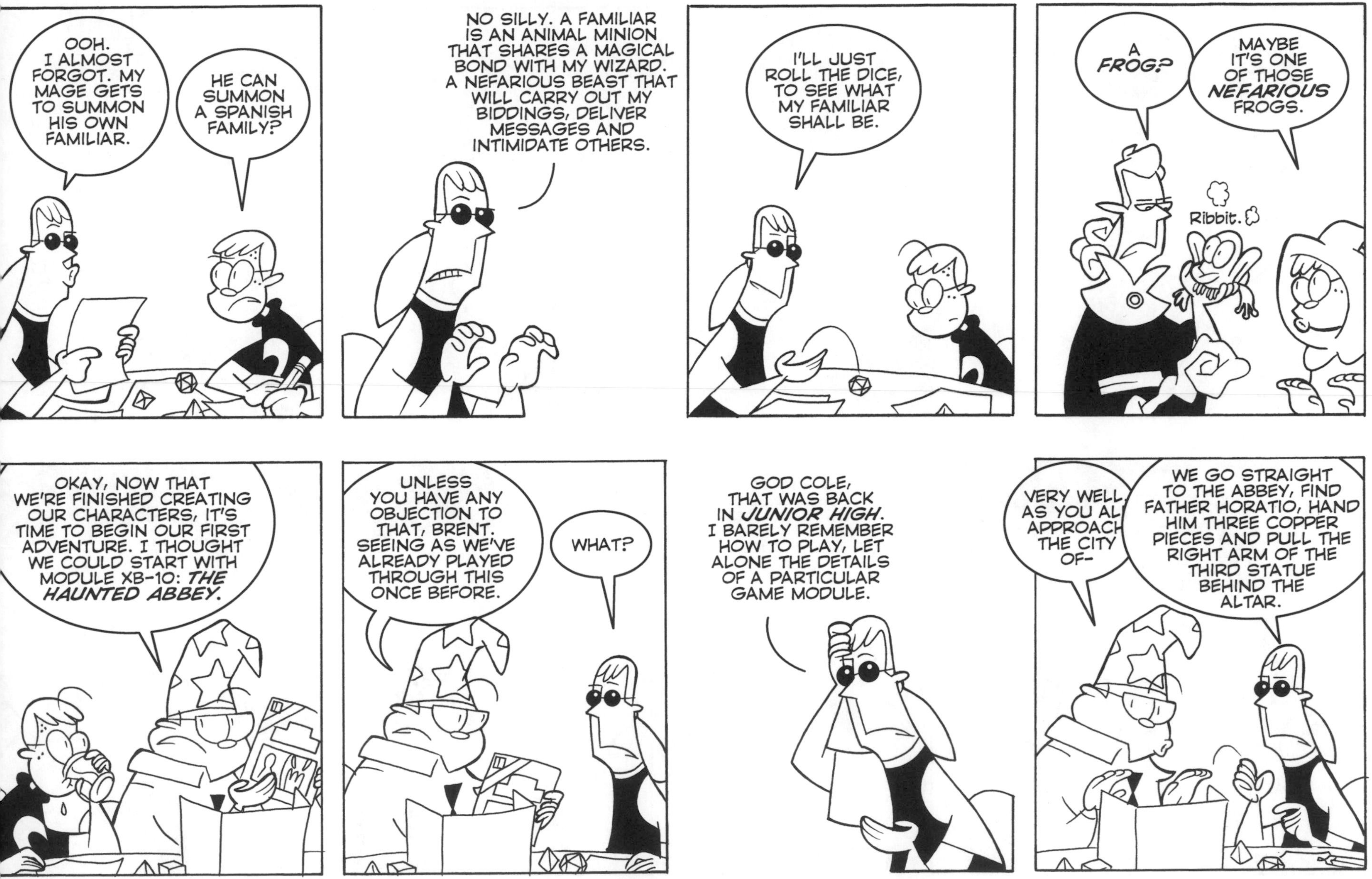
OOH. I ALMOST FORGOT. MY MAGE GETS TO SUMMON HIS OWN FAMILIAR.
HE CAN SUMMON A SPANISH FAMILY?
NO SILLY. A FAMILIAR IS AN ANIMAL MINION THAT SHARES A MAGICAL BOND WITH MY WIZARD. A NEFARIOUS BEAST THAT WILL CARRY OUT MY BIDDINGS, DELIVER MESSAGES AND INTIMIDATE OTHERS.
I'LL JUST ROLL THE DICE, TO SEE WHAT MY FAMILIAR SHALL BE.
A FROG?
MAYBE IT'S ONE OF THOSE NEFARIOUS FROGS.
Ribbit.
OKAY, NOW THAT WE'RE FINISHED CREATING OUR CHARACTERS, IT'S TIME TO BEGIN OUR FIRST ADVENTURE. I THOUGHT WE COULD START WITH MODULE XB-10: THE HAUNTED ABBEY.
UNLESS YOU HAVE ANY OBJECTION TO THAT, BRENT. SEEING AS WE'VE ALREADY PLAYED THROUGH THIS ONCE BEFORE.
WHAT?
GOD COLE, THAT WAS BACK IN JUNIOR HIGH. I BARELY REMEMBER HOW TO PLAY, LET ALONE THE DETAILS OF A PARTICULAR GAME MODULE.
VERY WELL. AS YOU AL APPROACH THE CITY OF-
WE GO STRAIGHT TO THE ABBEY, FIND FATHER HORATIO, HAND HIM THREE COPPER PIECES AND PULL THE RIGHT ARM OF THE THIRD STATUE BEHIND THE ALTAR.

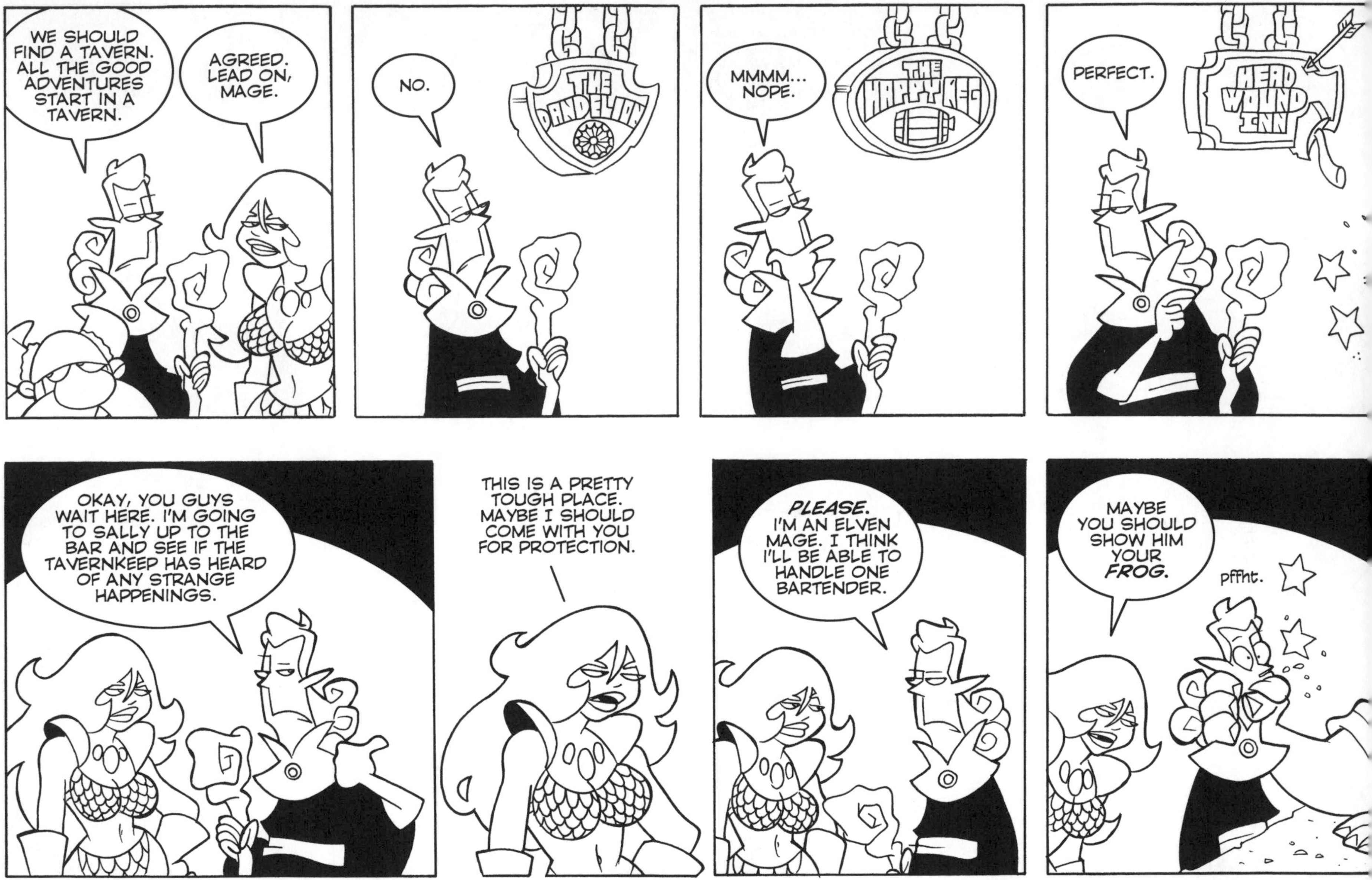
WE SHOULD FIND A TAVERN. ALL THE GOOD ADVENTURES START IN A TAVERN.
AGREED. LEAD ON, MAGE.
NO.
THE DANDELION
MMMM... NOPE.
THE HAPPY KEG
PERFECT.
HEAD WOUND INN
OKAY, YOU GUYS WAIT HERE. I'M GOING TO SALLY UP TO THE BAR AND SEE IF THE TAVERNKEEP HAS HEARD OF ANY STRANGE HAPPENINGS.
THIS IS A PRETTY TOUGH PLACE. MAYBE I SHOULD COME WITH YOU FOR PROTECTION.
PLEASE. I'M AN ELVEN MAGE. I THINK I'LL BE ABLE TO HANDLE ONE BARTENDER.
MAYBE YOU SHOULD SHOW HIM YOUR *FROG*.
pffht.

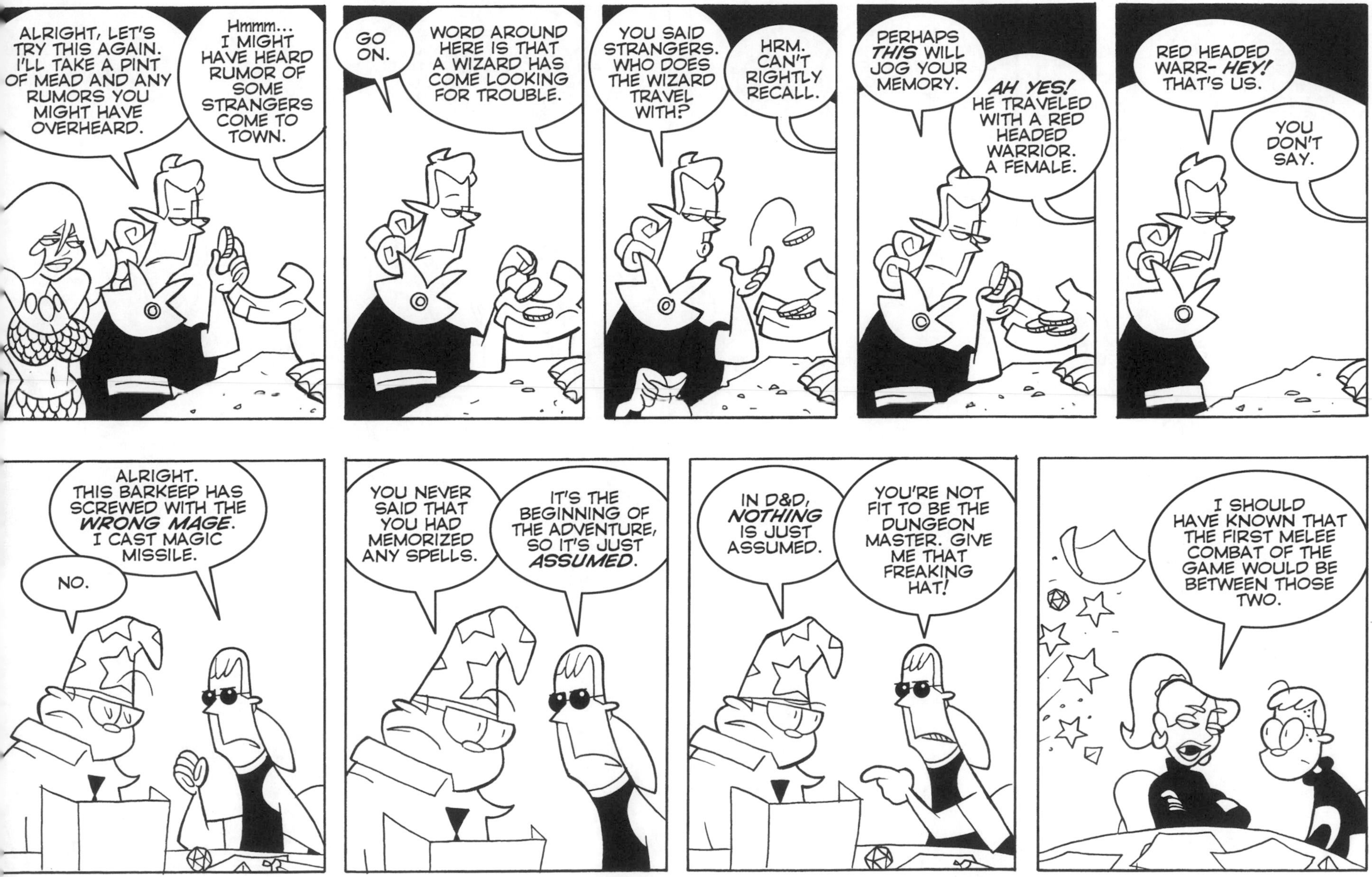
ALRIGHT, LET'S TRY THIS AGAIN. I'LL TAKE A PINT OF MEAD AND ANY RUMORS YOU MIGHT HAVE OVERHEARD.
Hmmm... I MIGHT HAVE HEARD RUMOR OF SOME STRANGERS COME TO TOWN.
GO ON.
WORD AROUND HERE IS THAT A WIZARD HAS COME LOOKING FOR TROUBLE.
YOU SAID STRANGERS. WHO DOES THE WIZARD TRAVEL WITH?
HRM. CAN'T RIGHTLY RECALL.
PERHAPS *THIS* WILL JOG YOUR MEMORY.
AH YES! HE TRAVELED WITH A RED HEADED WARRIOR. A FEMALE.
RED HEADED WARR- *HEY!* THAT'S US.
YOU DON'T SAY.
ALRIGHT. THIS BARKEEP HAS SCREWED WITH THE *WRONG MAGE*. I CAST MAGIC MISSILE.
NO.
YOU NEVER SAID THAT YOU HAD MEMORIZED ANY SPELLS.
IT'S THE BEGINNING OF THE ADVENTURE, SO IT'S JUST *ASSUMED*.
IN D&D, *NOTHING* IS JUST ASSUMED.
YOU'RE NOT FIT TO BE THE DUNGEON MASTER. GIVE ME THAT FREAKING HAT!
I SHOULD HAVE KNOWN THAT THE FIRST MELEE COMBAT OF THE GAME WOULD BE BETWEEN THOSE TWO.

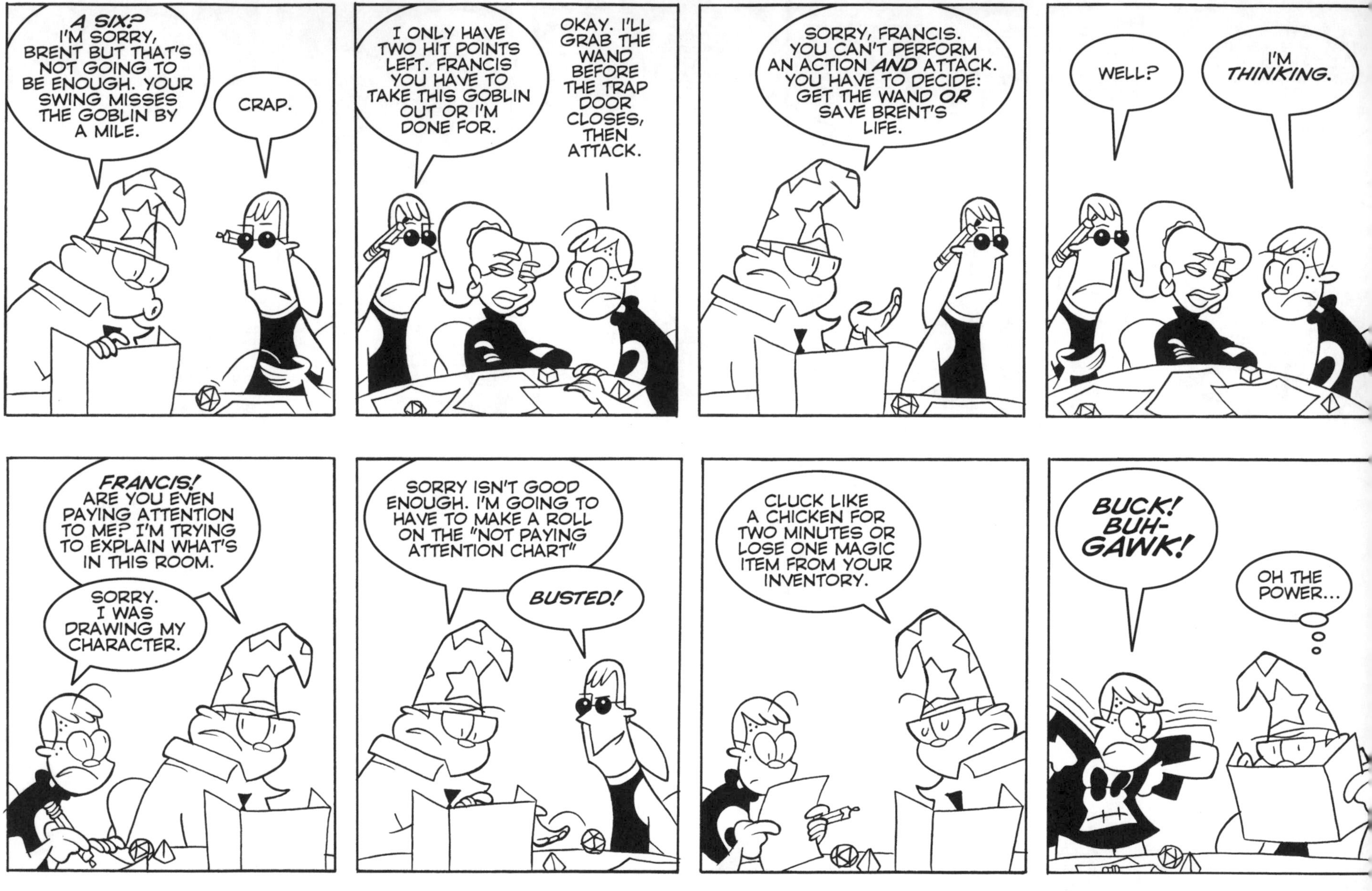
A SIX? I'M SORRY, BRENT BUT THAT'S NOT GOING TO BE ENOUGH. YOUR SWING MISSES THE GOBLIN BY A MILE.
CRAP.
I ONLY HAVE TWO HIT POINTS LEFT. FRANCIS YOU HAVE TO TAKE THIS GOBLIN OUT OR I'M DONE FOR.
OKAY. I'LL GRAB THE WAND BEFORE THE TRAP DOOR CLOSES, THEN ATTACK.
SORRY, FRANCIS. YOU CAN'T PERFORM AN ACTION AND ATTACK. YOU HAVE TO DECIDE: GET THE WAND OR SAVE BRENT'S LIFE.
WELL?
I'M THINKING.
FRANCIS! ARE YOU EVEN PAYING ATTENTION TO ME? I'M TRYING TO EXPLAIN WHAT'S IN THIS ROOM.
SORRY. I WAS DRAWING MY CHARACTER.
SORRY ISN'T GOOD ENOUGH. I'M GOING TO HAVE TO MAKE A ROLL ON THE "NOT PAYING ATTENTION CHART"
BUSTED!
CLUCK LIKE A CHICKEN FOR TWO MINUTES OR LOSE ONE MAGIC ITEM FROM YOUR INVENTORY.
BUCK! BUH-GAWK!
OH THE POWER...

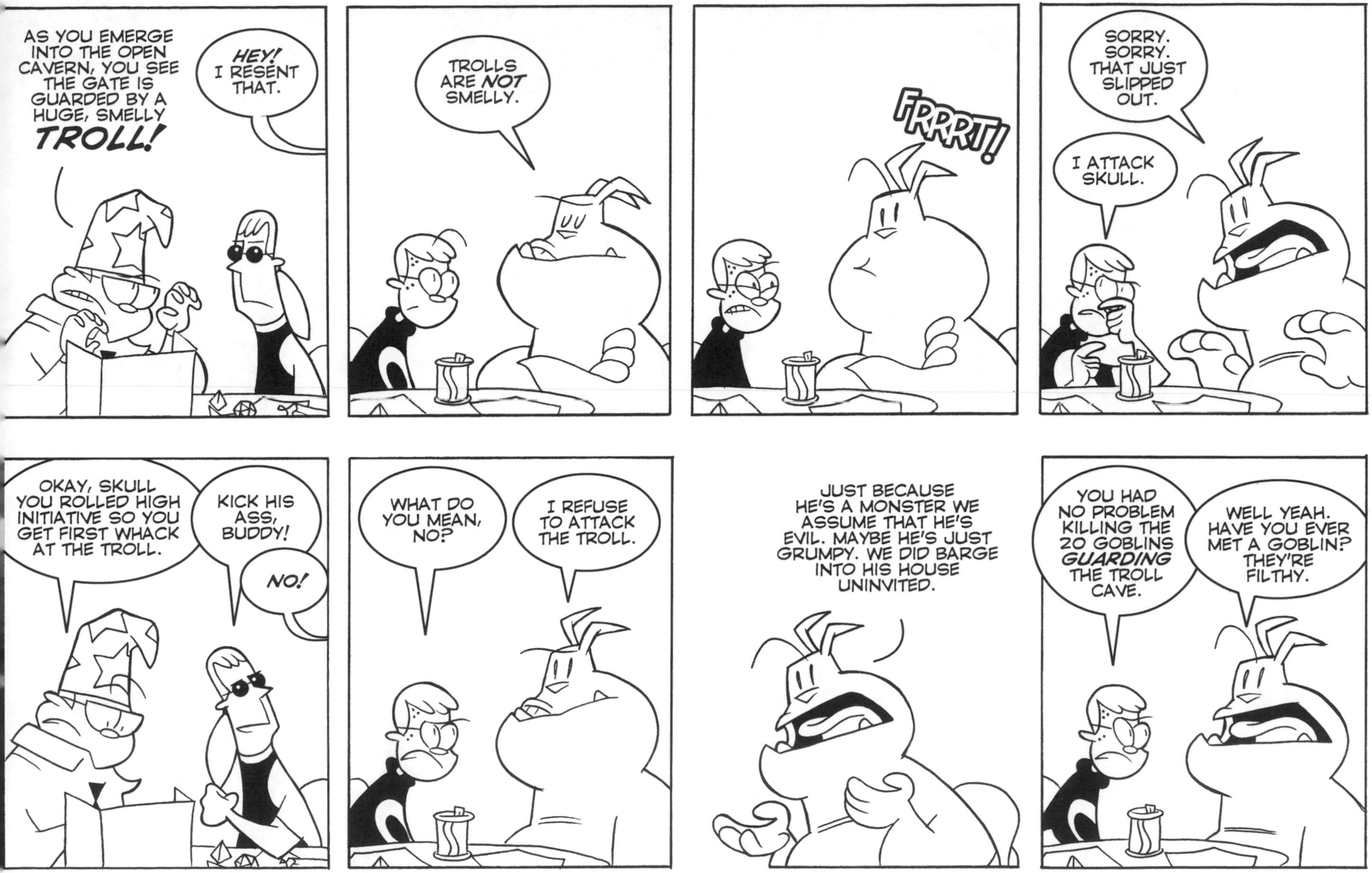
AS YOU EMERGE INTO THE OPEN CAVERN, YOU SEE THE GATE IS GUARDED BY A HUGE, SMELLY *TROLL!*
HEY! I RESENT THAT.
TROLLS ARE *NOT* SMELLY.
FRRRT!
SORRY. SORRY. THAT JUST SLIPPED OUT.
I ATTACK SKULL.
OKAY, SKULL YOU ROLLED HIGH INITIATIVE SO YOU GET FIRST WHACK AT THE TROLL.
KICK HIS ASS, BUDDY!
NO!
WHAT DO YOU MEAN, NO?
I REFUSE TO ATTACK THE TROLL.
JUST BECAUSE HE'S A MONSTER WE ASSUME THAT HE'S EVIL. MAYBE HE'S JUST GRUMPY. WE DID BARGE INTO HIS HOUSE UNINVITED.
YOU HAD NO PROBLEM KILLING THE 20 GOBLINS *GUARDING* THE TROLL CAVE.
WELL YEAH. HAVE YOU EVER MET A GOBLIN? THEY'RE FILTHY.

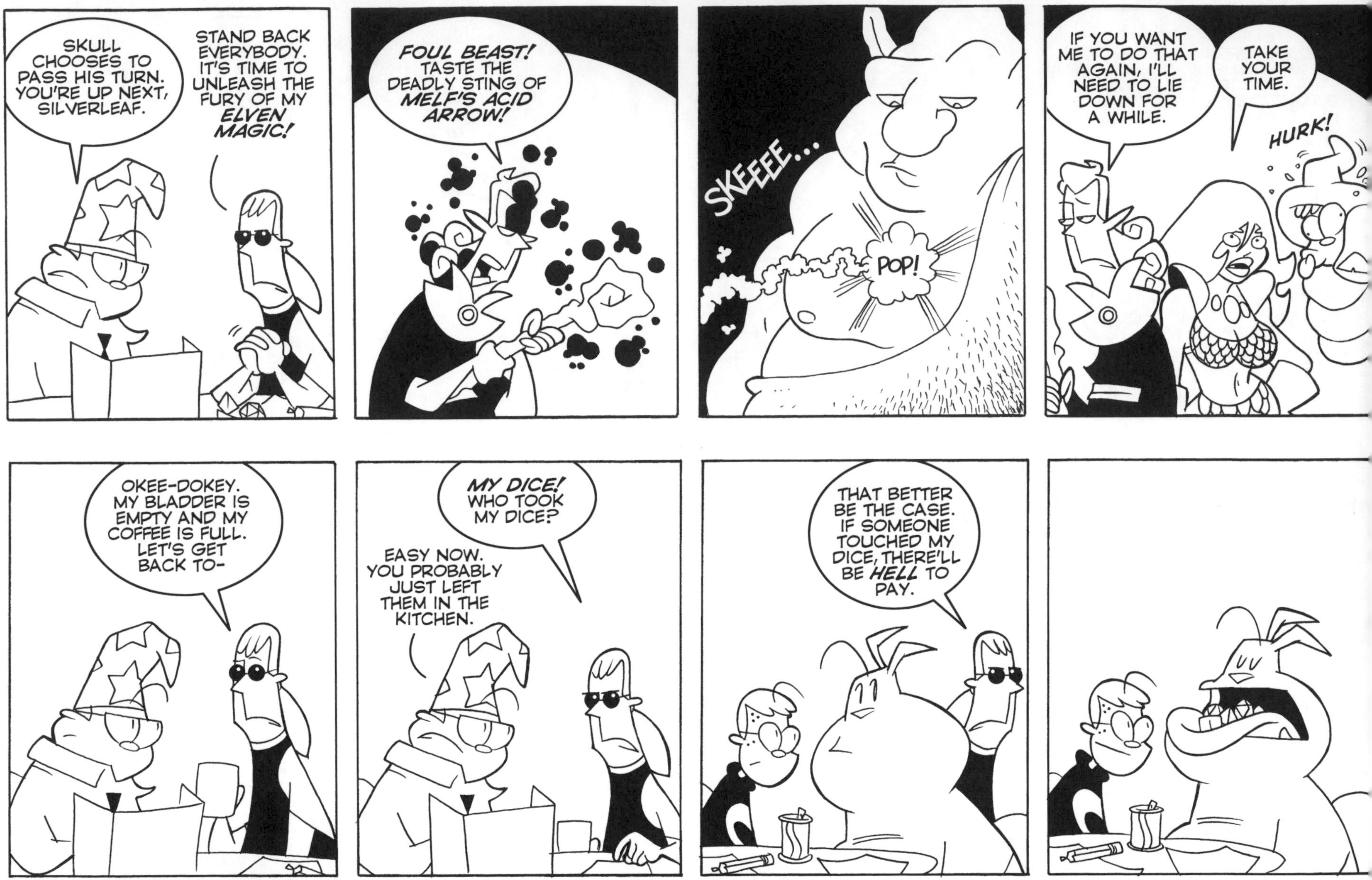
SKULL CHOOSES TO PASS HIS TURN. YOU'RE UP NEXT, SILVERLEAF.
STAND BACK EVERYBODY. IT'S TIME TO UNLEASH THE FURY OF MY ELVEN MAGIC!
FOUL BEAST! TASTE THE DEADLY STING OF MELF'S ACID ARROW!
SKEEEE...
POP!
IF YOU WANT ME TO DO THAT AGAIN, I'LL NEED TO LIE DOWN FOR A WHILE.
TAKE YOUR TIME.
HURK!
OKEE-DOKEY. MY BLADDER IS EMPTY AND MY COFFEE IS FULL. LET'S GET BACK TO-
MY DICE! WHO TOOK MY DICE?
EASY NOW. YOU PROBABLY JUST LEFT THEM IN THE KITCHEN.
THAT BETTER BE THE CASE. IF SOMEONE TOUCHED MY DICE, THERE'LL BE HELL TO PAY.

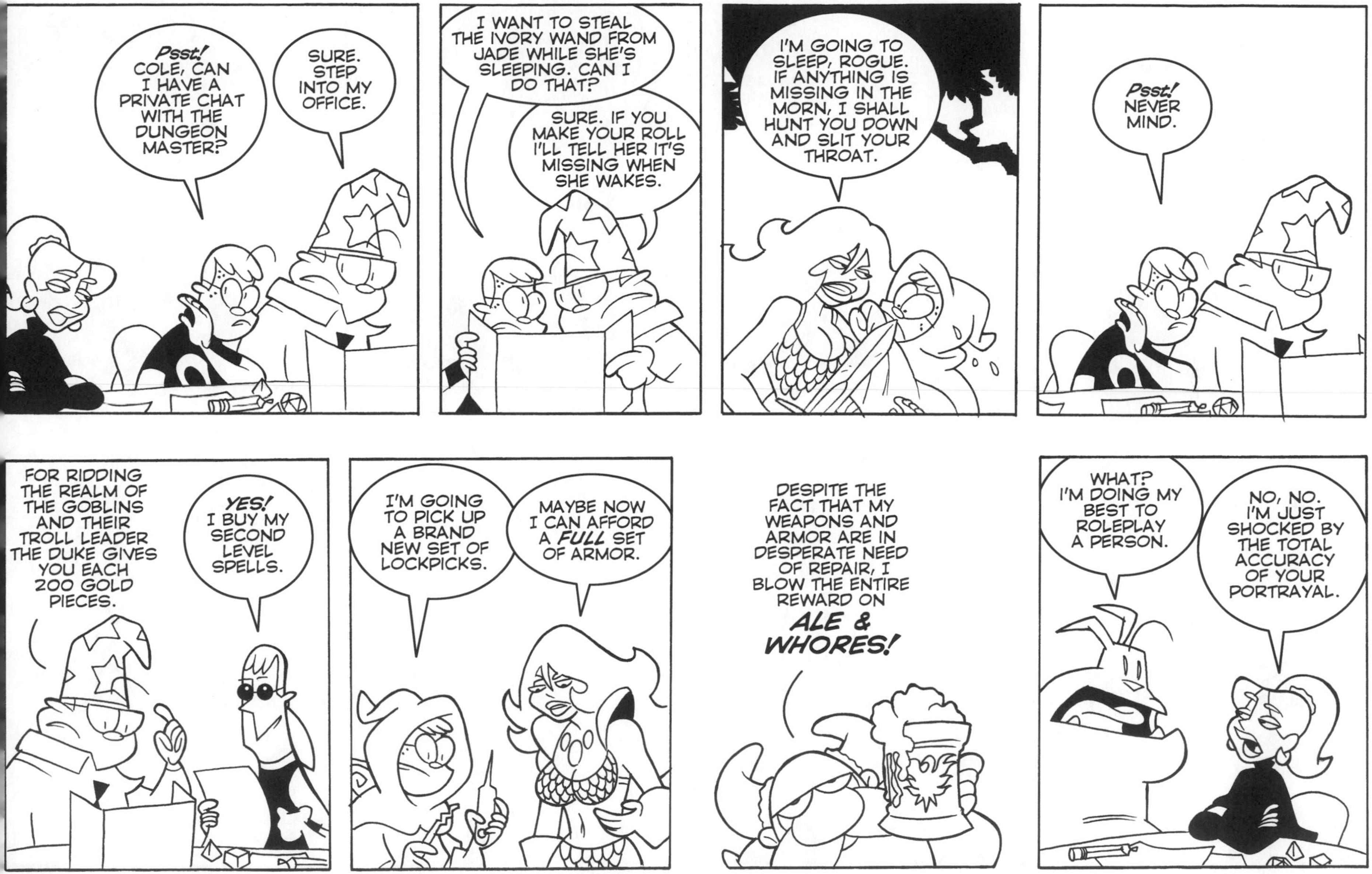

Psst! COLE, CAN I HAVE A PRIVATE CHAT WITH THE DUNGEON MASTER?
SURE. STEP INTO MY OFFICE.
I WANT TO STEAL THE IVORY WAND FROM JADE WHILE SHE'S SLEEPING. CAN I DO THAT?
SURE. IF YOU MAKE YOUR ROLL I'LL TELL HER IT'S MISSING WHEN SHE WAKES.
I'M GOING TO SLEEP, ROGUE. IF ANYTHING IS MISSING IN THE MORN, I SHALL HUNT YOU DOWN AND SLIT YOUR THROAT.
Psst! NEVER MIND.
FOR RIDDING THE REALM OF THE GOBLINS AND THEIR TROLL LEADER THE DUKE GIVES YOU EACH 200 GOLD PIECES.
YES! I BUY MY SECOND LEVEL SPELLS.
I'M GOING TO PICK UP A BRAND NEW SET OF LOCKPICKS.
MAYBE NOW I CAN AFFORD A FULL SET OF ARMOR.
DESPITE THE FACT THAT MY WEAPONS AND ARMOR ARE IN DESPERATE NEED OF REPAIR, I BLOW THE ENTIRE REWARD ON ALE & WHORES!
WHAT? I'M DOING MY BEST TO ROLEPLAY A PERSON.
NO, NO. I'M JUST SHOCKED BY THE TOTAL ACCURACY OF YOUR PORTRAYAL.

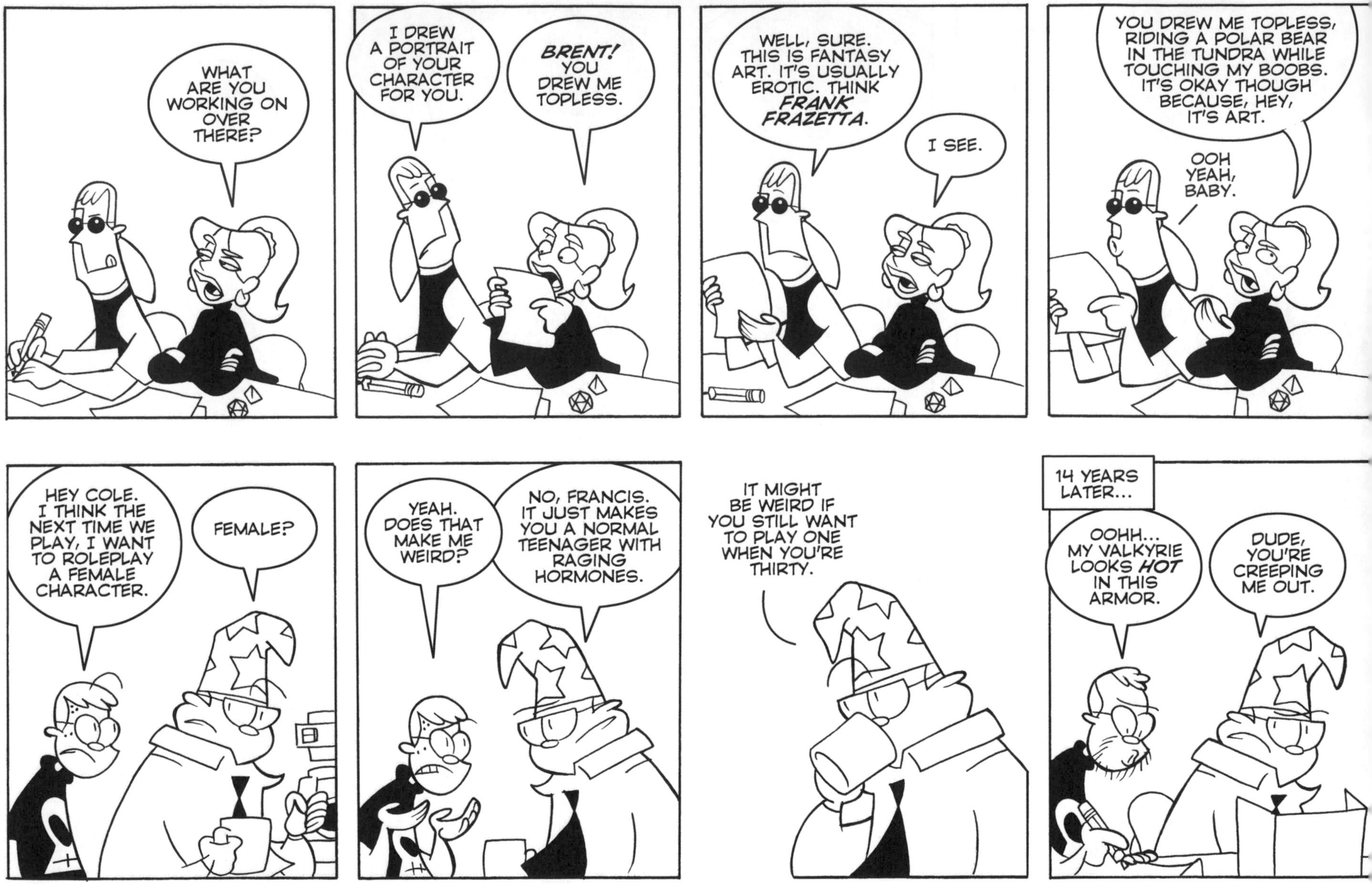
WHAT ARE YOU WORKING ON OVER THERE?
I DREW A PORTRAIT OF YOUR CHARACTER FOR YOU.
BRENT! YOU DREW ME TOPLESS.
WELL, SURE. THIS IS FANTASY ART. IT'S USUALLY EROTIC. THINK FRANK FRAZETTA.
I SEE.
YOU DREW ME TOPLESS, RIDING A POLAR BEAR IN THE TUNDRA WHILE TOUCHING MY BOOBS. IT'S OKAY THOUGH BECAUSE, HEY, IT'S ART.
OOH YEAH, BABY.
HEY COLE. I THINK THE NEXT TIME WE PLAY, I WANT TO ROLEPLAY A FEMALE CHARACTER.
FEMALE?
YEAH. DOES THAT MAKE ME WEIRD?
NO, FRANCIS. IT JUST MAKES YOU A NORMAL TEENAGER WITH RAGING HORMONES.
IT MIGHT BE WEIRD IF YOU STILL WANT TO PLAY ONE WHEN YOU'RE THIRTY.
14 YEARS LATER...
OOHH... MY VALKYRIE LOOKS HOT IN THIS ARMOR.
DUDE, YOU'RE CREEPING ME OUT.

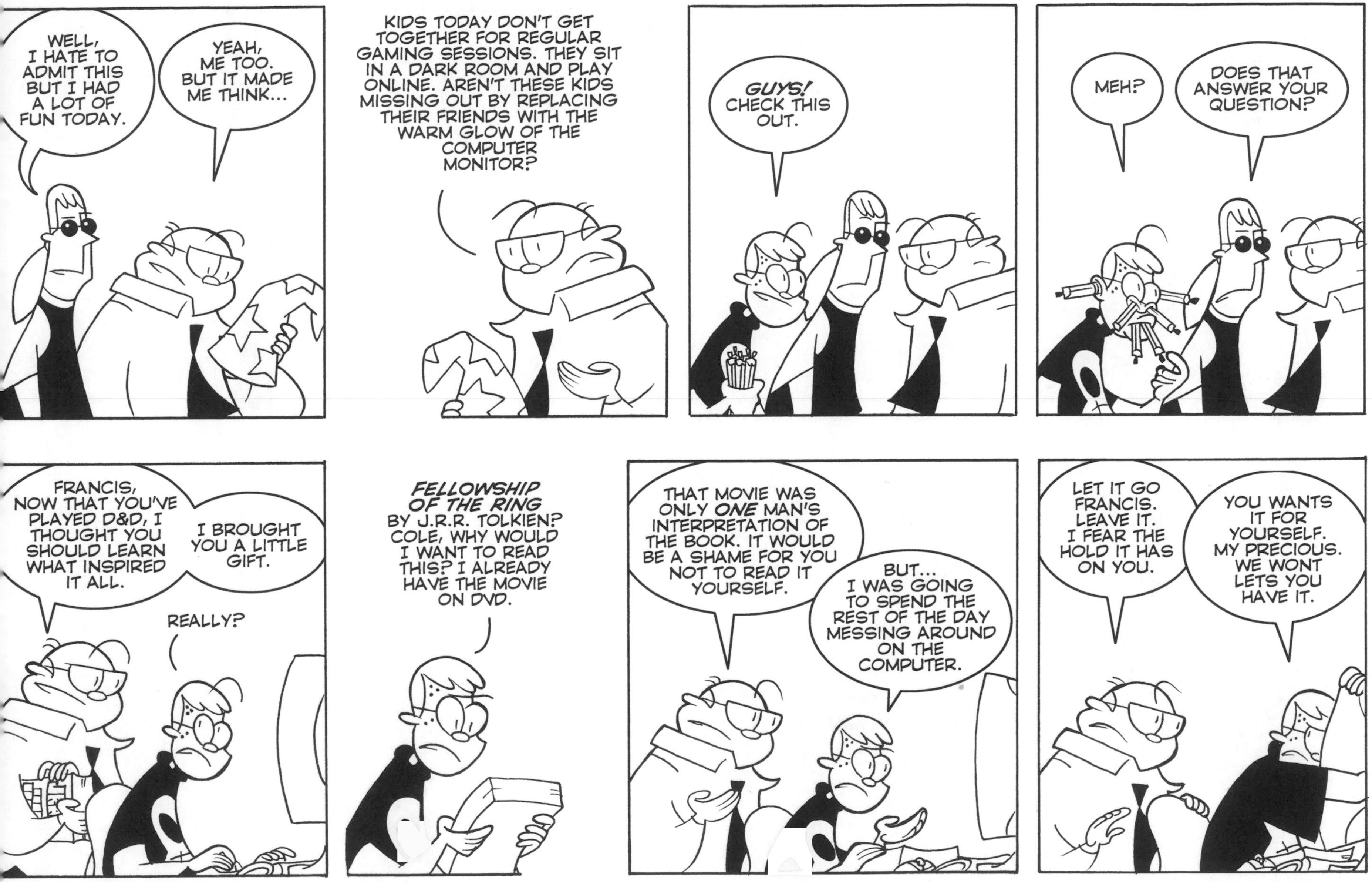
WELL, I HATE TO ADMIT THIS BUT I HAD A LOT OF FUN TODAY.
YEAH, ME TOO. BUT IT MADE ME THINK...
KIDS TODAY DON'T GET TOGETHER FOR REGULAR GAMING SESSIONS. THEY SIT IN A DARK ROOM AND PLAY ONLINE. AREN'T THESE KIDS MISSING OUT BY REPLACING THEIR FRIENDS WITH THE WARM GLOW OF THE COMPUTER MONITOR?
GUYS! CHECK THIS OUT.
MEH?
DOES THAT ANSWER YOUR QUESTION?
FRANCIS, NOW THAT YOU'VE PLAYED D&D, I THOUGHT YOU SHOULD LEARN WHAT INSPIRED IT ALL.
I BROUGHT YOU A LITTLE GIFT.
REALLY?
FELLOWSHIP OF THE RING BY J.R.R. TOLKIEN? COLE, WHY WOULD I WANT TO READ THIS? I ALREADY HAVE THE MOVIE ON DVD.
THAT MOVIE WAS ONLY ONE MAN'S INTERPRETATION OF THE BOOK. IT WOULD BE A SHAME FOR YOU NOT TO READ IT YOURSELF.
BUT... I WAS GOING TO SPEND THE REST OF THE DAY MESSING AROUND ON THE COMPUTER.
LET IT GO FRANCIS. LEAVE IT. I FEAR THE HOLD IT HAS ON YOU.
YOU WANTS IT FOR YOURSELF. MY PRECIOUS. WE WONT LETS YOU HAVE IT.

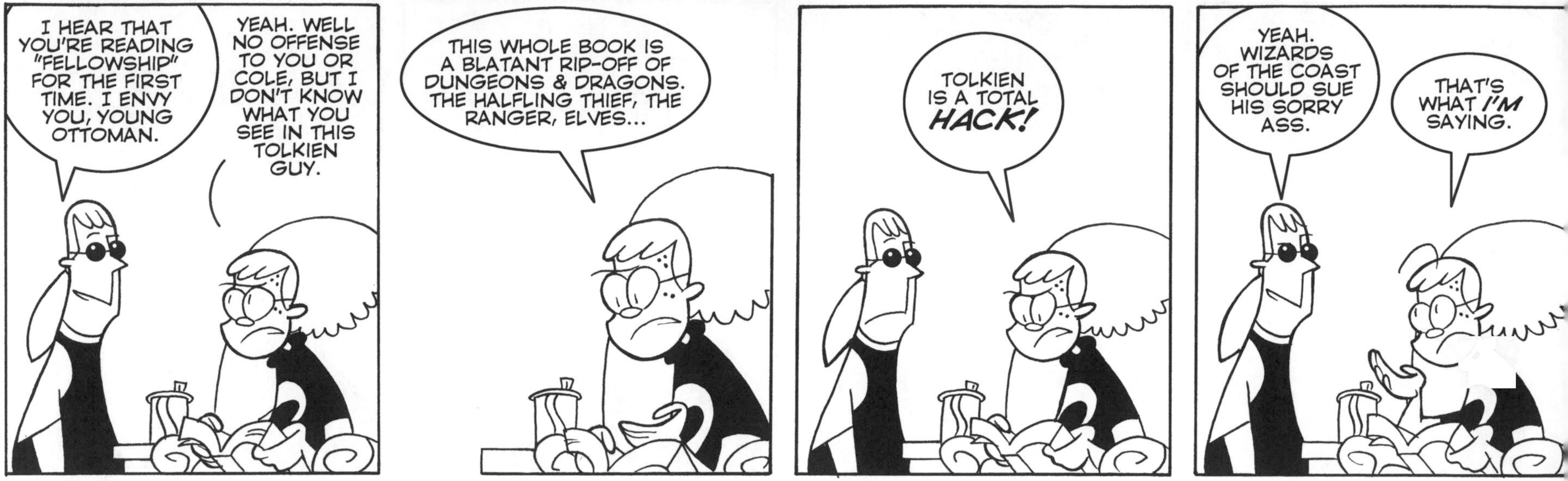
I HEAR THAT YOU'RE READING "FELLOWSHIP" FOR THE FIRST TIME. I ENVY YOU, YOUNG OTTOMAN.
YEAH. WELL NO OFFENSE TO YOU OR COLE, BUT I DON'T KNOW WHAT YOU SEE IN THIS TOLKIEN GUY.
THIS WHOLE BOOK IS A BLATANT RIP-OFF OF DUNGEONS & DRAGONS. THE HALFLING THIEF, THE RANGER, ELVES...
TOLKIEN IS A TOTAL *HACK!*
YEAH. WIZARDS OF THE COAST SHOULD SUE HIS SORRY ASS.
THAT'S WHAT *I'M* SAYING.

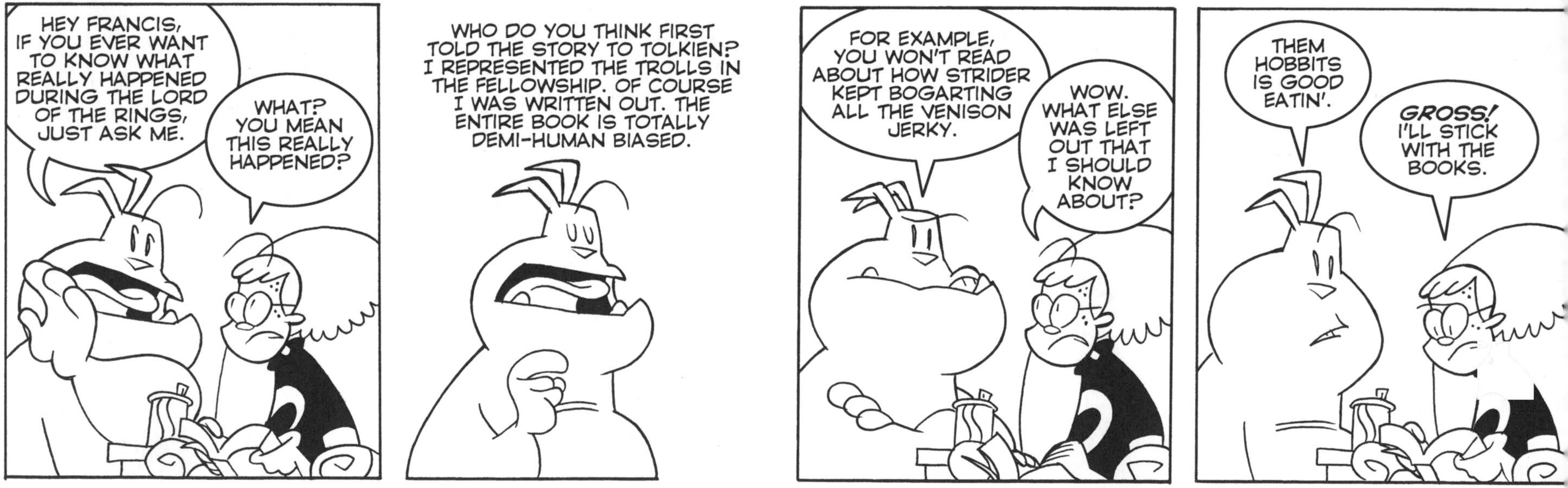
HEY FRANCIS, IF YOU EVER WANT TO KNOW WHAT REALLY HAPPENED DURING THE LORD OF THE RINGS, JUST ASK ME.
WHAT? YOU MEAN THIS REALLY HAPPENED?
WHO DO YOU THINK FIRST TOLD THE STORY TO TOLKIEN? I REPRESENTED THE TROLLS IN THE FELLOWSHIP. OF COURSE I WAS WRITTEN OUT. THE ENTIRE BOOK IS TOTALLY DEMI-HUMAN BIASED.
FOR EXAMPLE, YOU WON'T READ ABOUT HOW STRIDER KEPT BOGARTING ALL THE VENISON JERKY.
WOW. WHAT ELSE WAS LEFT OUT THAT I SHOULD KNOW ABOUT?
THEM HOBBITS IS GOOD EATIN'.
GROSS! I'LL STICK WITH THE BOOKS.

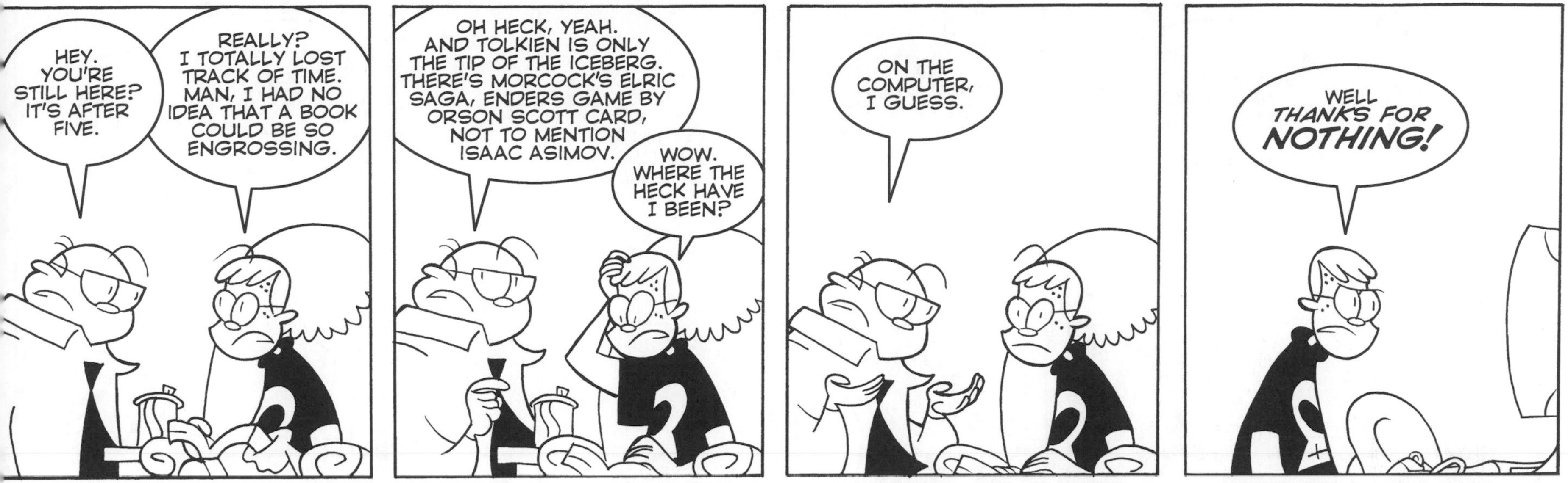
HEY. YOU'RE STILL HERE? IT'S AFTER FIVE.
REALLY? I TOTALLY LOST TRACK OF TIME. MAN, I HAD NO IDEA THAT A BOOK COULD BE SO ENGROSSING.
OH HECK, YEAH. AND TOLKIEN IS ONLY THE TIP OF THE ICEBERG. THERE'S MORCOCK'S ELRIC SAGA, ENDERS GAME BY ORSON SCOTT CARD, NOT TO MENTION ISAAC ASIMOV.
WOW. WHERE THE HECK HAVE I BEEN?
ON THE COMPUTER, I GUESS.
WELL *THANKS FOR* ***NOTHING!***

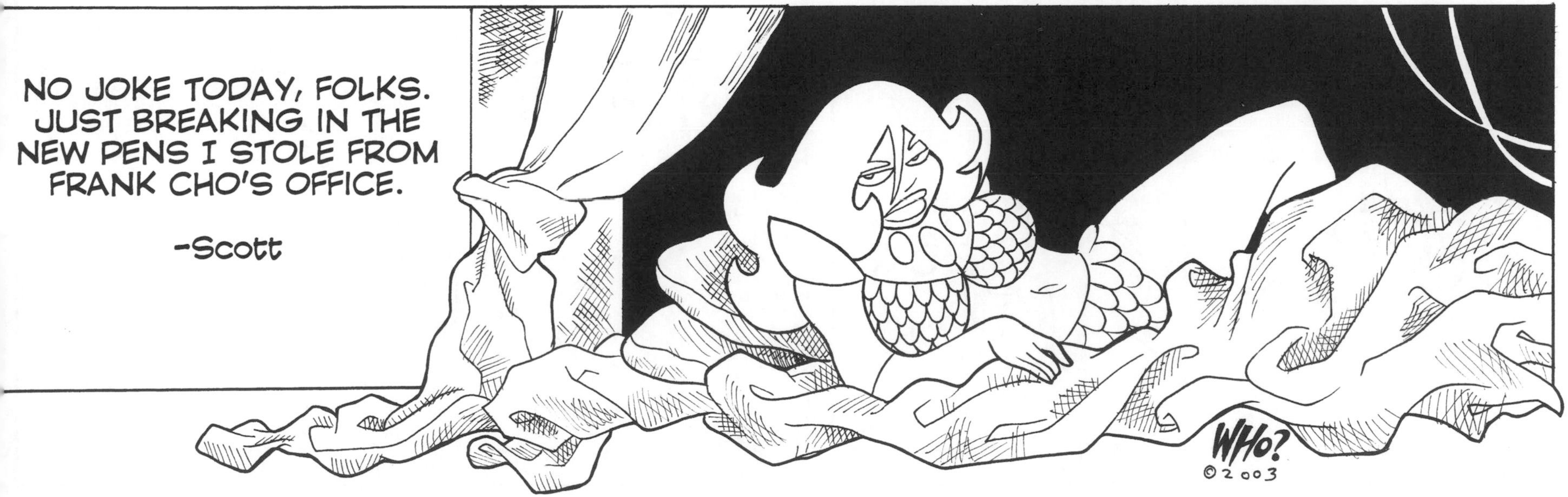
NO JOKE TODAY, FOLKS. JUST BREAKING IN THE NEW PENS I STOLE FROM FRANK CHO'S OFFICE.
-Scott
WHO?
©2003

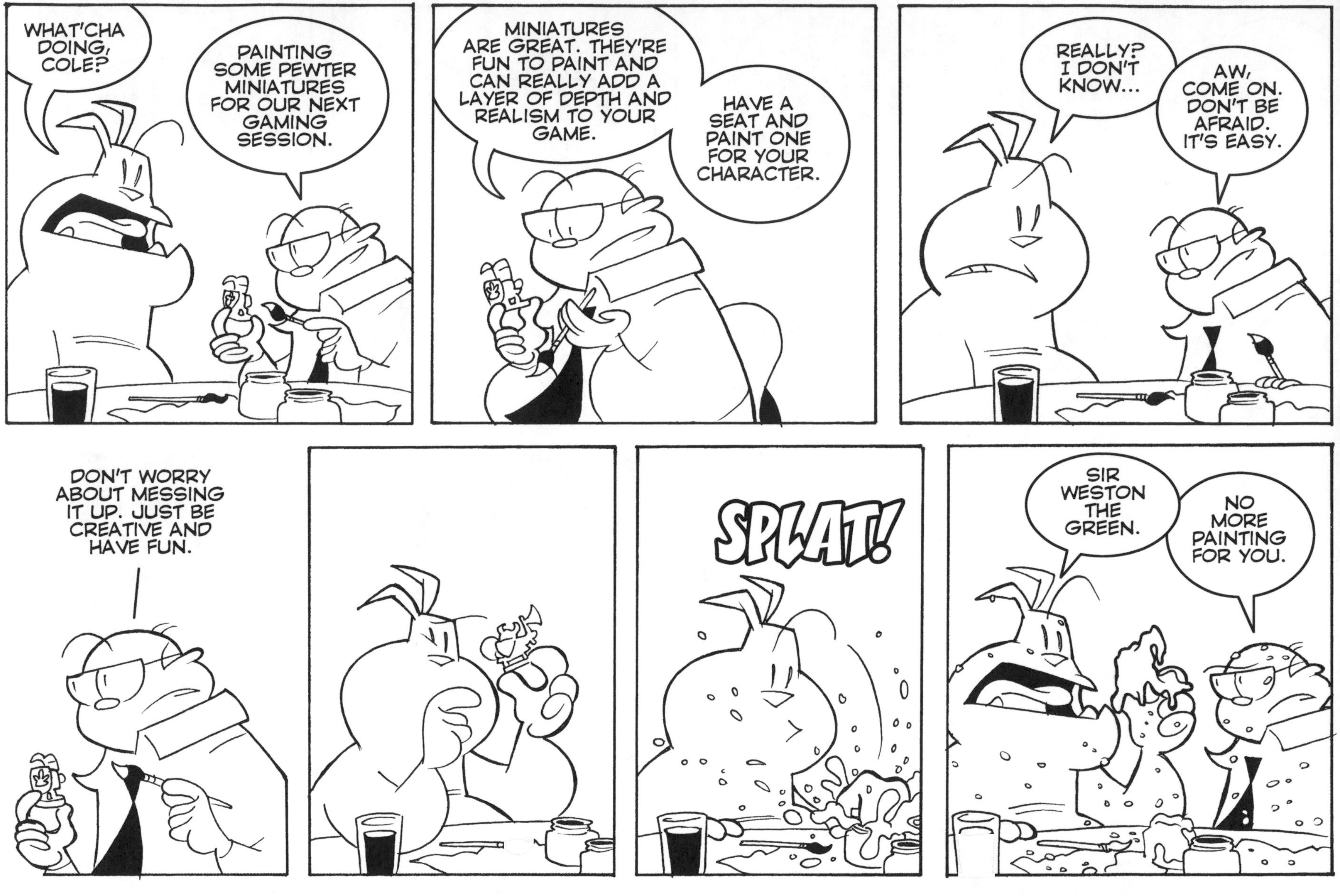
WHAT'CHA DOING, COLE?
PAINTING SOME PEWTER MINIATURES FOR OUR NEXT GAMING SESSION.
MINIATURES ARE GREAT. THEY'RE FUN TO PAINT AND CAN REALLY ADD A LAYER OF DEPTH AND REALISM TO YOUR GAME.
HAVE A SEAT AND PAINT ONE FOR YOUR CHARACTER.
REALLY? I DON'T KNOW...
AW, COME ON. DON'T BE AFRAID. IT'S EASY.
DON'T WORRY ABOUT MESSING IT UP. JUST BE CREATIVE AND HAVE FUN.
SPLAT!
SIR WESTON THE GREEN.
NO MORE PAINTING FOR YOU.

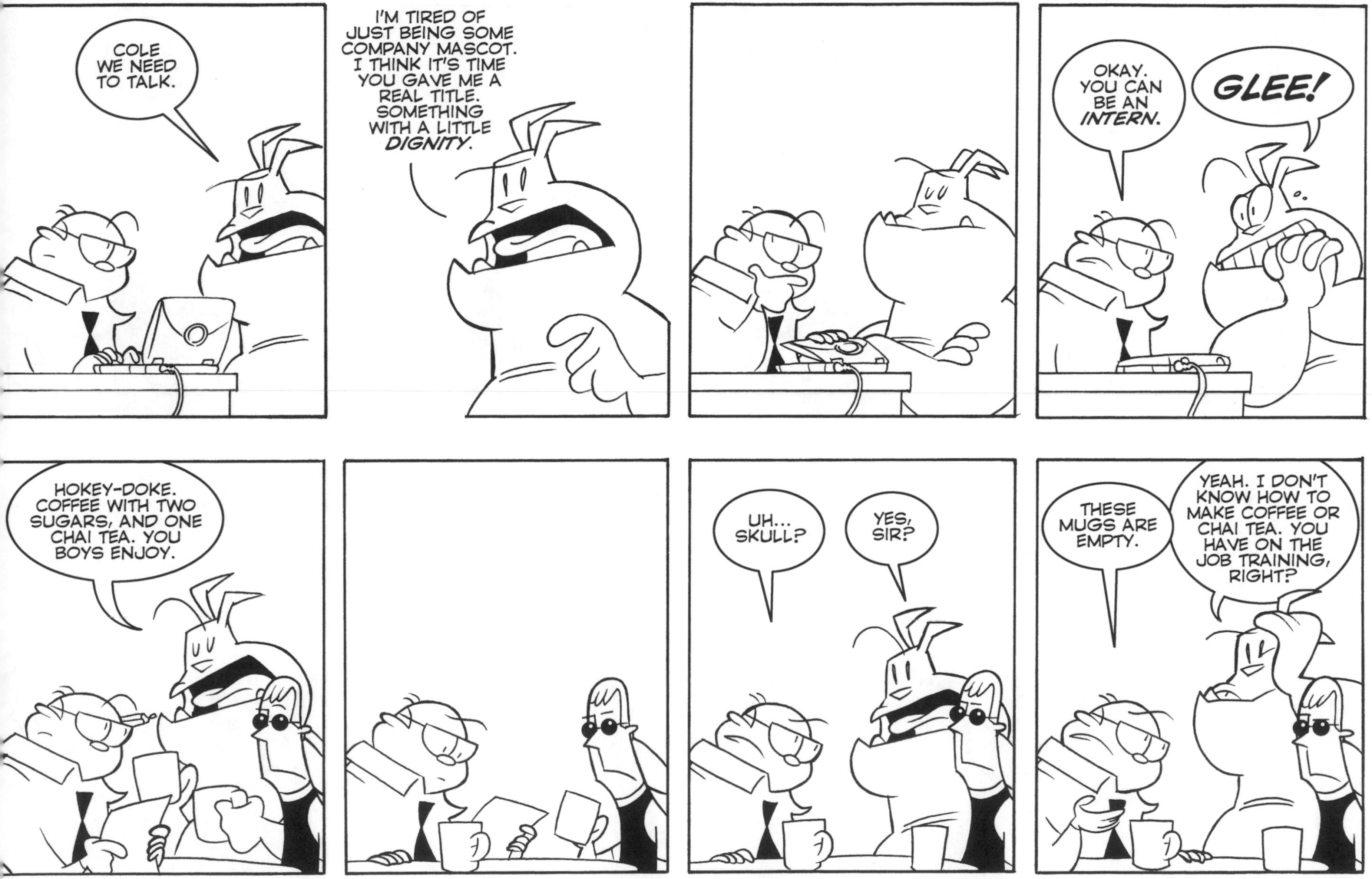
COLE WE NEED TO TALK.
I'M TIRED OF JUST BEING SOME COMPANY MASCOT. I THINK IT'S TIME YOU GAVE ME A REAL TITLE. SOMETHING WITH A LITTLE *DIGNITY*.
OKAY. YOU CAN BE AN *INTERN*.
GLEE!
HOKEY-DOKE. COFFEE WITH TWO SUGARS, AND ONE CHAI TEA. YOU BOYS ENJOY.
UH... SKULL?
YES, SIR?
THESE MUGS ARE EMPTY.
YEAH. I DON'T KNOW HOW TO MAKE COFFEE OR CHAI TEA. YOU HAVE ON THE JOB TRAINING, RIGHT?

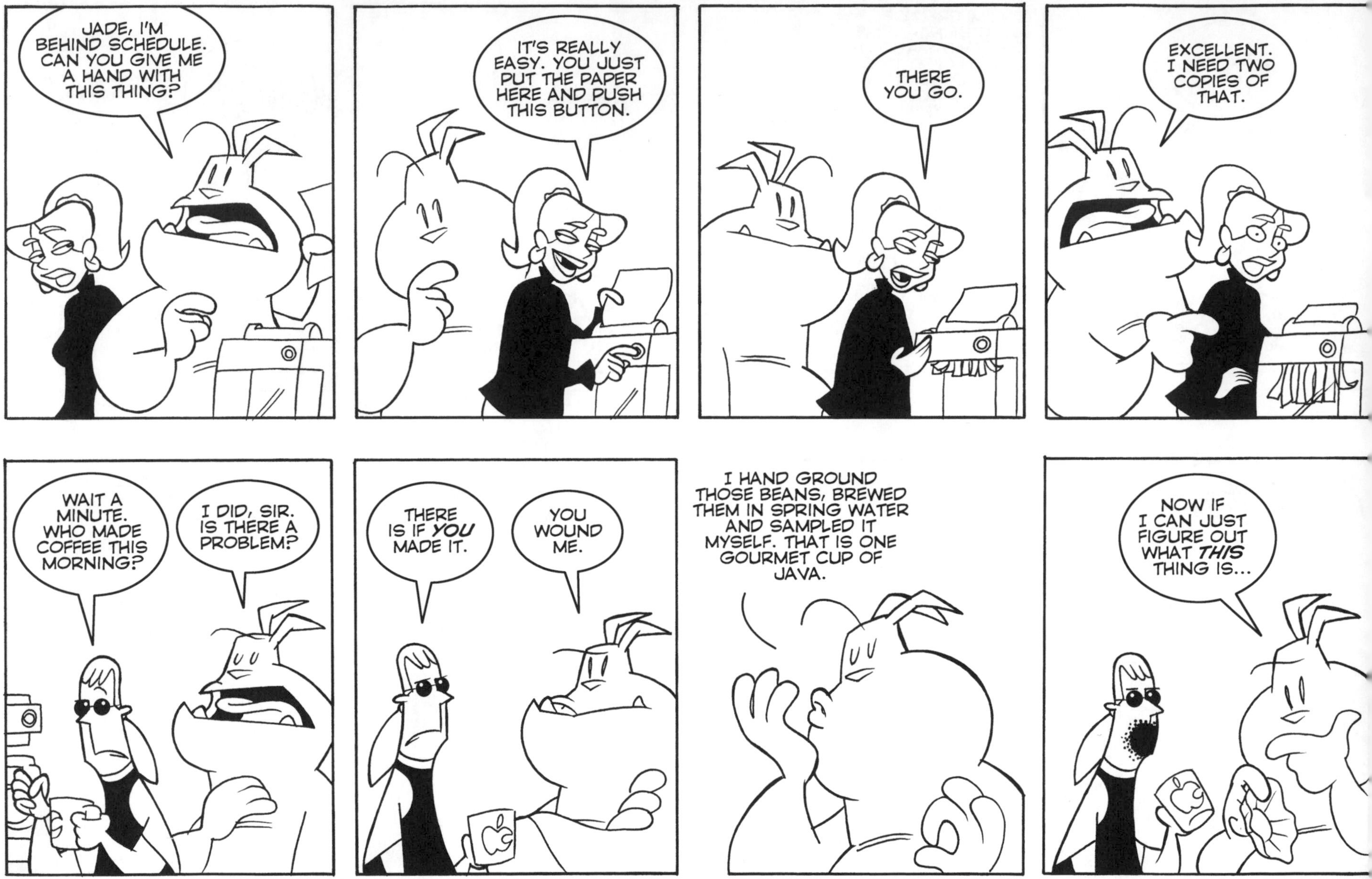
JADE, I'M BEHIND SCHEDULE. CAN YOU GIVE ME A HAND WITH THIS THING?
IT'S REALLY EASY. YOU JUST PUT THE PAPER HERE AND PUSH THIS BUTTON.
THERE YOU GO.
EXCELLENT. I NEED TWO COPIES OF THAT.
WAIT A MINUTE. WHO MADE COFFEE THIS MORNING?
I DID, SIR. IS THERE A PROBLEM?
THERE IS IF *YOU* MADE IT.
YOU WOUND ME.
I HAND GROUND THOSE BEANS, BREWED THEM IN SPRING WATER AND SAMPLED IT MYSELF. THAT IS ONE GOURMET CUP OF JAVA.
NOW IF I CAN JUST FIGURE OUT WHAT *THIS* THING IS...

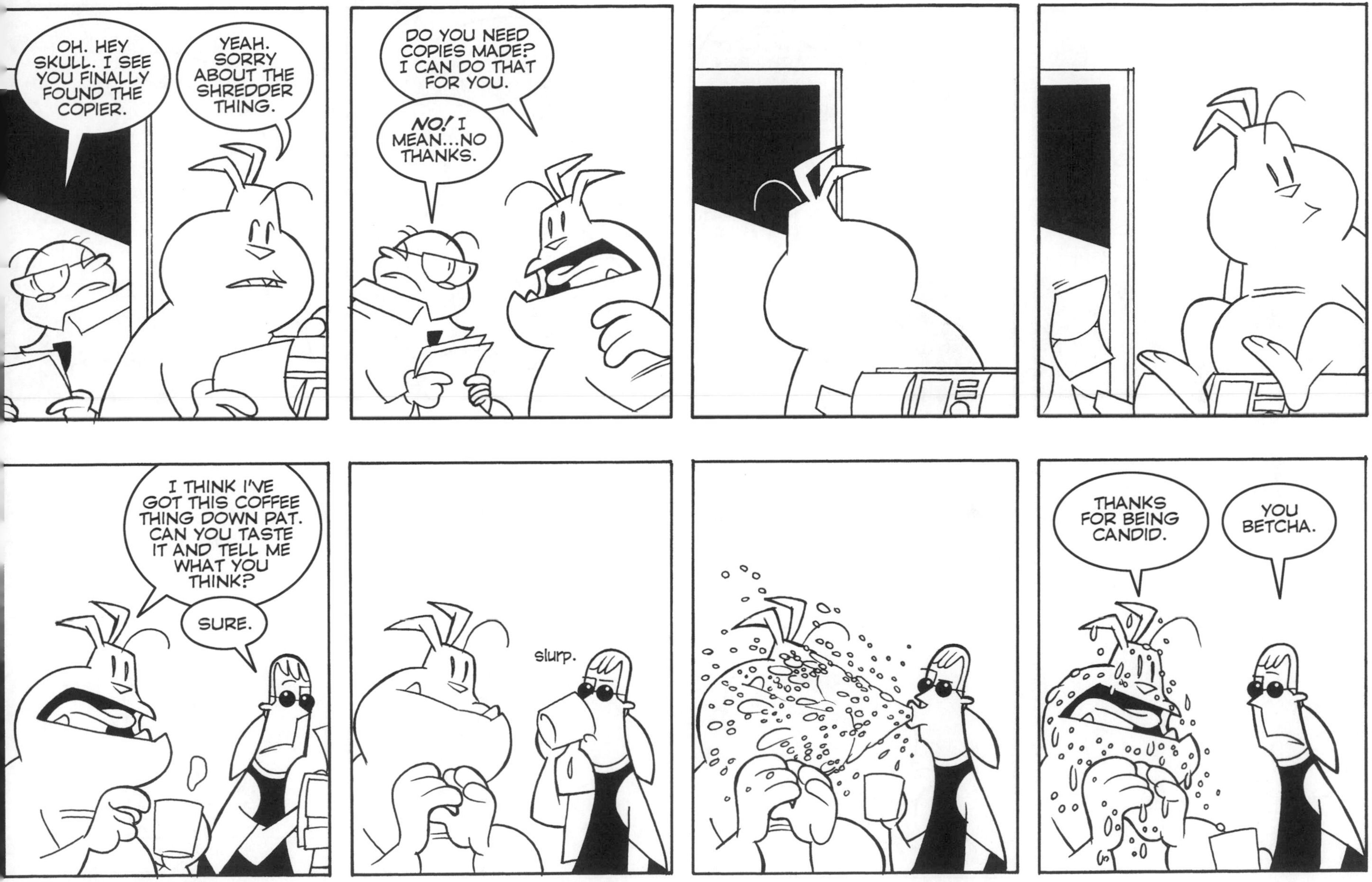
OH. HEY SKULL. I SEE YOU FINALLY FOUND THE COPIER.
YEAH. SORRY ABOUT THE SHREDDER THING.
DO YOU NEED COPIES MADE? I CAN DO THAT FOR YOU.
NO! I MEAN...NO THANKS.
I THINK I'VE GOT THIS COFFEE THING DOWN PAT. CAN YOU TASTE IT AND TELL ME WHAT YOU THINK?
SURE.
slurp.
THANKS FOR BEING CANDID.
YOU BETCHA.

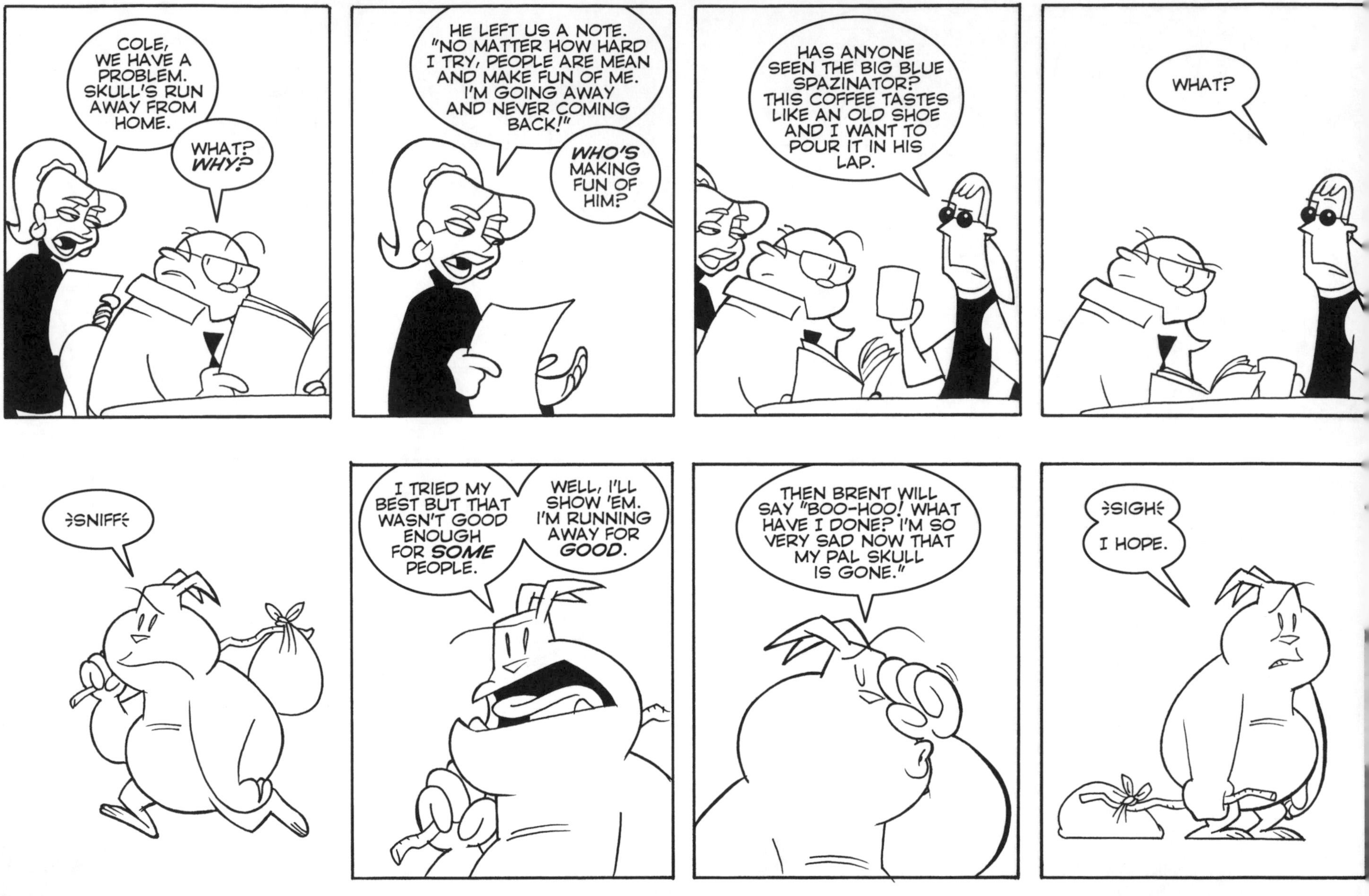
COLE, WE HAVE A PROBLEM. SKULL'S RUN AWAY FROM HOME.
WHAT? WHY?
HE LEFT US A NOTE. "NO MATTER HOW HARD I TRY, PEOPLE ARE MEAN AND MAKE FUN OF ME. I'M GOING AWAY AND NEVER COMING BACK!"
WHO'S MAKING FUN OF HIM?
HAS ANYONE SEEN THE BIG BLUE SPAZINATOR? THIS COFFEE TASTES LIKE AN OLD SHOE AND I WANT TO POUR IT IN HIS LAP.
WHAT?
SNIFF
I TRIED MY BEST BUT THAT WASN'T GOOD ENOUGH FOR SOME PEOPLE.
WELL, I'LL SHOW 'EM. I'M RUNNING AWAY FOR GOOD.
THEN BRENT WILL SAY "BOO-HOO! WHAT HAVE I DONE? I'M SO VERY SAD NOW THAT MY PAL SKULL IS GONE."
SIGH
I HOPE.

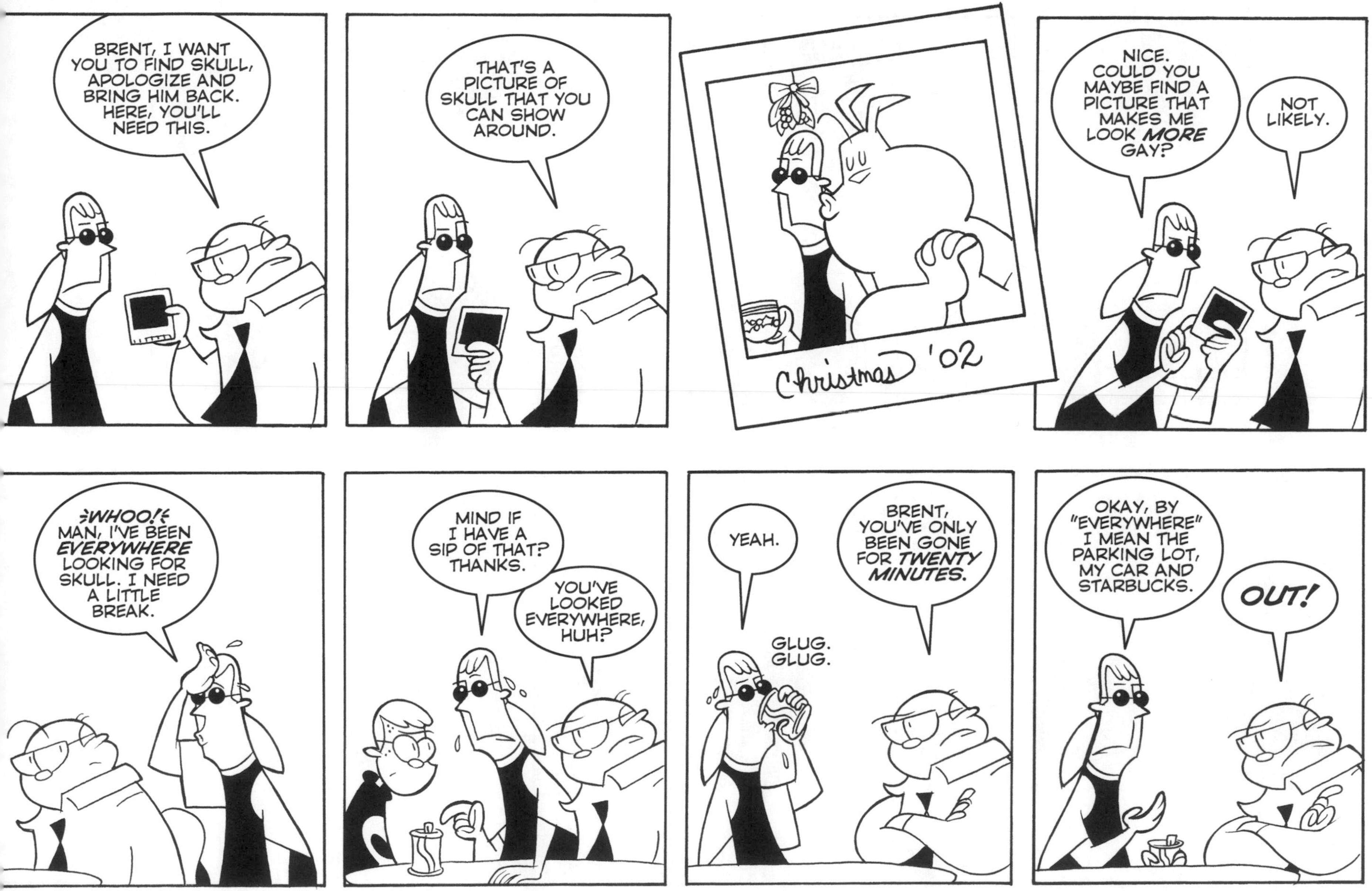
BRENT, I WANT YOU TO FIND SKULL, APOLOGIZE AND BRING HIM BACK. HERE, YOU'LL NEED THIS.
THAT'S A PICTURE OF SKULL THAT YOU CAN SHOW AROUND.
Christmas '02
NICE. COULD YOU MAYBE FIND A PICTURE THAT MAKES ME LOOK *MORE* GAY?
NOT LIKELY.
WHOO! MAN, I'VE BEEN *EVERYWHERE* LOOKING FOR SKULL. I NEED A LITTLE BREAK.
MIND IF I HAVE A SIP OF THAT? THANKS.
YOU'VE LOOKED EVERYWHERE, HUH?
YEAH.
GLUG. GLUG.
BRENT, YOU'VE ONLY BEEN GONE FOR *TWENTY MINUTES.*
OKAY, BY "EVERYWHERE" I MEAN THE PARKING LOT, MY CAR AND STARBUCKS.
OUT!

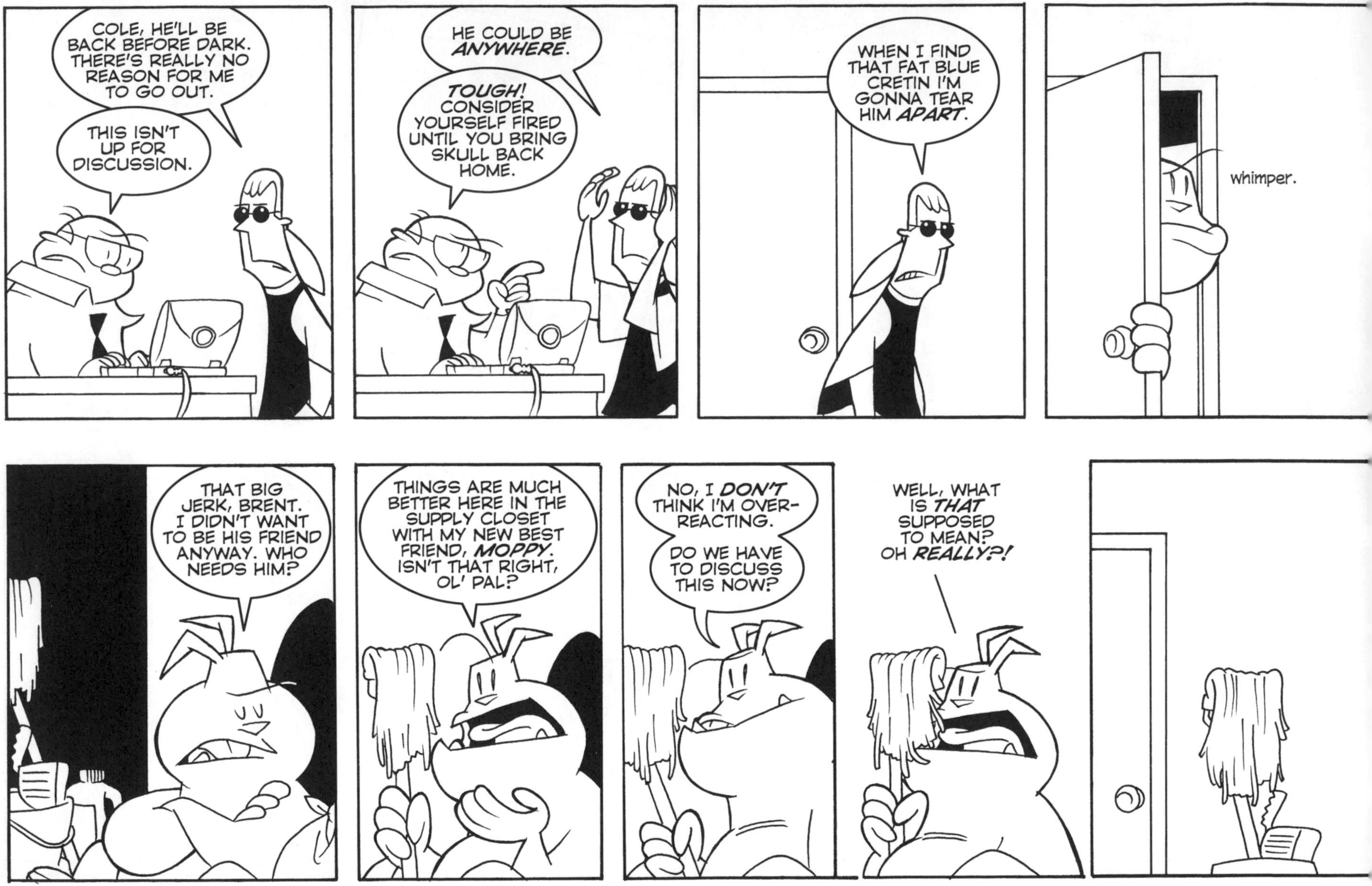
COLE, HE'LL BE BACK BEFORE DARK. THERE'S REALLY NO REASON FOR ME TO GO OUT.
THIS ISN'T UP FOR DISCUSSION.
HE COULD BE *ANYWHERE*.
TOUGH! CONSIDER YOURSELF FIRED UNTIL YOU BRING SKULL BACK HOME.
WHEN I FIND THAT FAT BLUE CRETIN I'M GONNA TEAR HIM *APART*.
whimper.
THAT BIG JERK, BRENT. I DIDN'T WANT TO BE HIS FRIEND ANYWAY. WHO NEEDS HIM?
THINGS ARE MUCH BETTER HERE IN THE SUPPLY CLOSET WITH MY NEW BEST FRIEND, *MOPPY*. ISN'T THAT RIGHT, OL' PAL?
NO, I *DON'T* THINK I'M OVER-REACTING.
DO WE HAVE TO DISCUSS THIS NOW?
WELL, WHAT IS *THAT* SUPPOSED TO MEAN? OH *REALLY?!*

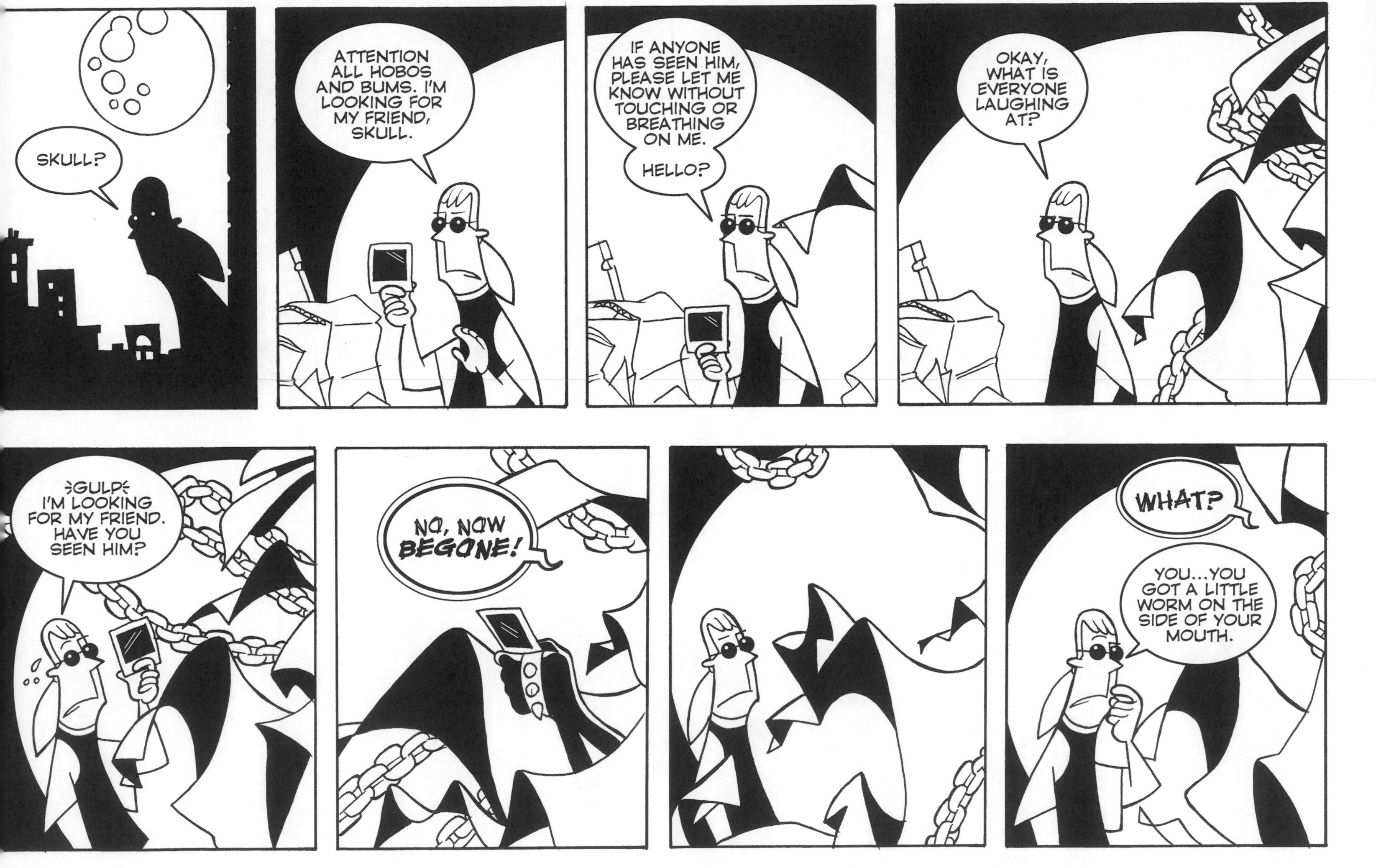
SKULL?
ATTENTION ALL HOBOS AND BUMS. I'M LOOKING FOR MY FRIEND, SKULL.
IF ANYONE HAS SEEN HIM, PLEASE LET ME KNOW WITHOUT TOUCHING OR BREATHING ON ME.
HELLO?
OKAY, WHAT IS EVERYONE LAUGHING AT?
GULP I'M LOOKING FOR MY FRIEND. HAVE YOU SEEN HIM?
NO, NOW BEGONE!
WHAT?
YOU...YOU GOT A LITTLE WORM ON THE SIDE OF YOUR MOUTH.

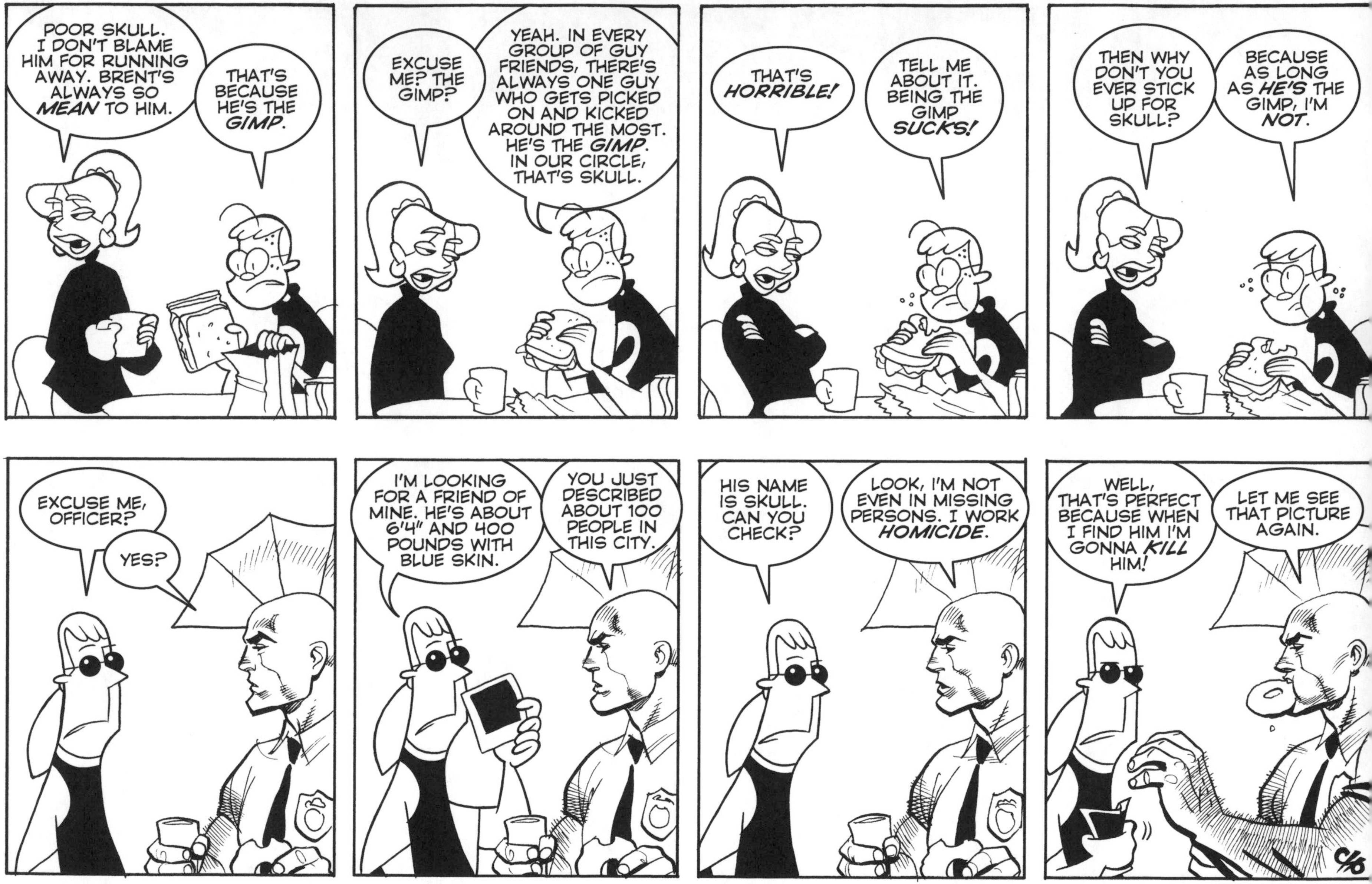
POOR SKULL. I DON'T BLAME HIM FOR RUNNING AWAY. BRENT'S ALWAYS SO *MEAN* TO HIM.
THAT'S BECAUSE HE'S THE *GIMP*.
EXCUSE ME? THE GIMP?
YEAH. IN EVERY GROUP OF GUY FRIENDS, THERE'S ALWAYS ONE GUY WHO GETS PICKED ON AND KICKED AROUND THE MOST. HE'S THE *GIMP*. IN OUR CIRCLE, THAT'S SKULL.
THAT'S *HORRIBLE!*
TELL ME ABOUT IT. BEING THE GIMP *SUCKS!*
THEN WHY DON'T YOU EVER STICK UP FOR SKULL?
BECAUSE AS LONG AS *HE'S* THE GIMP, I'M *NOT*.
EXCUSE ME, OFFICER?
YES?
I'M LOOKING FOR A FRIEND OF MINE. HE'S ABOUT 6'4" AND 400 POUNDS WITH BLUE SKIN.
YOU JUST DESCRIBED ABOUT 100 PEOPLE IN THIS CITY.
HIS NAME IS SKULL. CAN YOU CHECK?
LOOK, I'M NOT EVEN IN MISSING PERSONS. I WORK *HOMICIDE*.
WELL, THAT'S PERFECT BECAUSE WHEN I FIND HIM I'M GONNA *KILL* HIM!
LET ME SEE THAT PICTURE AGAIN.

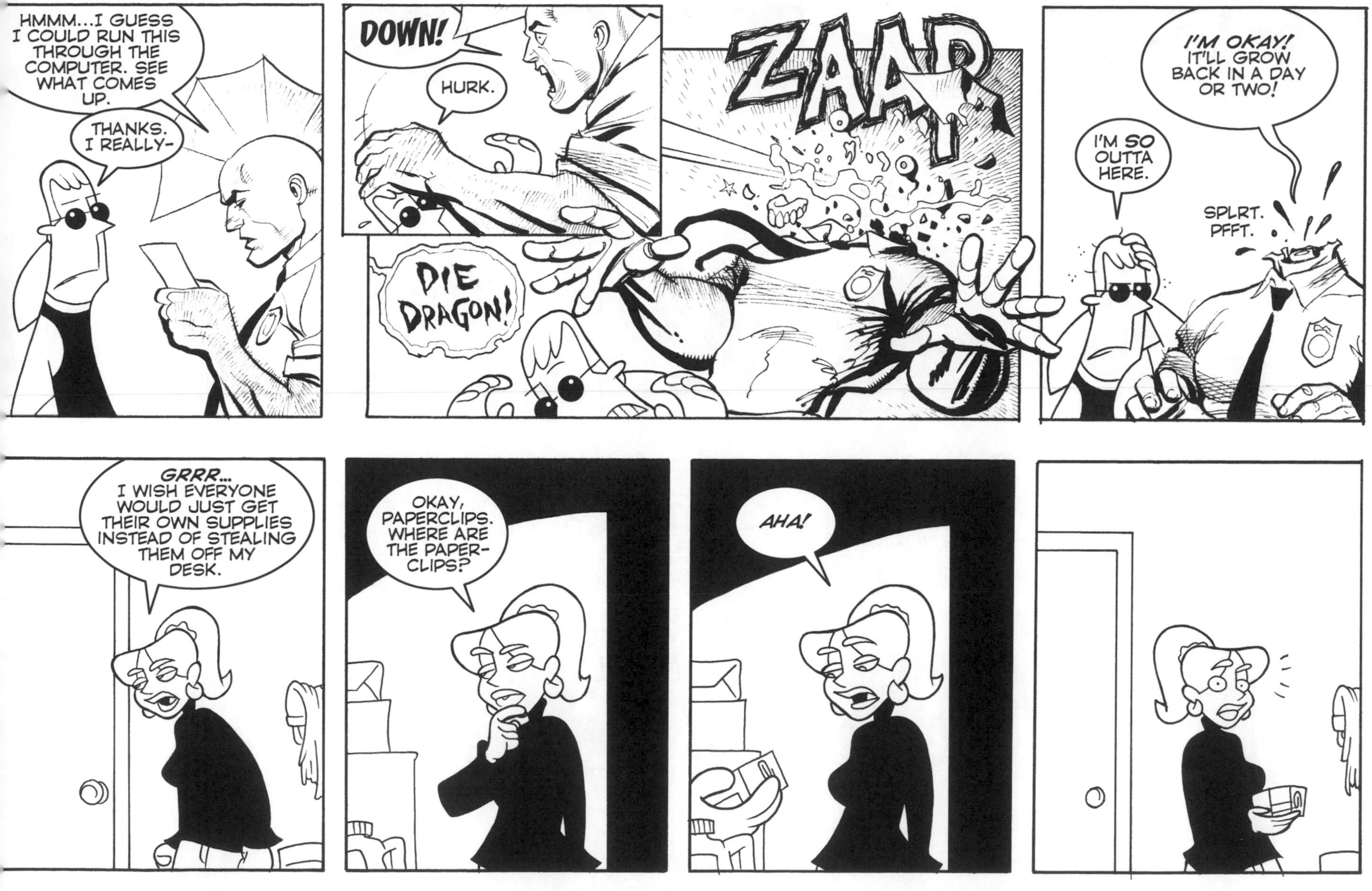
HMMM...I GUESS I COULD RUN THIS THROUGH THE COMPUTER. SEE WHAT COMES UP.
THANKS. I REALLY-
DOWN!
HURK.
ZAAP
DIE DRAGON!
I'M SO OUTTA HERE.
I'M OKAY! IT'LL GROW BACK IN A DAY OR TWO!
SPLRT. PFFT.
GRRR... I WISH EVERYONE WOULD JUST GET THEIR OWN SUPPLIES INSTEAD OF STEALING THEM OFF MY DESK.
OKAY, PAPERCLIPS. WHERE ARE THE PAPER-CLIPS?
AHA!

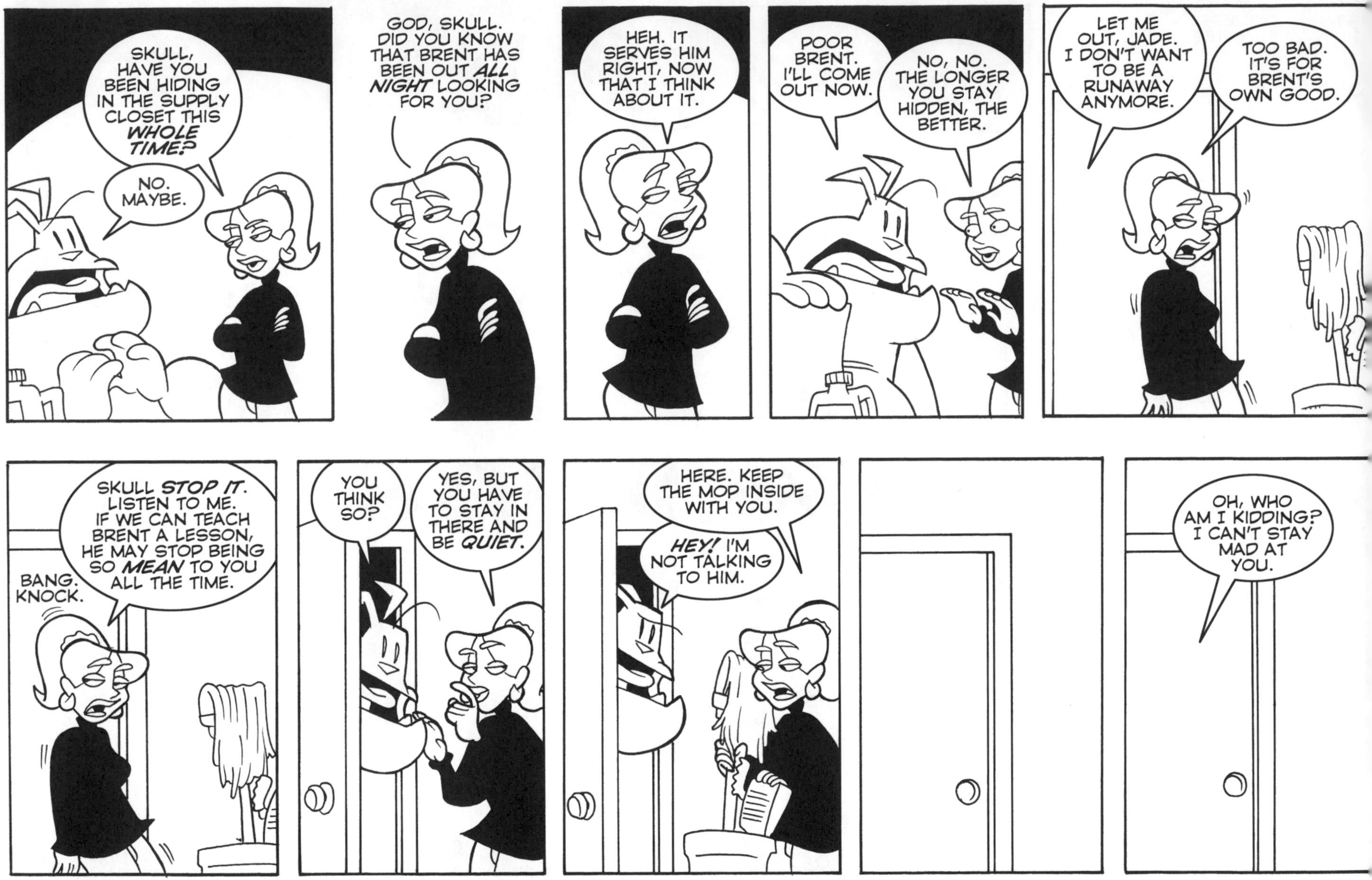

SKULL, HAVE YOU BEEN HIDING IN THE SUPPLY CLOSET THIS *WHOLE TIME?*
NO. MAYBE.
GOD, SKULL. DID YOU KNOW THAT BRENT HAS BEEN OUT *ALL NIGHT* LOOKING FOR YOU?
HEH. IT SERVES HIM RIGHT, NOW THAT I THINK ABOUT IT.
POOR BRENT. I'LL COME OUT NOW.
NO, NO. THE LONGER YOU STAY HIDDEN, THE BETTER.
LET ME OUT, JADE. I DON'T WANT TO BE A RUNAWAY ANYMORE.
TOO BAD. IT'S FOR BRENT'S OWN GOOD.
BANG. KNOCK.
SKULL *STOP IT*. LISTEN TO ME. IF WE CAN TEACH BRENT A LESSON, HE MAY STOP BEING SO *MEAN* TO YOU ALL THE TIME.
YOU THINK SO?
YES, BUT YOU HAVE TO STAY IN THERE AND BE *QUIET*.
HERE. KEEP THE MOP INSIDE WITH YOU.
HEY! I'M NOT TALKING TO HIM.
OH, WHO AM I KIDDING? I CAN'T STAY MAD AT YOU.

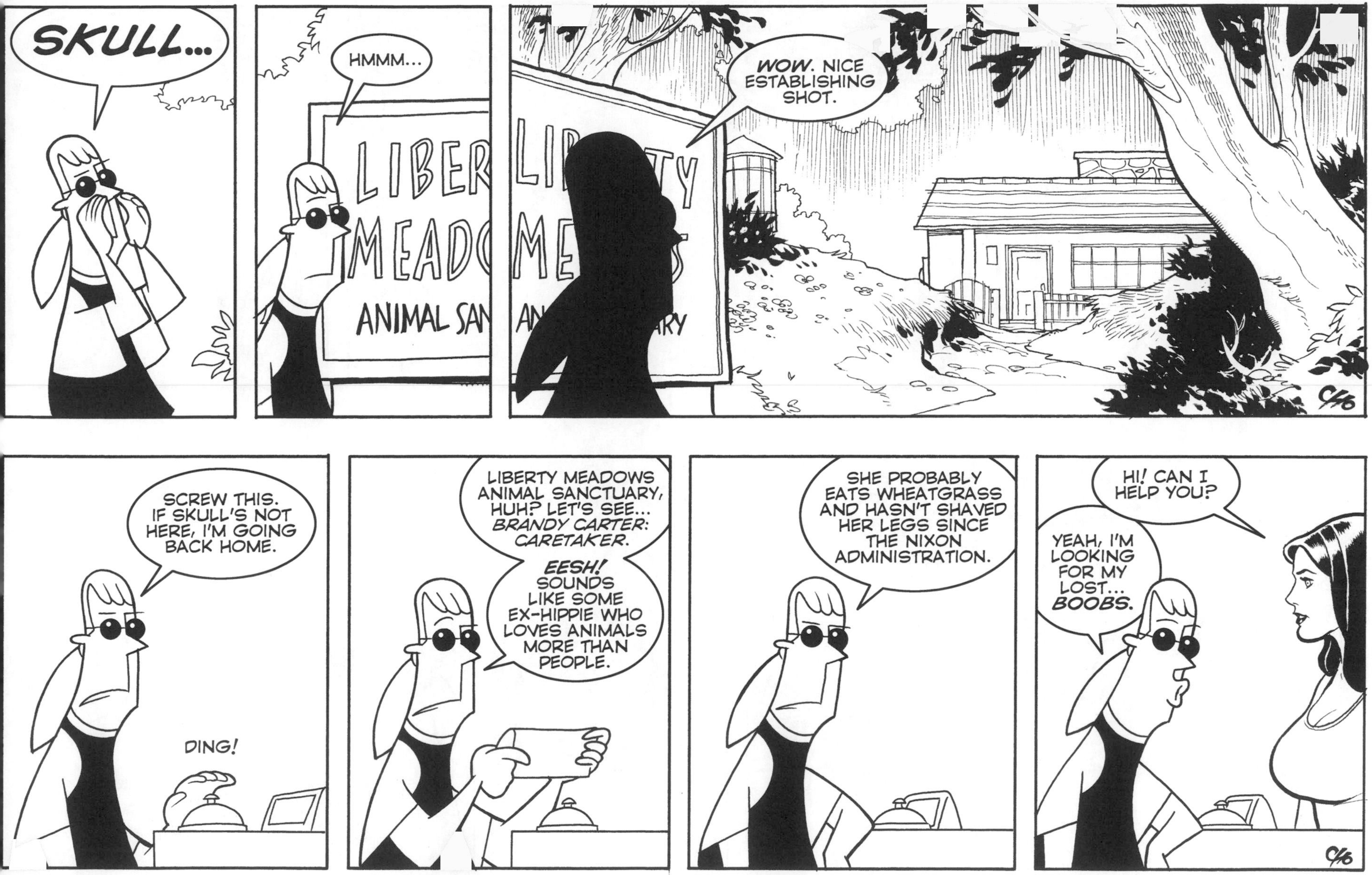
SKULL...
HMMM...
LIBER
MEADO
ANIMAL SAN
WOW. NICE ESTABLISHING SHOT.
SCREW THIS. IF SKULL'S NOT HERE, I'M GOING BACK HOME.
DING!
LIBERTY MEADOWS ANIMAL SANCTUARY, HUH? LET'S SEE... BRANDY CARTER: CARETAKER.
EESH! SOUNDS LIKE SOME EX-HIPPIE WHO LOVES ANIMALS MORE THAN PEOPLE.
SHE PROBABLY EATS WHEATGRASS AND HASN'T SHAVED HER LEGS SINCE THE NIXON ADMINISTRATION.
HI! CAN I HELP YOU?
YEAH, I'M LOOKING FOR MY LOST... BOOBS.

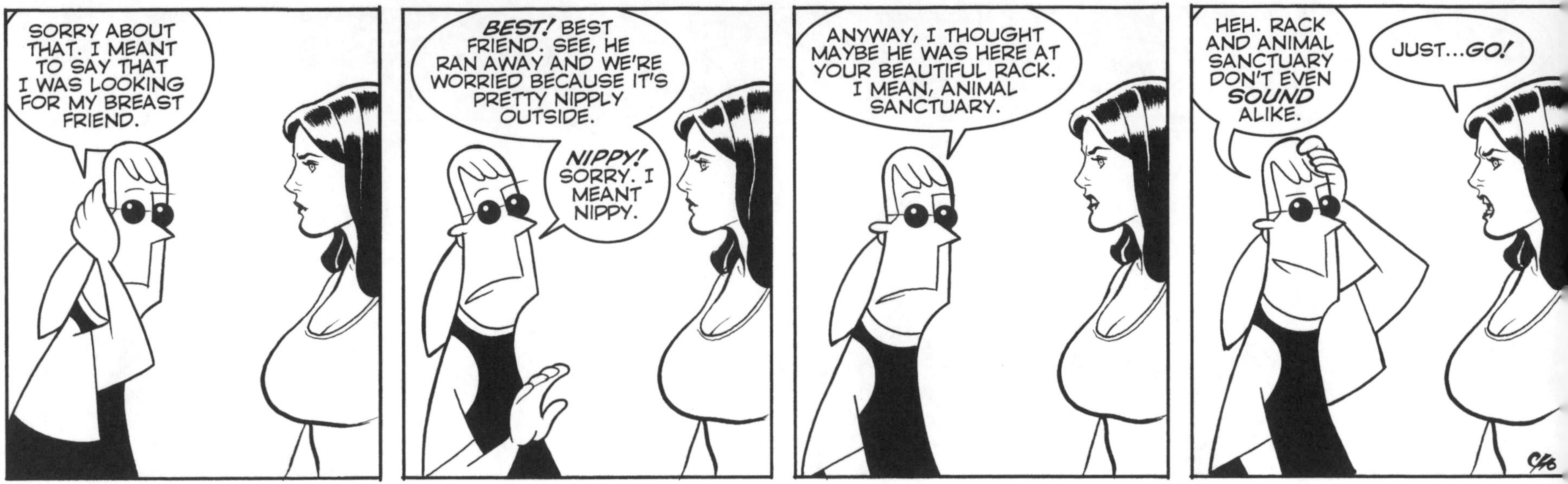
SORRY ABOUT THAT. I MEANT TO SAY THAT I WAS LOOKING FOR MY BREAST FRIEND.
BEST! BEST FRIEND. SEE, HE RAN AWAY AND WE'RE WORRIED BECAUSE IT'S PRETTY NIPPLY OUTSIDE.
NIPPY! SORRY. I MEANT NIPPY.
ANYWAY, I THOUGHT MAYBE HE WAS HERE AT YOUR BEAUTIFUL RACK. I MEAN, ANIMAL SANCTUARY.
HEH. RACK AND ANIMAL SANCTUARY DON'T EVEN SOUND ALIKE.
JUST...GO!

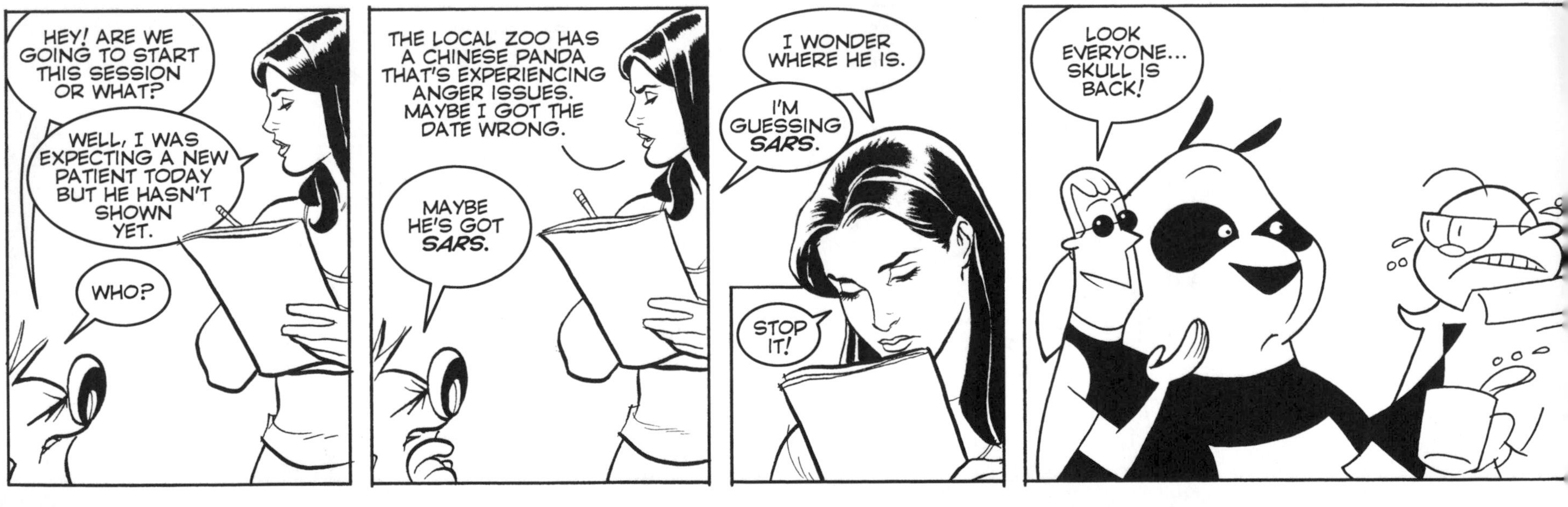
HEY! ARE WE GOING TO START THIS SESSION OR WHAT?
WELL, I WAS EXPECTING A NEW PATIENT TODAY BUT HE HASN'T SHOWN YET.
WHO?
THE LOCAL ZOO HAS A CHINESE PANDA THAT'S EXPERIENCING ANGER ISSUES. MAYBE I GOT THE DATE WRONG.
MAYBE HE'S GOT SARS.
I WONDER WHERE HE IS.
I'M GUESSING SARS.
STOP IT!
LOOK EVERYONE... SKULL IS BACK!

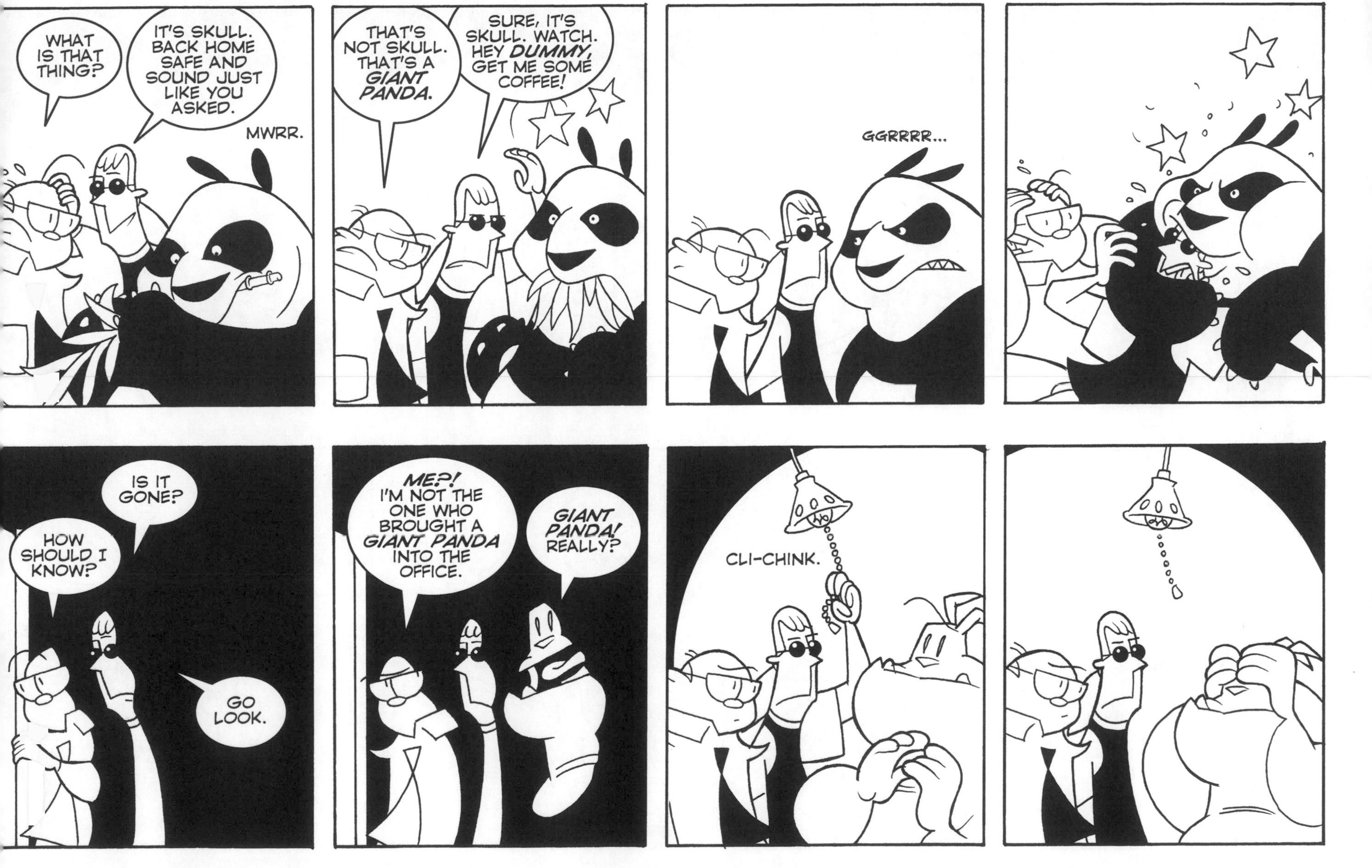
WHAT IS THAT THING?
IT'S SKULL. BACK HOME SAFE AND SOUND JUST LIKE YOU ASKED.
MWRR.
THAT'S NOT SKULL. THAT'S A GIANT PANDA.
SURE, IT'S SKULL. WATCH. HEY DUMMY, GET ME SOME COFFEE!
GGRRRR...
IS IT GONE?
HOW SHOULD I KNOW?
GO LOOK.
ME?! I'M NOT THE ONE WHO BROUGHT A GIANT PANDA INTO THE OFFICE.
GIANT PANDA! REALLY?
CLI-CHINK.

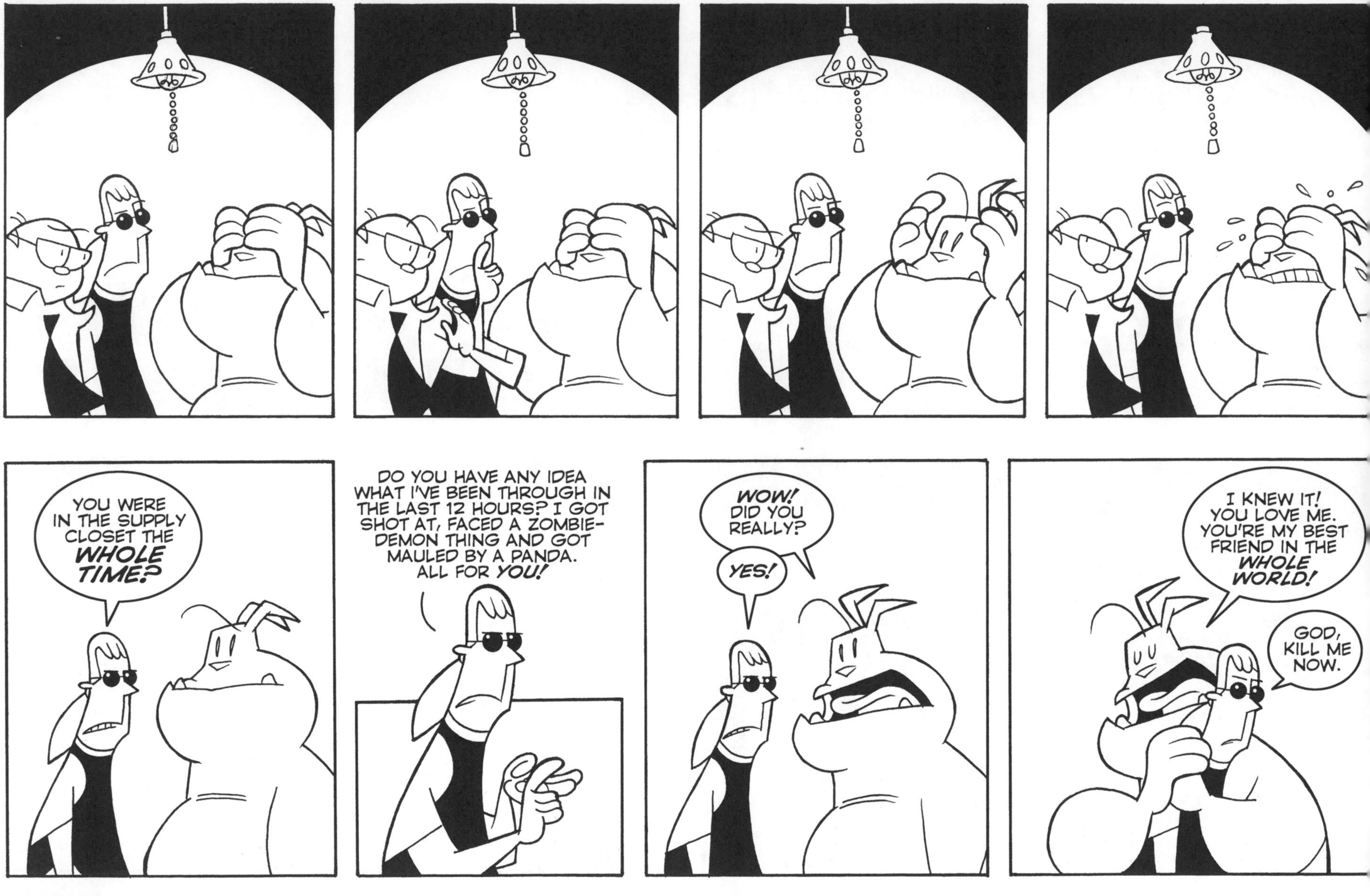
YOU WERE IN THE SUPPLY CLOSET THE WHOLE TIME?
DO YOU HAVE ANY IDEA WHAT I'VE BEEN THROUGH IN THE LAST 12 HOURS? I GOT SHOT AT, FACED A ZOMBIE-DEMON THING AND GOT MAULED BY A PANDA. ALL FOR YOU!
WOW! DID YOU REALLY?
YES!
I KNEW IT! YOU LOVE ME. YOU'RE MY BEST FRIEND IN THE WHOLE WORLD!
GOD, KILL ME NOW.

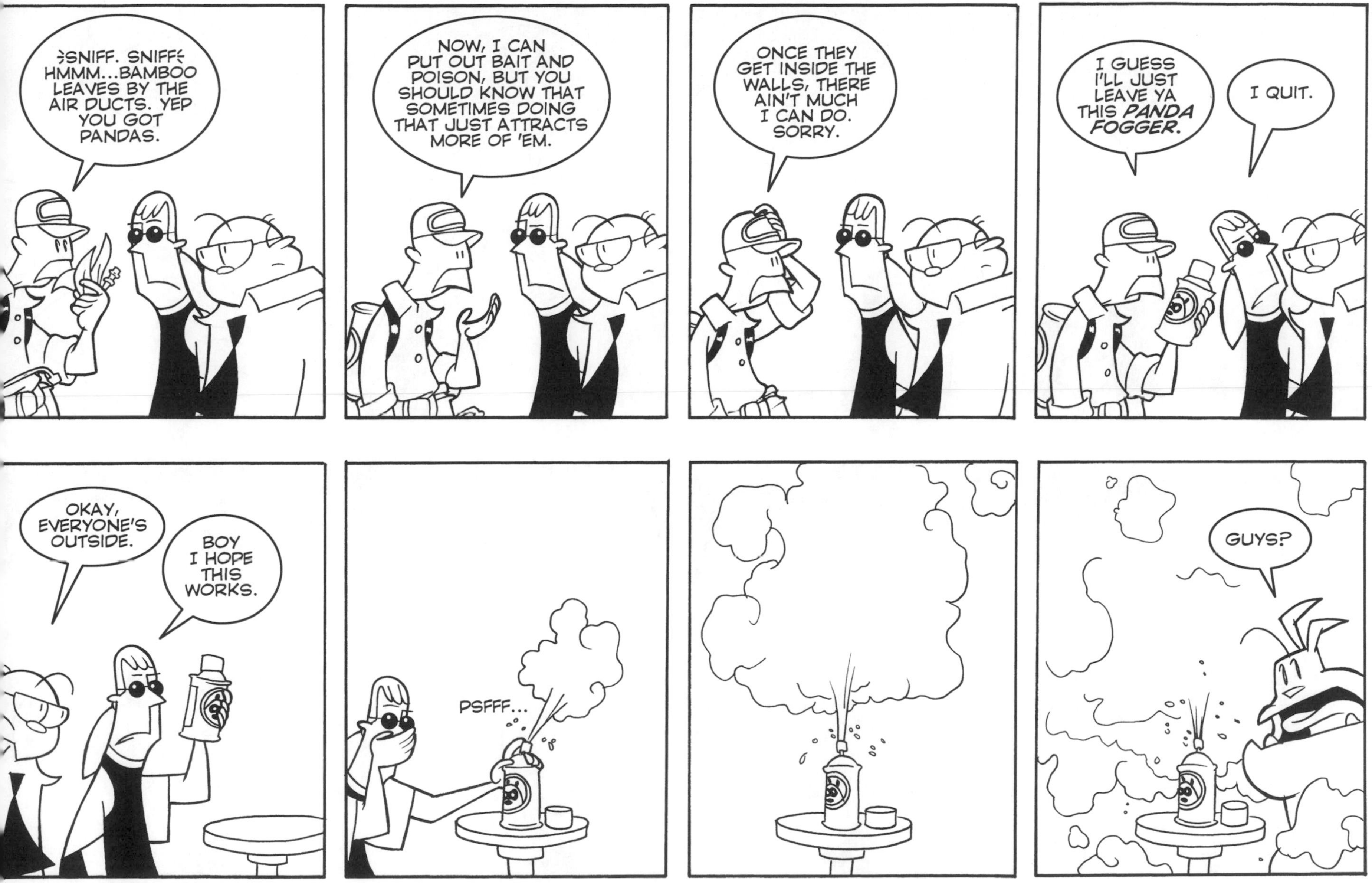

SNIFF. SNIFF HMMM...BAMBOO LEAVES BY THE AIR DUCTS. YEP YOU GOT PANDAS.
NOW, I CAN PUT OUT BAIT AND POISON, BUT YOU SHOULD KNOW THAT SOMETIMES DOING THAT JUST ATTRACTS MORE OF 'EM.
ONCE THEY GET INSIDE THE WALLS, THERE AIN'T MUCH I CAN DO. SORRY.
I GUESS I'LL JUST LEAVE YA THIS *PANDA FOGGER.*
I QUIT.
OKAY, EVERYONE'S OUTSIDE.
BOY I HOPE THIS WORKS.
PSFFF...
GUYS?

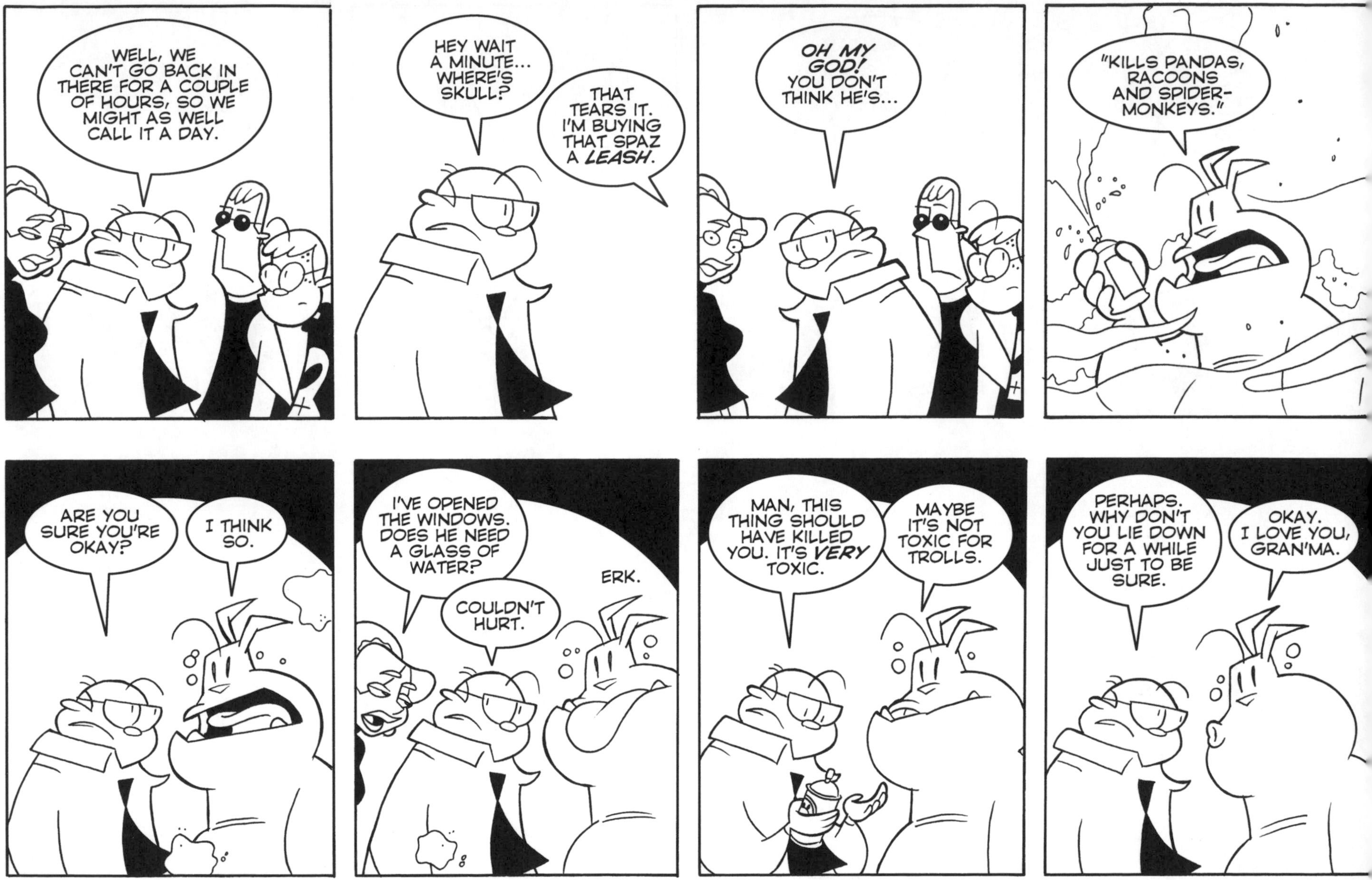
WELL, WE CAN'T GO BACK IN THERE FOR A COUPLE OF HOURS, SO WE MIGHT AS WELL CALL IT A DAY.
HEY WAIT A MINUTE... WHERE'S SKULL?
THAT TEARS IT. I'M BUYING THAT SPAZ A *LEASH*.
OH MY GOD! YOU DON'T THINK HE'S...
"KILLS PANDAS, RACOONS AND SPIDER-MONKEYS."
ARE YOU SURE YOU'RE OKAY?
I THINK SO.
I'VE OPENED THE WINDOWS. DOES HE NEED A GLASS OF WATER?
COULDN'T HURT.
ERK.
MAN, THIS THING SHOULD HAVE KILLED YOU. IT'S *VERY* TOXIC.
MAYBE IT'S NOT TOXIC FOR TROLLS.
PERHAPS. WHY DON'T YOU LIE DOWN FOR A WHILE JUST TO BE SURE.
OKAY. I LOVE YOU, GRAN'MA.

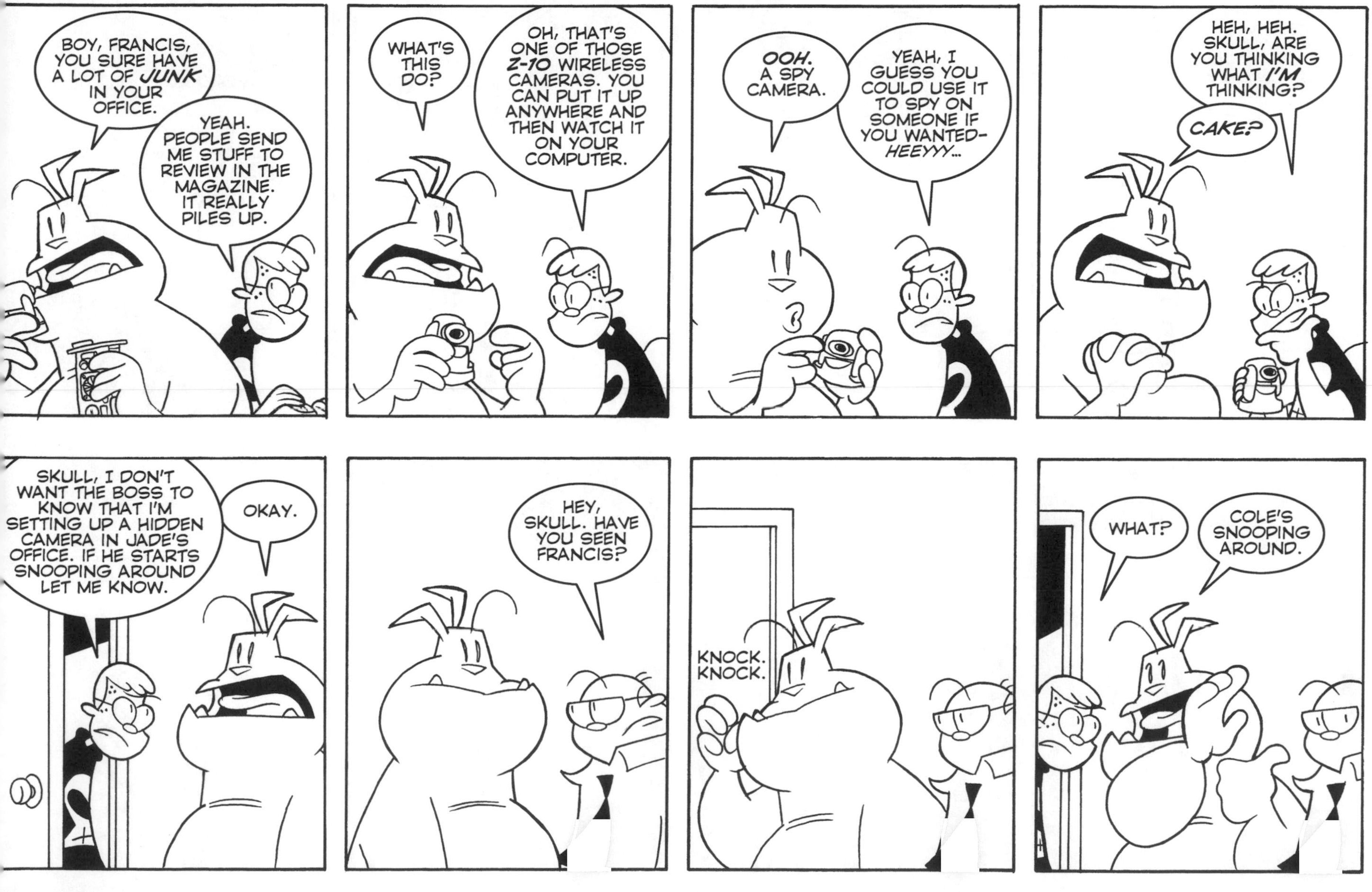
BOY, FRANCIS, YOU SURE HAVE A LOT OF JUNK IN YOUR OFFICE.
YEAH. PEOPLE SEND ME STUFF TO REVIEW IN THE MAGAZINE. IT REALLY PILES UP.
WHAT'S THIS DO?
OH, THAT'S ONE OF THOSE Z-10 WIRELESS CAMERAS. YOU CAN PUT IT UP ANYWHERE AND THEN WATCH IT ON YOUR COMPUTER.
OOH. A SPY CAMERA.
YEAH, I GUESS YOU COULD USE IT TO SPY ON SOMEONE IF YOU WANTED- HEEYYY...
HEH, HEH. SKULL, ARE YOU THINKING WHAT I'M THINKING?
CAKE?
SKULL, I DON'T WANT THE BOSS TO KNOW THAT I'M SETTING UP A HIDDEN CAMERA IN JADE'S OFFICE. IF HE STARTS SNOOPING AROUND LET ME KNOW.
OKAY.
HEY, SKULL. HAVE YOU SEEN FRANCIS?
KNOCK. KNOCK.
WHAT?
COLE'S SNOOPING AROUND.

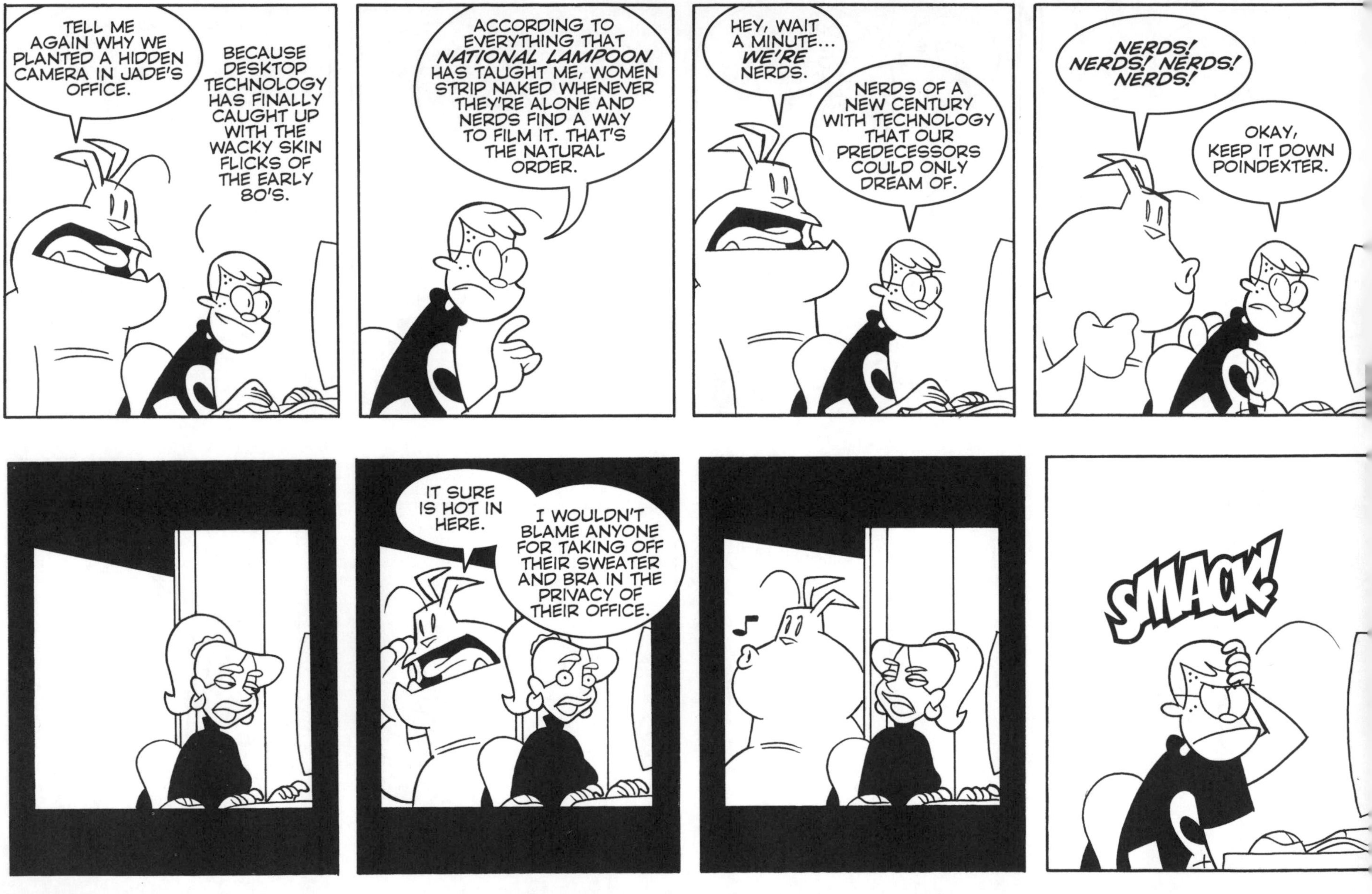
TELL ME AGAIN WHY WE PLANTED A HIDDEN CAMERA IN JADE'S OFFICE.
BECAUSE DESKTOP TECHNOLOGY HAS FINALLY CAUGHT UP WITH THE WACKY SKIN FLICKS OF THE EARLY 80'S.
ACCORDING TO EVERYTHING THAT NATIONAL LAMPOON HAS TAUGHT ME, WOMEN STRIP NAKED WHENEVER THEY'RE ALONE AND NERDS FIND A WAY TO FILM IT. THAT'S THE NATURAL ORDER.
HEY, WAIT A MINUTE... WE'RE NERDS.
NERDS OF A NEW CENTURY WITH TECHNOLOGY THAT OUR PREDECESSORS COULD ONLY DREAM OF.
NERDS! NERDS! NERDS! NERDS!
OKAY, KEEP IT DOWN POINDEXTER.
IT SURE IS HOT IN HERE.
I WOULDN'T BLAME ANYONE FOR TAKING OFF THEIR SWEATER AND BRA IN THE PRIVACY OF THEIR OFFICE.
SMACK!

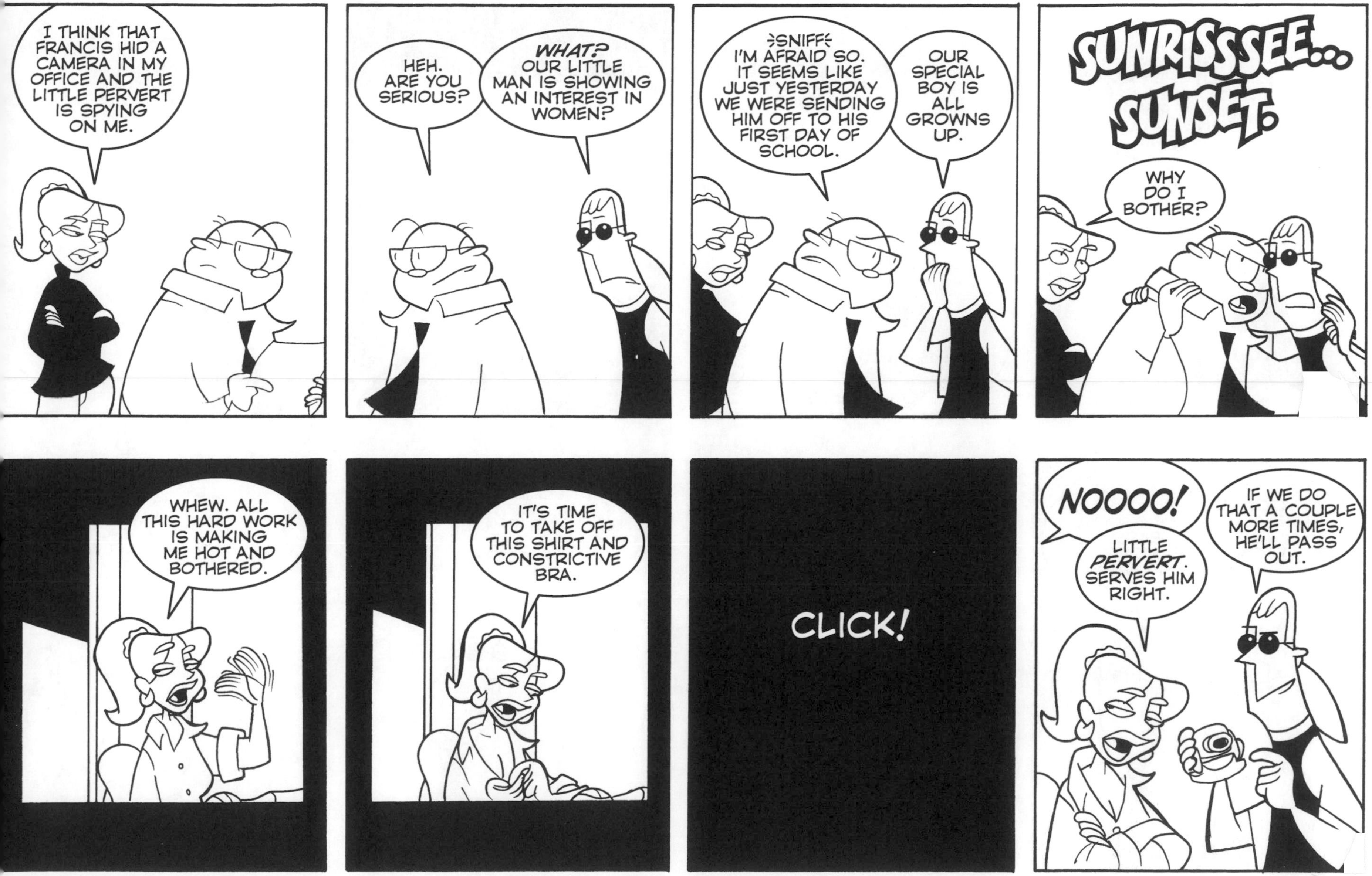
I THINK THAT FRANCIS HID A CAMERA IN MY OFFICE AND THE LITTLE PERVERT IS SPYING ON ME.
HEH. ARE YOU SERIOUS?
WHAT? OUR LITTLE MAN IS SHOWING AN INTEREST IN WOMEN?
SNIFF I'M AFRAID SO. IT SEEMS LIKE JUST YESTERDAY WE WERE SENDING HIM OFF TO HIS FIRST DAY OF SCHOOL.
OUR SPECIAL BOY IS ALL GROWNS UP.
SUNRISSSEE... SUNSET.
WHY DO I BOTHER?
WHEW. ALL THIS HARD WORK IS MAKING ME HOT AND BOTHERED.
IT'S TIME TO TAKE OFF THIS SHIRT AND CONSTRICTIVE BRA.
CLICK!
NOOOO!
LITTLE PERVERT. SERVES HIM RIGHT.
IF WE DO THAT A COUPLE MORE TIMES, HE'LL PASS OUT.

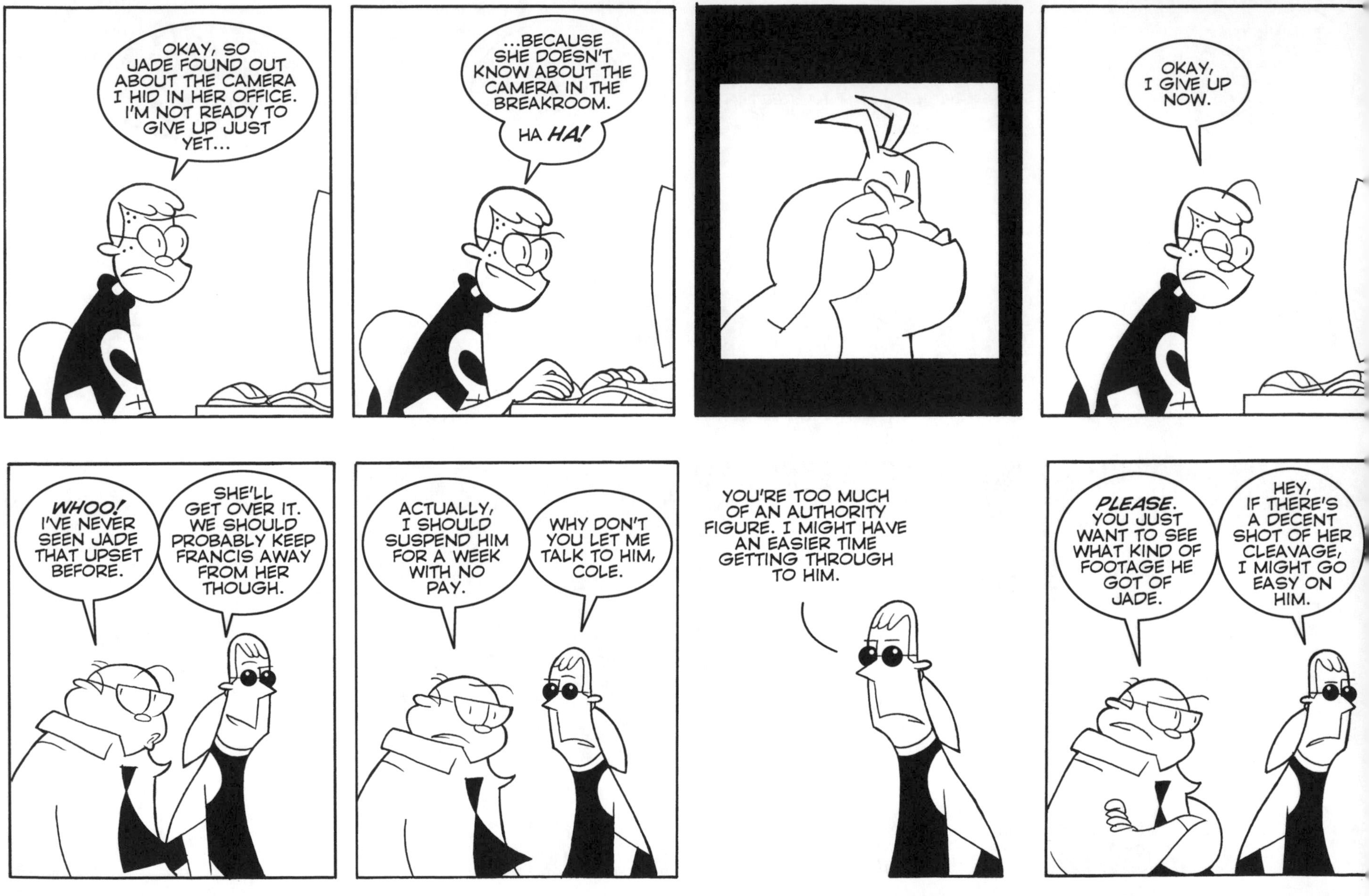
OKAY, SO JADE FOUND OUT ABOUT THE CAMERA I HID IN HER OFFICE. I'M NOT READY TO GIVE UP JUST YET...
...BECAUSE SHE DOESN'T KNOW ABOUT THE CAMERA IN THE BREAKROOM.
HA *HA!*
OKAY, I GIVE UP NOW.
WHOO! I'VE NEVER SEEN JADE THAT UPSET BEFORE.
SHE'LL GET OVER IT. WE SHOULD PROBABLY KEEP FRANCIS AWAY FROM HER THOUGH.
ACTUALLY, I SHOULD SUSPEND HIM FOR A WEEK WITH NO PAY.
WHY DON'T YOU LET ME TALK TO HIM, COLE.
YOU'RE TOO MUCH OF AN AUTHORITY FIGURE. I MIGHT HAVE AN EASIER TIME GETTING THROUGH TO HIM.
PLEASE. YOU JUST WANT TO SEE WHAT KIND OF FOOTAGE HE GOT OF JADE.
HEY, IF THERE'S A DECENT SHOT OF HER CLEAVAGE, I MIGHT GO EASY ON HIM.

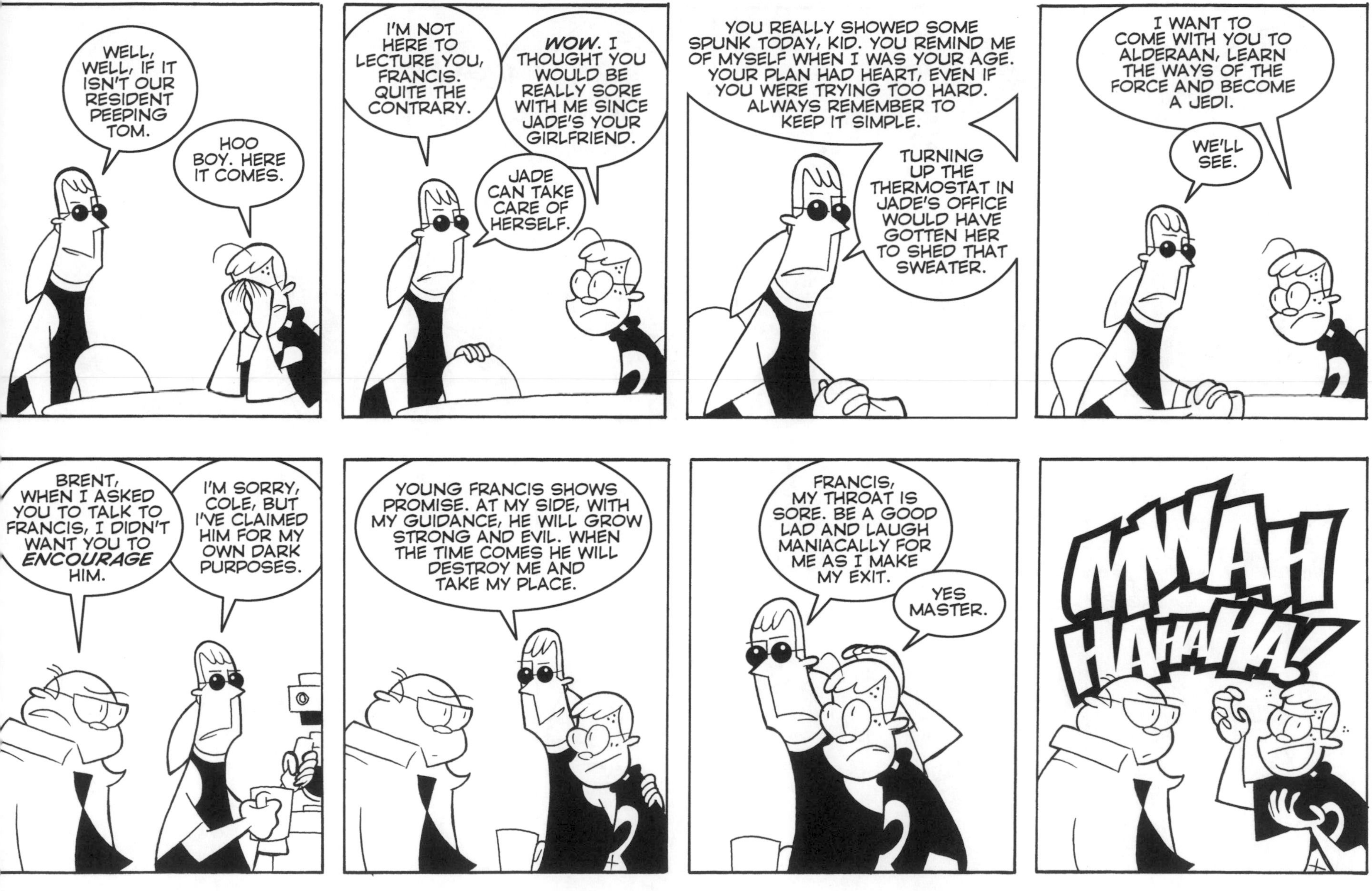
WELL, WELL, IF IT ISN'T OUR RESIDENT PEEPING TOM.
HOO BOY. HERE IT COMES.
I'M NOT HERE TO LECTURE YOU, FRANCIS. QUITE THE CONTRARY.
WOW. I THOUGHT YOU WOULD BE REALLY SORE WITH ME SINCE JADE'S YOUR GIRLFRIEND.
JADE CAN TAKE CARE OF HERSELF.
YOU REALLY SHOWED SOME SPUNK TODAY, KID. YOU REMIND ME OF MYSELF WHEN I WAS YOUR AGE. YOUR PLAN HAD HEART, EVEN IF YOU WERE TRYING TOO HARD. ALWAYS REMEMBER TO KEEP IT SIMPLE.
TURNING UP THE THERMOSTAT IN JADE'S OFFICE WOULD HAVE GOTTEN HER TO SHED THAT SWEATER.
I WANT TO COME WITH YOU TO ALDERAAN, LEARN THE WAYS OF THE FORCE AND BECOME A JEDI.
WE'LL SEE.
BRENT, WHEN I ASKED YOU TO TALK TO FRANCIS, I DIDN'T WANT YOU TO ENCOURAGE HIM.
I'M SORRY, COLE, BUT I'VE CLAIMED HIM FOR MY OWN DARK PURPOSES.
YOUNG FRANCIS SHOWS PROMISE. AT MY SIDE, WITH MY GUIDANCE, HE WILL GROW STRONG AND EVIL. WHEN THE TIME COMES HE WILL DESTROY ME AND TAKE MY PLACE.
FRANCIS, MY THROAT IS SORE. BE A GOOD LAD AND LAUGH MANIACALLY FOR ME AS I MAKE MY EXIT.
YES MASTER.
MWAH HAHAHA!

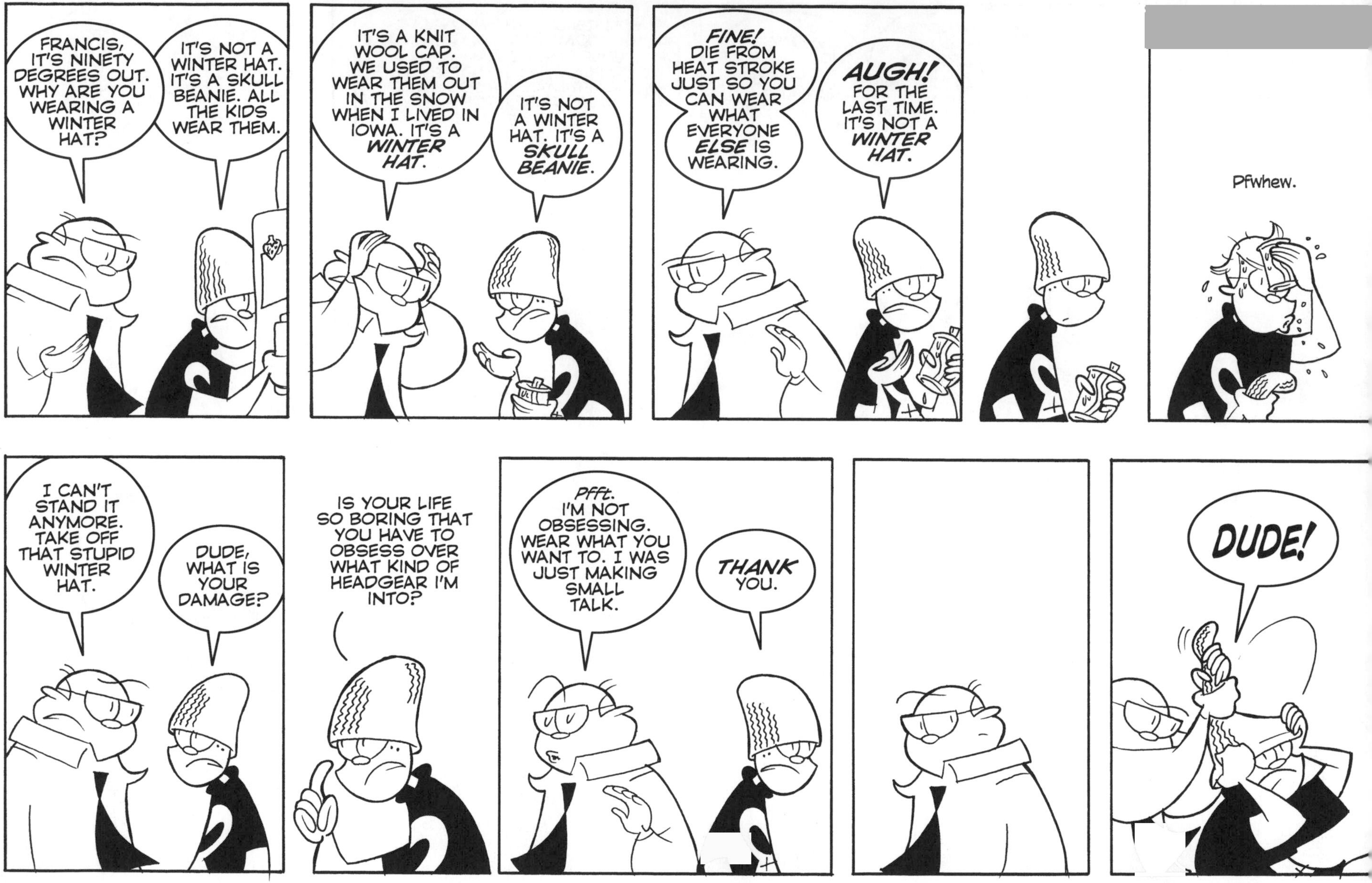
FRANCIS, IT'S NINETY DEGREES OUT. WHY ARE YOU WEARING A WINTER HAT?
IT'S NOT A WINTER HAT. IT'S A SKULL BEANIE. ALL THE KIDS WEAR THEM.
IT'S A KNIT WOOL CAP. WE USED TO WEAR THEM OUT IN THE SNOW WHEN I LIVED IN IOWA. IT'S A *WINTER HAT*.
IT'S NOT A WINTER HAT. IT'S A *SKULL BEANIE*.
FINE! DIE FROM HEAT STROKE JUST SO YOU CAN WEAR WHAT EVERYONE *ELSE* IS WEARING.
AUGH! FOR THE LAST TIME. IT'S NOT A *WINTER HAT*.
Pfwhew.
I CAN'T STAND IT ANYMORE. TAKE OFF THAT STUPID WINTER HAT.
DUDE, WHAT IS YOUR DAMAGE?
IS YOUR LIFE SO BORING THAT YOU HAVE TO OBSESS OVER WHAT KIND OF HEADGEAR I'M INTO?
Pfft. I'M NOT OBSESSING. WEAR WHAT YOU WANT TO. I WAS JUST MAKING SMALL TALK.
THANK YOU.
DUDE!

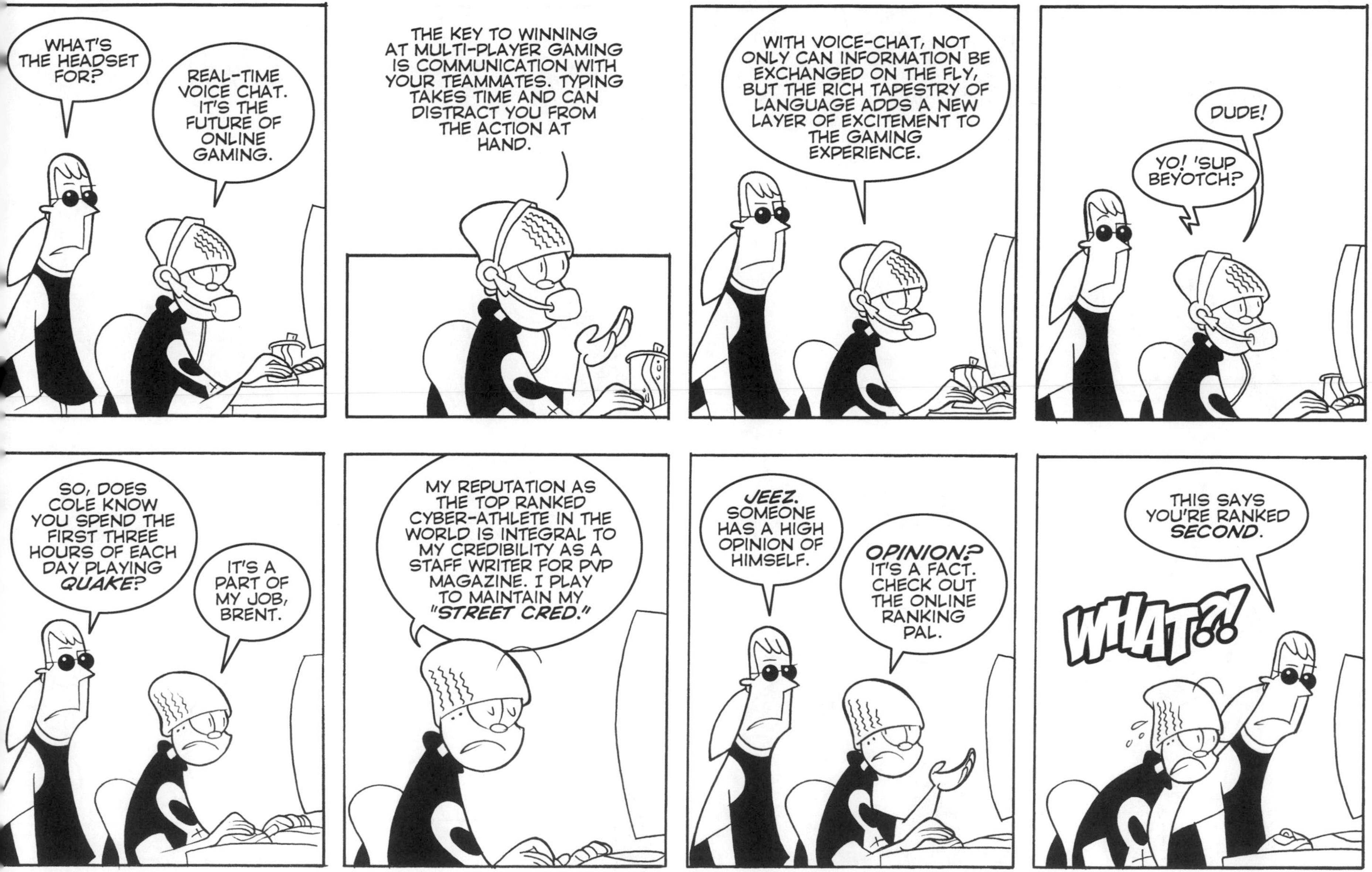
WHAT'S THE HEADSET FOR?
REAL-TIME VOICE CHAT. IT'S THE FUTURE OF ONLINE GAMING.
THE KEY TO WINNING AT MULTI-PLAYER GAMING IS COMMUNICATION WITH YOUR TEAMMATES. TYPING TAKES TIME AND CAN DISTRACT YOU FROM THE ACTION AT HAND.
WITH VOICE-CHAT, NOT ONLY CAN INFORMATION BE EXCHANGED ON THE FLY, BUT THE RICH TAPESTRY OF LANGUAGE ADDS A NEW LAYER OF EXCITEMENT TO THE GAMING EXPERIENCE.
YO! 'SUP BEYOTCH?
DUDE!
SO, DOES COLE KNOW YOU SPEND THE FIRST THREE HOURS OF EACH DAY PLAYING *QUAKE*?
IT'S A PART OF MY JOB, BRENT.
MY REPUTATION AS THE TOP RANKED CYBER-ATHLETE IN THE WORLD IS INTEGRAL TO MY CREDIBILITY AS A STAFF WRITER FOR PVP MAGAZINE. I PLAY TO MAINTAIN MY *"STREET CRED."*
JEEZ. SOMEONE HAS A HIGH OPINION OF HIMSELF.
OPINION? IT'S A FACT. CHECK OUT THE ONLINE RANKING PAL.
THIS SAYS YOU'RE RANKED *SECOND*.
WHAT?!

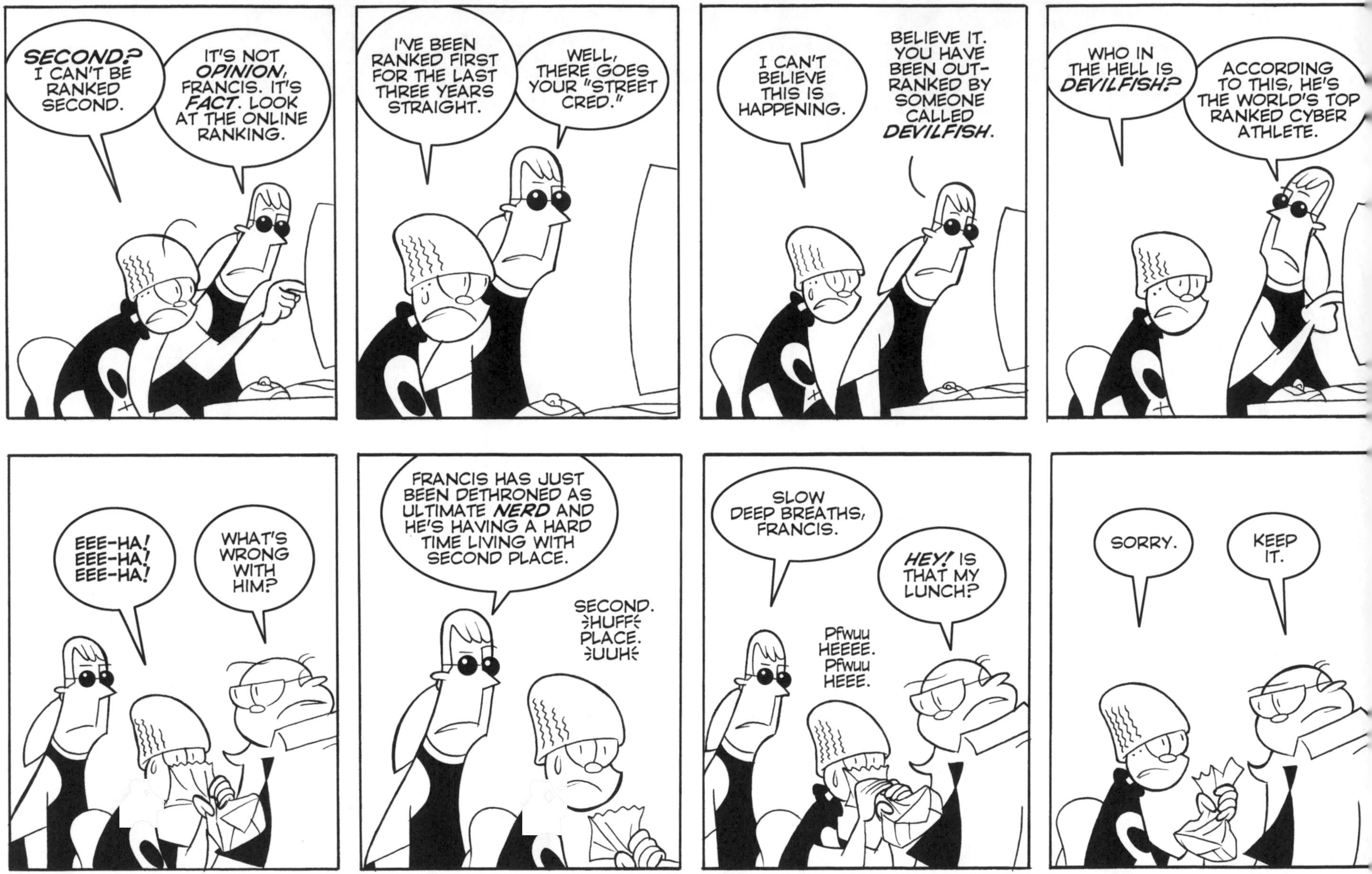
SECOND? I CAN'T BE RANKED SECOND.
IT'S NOT OPINION, FRANCIS. IT'S FACT. LOOK AT THE ONLINE RANKING.
I'VE BEEN RANKED FIRST FOR THE LAST THREE YEARS STRAIGHT.
WELL, THERE GOES YOUR "STREET CRED."
I CAN'T BELIEVE THIS IS HAPPENING.
BELIEVE IT. YOU HAVE BEEN OUT-RANKED BY SOMEONE CALLED DEVILFISH.
WHO IN THE HELL IS DEVILFISH?
ACCORDING TO THIS, HE'S THE WORLD'S TOP RANKED CYBER ATHLETE.
EEE-HA! EEE-HA! EEE-HA!
WHAT'S WRONG WITH HIM?
FRANCIS HAS JUST BEEN DETHRONED AS ULTIMATE NERD AND HE'S HAVING A HARD TIME LIVING WITH SECOND PLACE.
SECOND. HUFF PLACE. UUH
SLOW DEEP BREATHS, FRANCIS.
Pfwuu HEEEE. Pfwuu HEEE.
HEY! IS THAT MY LUNCH?
SORRY.
KEEP IT.

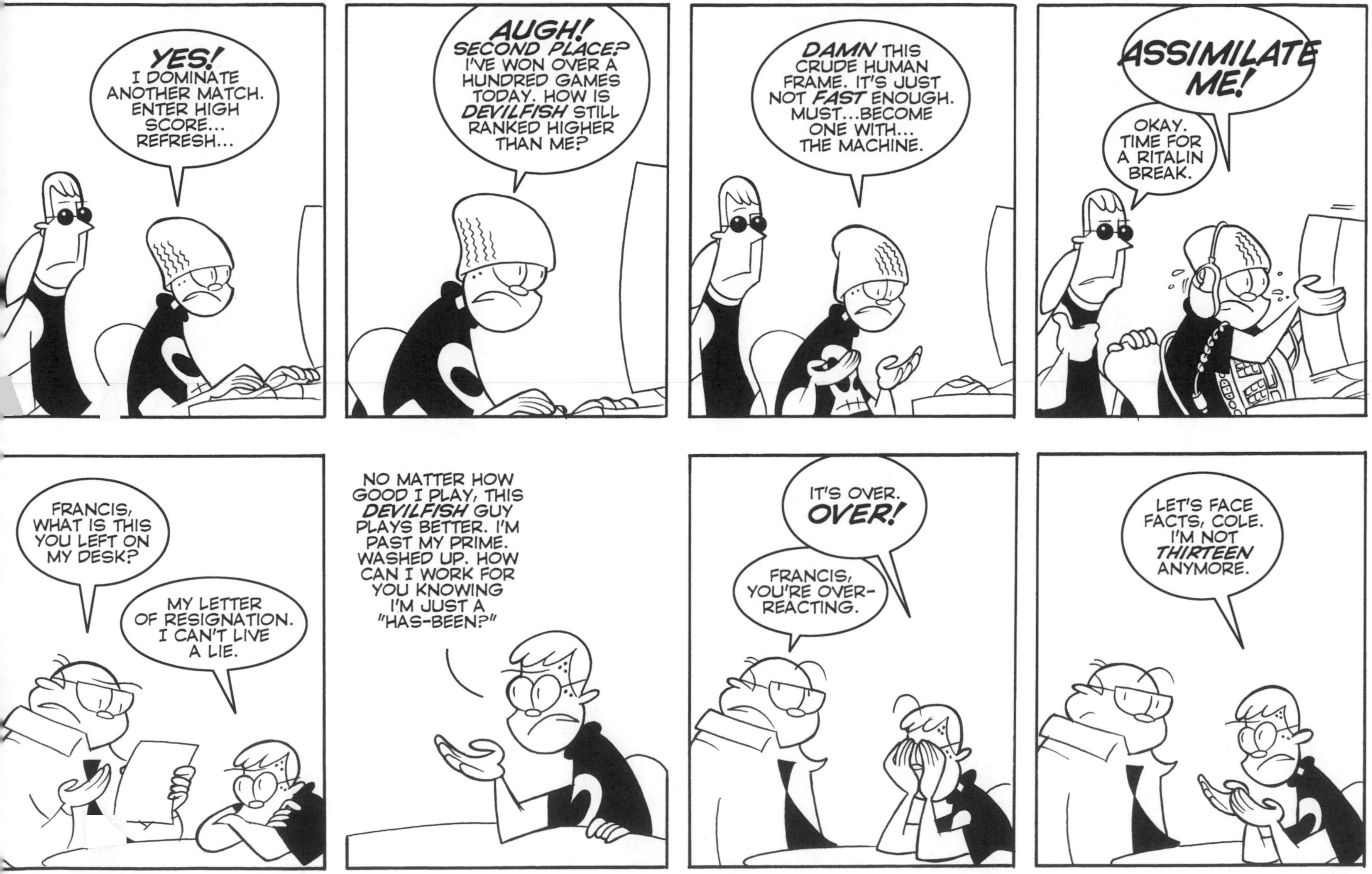
YES! I DOMINATE ANOTHER MATCH. ENTER HIGH SCORE... REFRESH...
AUGH! SECOND PLACE? I'VE WON OVER A HUNDRED GAMES TODAY. HOW IS DEVILFISH STILL RANKED HIGHER THAN ME?
DAMN THIS CRUDE HUMAN FRAME. IT'S JUST NOT FAST ENOUGH. MUST...BECOME ONE WITH... THE MACHINE.
ASSIMILATE ME!
OKAY. TIME FOR A RITALIN BREAK.
FRANCIS, WHAT IS THIS YOU LEFT ON MY DESK?
MY LETTER OF RESIGNATION. I CAN'T LIVE A LIE.
NO MATTER HOW GOOD I PLAY, THIS DEVILFISH GUY PLAYS BETTER. I'M PAST MY PRIME. WASHED UP. HOW CAN I WORK FOR YOU KNOWING I'M JUST A "HAS-BEEN?"
IT'S OVER. OVER!
FRANCIS, YOU'RE OVER-REACTING.
LET'S FACE FACTS, COLE. I'M NOT THIRTEEN ANYMORE.

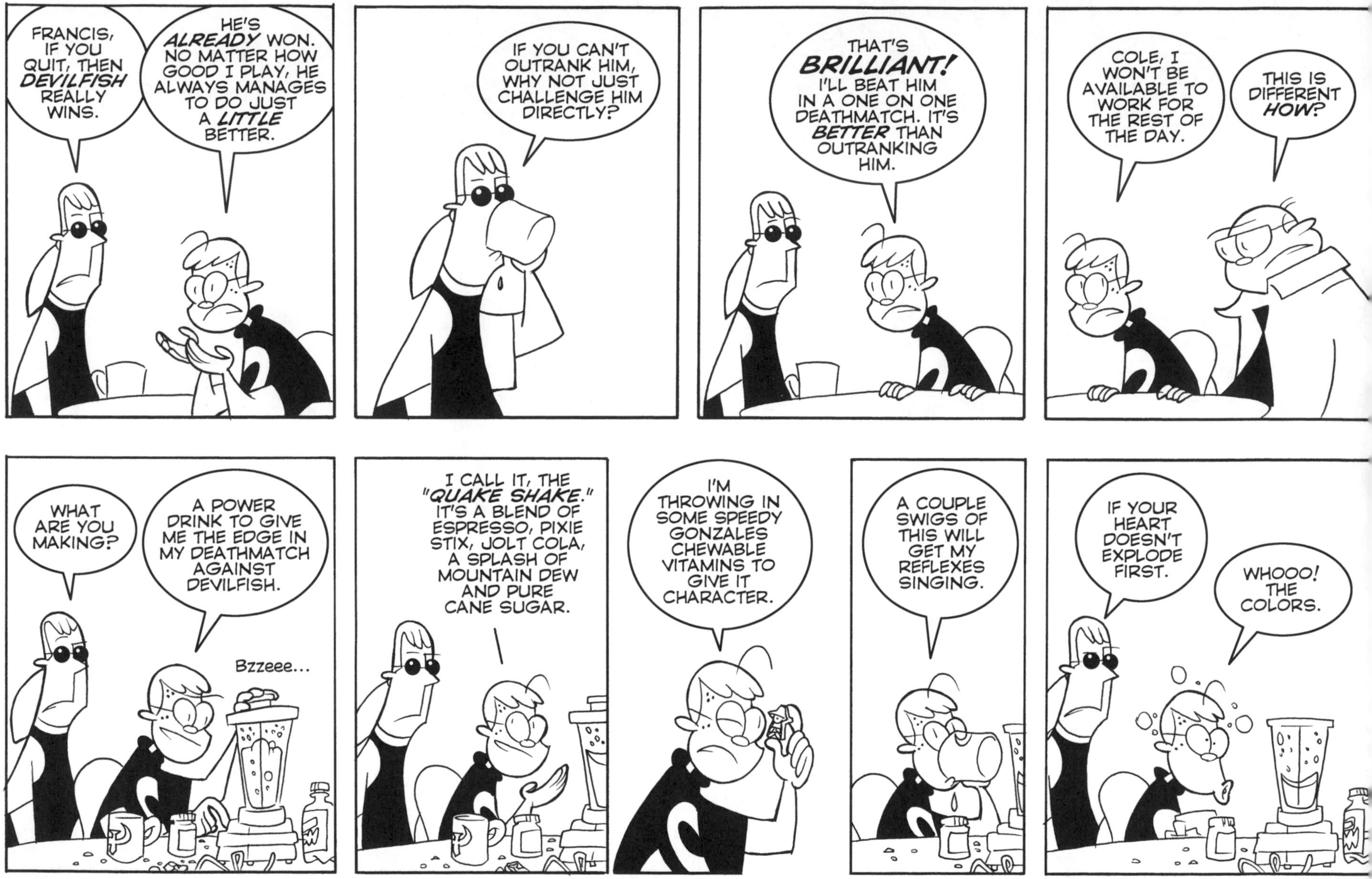
FRANCIS, IF YOU QUIT, THEN DEVILFISH REALLY WINS.
HE'S ALREADY WON. NO MATTER HOW GOOD I PLAY, HE ALWAYS MANAGES TO DO JUST A LITTLE BETTER.
IF YOU CAN'T OUTRANK HIM, WHY NOT JUST CHALLENGE HIM DIRECTLY?
THAT'S BRILLIANT! I'LL BEAT HIM IN A ONE ON ONE DEATHMATCH. IT'S BETTER THAN OUTRANKING HIM.
COLE, I WON'T BE AVAILABLE TO WORK FOR THE REST OF THE DAY.
THIS IS DIFFERENT HOW?
WHAT ARE YOU MAKING?
A POWER DRINK TO GIVE ME THE EDGE IN MY DEATHMATCH AGAINST DEVILFISH.
Bzzeee...
I CALL IT, THE "QUAKE SHAKE." IT'S A BLEND OF ESPRESSO, PIXIE STIX, JOLT COLA, A SPLASH OF MOUNTAIN DEW AND PURE CANE SUGAR.
I'M THROWING IN SOME SPEEDY GONZALES CHEWABLE VITAMINS TO GIVE IT CHARACTER.
A COUPLE SWIGS OF THIS WILL GET MY REFLEXES SINGING.
IF YOUR HEART DOESN'T EXPLODE FIRST.
WHOOO! THE COLORS.

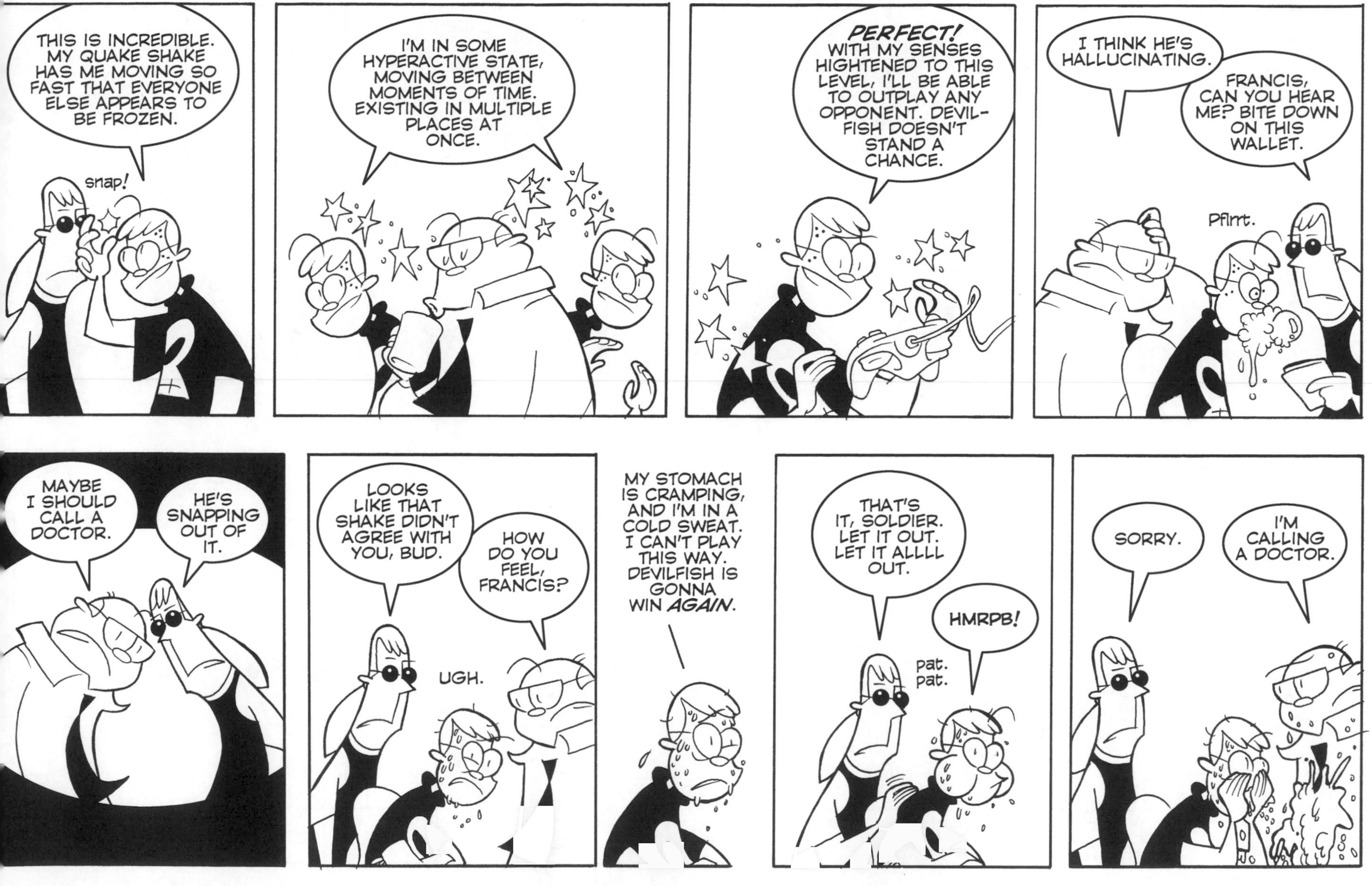
THIS IS INCREDIBLE. MY QUAKE SHAKE HAS ME MOVING SO FAST THAT EVERYONE ELSE APPEARS TO BE FROZEN.
snap!
I'M IN SOME HYPERACTIVE STATE, MOVING BETWEEN MOMENTS OF TIME. EXISTING IN MULTIPLE PLACES AT ONCE.
PERFECT! WITH MY SENSES HIGHTENED TO THIS LEVEL, I'LL BE ABLE TO OUTPLAY ANY OPPONENT. DEVIL-FISH DOESN'T STAND A CHANCE.
I THINK HE'S HALLUCINATING.
FRANCIS, CAN YOU HEAR ME? BITE DOWN ON THIS WALLET.
Pflrrt.
MAYBE I SHOULD CALL A DOCTOR.
HE'S SNAPPING OUT OF IT.
LOOKS LIKE THAT SHAKE DIDN'T AGREE WITH YOU, BUD.
HOW DO YOU FEEL, FRANCIS?
UGH.
MY STOMACH IS CRAMPING, AND I'M IN A COLD SWEAT. I CAN'T PLAY THIS WAY. DEVILFISH IS GONNA WIN AGAIN.
THAT'S IT, SOLDIER. LET IT OUT. LET IT ALLLL OUT.
pat. pat.
HMRPB!
SORRY.
I'M CALLING A DOCTOR.

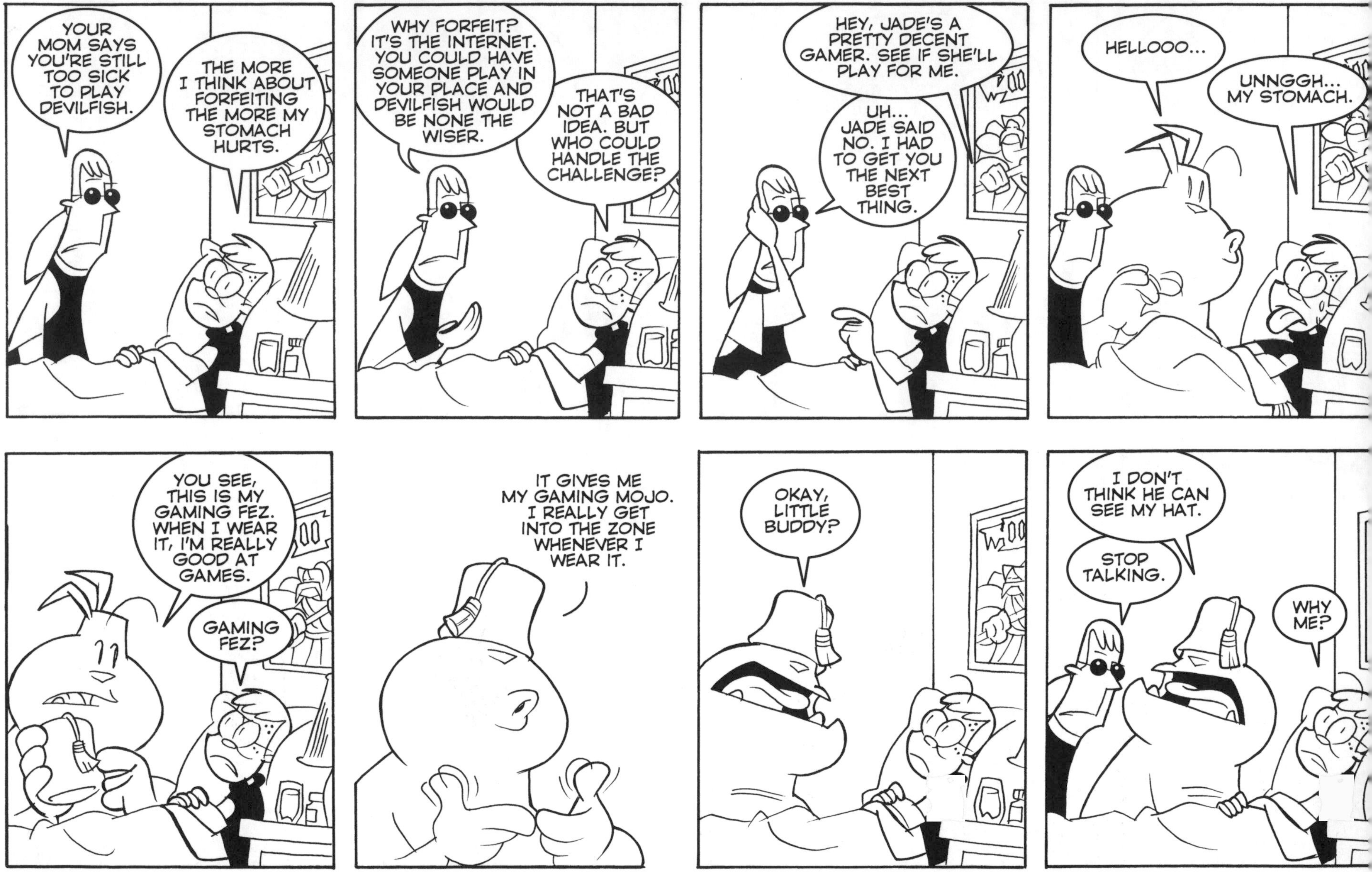
YOUR MOM SAYS YOU'RE STILL TOO SICK TO PLAY DEVILFISH.
THE MORE I THINK ABOUT FORFEITING THE MORE MY STOMACH HURTS.
WHY FORFEIT? IT'S THE INTERNET. YOU COULD HAVE SOMEONE PLAY IN YOUR PLACE AND DEVILFISH WOULD BE NONE THE WISER.
THAT'S NOT A BAD IDEA. BUT WHO COULD HANDLE THE CHALLENGE?
HEY, JADE'S A PRETTY DECENT GAMER. SEE IF SHE'LL PLAY FOR ME.
UH... JADE SAID NO. I HAD TO GET YOU THE NEXT BEST THING.
HELLOOO...
UNNGGH... MY STOMACH.
YOU SEE, THIS IS MY GAMING FEZ. WHEN I WEAR IT, I'M REALLY GOOD AT GAMES.
GAMING FEZ?
IT GIVES ME MY GAMING MOJO. I REALLY GET INTO THE ZONE WHENEVER I WEAR IT.
OKAY, LITTLE BUDDY?
I DON'T THINK HE CAN SEE MY HAT.
STOP TALKING.
WHY ME?

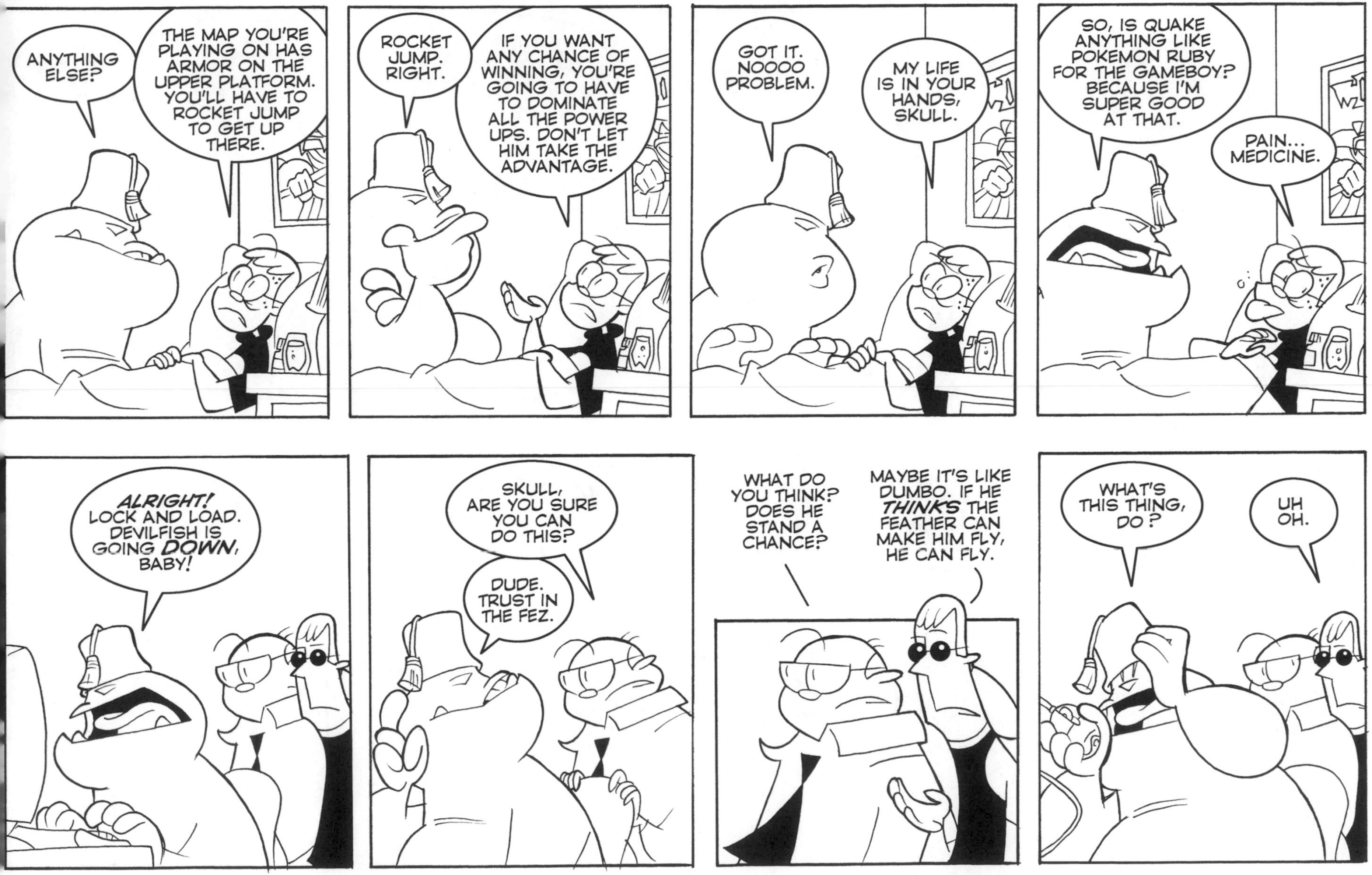
ANYTHING ELSE?
THE MAP YOU'RE PLAYING ON HAS ARMOR ON THE UPPER PLATFORM. YOU'LL HAVE TO ROCKET JUMP TO GET UP THERE.
ROCKET JUMP. RIGHT.
IF YOU WANT ANY CHANCE OF WINNING, YOU'RE GOING TO HAVE TO DOMINATE ALL THE POWER UPS. DON'T LET HIM TAKE THE ADVANTAGE.
GOT IT. NOOOO PROBLEM.
MY LIFE IS IN YOUR HANDS, SKULL.
SO, IS QUAKE ANYTHING LIKE POKEMON RUBY FOR THE GAMEBOY? BECAUSE I'M SUPER GOOD AT THAT.
PAIN... MEDICINE.
ALRIGHT! LOCK AND LOAD. DEVILFISH IS GOING ***DOWN***, BABY!
SKULL, ARE YOU SURE YOU CAN DO THIS?
DUDE. TRUST IN THE FEZ.
WHAT DO YOU THINK? DOES HE STAND A CHANCE?
MAYBE IT'S LIKE DUMBO. IF HE ***THINKS*** THE FEATHER CAN MAKE HIM FLY, HE CAN FLY.
WHAT'S THIS THING, DO?
UH OH.

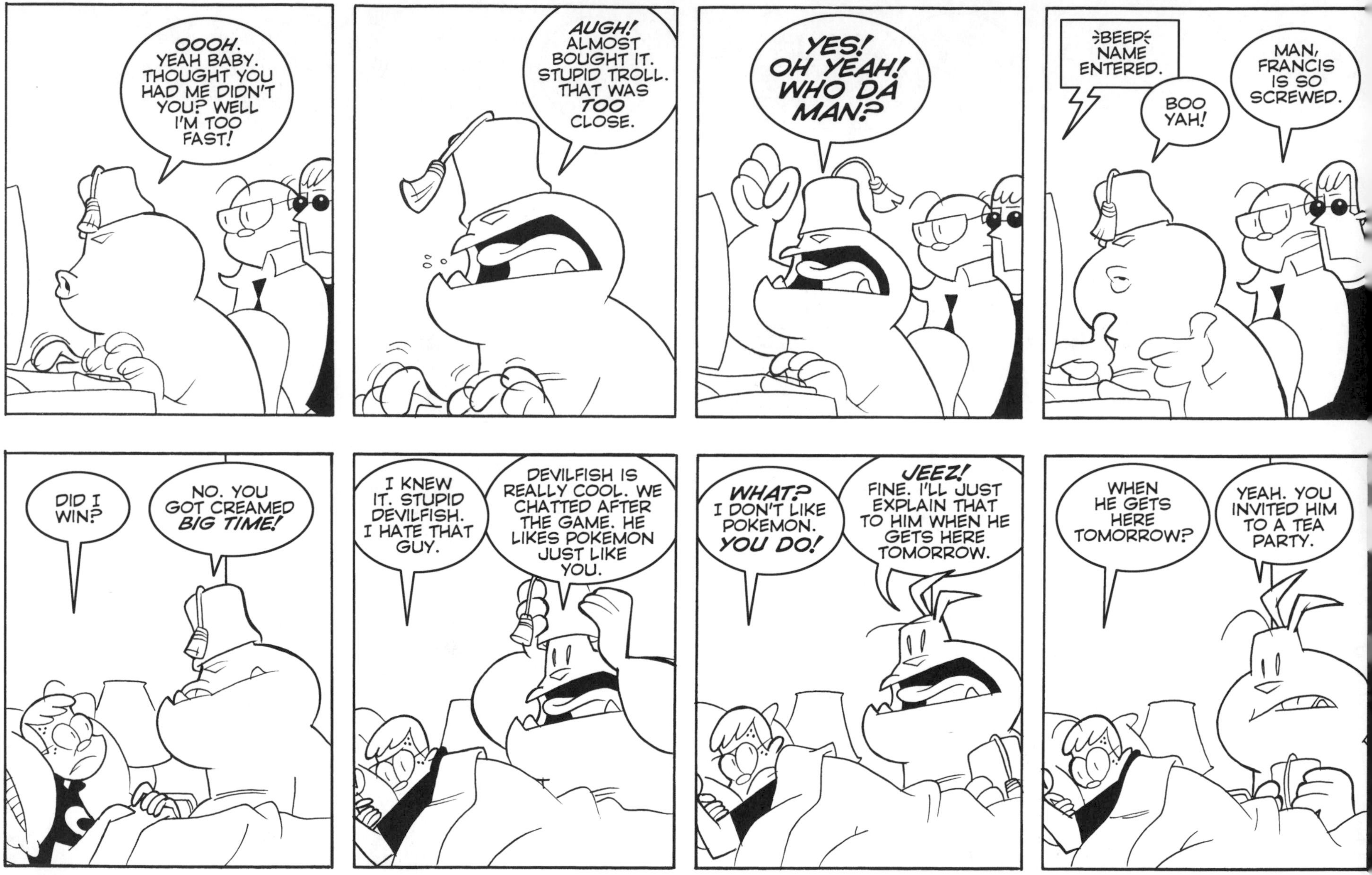
OOOH. YEAH BABY. THOUGHT YOU HAD ME DIDN'T YOU? WELL I'M TOO FAST!
AUGH! ALMOST BOUGHT IT. STUPID TROLL. THAT WAS TOO CLOSE.
YES! OH YEAH! WHO DA MAN?
BEEP NAME ENTERED.
BOO YAH!
MAN, FRANCIS IS SO SCREWED.
DID I WIN?
NO. YOU GOT CREAMED BIG TIME!
I KNEW IT. STUPID DEVILFISH. I HATE THAT GUY.
DEVILFISH IS REALLY COOL. WE CHATTED AFTER THE GAME. HE LIKES POKEMON JUST LIKE YOU.
WHAT? I DON'T LIKE POKEMON. YOU DO!
JEEZ! FINE. I'LL JUST EXPLAIN THAT TO HIM WHEN HE GETS HERE TOMORROW.
WHEN HE GETS HERE TOMORROW?
YEAH. YOU INVITED HIM TO A TEA PARTY.

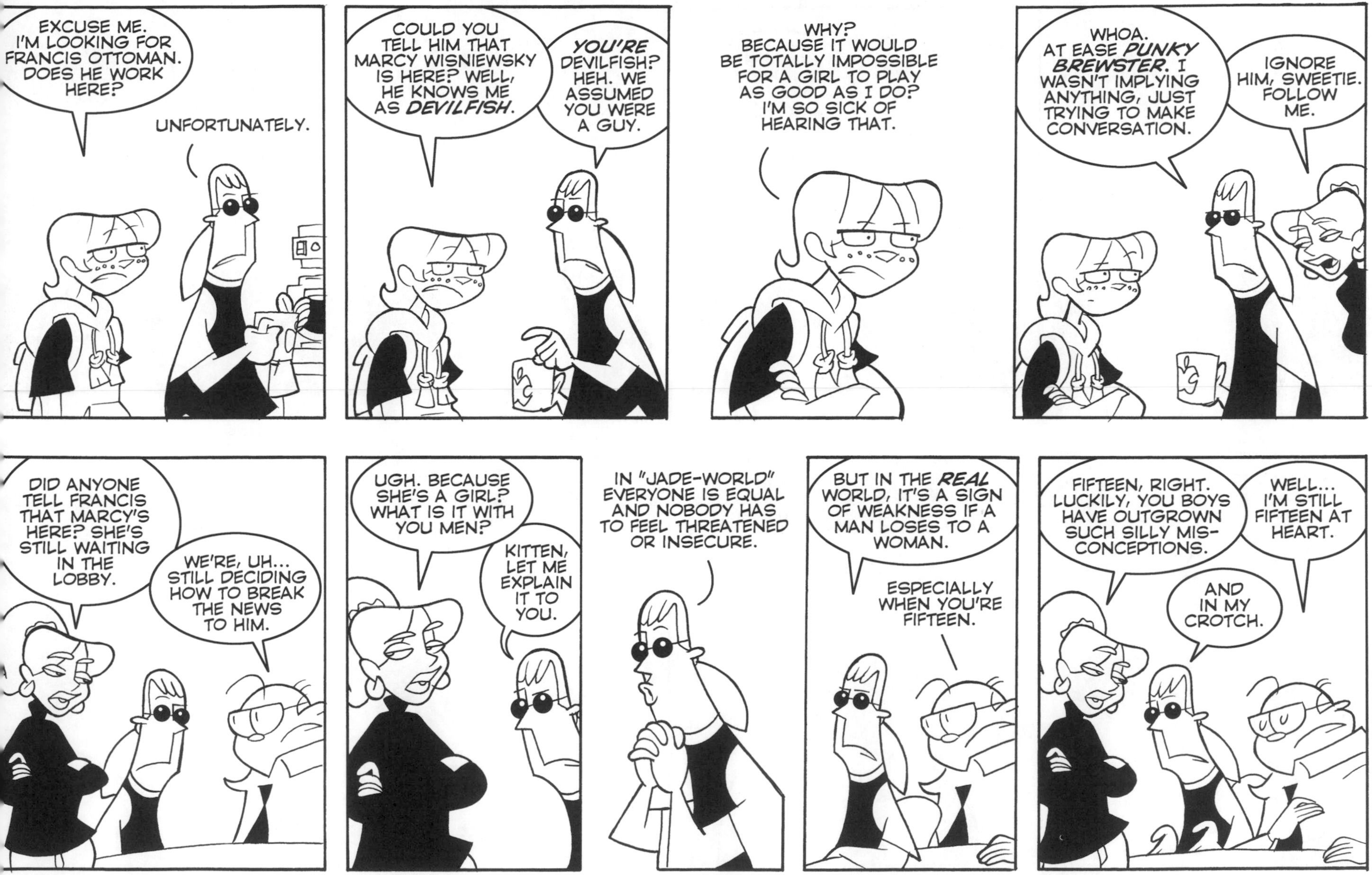

EXCUSE ME. I'M LOOKING FOR FRANCIS OTTOMAN. DOES HE WORK HERE?
UNFORTUNATELY.
COULD YOU TELL HIM THAT MARCY WISNIEWSKY IS HERE? WELL, HE KNOWS ME AS DEVILFISH.
YOU'RE DEVILFISH? HEH. WE ASSUMED YOU WERE A GUY.
WHY? BECAUSE IT WOULD BE TOTALLY IMPOSSIBLE FOR A GIRL TO PLAY AS GOOD AS I DO? I'M SO SICK OF HEARING THAT.
WHOA. AT EASE PUNKY BREWSTER. I WASN'T IMPLYING ANYTHING, JUST TRYING TO MAKE CONVERSATION.
IGNORE HIM, SWEETIE. FOLLOW ME.
DID ANYONE TELL FRANCIS THAT MARCY'S HERE? SHE'S STILL WAITING IN THE LOBBY.
WE'RE, UH... STILL DECIDING HOW TO BREAK THE NEWS TO HIM.
UGH. BECAUSE SHE'S A GIRL? WHAT IS IT WITH YOU MEN?
KITTEN, LET ME EXPLAIN IT TO YOU.
IN "JADE-WORLD" EVERYONE IS EQUAL AND NOBODY HAS TO FEEL THREATENED OR INSECURE.
BUT IN THE REAL WORLD, IT'S A SIGN OF WEAKNESS IF A MAN LOSES TO A WOMAN.
ESPECIALLY WHEN YOU'RE FIFTEEN.
FIFTEEN, RIGHT. LUCKILY, YOU BOYS HAVE OUTGROWN SUCH SILLY MIS-CONCEPTIONS.
WELL... I'M STILL FIFTEEN AT HEART.
AND IN MY CROTCH.

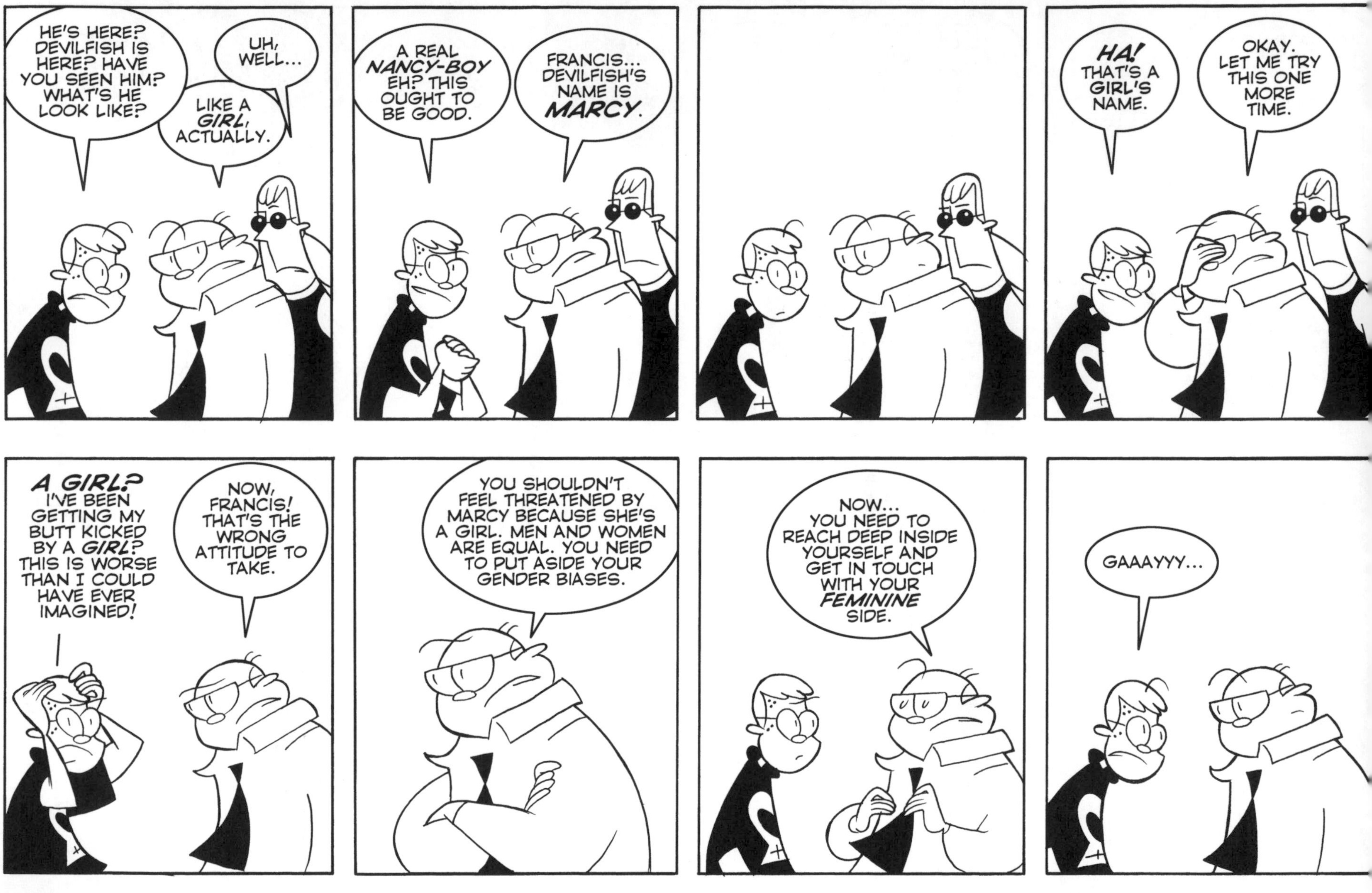
HE'S HERE? DEVILFISH IS HERE? HAVE YOU SEEN HIM? WHAT'S HE LOOK LIKE?
UH, WELL...
LIKE A *GIRL*, ACTUALLY.
A REAL *NANCY-BOY* EH? THIS OUGHT TO BE GOOD.
FRANCIS... DEVILFISH'S NAME IS *MARCY*.
HA! THAT'S A *GIRL'S* NAME.
OKAY. LET ME TRY THIS ONE MORE TIME.
A GIRL? I'VE BEEN GETTING MY BUTT KICKED BY A *GIRL*? THIS IS WORSE THAN I COULD HAVE EVER IMAGINED!
NOW, FRANCIS! THAT'S THE WRONG ATTITUDE TO TAKE.
YOU SHOULDN'T FEEL THREATENED BY MARCY BECAUSE SHE'S A GIRL. MEN AND WOMEN ARE EQUAL. YOU NEED TO PUT ASIDE YOUR GENDER BIASES.
NOW... YOU NEED TO REACH DEEP INSIDE YOURSELF AND GET IN TOUCH WITH YOUR *FEMININE* SIDE.
GAAAYYY...

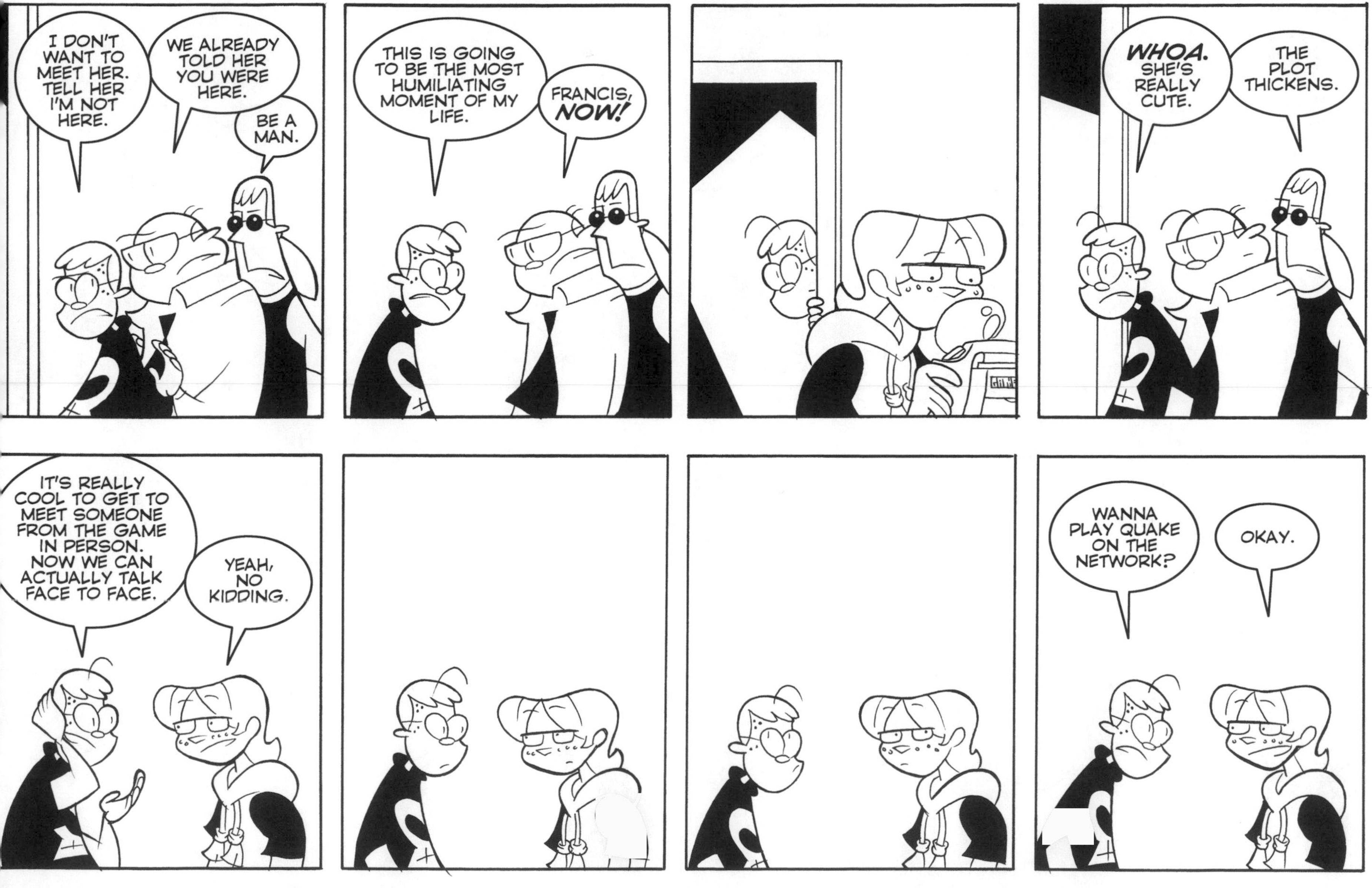
I DON'T WANT TO MEET HER. TELL HER I'M NOT HERE.
WE ALREADY TOLD HER YOU WERE HERE.
BE A MAN.
THIS IS GOING TO BE THE MOST HUMILIATING MOMENT OF MY LIFE.
FRANCIS, NOW!
WHOA. SHE'S REALLY CUTE.
THE PLOT THICKENS.
IT'S REALLY COOL TO GET TO MEET SOMEONE FROM THE GAME IN PERSON. NOW WE CAN ACTUALLY TALK FACE TO FACE.
YEAH, NO KIDDING.
WANNA PLAY QUAKE ON THE NETWORK?
OKAY.

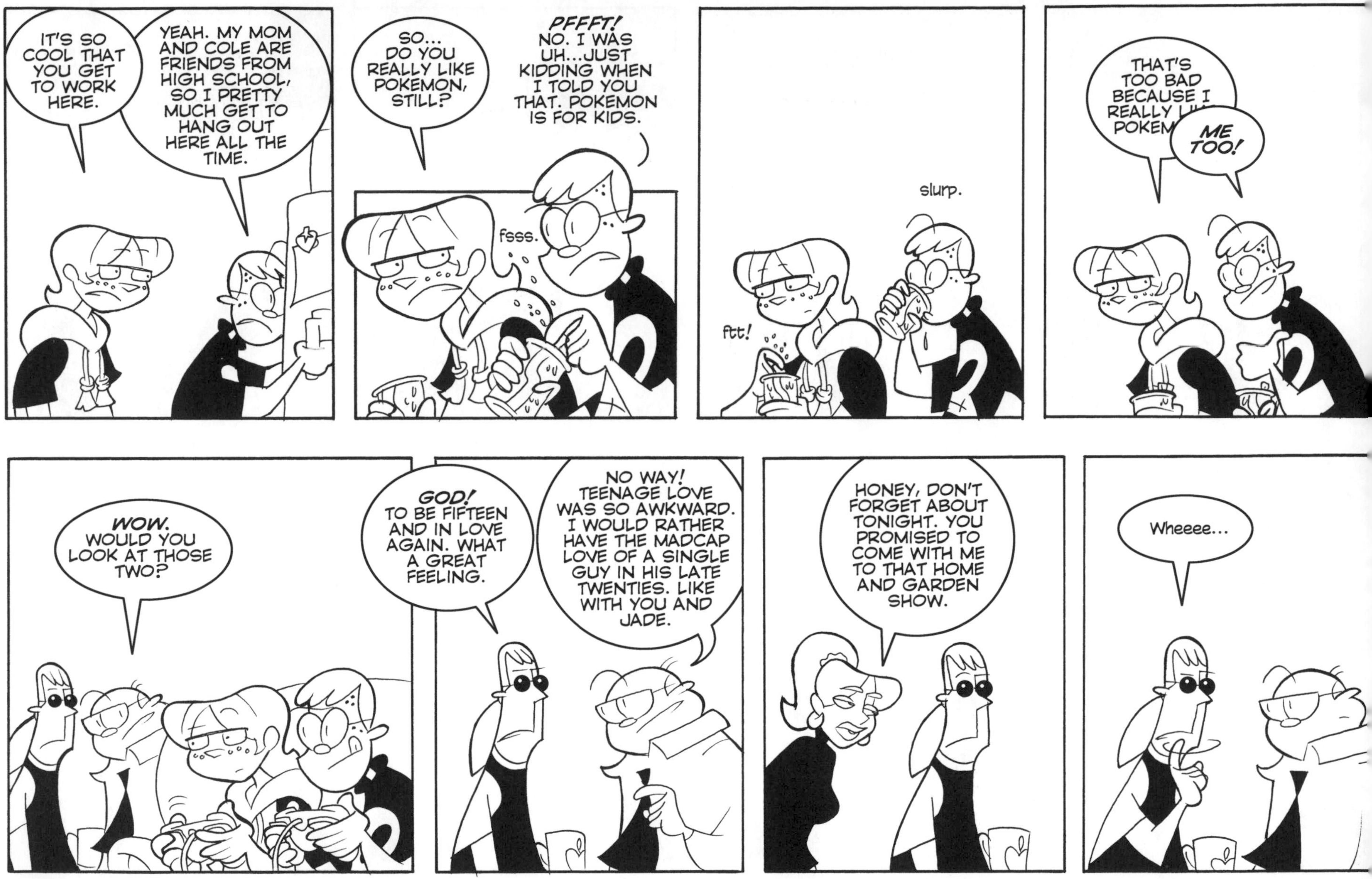

IT'S SO COOL THAT YOU GET TO WORK HERE.
YEAH. MY MOM AND COLE ARE FRIENDS FROM HIGH SCHOOL, SO I PRETTY MUCH GET TO HANG OUT HERE ALL THE TIME.
SO... DO YOU REALLY LIKE POKEMON, STILL?
PFFFT! NO. I WAS UH...JUST KIDDING WHEN I TOLD YOU THAT. POKEMON IS FOR KIDS.
fsss.
slurp.
ftt!
THAT'S TOO BAD BECAUSE I REALLY LI POKEM
ME TOO!
WOW. WOULD YOU LOOK AT THOSE TWO?
GOD! TO BE FIFTEEN AND IN LOVE AGAIN. WHAT A GREAT FEELING.
NO WAY! TEENAGE LOVE WAS SO AWKWARD. I WOULD RATHER HAVE THE MADCAP LOVE OF A SINGLE GUY IN HIS LATE TWENTIES. LIKE WITH YOU AND JADE.
HONEY, DON'T FORGET ABOUT TONIGHT. YOU PROMISED TO COME WITH ME TO THAT HOME AND GARDEN SHOW.
Wheeee...

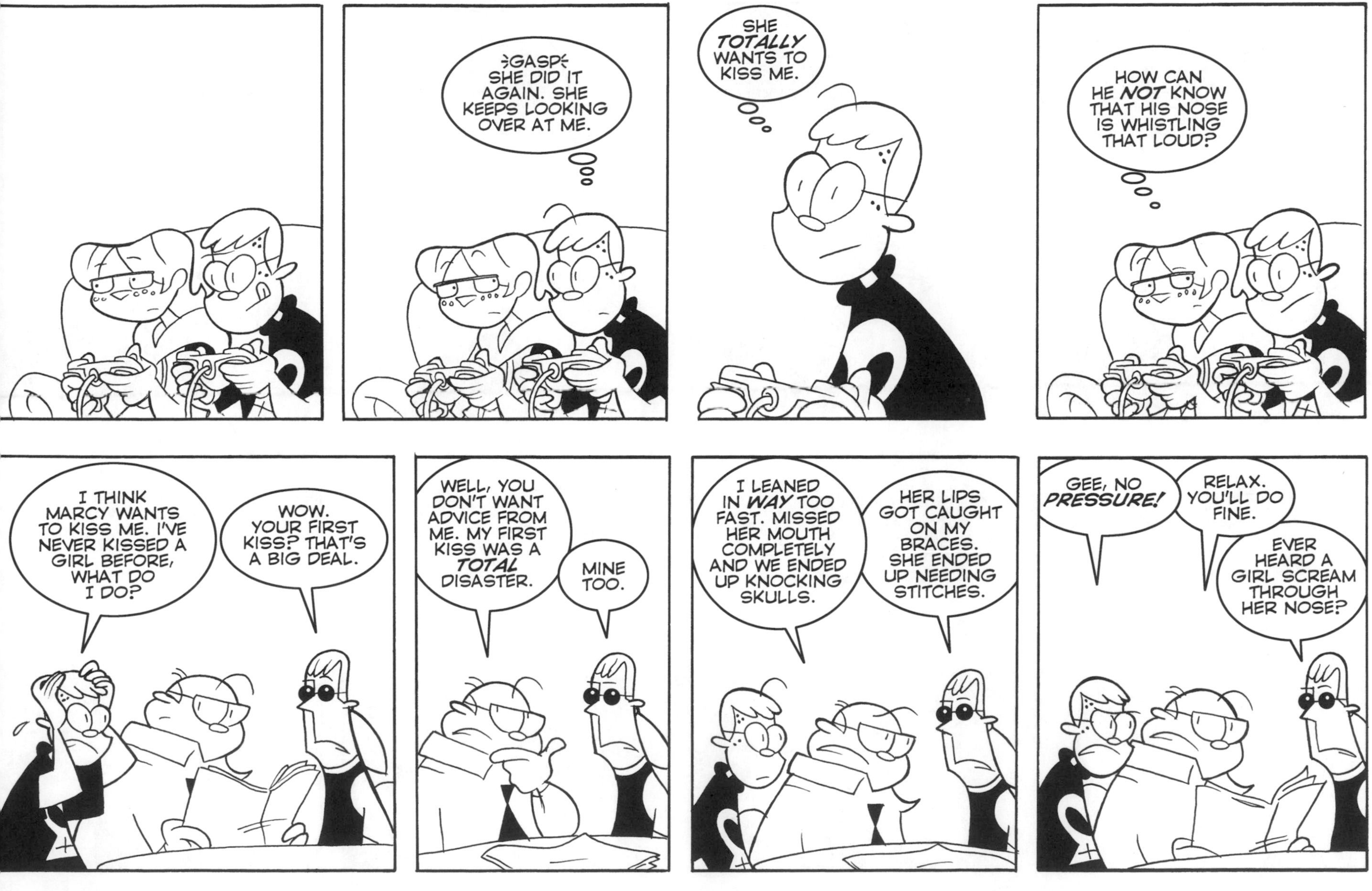

≶GASP≷ SHE DID IT AGAIN. SHE KEEPS LOOKING OVER AT ME.
SHE *TOTALLY* WANTS TO KISS ME.
HOW CAN HE *NOT* KNOW THAT HIS NOSE IS WHISTLING THAT LOUD?
I THINK MARCY WANTS TO KISS ME. I'VE NEVER KISSED A GIRL BEFORE, WHAT DO I DO?
WOW. YOUR FIRST KISS? THAT'S A BIG DEAL.
WELL, YOU DON'T WANT ADVICE FROM ME. MY FIRST KISS WAS A *TOTAL* DISASTER.
MINE TOO.
I LEANED IN *WAY* TOO FAST. MISSED HER MOUTH COMPLETELY AND WE ENDED UP KNOCKING SKULLS.
HER LIPS GOT CAUGHT ON MY BRACES. SHE ENDED UP NEEDING STITCHES.
GEE, NO *PRESSURE!*
RELAX. YOU'LL DO FINE.
EVER HEARD A GIRL SCREAM THROUGH HER NOSE?

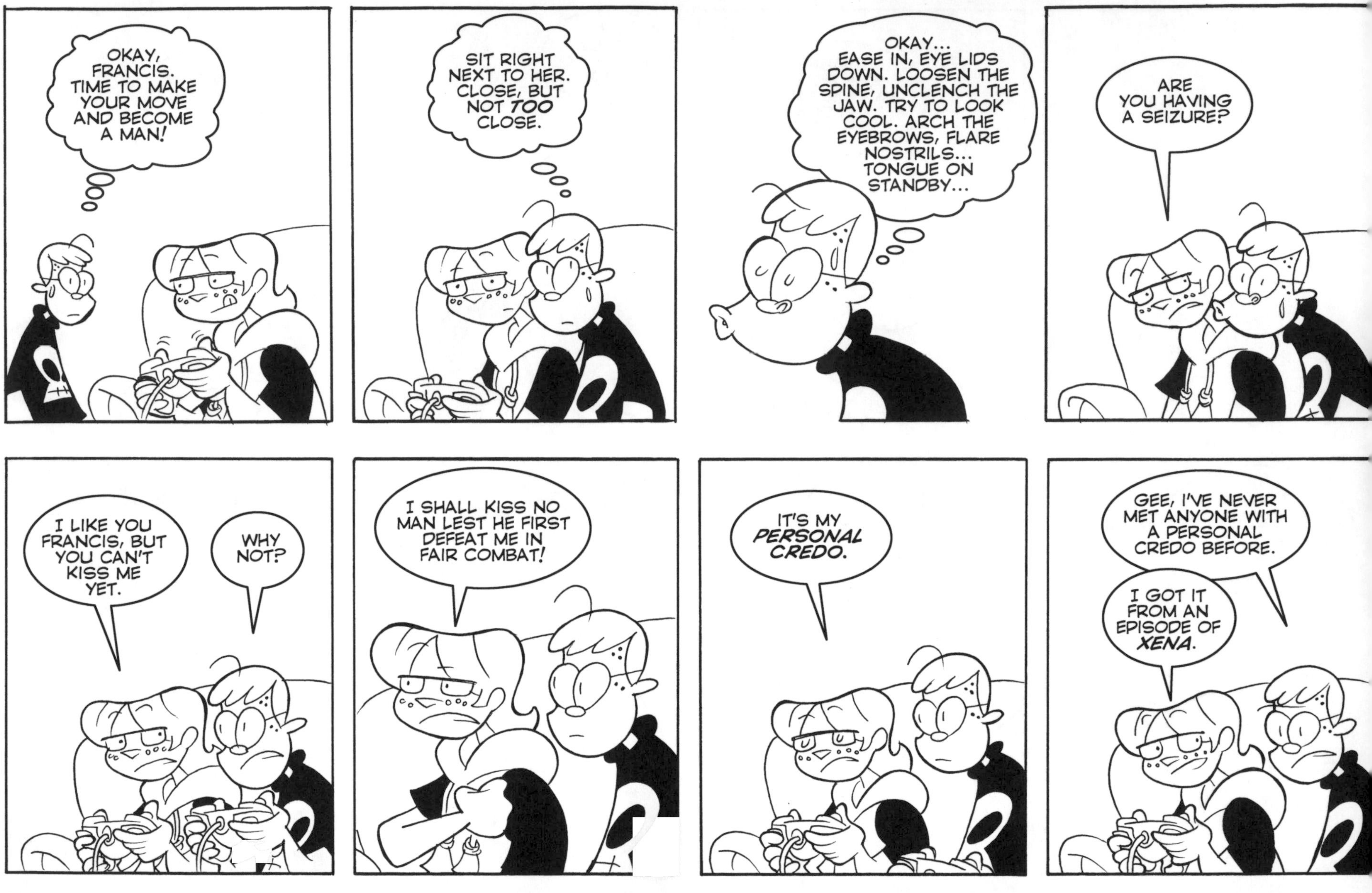
OKAY, FRANCIS. TIME TO MAKE YOUR MOVE AND BECOME A MAN!
SIT RIGHT NEXT TO HER. CLOSE, BUT NOT TOO CLOSE.
OKAY... EASE IN, EYE LIDS DOWN. LOOSEN THE SPINE, UNCLENCH THE JAW. TRY TO LOOK COOL. ARCH THE EYEBROWS, FLARE NOSTRILS... TONGUE ON STANDBY...
ARE YOU HAVING A SEIZURE?
I LIKE YOU FRANCIS, BUT YOU CAN'T KISS ME YET.
WHY NOT?
I SHALL KISS NO MAN LEST HE FIRST DEFEAT ME IN FAIR COMBAT!
IT'S MY PERSONAL CREDO.
GEE, I'VE NEVER MET ANYONE WITH A PERSONAL CREDO BEFORE.
I GOT IT FROM AN EPISODE OF XENA.

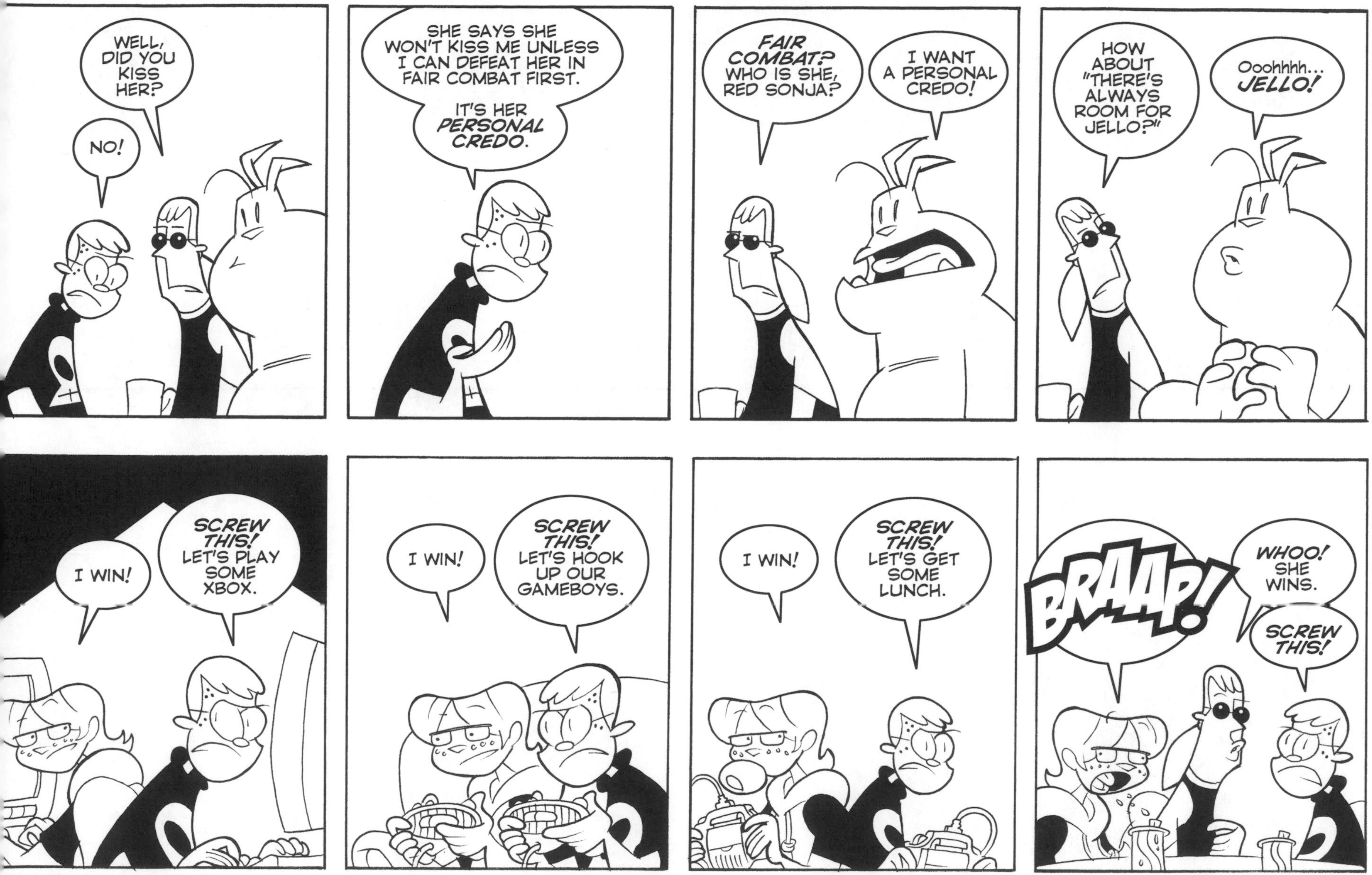
WELL, DID YOU KISS HER?
NO!
SHE SAYS SHE WON'T KISS ME UNLESS I CAN DEFEAT HER IN FAIR COMBAT FIRST.
IT'S HER PERSONAL CREDO.
FAIR COMBAT? WHO IS SHE, RED SONJA?
I WANT A PERSONAL CREDO!
HOW ABOUT "THERE'S ALWAYS ROOM FOR JELLO?"
Ooohhhh... JELLO!
I WIN!
SCREW THIS! LET'S PLAY SOME XBOX.
I WIN!
SCREW THIS! LET'S HOOK UP OUR GAMEBOYS.
I WIN!
SCREW THIS! LET'S GET SOME LUNCH.
BRAAAP!
WHOO! SHE WINS.
SCREW THIS!

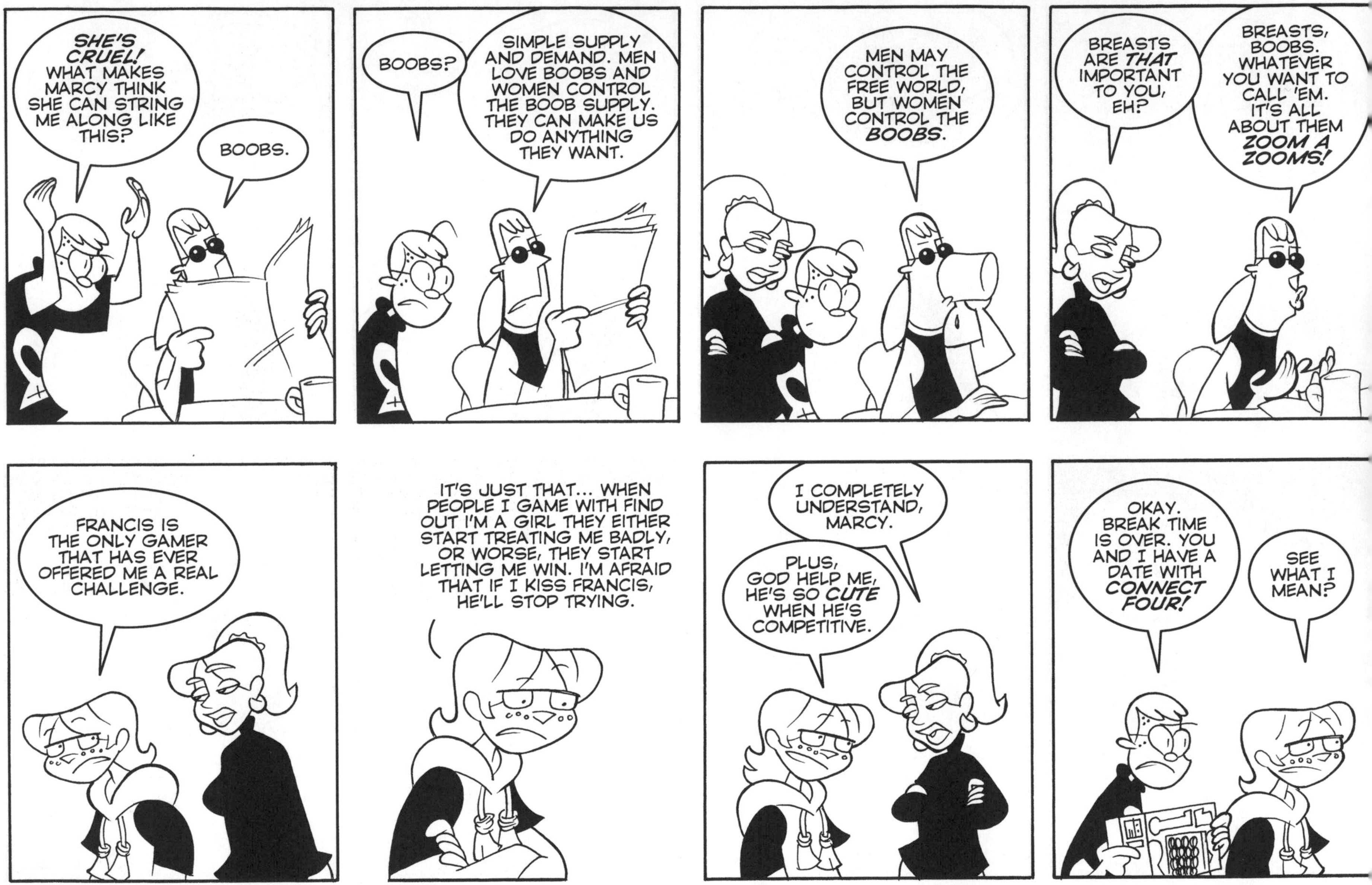
SHE'S CRUEL! WHAT MAKES MARCY THINK SHE CAN STRING ME ALONG LIKE THIS?
BOOBS.
BOOBS?
SIMPLE SUPPLY AND DEMAND. MEN LOVE BOOBS AND WOMEN CONTROL THE BOOB SUPPLY. THEY CAN MAKE US DO ANYTHING THEY WANT.
MEN MAY CONTROL THE FREE WORLD, BUT WOMEN CONTROL THE BOOBS.
BREASTS ARE THAT IMPORTANT TO YOU, EH?
BREASTS, BOOBS. WHATEVER YOU WANT TO CALL 'EM. IT'S ALL ABOUT THEM ZOOM A ZOOMS!
FRANCIS IS THE ONLY GAMER THAT HAS EVER OFFERED ME A REAL CHALLENGE.
IT'S JUST THAT... WHEN PEOPLE I GAME WITH FIND OUT I'M A GIRL THEY EITHER START TREATING ME BADLY, OR WORSE, THEY START LETTING ME WIN. I'M AFRAID THAT IF I KISS FRANCIS, HE'LL STOP TRYING.
I COMPLETELY UNDERSTAND, MARCY.
PLUS, GOD HELP ME, HE'S SO CUTE WHEN HE'S COMPETITIVE.
OKAY. BREAK TIME IS OVER. YOU AND I HAVE A DATE WITH CONNECT FOUR!
SEE WHAT I MEAN?

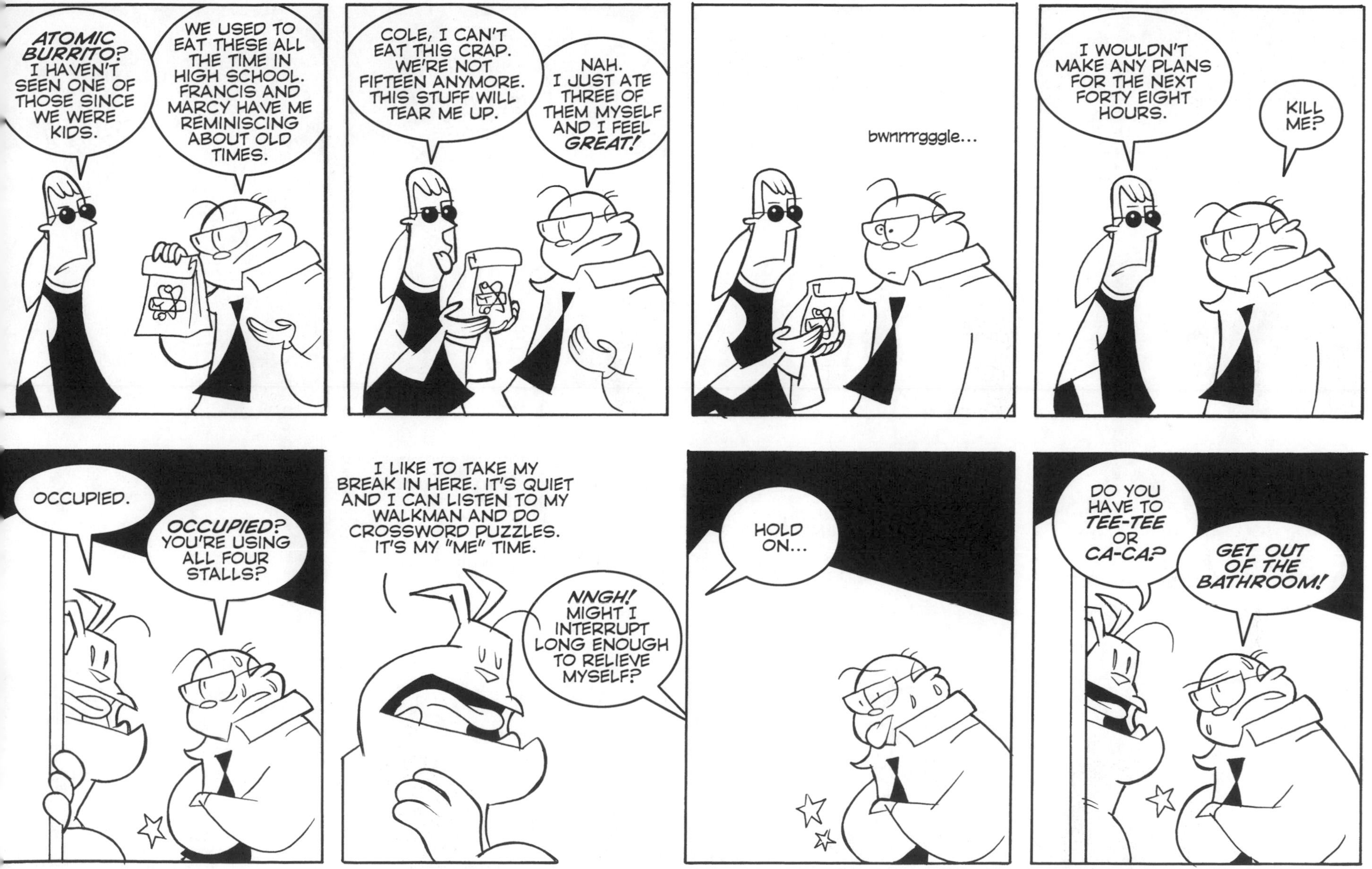
ATOMIC BURRITO? I HAVEN'T SEEN ONE OF THOSE SINCE WE WERE KIDS.
WE USED TO EAT THESE ALL THE TIME IN HIGH SCHOOL. FRANCIS AND MARCY HAVE ME REMINISCING ABOUT OLD TIMES.
COLE, I CAN'T EAT THIS CRAP. WE'RE NOT FIFTEEN ANYMORE. THIS STUFF WILL TEAR ME UP.
NAH. I JUST ATE THREE OF THEM MYSELF AND I FEEL GREAT!
bwnrrrgggle...
I WOULDN'T MAKE ANY PLANS FOR THE NEXT FORTY EIGHT HOURS.
KILL ME?
OCCUPIED.
OCCUPIED? YOU'RE USING ALL FOUR STALLS?
I LIKE TO TAKE MY BREAK IN HERE. IT'S QUIET AND I CAN LISTEN TO MY WALKMAN AND DO CROSSWORD PUZZLES. IT'S MY "ME" TIME.
NNGH! MIGHT I INTERRUPT LONG ENOUGH TO RELIEVE MYSELF?
HOLD ON...
DO YOU HAVE TO TEE-TEE OR CA-CA?
GET OUT OF THE BATHROOM!

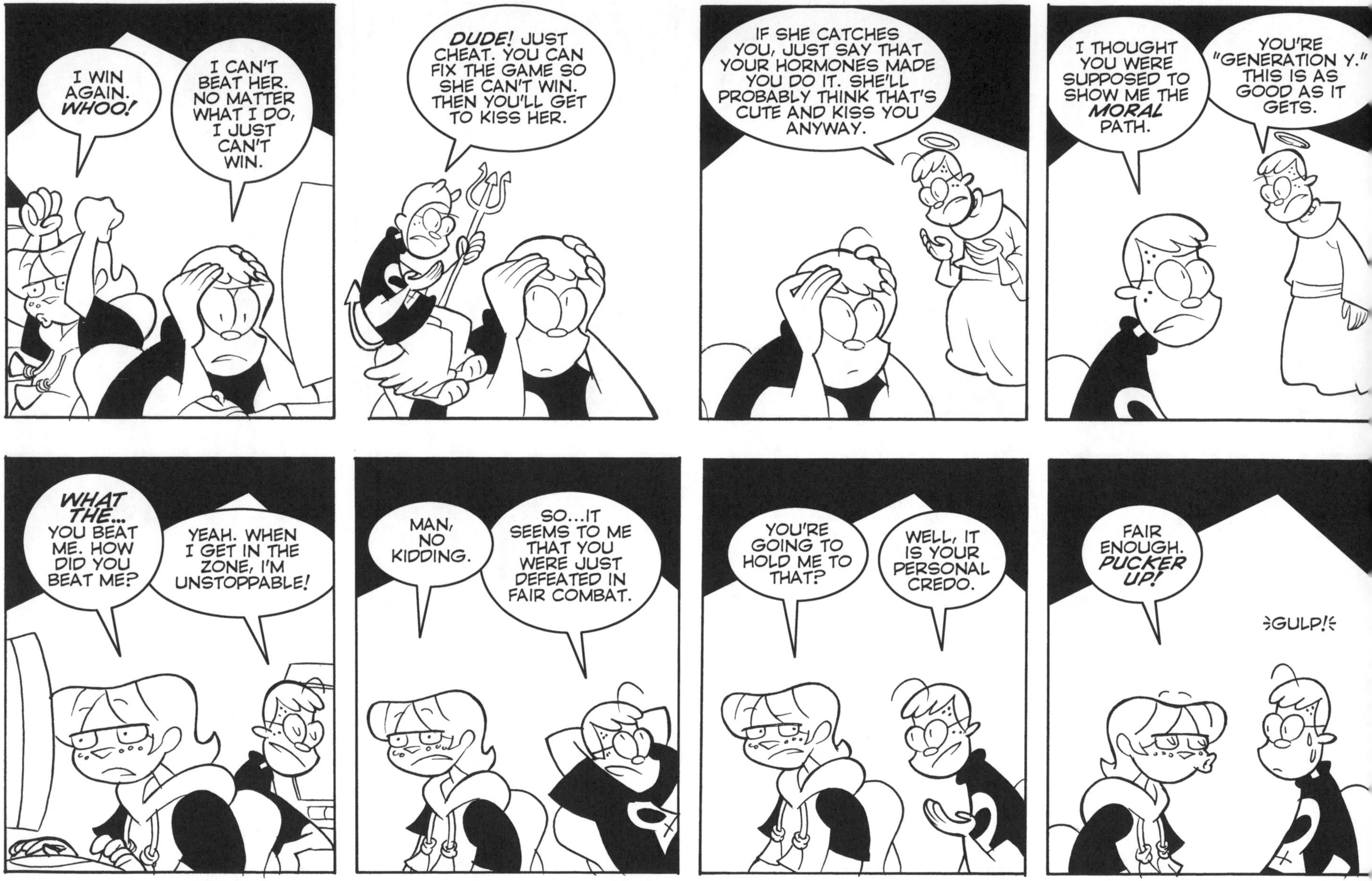
I WIN AGAIN. WHOO!
I CAN'T BEAT HER. NO MATTER WHAT I DO, I JUST CAN'T WIN.
DUDE! JUST CHEAT. YOU CAN FIX THE GAME SO SHE CAN'T WIN. THEN YOU'LL GET TO KISS HER.
IF SHE CATCHES YOU, JUST SAY THAT YOUR HORMONES MADE YOU DO IT. SHE'LL PROBABLY THINK THAT'S CUTE AND KISS YOU ANYWAY.
I THOUGHT YOU WERE SUPPOSED TO SHOW ME THE MORAL PATH.
YOU'RE "GENERATION Y." THIS IS AS GOOD AS IT GETS.
WHAT THE... YOU BEAT ME. HOW DID YOU BEAT ME?
YEAH. WHEN I GET IN THE ZONE, I'M UNSTOPPABLE!
MAN, NO KIDDING.
SO...IT SEEMS TO ME THAT YOU WERE JUST DEFEATED IN FAIR COMBAT.
YOU'RE GOING TO HOLD ME TO THAT?
WELL, IT IS YOUR PERSONAL CREDO.
FAIR ENOUGH. PUCKER UP!
GULP!

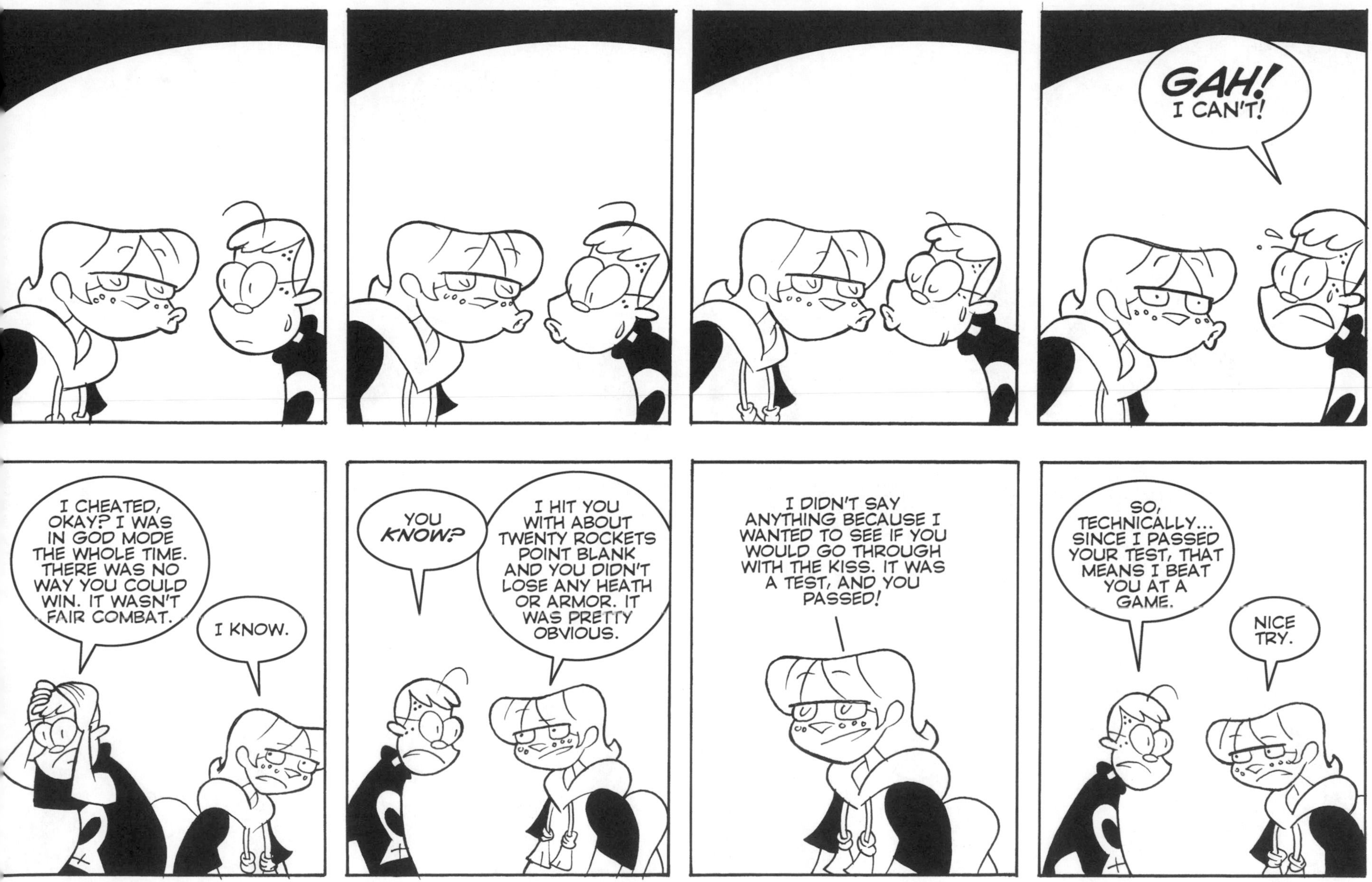
GAH! I CAN'T!
I CHEATED, OKAY? I WAS IN GOD MODE THE WHOLE TIME. THERE WAS NO WAY YOU COULD WIN. IT WASN'T FAIR COMBAT.
I KNOW.
YOU KNOW?
I HIT YOU WITH ABOUT TWENTY ROCKETS POINT BLANK AND YOU DIDN'T LOSE ANY HEATH OR ARMOR. IT WAS PRETTY OBVIOUS.
I DIDN'T SAY ANYTHING BECAUSE I WANTED TO SEE IF YOU WOULD GO THROUGH WITH THE KISS. IT WAS A TEST, AND YOU PASSED!
SO, TECHNICALLY... SINCE I PASSED YOUR TEST, THAT MEANS I BEAT YOU AT A GAME.
NICE TRY.

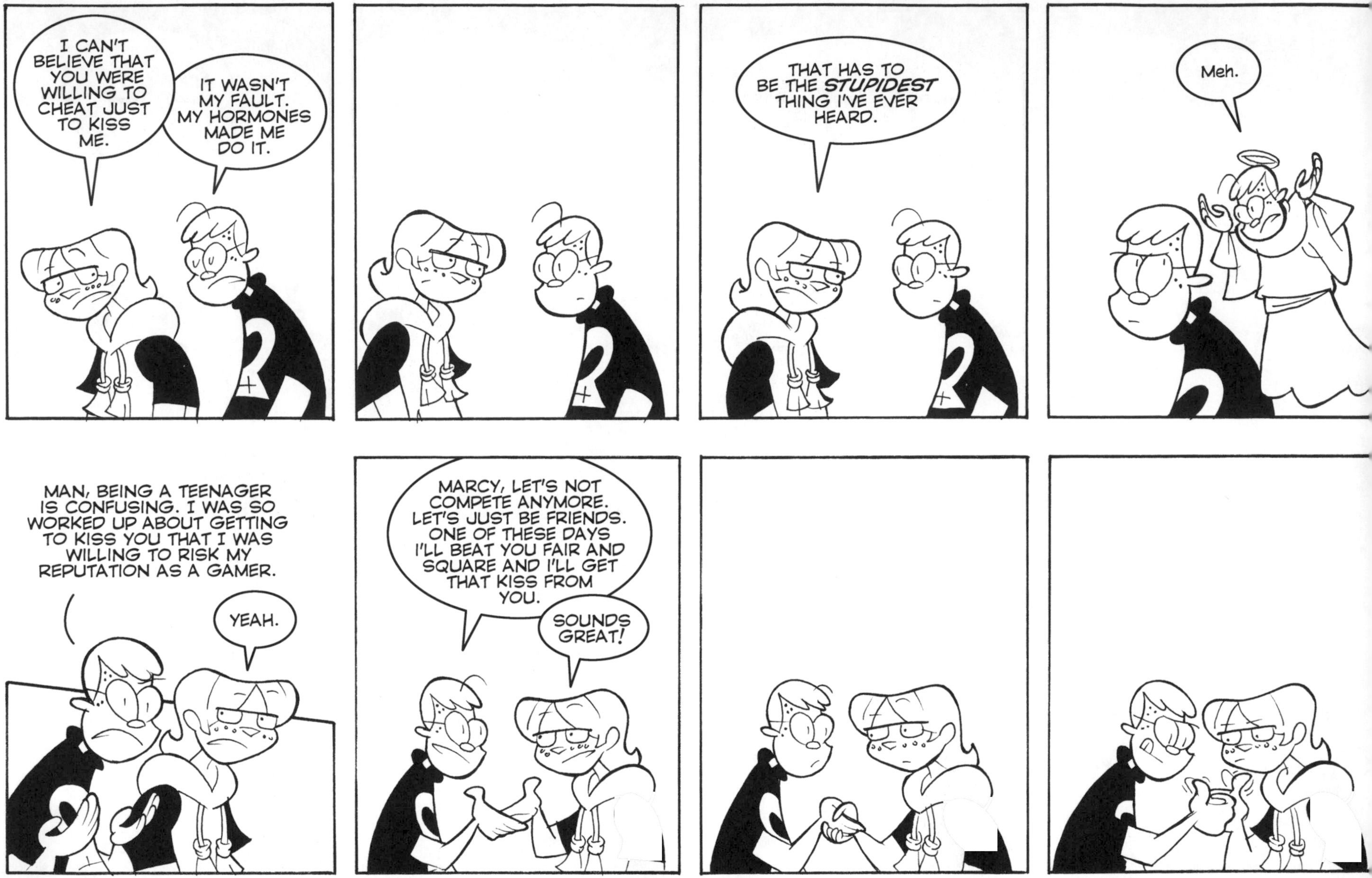
I CAN'T BELIEVE THAT YOU WERE WILLING TO CHEAT JUST TO KISS ME.
IT WASN'T MY FAULT. MY HORMONES MADE ME DO IT.
THAT HAS TO BE THE STUPIDEST THING I'VE EVER HEARD.
Meh.
MAN, BEING A TEENAGER IS CONFUSING. I WAS SO WORKED UP ABOUT GETTING TO KISS YOU THAT I WAS WILLING TO RISK MY REPUTATION AS A GAMER.
YEAH.
MARCY, LET'S NOT COMPETE ANYMORE. LET'S JUST BE FRIENDS. ONE OF THESE DAYS I'LL BEAT YOU FAIR AND SQUARE AND I'LL GET THAT KISS FROM YOU.
SOUNDS GREAT!

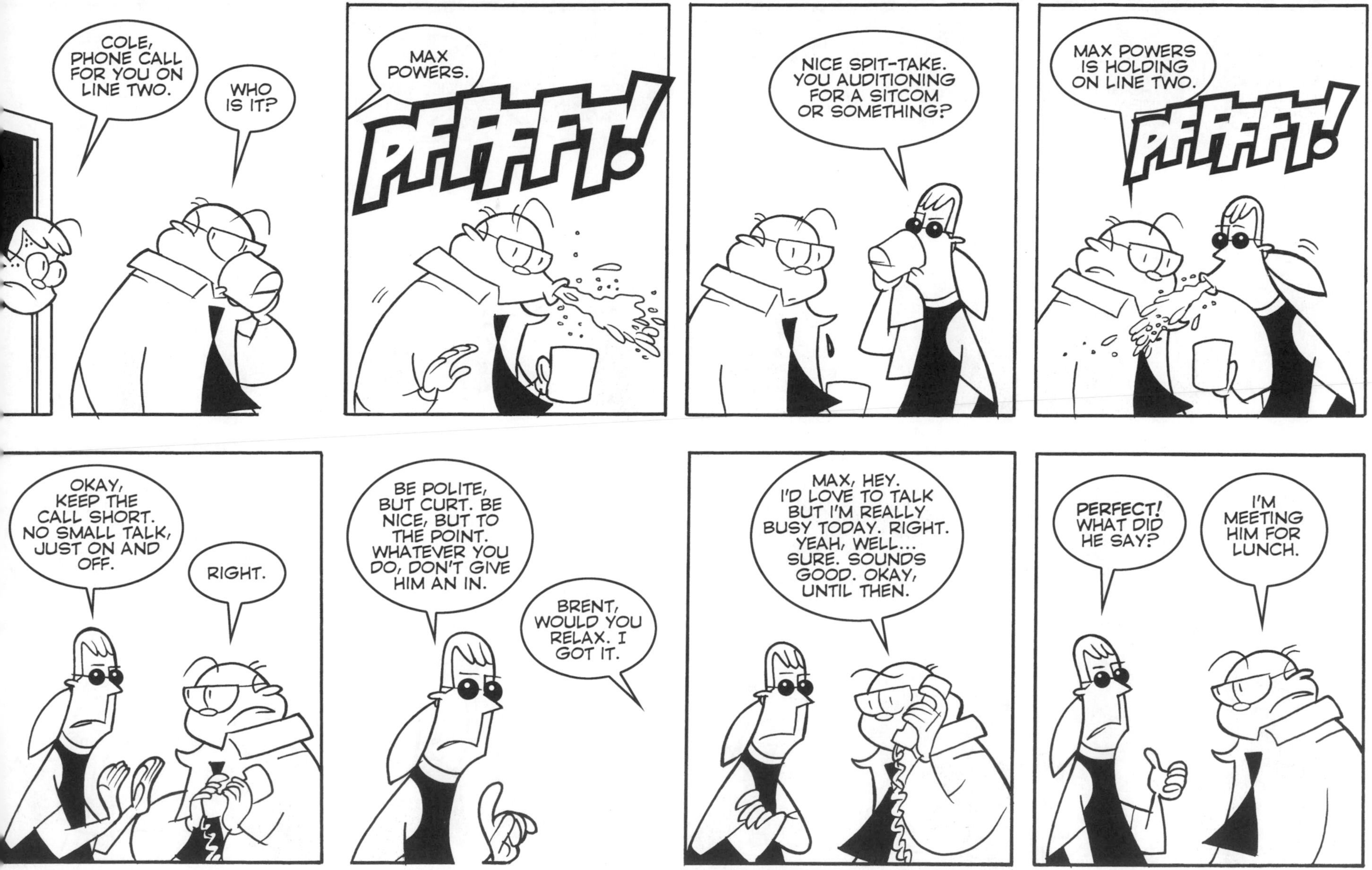
COLE, PHONE CALL FOR YOU ON LINE TWO.
WHO IS IT?
MAX POWERS.
PFFFFT!
NICE SPIT-TAKE. YOU AUDITIONING FOR A SITCOM OR SOMETHING?
MAX POWERS IS HOLDING ON LINE TWO.
PFFFFT!
OKAY, KEEP THE CALL SHORT. NO SMALL TALK, JUST ON AND OFF.
RIGHT.
BE POLITE, BUT CURT. BE NICE, BUT TO THE POINT. WHATEVER YOU DO, DON'T GIVE HIM AN IN.
BRENT, WOULD YOU RELAX. I GOT IT.
MAX, HEY. I'D LOVE TO TALK BUT I'M REALLY BUSY TODAY. RIGHT. YEAH, WELL... SURE. SOUNDS GOOD. OKAY, UNTIL THEN.
PERFECT! WHAT DID HE SAY?
I'M MEETING HIM FOR LUNCH.

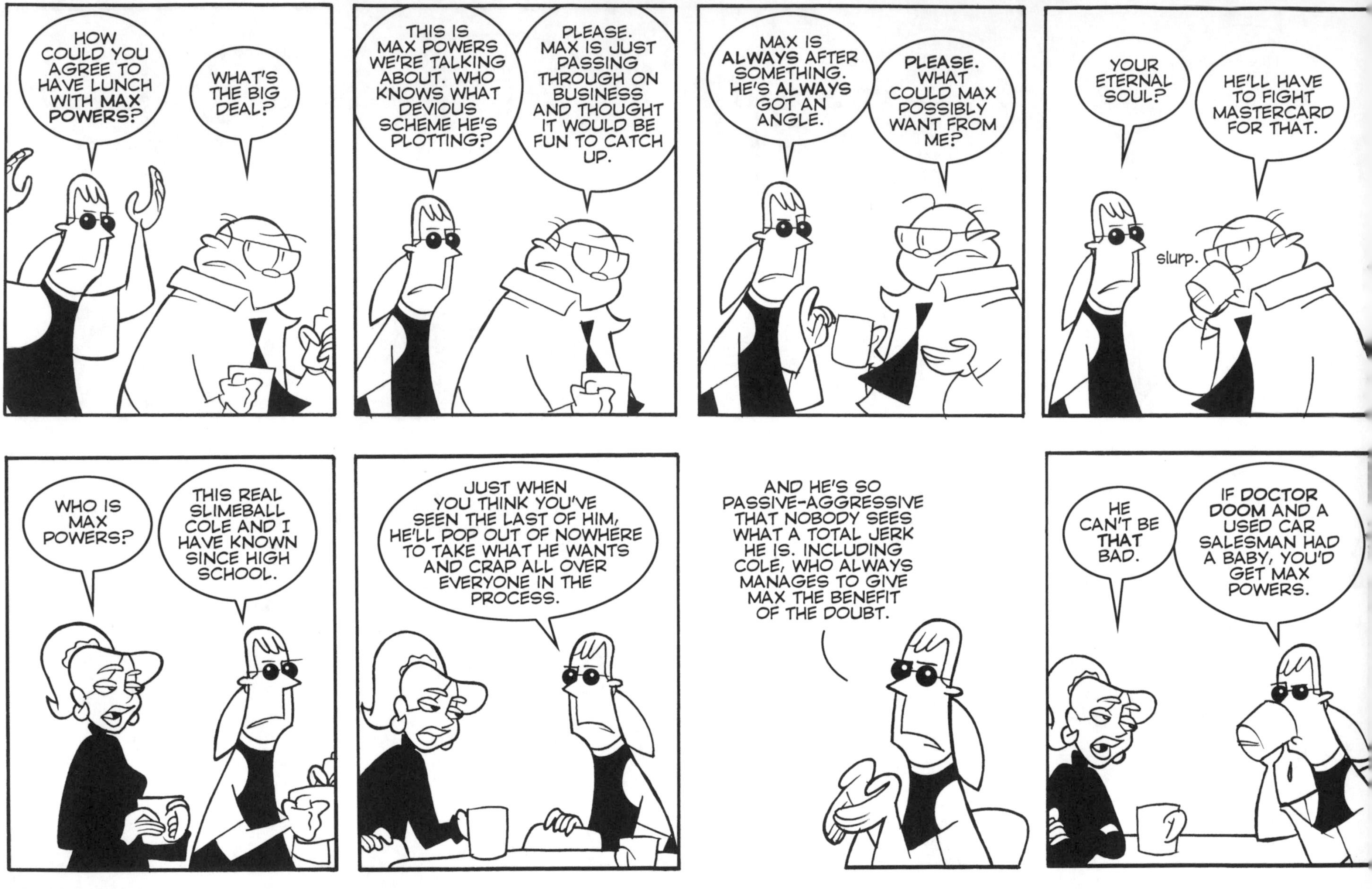
HOW COULD YOU AGREE TO HAVE LUNCH WITH MAX POWERS?
WHAT'S THE BIG DEAL?
THIS IS MAX POWERS WE'RE TALKING ABOUT. WHO KNOWS WHAT DEVIOUS SCHEME HE'S PLOTTING?
PLEASE. MAX IS JUST PASSING THROUGH ON BUSINESS AND THOUGHT IT WOULD BE FUN TO CATCH UP.
MAX IS ALWAYS AFTER SOMETHING. HE'S ALWAYS GOT AN ANGLE.
PLEASE. WHAT COULD MAX POSSIBLY WANT FROM ME?
YOUR ETERNAL SOUL?
HE'LL HAVE TO FIGHT MASTERCARD FOR THAT.
slurp.
WHO IS MAX POWERS?
THIS REAL SLIMEBALL COLE AND I HAVE KNOWN SINCE HIGH SCHOOL.
JUST WHEN YOU THINK YOU'VE SEEN THE LAST OF HIM, HE'LL POP OUT OF NOWHERE TO TAKE WHAT HE WANTS AND CRAP ALL OVER EVERYONE IN THE PROCESS.
AND HE'S SO PASSIVE-AGGRESSIVE THAT NOBODY SEES WHAT A TOTAL JERK HE IS. INCLUDING COLE, WHO ALWAYS MANAGES TO GIVE MAX THE BENEFIT OF THE DOUBT.
HE CAN'T BE THAT BAD.
IF DOCTOR DOOM AND A USED CAR SALESMAN HAD A BABY, YOU'D GET MAX POWERS.

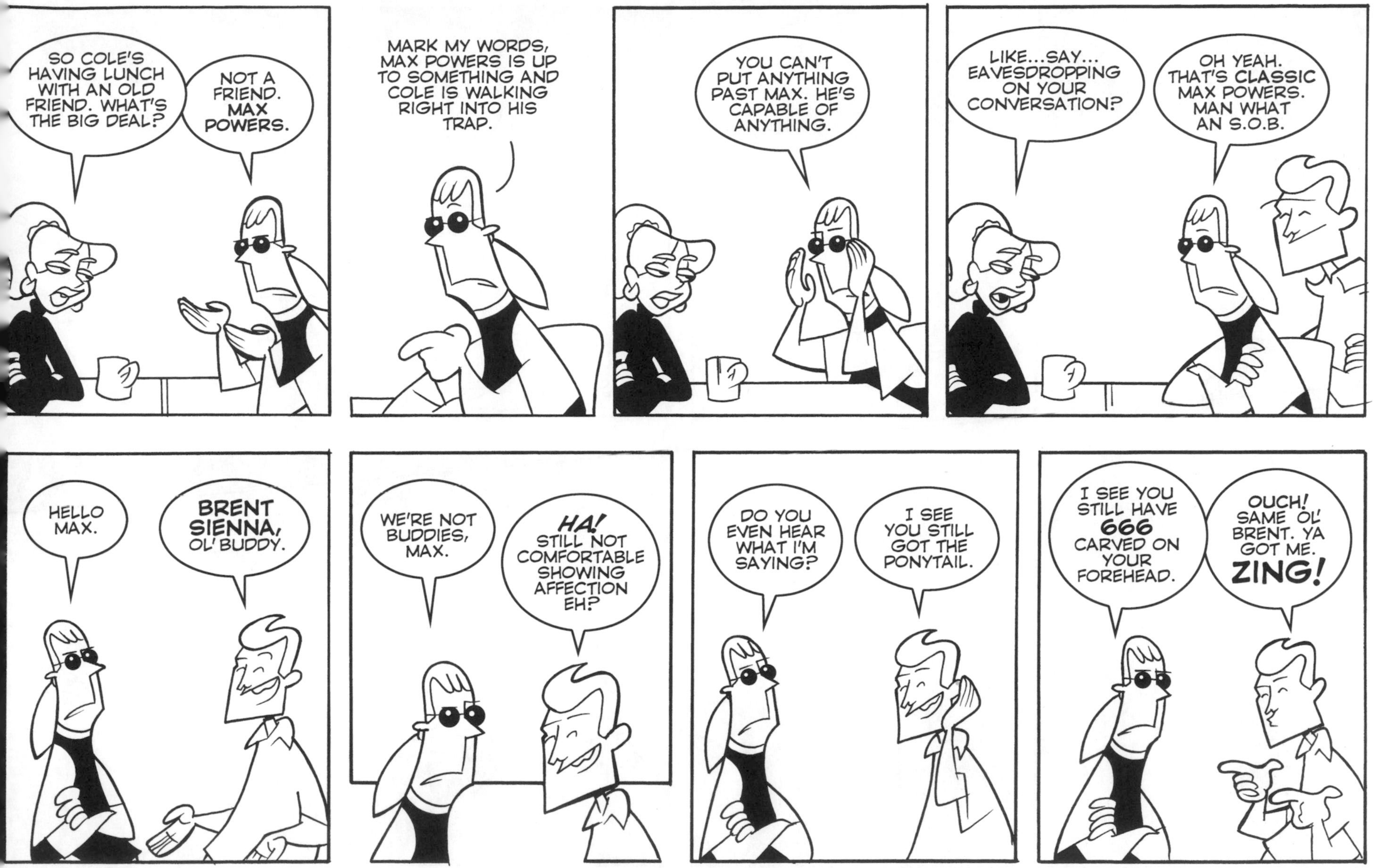
SO COLE'S HAVING LUNCH WITH AN OLD FRIEND. WHAT'S THE BIG DEAL?
NOT A FRIEND. MAX POWERS.
MARK MY WORDS, MAX POWERS IS UP TO SOMETHING AND COLE IS WALKING RIGHT INTO HIS TRAP.
YOU CAN'T PUT ANYTHING PAST MAX. HE'S CAPABLE OF ANYTHING.
LIKE...SAY... EAVESDROPPING ON YOUR CONVERSATION?
OH YEAH. THAT'S CLASSIC MAX POWERS. MAN WHAT AN S.O.B.
HELLO MAX.
BRENT SIENNA, OL' BUDDY.
WE'RE NOT BUDDIES, MAX.
HA! STILL NOT COMFORTABLE SHOWING AFFECTION EH?
DO YOU EVEN HEAR WHAT I'M SAYING?
I SEE YOU STILL GOT THE PONYTAIL.
I SEE YOU STILL HAVE 666 CARVED ON YOUR FOREHEAD.
OUCH! SAME OL' BRENT. YA GOT ME. ZING!

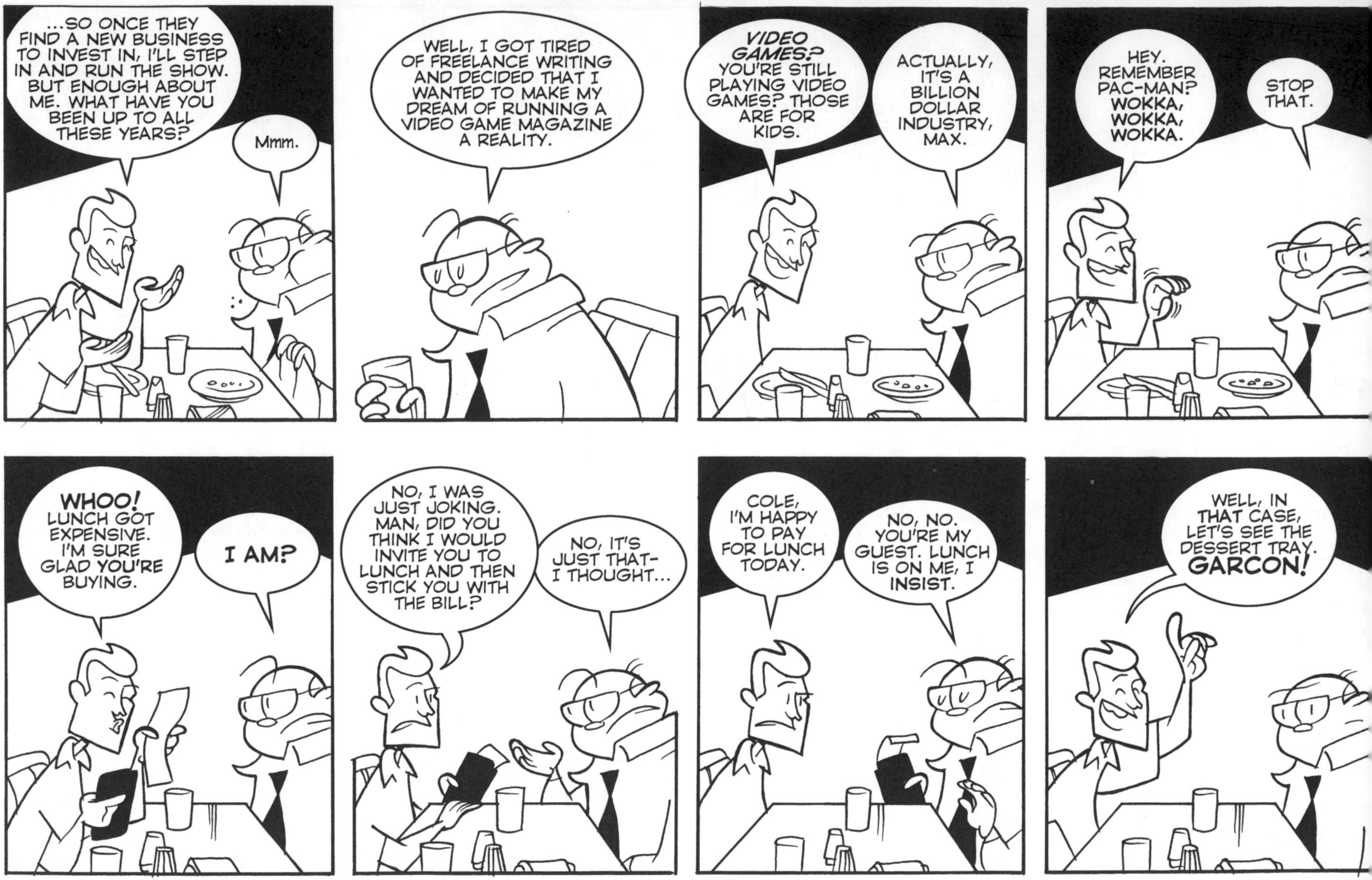
...SO ONCE THEY FIND A NEW BUSINESS TO INVEST IN, I'LL STEP IN AND RUN THE SHOW. BUT ENOUGH ABOUT ME. WHAT HAVE YOU BEEN UP TO ALL THESE YEARS?
Mmm.
WELL, I GOT TIRED OF FREELANCE WRITING AND DECIDED THAT I WANTED TO MAKE MY DREAM OF RUNNING A VIDEO GAME MAGAZINE A REALITY.
VIDEO GAMES? YOU'RE STILL PLAYING VIDEO GAMES? THOSE ARE FOR KIDS.
ACTUALLY, IT'S A BILLION DOLLAR INDUSTRY, MAX.
HEY. REMEMBER PAC-MAN? WOKKA, WOKKA, WOKKA.
STOP THAT.
WHOO! LUNCH GOT EXPENSIVE. I'M SURE GLAD YOU'RE BUYING.
I AM?
NO, I WAS JUST JOKING. MAN, DID YOU THINK I WOULD INVITE YOU TO LUNCH AND THEN STICK YOU WITH THE BILL?
NO, IT'S JUST THAT- I THOUGHT...
COLE, I'M HAPPY TO PAY FOR LUNCH TODAY.
NO, NO. YOU'RE MY GUEST. LUNCH IS ON ME, I INSIST.
WELL, IN THAT CASE, LET'S SEE THE DESSERT TRAY. GARCON!

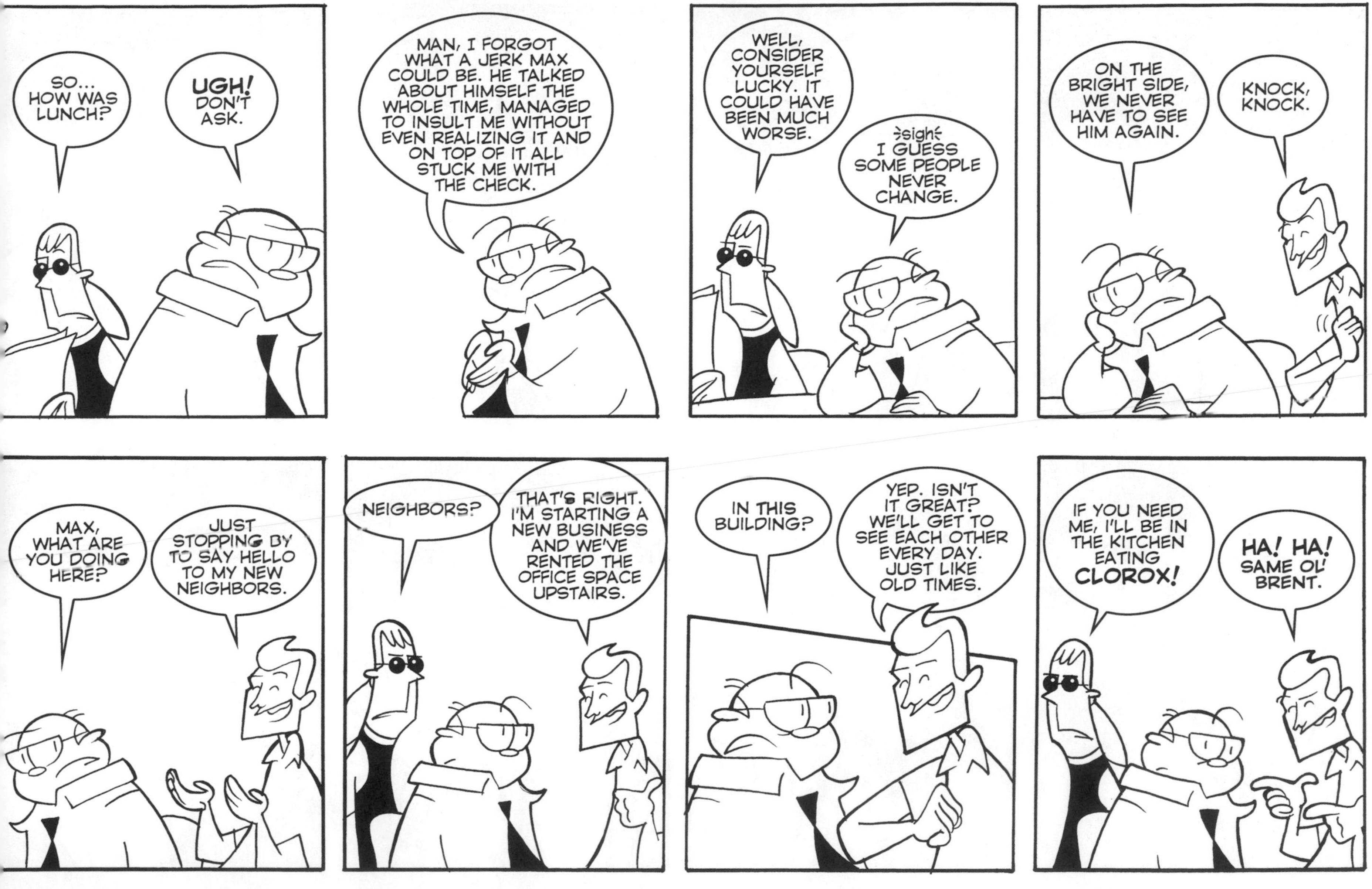
SO... HOW WAS LUNCH?
UGH! DON'T ASK.
MAN, I FORGOT WHAT A JERK MAX COULD BE. HE TALKED ABOUT HIMSELF THE WHOLE TIME, MANAGED TO INSULT ME WITHOUT EVEN REALIZING IT AND ON TOP OF IT ALL STUCK ME WITH THE CHECK.
WELL, CONSIDER YOURSELF LUCKY. IT COULD HAVE BEEN MUCH WORSE.
sigh I GUESS SOME PEOPLE NEVER CHANGE.
ON THE BRIGHT SIDE, WE NEVER HAVE TO SEE HIM AGAIN.
KNOCK, KNOCK.
MAX, WHAT ARE YOU DOING HERE?
JUST STOPPING BY TO SAY HELLO TO MY NEW NEIGHBORS.
NEIGHBORS?
THAT'S RIGHT. I'M STARTING A NEW BUSINESS AND WE'VE RENTED THE OFFICE SPACE UPSTAIRS.
IN THIS BUILDING?
YEP. ISN'T IT GREAT? WE'LL GET TO SEE EACH OTHER EVERY DAY. JUST LIKE OLD TIMES.
IF YOU NEED ME, I'LL BE IN THE KITCHEN EATING CLOROX!
HA! HA! SAME OL' BRENT.

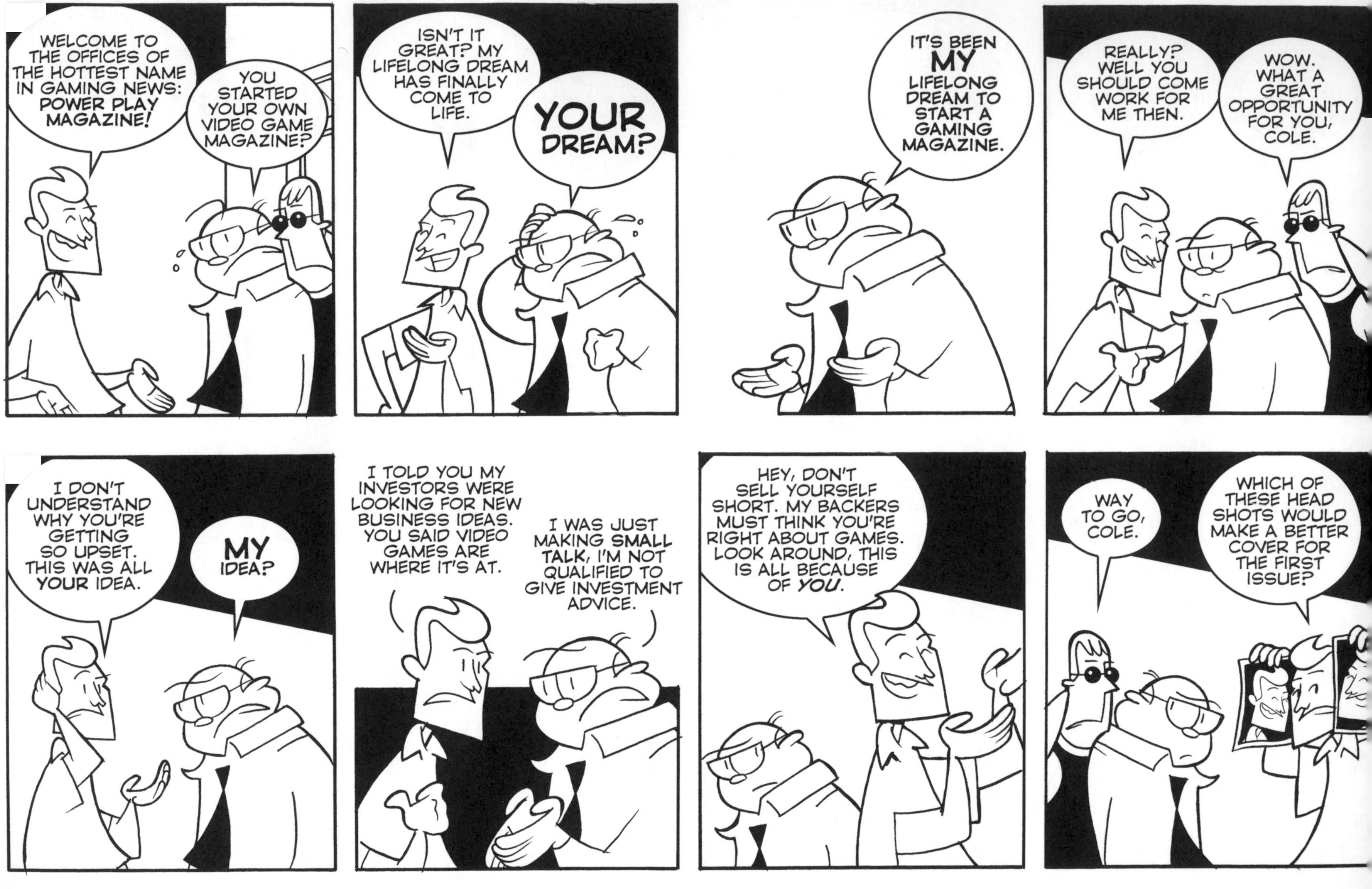
WELCOME TO THE OFFICES OF THE HOTTEST NAME IN GAMING NEWS: POWER PLAY MAGAZINE!
YOU STARTED YOUR OWN VIDEO GAME MAGAZINE?
ISN'T IT GREAT? MY LIFELONG DREAM HAS FINALLY COME TO LIFE.
YOUR DREAM?
IT'S BEEN MY LIFELONG DREAM TO START A GAMING MAGAZINE.
REALLY? WELL YOU SHOULD COME WORK FOR ME THEN.
WOW. WHAT A GREAT OPPORTUNITY FOR YOU, COLE.
I DON'T UNDERSTAND WHY YOU'RE GETTING SO UPSET. THIS WAS ALL YOUR IDEA.
MY IDEA?
I TOLD YOU MY INVESTORS WERE LOOKING FOR NEW BUSINESS IDEAS. YOU SAID VIDEO GAMES ARE WHERE IT'S AT.
I WAS JUST MAKING SMALL TALK, I'M NOT QUALIFIED TO GIVE INVESTMENT ADVICE.
HEY, DON'T SELL YOURSELF SHORT. MY BACKERS MUST THINK YOU'RE RIGHT ABOUT GAMES. LOOK AROUND, THIS IS ALL BECAUSE OF YOU.
WAY TO GO, COLE.
WHICH OF THESE HEAD SHOTS WOULD MAKE A BETTER COVER FOR THE FIRST ISSUE?

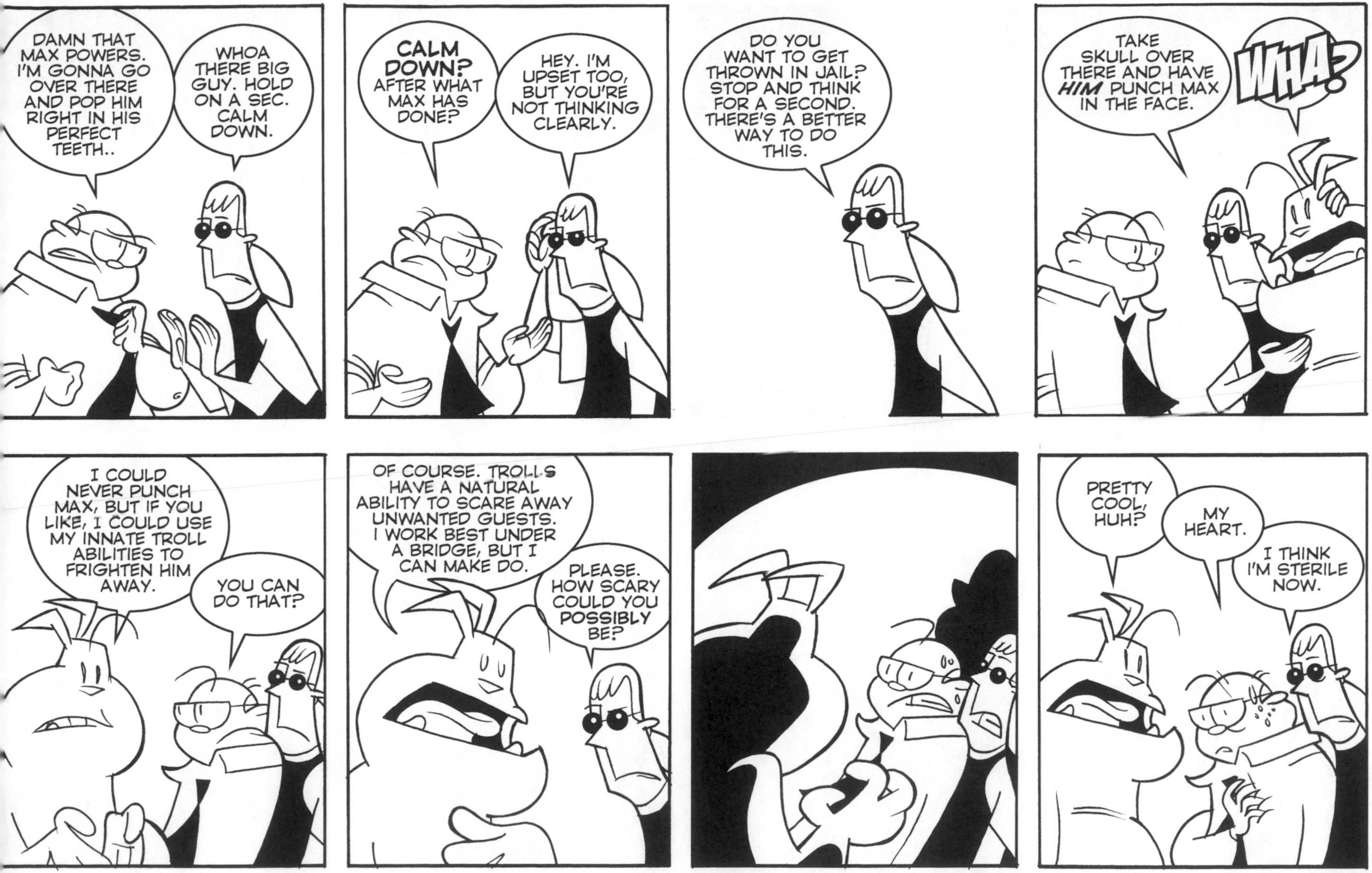
DAMN THAT MAX POWERS. I'M GONNA GO OVER THERE AND POP HIM RIGHT IN HIS PERFECT TEETH..
WHOA THERE BIG GUY. HOLD ON A SEC. CALM DOWN.
CALM DOWN? AFTER WHAT MAX HAS DONE?
HEY. I'M UPSET TOO, BUT YOU'RE NOT THINKING CLEARLY.
DO YOU WANT TO GET THROWN IN JAIL? STOP AND THINK FOR A SECOND. THERE'S A BETTER WAY TO DO THIS.
TAKE SKULL OVER THERE AND HAVE HIM PUNCH MAX IN THE FACE.
WHA?
I COULD NEVER PUNCH MAX, BUT IF YOU LIKE, I COULD USE MY INNATE TROLL ABILITIES TO FRIGHTEN HIM AWAY.
YOU CAN DO THAT?
OF COURSE. TROLLS HAVE A NATURAL ABILITY TO SCARE AWAY UNWANTED GUESTS. I WORK BEST UNDER A BRIDGE, BUT I CAN MAKE DO.
PLEASE. HOW SCARY COULD YOU POSSIBLY BE?
PRETTY COOL, HUH?
MY HEART.
I THINK I'M STERILE NOW.

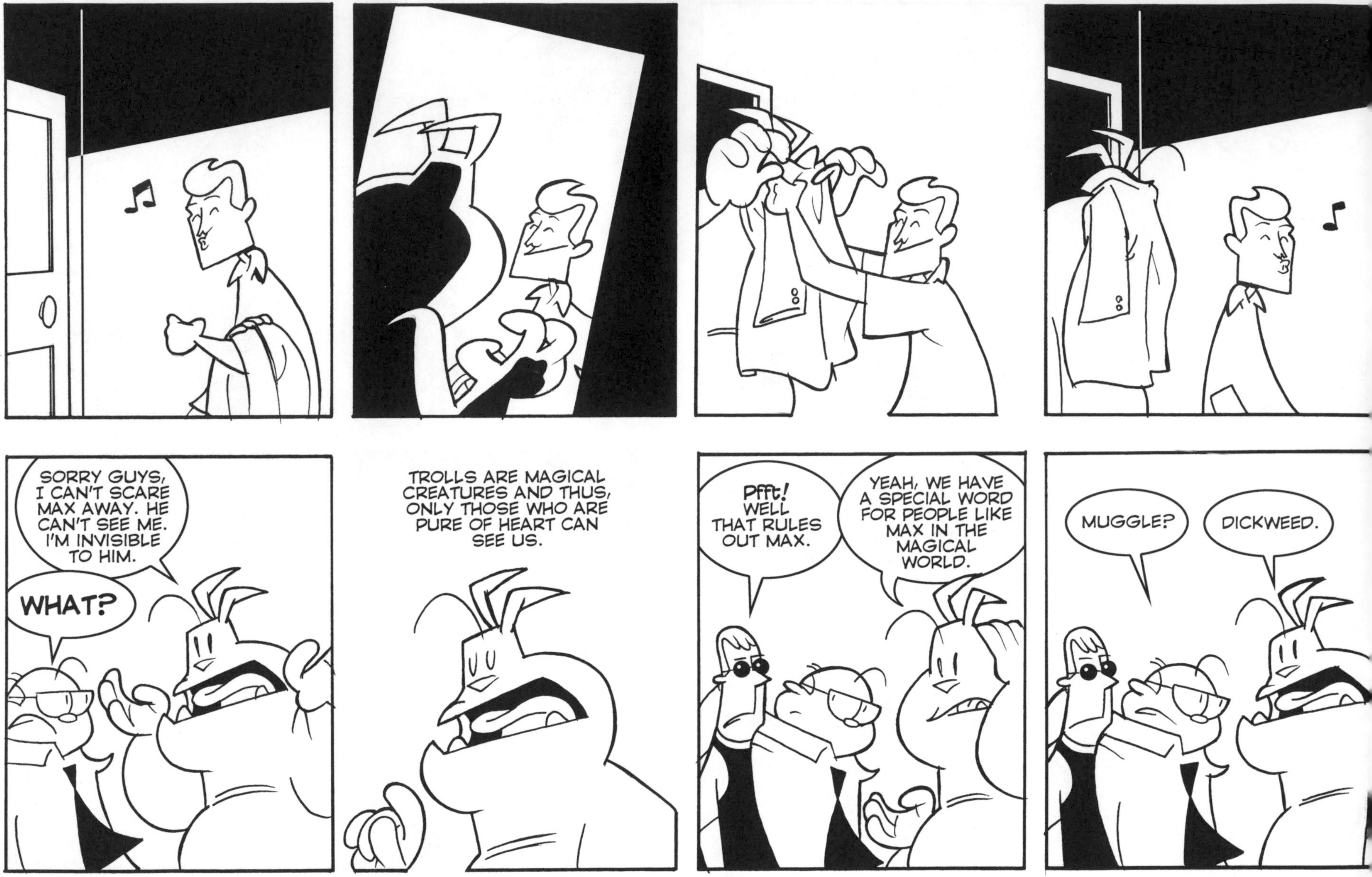
SORRY GUYS, I CAN'T SCARE MAX AWAY. HE CAN'T SEE ME. I'M INVISIBLE TO HIM.
WHAT?
TROLLS ARE MAGICAL CREATURES AND THUS, ONLY THOSE WHO ARE PURE OF HEART CAN SEE US.
Pfft! WELL THAT RULES OUT MAX.
YEAH, WE HAVE A SPECIAL WORD FOR PEOPLE LIKE MAX IN THE MAGICAL WORLD.
MUGGLE?
DICKWEED.

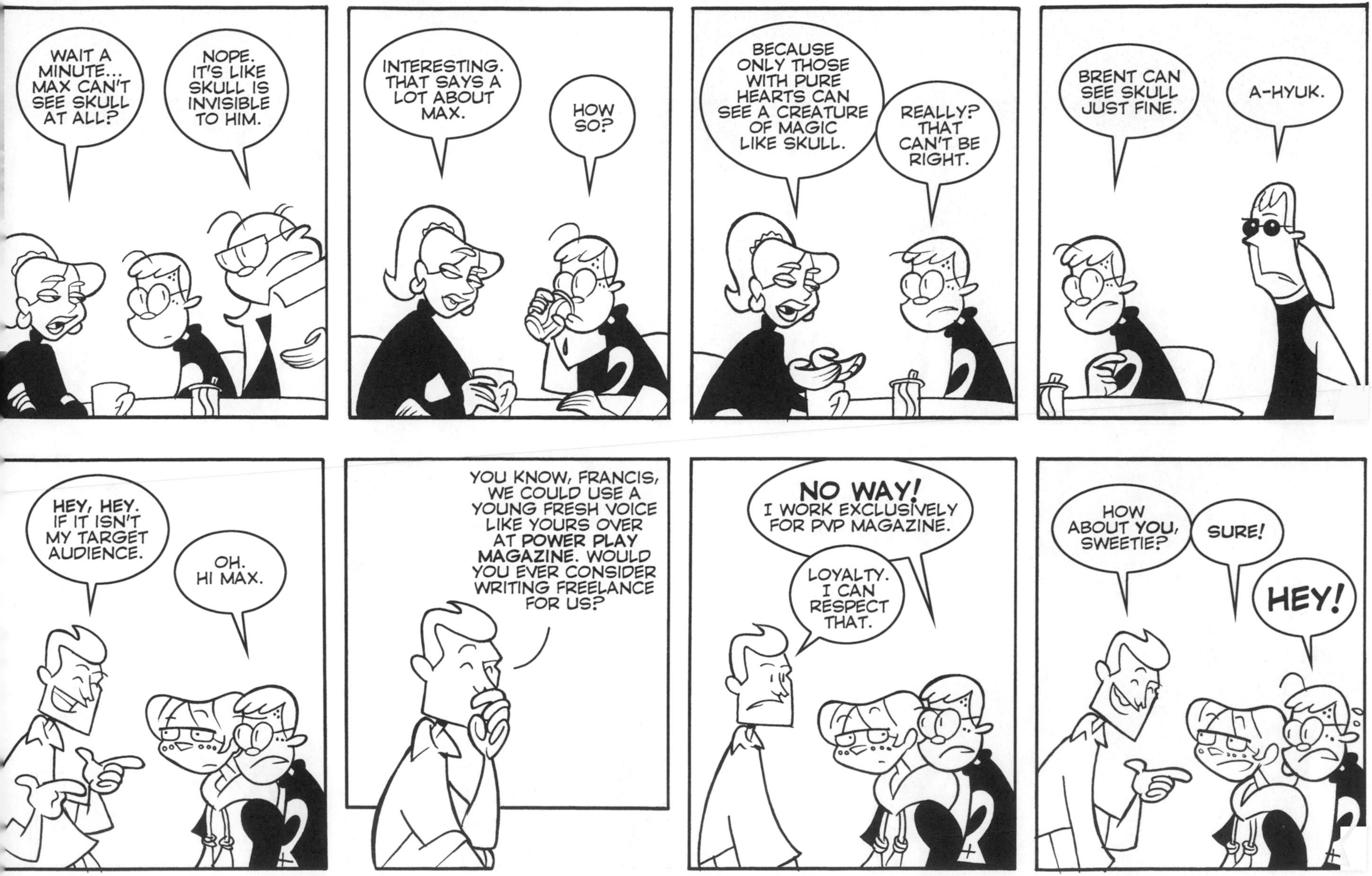
WAIT A MINUTE... MAX CAN'T SEE SKULL AT ALL?
NOPE. IT'S LIKE SKULL IS INVISIBLE TO HIM.
INTERESTING. THAT SAYS A LOT ABOUT MAX.
HOW SO?
BECAUSE ONLY THOSE WITH PURE HEARTS CAN SEE A CREATURE OF MAGIC LIKE SKULL.
REALLY? THAT CAN'T BE RIGHT.
BRENT CAN SEE SKULL JUST FINE.
A-HYUK.
HEY, HEY. IF IT ISN'T MY TARGET AUDIENCE.
OH. HI MAX.
YOU KNOW, FRANCIS, WE COULD USE A YOUNG FRESH VOICE LIKE YOURS OVER AT POWER PLAY MAGAZINE. WOULD YOU EVER CONSIDER WRITING FREELANCE FOR US?
NO WAY! I WORK EXCLUSIVELY FOR PVP MAGAZINE.
LOYALTY. I CAN RESPECT THAT.
HOW ABOUT YOU, SWEETIE?
SURE!
HEY!

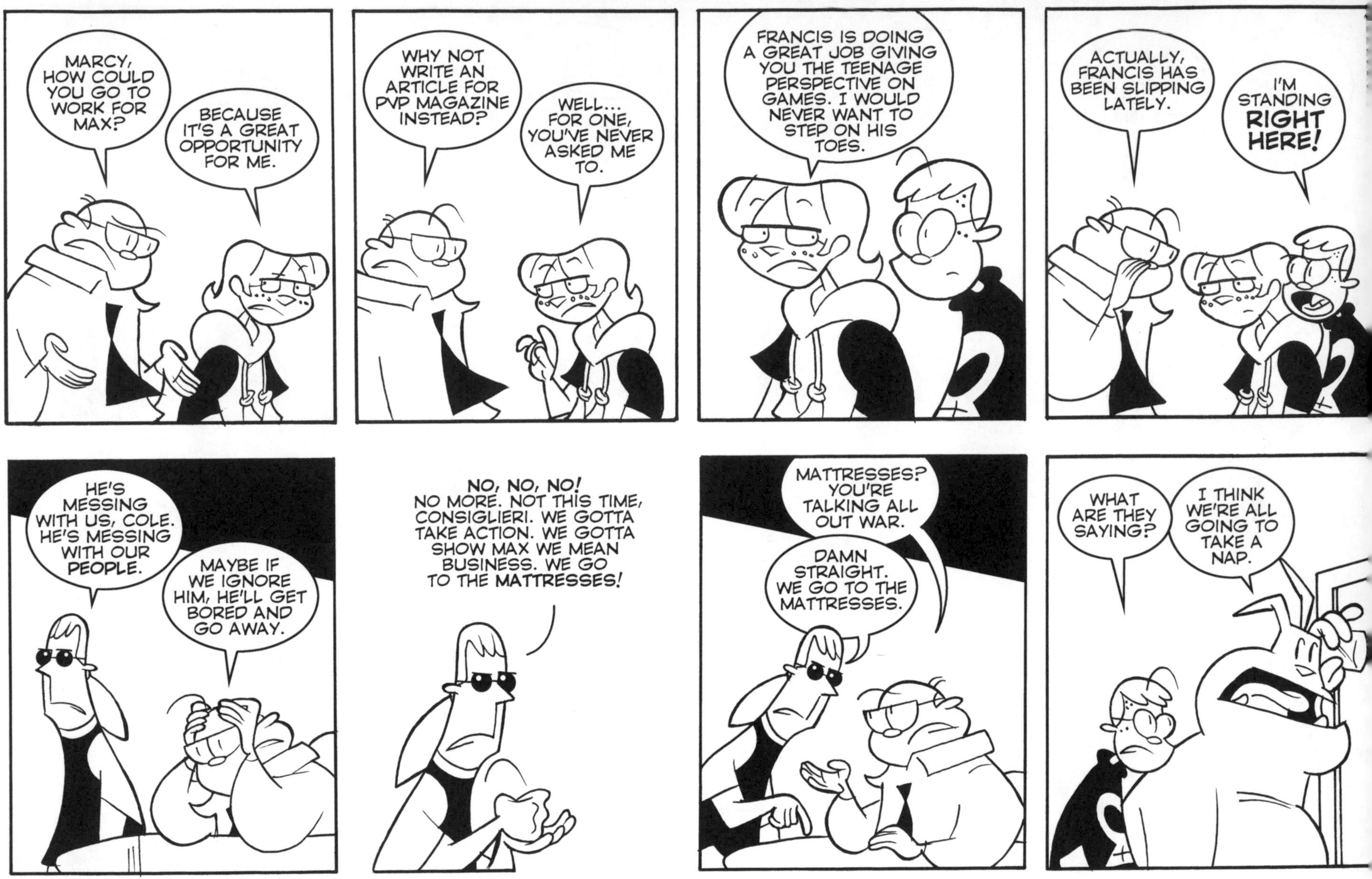
MARCY, HOW COULD YOU GO TO WORK FOR MAX?
BECAUSE IT'S A GREAT OPPORTUNITY FOR ME.
WHY NOT WRITE AN ARTICLE FOR PVP MAGAZINE INSTEAD?
WELL... FOR ONE, YOU'VE NEVER ASKED ME TO.
FRANCIS IS DOING A GREAT JOB GIVING YOU THE TEENAGE PERSPECTIVE ON GAMES. I WOULD NEVER WANT TO STEP ON HIS TOES.
ACTUALLY, FRANCIS HAS BEEN SLIPPING LATELY.
I'M STANDING **RIGHT HERE!**
HE'S MESSING WITH US, COLE. HE'S MESSING WITH OUR **PEOPLE**.
MAYBE IF WE IGNORE HIM, HE'LL GET BORED AND GO AWAY.
NO, NO, NO! NO MORE. NOT THIS TIME, CONSIGLIERI. WE GOTTA TAKE ACTION. WE GOTTA SHOW MAX WE MEAN BUSINESS. WE GO TO THE **MATTRESSES!**
MATTRESSES? YOU'RE TALKING ALL OUT WAR.
DAMN STRAIGHT. WE GO TO THE MATTRESSES.
WHAT ARE THEY SAYING?
I THINK WE'RE ALL GOING TO TAKE A NAP.

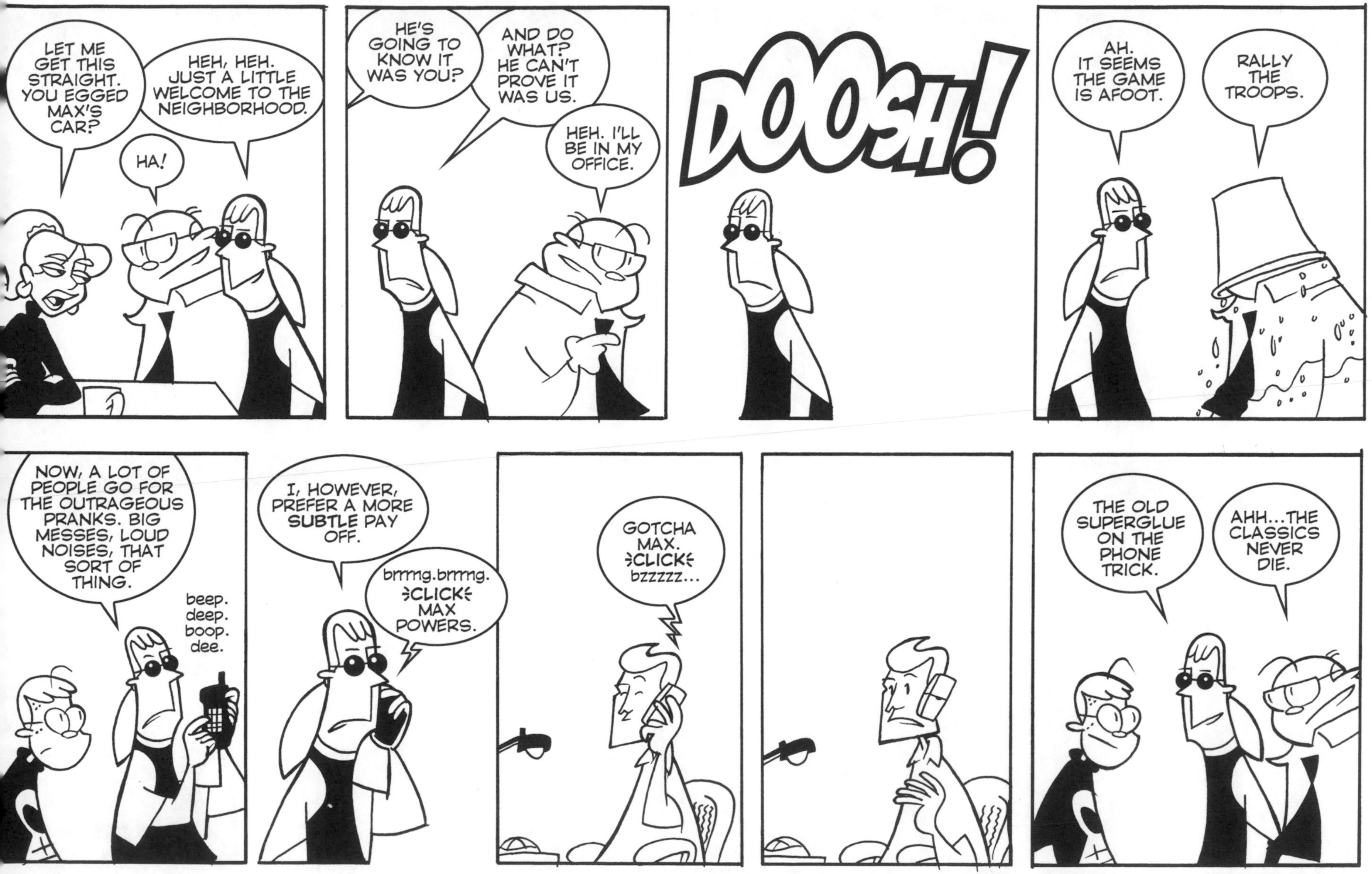
LET ME GET THIS STRAIGHT. YOU EGGED MAX'S CAR?
HEH, HEH. JUST A LITTLE WELCOME TO THE NEIGHBORHOOD.
HA!
HE'S GOING TO KNOW IT WAS YOU?
AND DO WHAT? HE CAN'T PROVE IT WAS US.
HEH. I'LL BE IN MY OFFICE.
DOOSH!
AH. IT SEEMS THE GAME IS AFOOT.
RALLY THE TROOPS.
NOW, A LOT OF PEOPLE GO FOR THE OUTRAGEOUS PRANKS. BIG MESSES, LOUD NOISES, THAT SORT OF THING.
beep. deep. boop. dee.
I, HOWEVER, PREFER A MORE SUBTLE PAY OFF.
brrrng.brrrng. CLICK MAX POWERS.
GOTCHA MAX. CLICK bzzzzz...
THE OLD SUPERGLUE ON THE PHONE TRICK.
AHH...THE CLASSICS NEVER DIE.

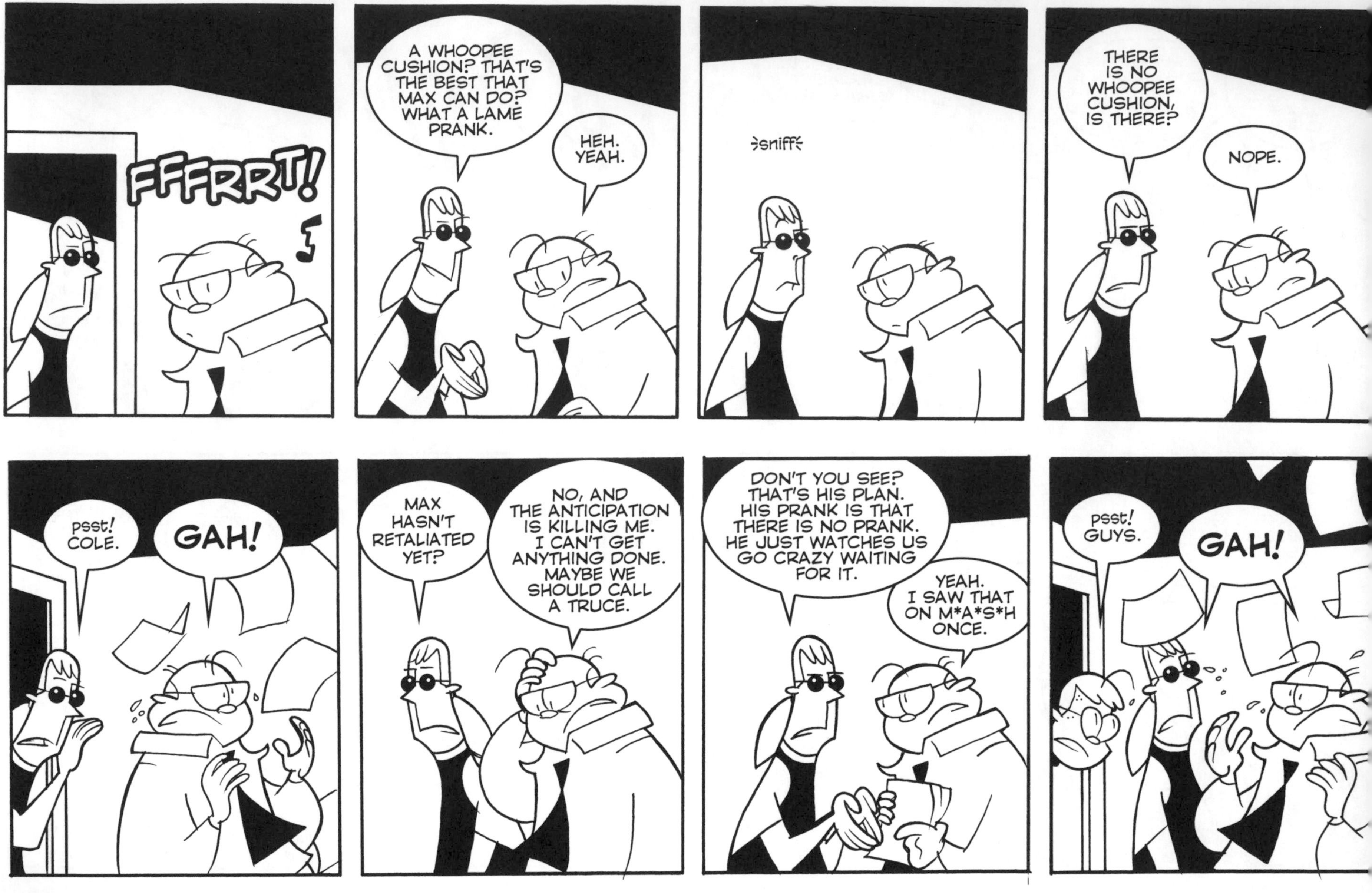
FFFRRT!
A WHOOPEE CUSHION? THAT'S THE BEST THAT MAX CAN DO? WHAT A LAME PRANK.
HEH. YEAH.
sniff
THERE IS NO WHOOPEE CUSHION, IS THERE?
NOPE.
psst! COLE.
GAH!
MAX HASN'T RETALIATED YET?
NO, AND THE ANTICIPATION IS KILLING ME. I CAN'T GET ANYTHING DONE. MAYBE WE SHOULD CALL A TRUCE.
DON'T YOU SEE? THAT'S HIS PLAN. HIS PRANK IS THAT THERE IS NO PRANK. HE JUST WATCHES US GO CRAZY WAITING FOR IT.
YEAH. I SAW THAT ON M*A*S*H ONCE.
psst! GUYS.
GAH!

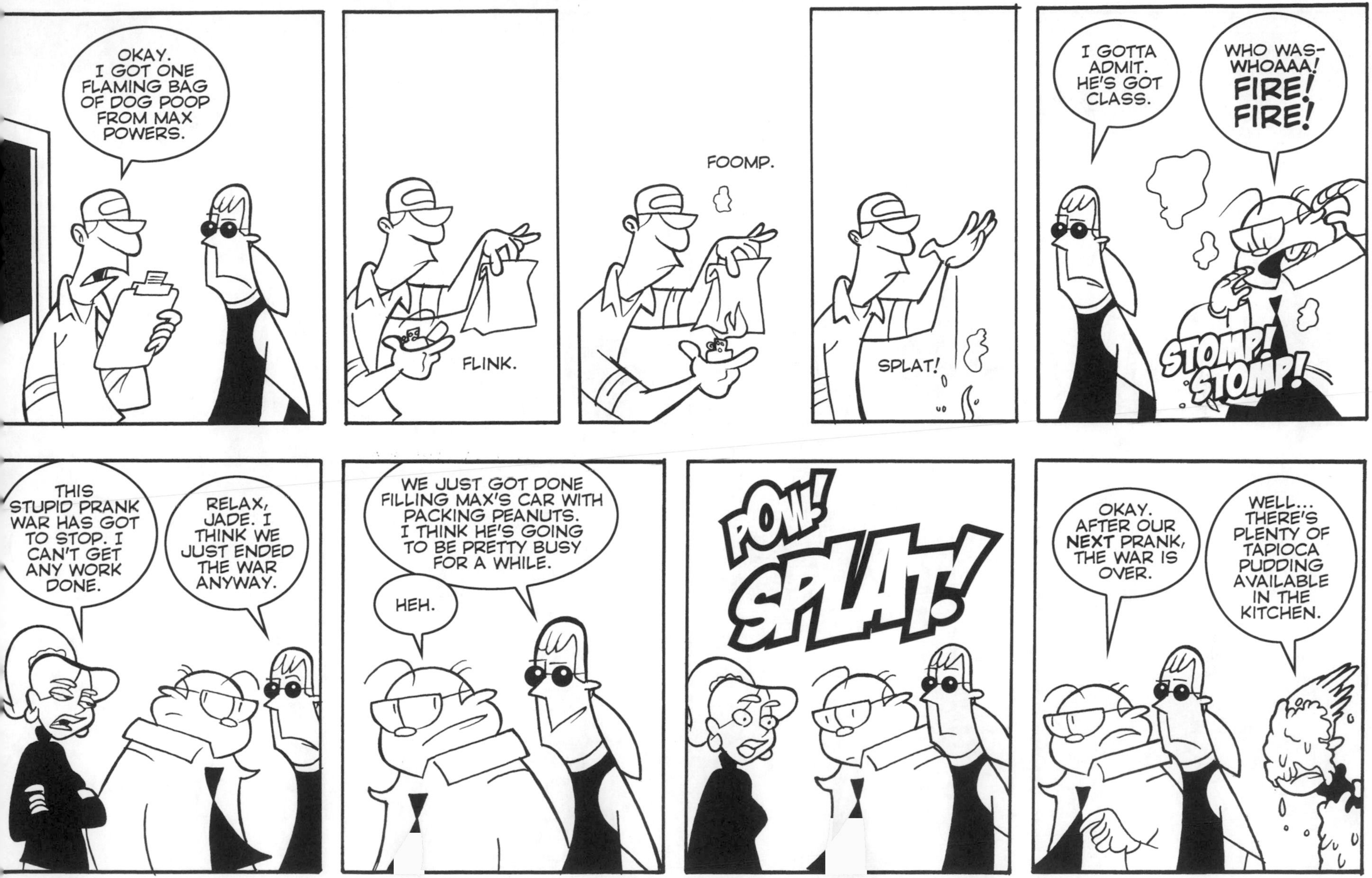
OKAY. I GOT ONE FLAMING BAG OF DOG POOP FROM MAX POWERS.
FLINK.
FOOMP.
SPLAT!
I GOTTA ADMIT. HE'S GOT CLASS.
WHO WAS- WHOAAA! FIRE! FIRE!
STOMP! STOMP!
THIS STUPID PRANK WAR HAS GOT TO STOP. I CAN'T GET ANY WORK DONE.
RELAX, JADE. I THINK WE JUST ENDED THE WAR ANYWAY.
WE JUST GOT DONE FILLING MAX'S CAR WITH PACKING PEANUTS. I THINK HE'S GOING TO BE PRETTY BUSY FOR A WHILE.
HEH.
POW!
SPLAT!
OKAY. AFTER OUR NEXT PRANK, THE WAR IS OVER.
WELL... THERE'S PLENTY OF TAPIOCA PUDDING AVAILABLE IN THE KITCHEN.

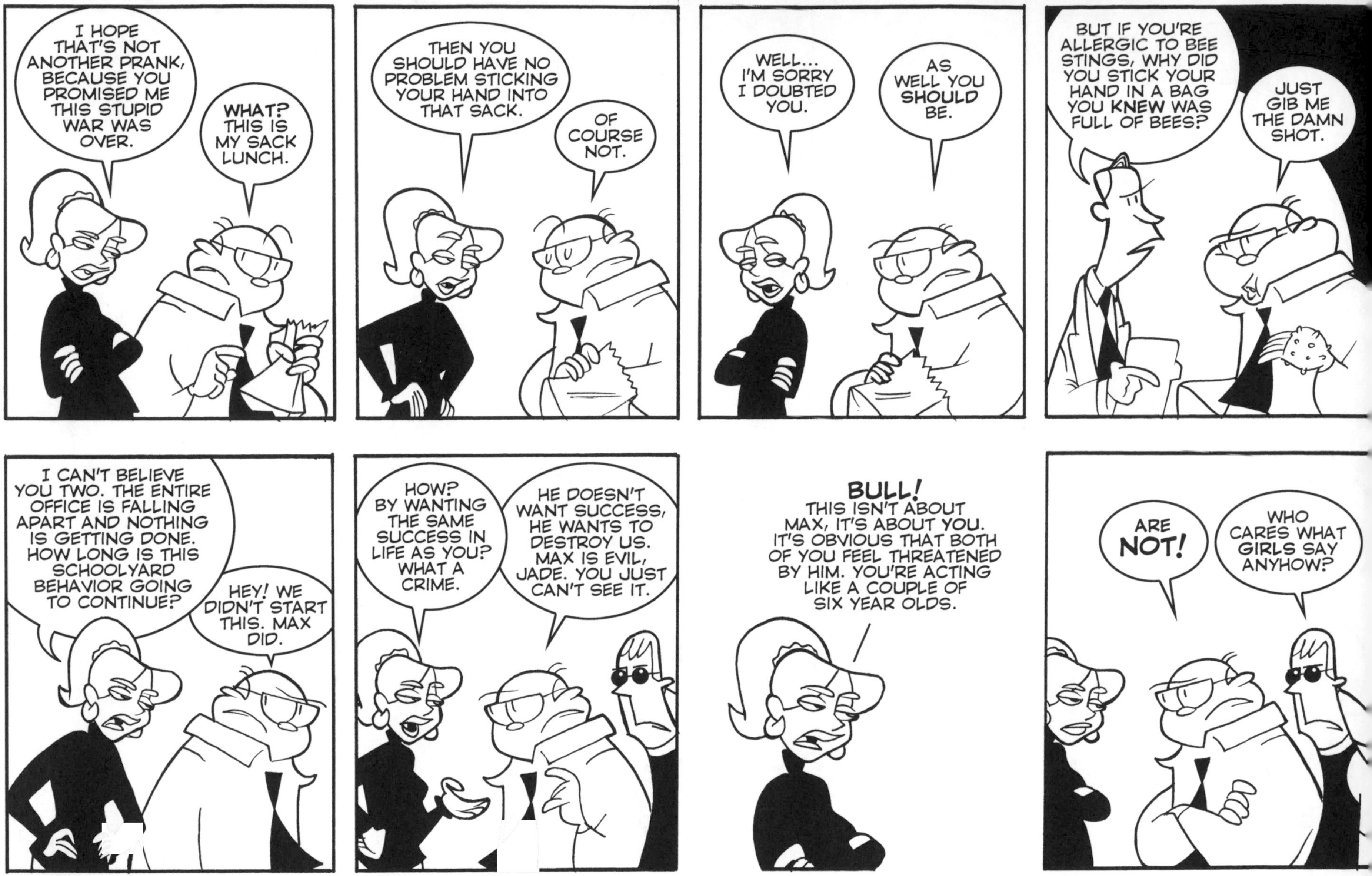
I HOPE THAT'S NOT ANOTHER PRANK, BECAUSE YOU PROMISED ME THIS STUPID WAR WAS OVER.
WHAT? THIS IS MY SACK LUNCH.
THEN YOU SHOULD HAVE NO PROBLEM STICKING YOUR HAND INTO THAT SACK.
OF COURSE NOT.
WELL... I'M SORRY I DOUBTED YOU.
AS WELL YOU SHOULD BE.
BUT IF YOU'RE ALLERGIC TO BEE STINGS, WHY DID YOU STICK YOUR HAND IN A BAG YOU KNEW WAS FULL OF BEES?
JUST GIB ME THE DAMN SHOT.
I CAN'T BELIEVE YOU TWO. THE ENTIRE OFFICE IS FALLING APART AND NOTHING IS GETTING DONE. HOW LONG IS THIS SCHOOLYARD BEHAVIOR GOING TO CONTINUE?
HEY! WE DIDN'T START THIS. MAX DID.
HOW? BY WANTING THE SAME SUCCESS IN LIFE AS YOU? WHAT A CRIME.
HE DOESN'T WANT SUCCESS, HE WANTS TO DESTROY US. MAX IS EVIL, JADE. YOU JUST CAN'T SEE IT.
BULL! THIS ISN'T ABOUT MAX, IT'S ABOUT YOU. IT'S OBVIOUS THAT BOTH OF YOU FEEL THREATENED BY HIM. YOU'RE ACTING LIKE A COUPLE OF SIX YEAR OLDS.
ARE NOT!
WHO CARES WHAT GIRLS SAY ANYHOW?

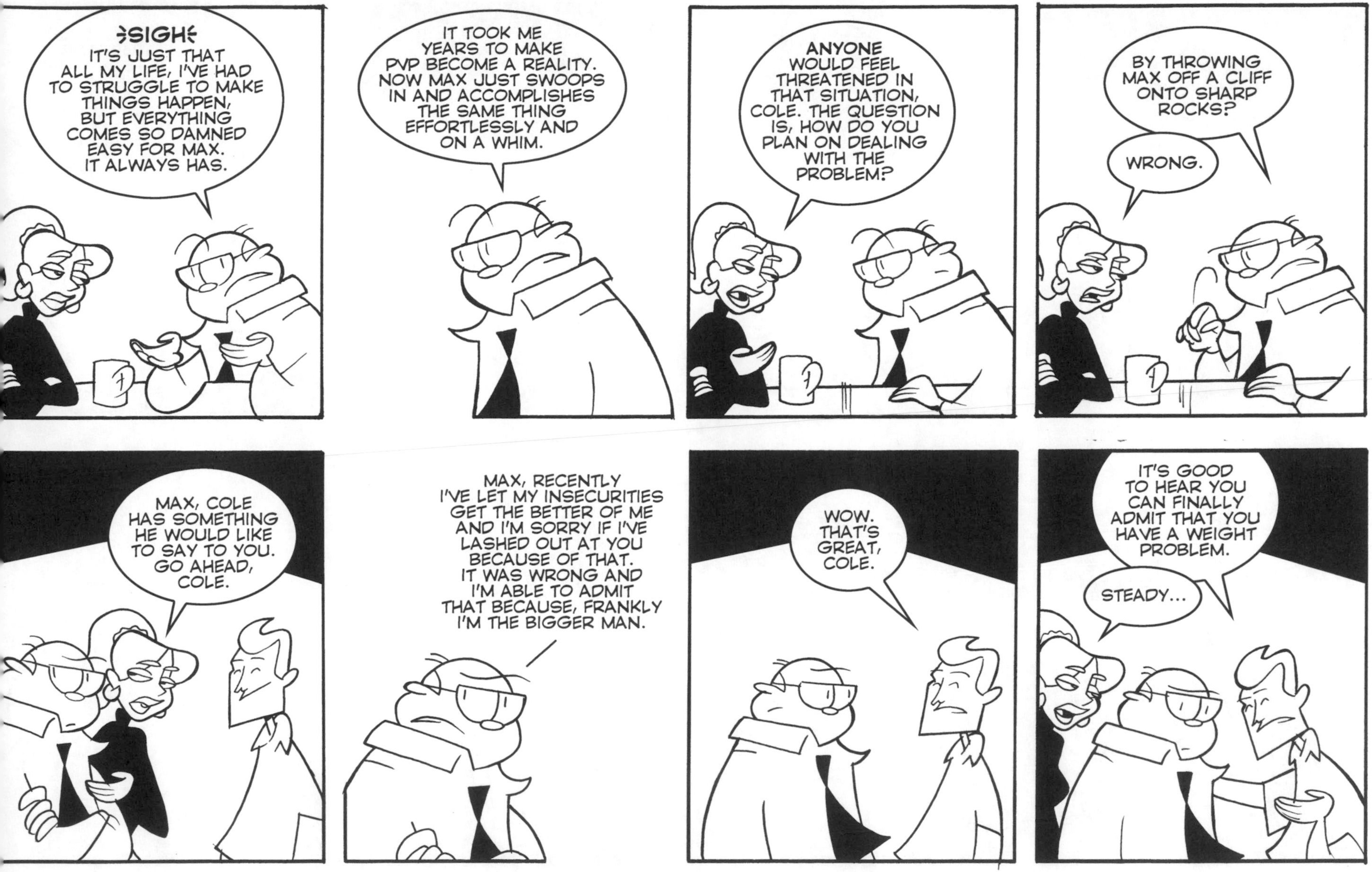

SIGH IT'S JUST THAT ALL MY LIFE, I'VE HAD TO STRUGGLE TO MAKE THINGS HAPPEN, BUT EVERYTHING COMES SO DAMNED EASY FOR MAX. IT ALWAYS HAS.
IT TOOK ME YEARS TO MAKE PVP BECOME A REALITY. NOW MAX JUST SWOOPS IN AND ACCOMPLISHES THE SAME THING EFFORTLESSLY AND ON A WHIM.
ANYONE WOULD FEEL THREATENED IN THAT SITUATION, COLE. THE QUESTION IS, HOW DO YOU PLAN ON DEALING WITH THE PROBLEM?
BY THROWING MAX OFF A CLIFF ONTO SHARP ROCKS?
WRONG.
MAX, COLE HAS SOMETHING HE WOULD LIKE TO SAY TO YOU. GO AHEAD, COLE.
MAX, RECENTLY I'VE LET MY INSECURITIES GET THE BETTER OF ME AND I'M SORRY IF I'VE LASHED OUT AT YOU BECAUSE OF THAT. IT WAS WRONG AND I'M ABLE TO ADMIT THAT BECAUSE, FRANKLY I'M THE BIGGER MAN.
WOW. THAT'S GREAT, COLE.
IT'S GOOD TO HEAR YOU CAN FINALLY ADMIT THAT YOU HAVE A WEIGHT PROBLEM.
STEADY...

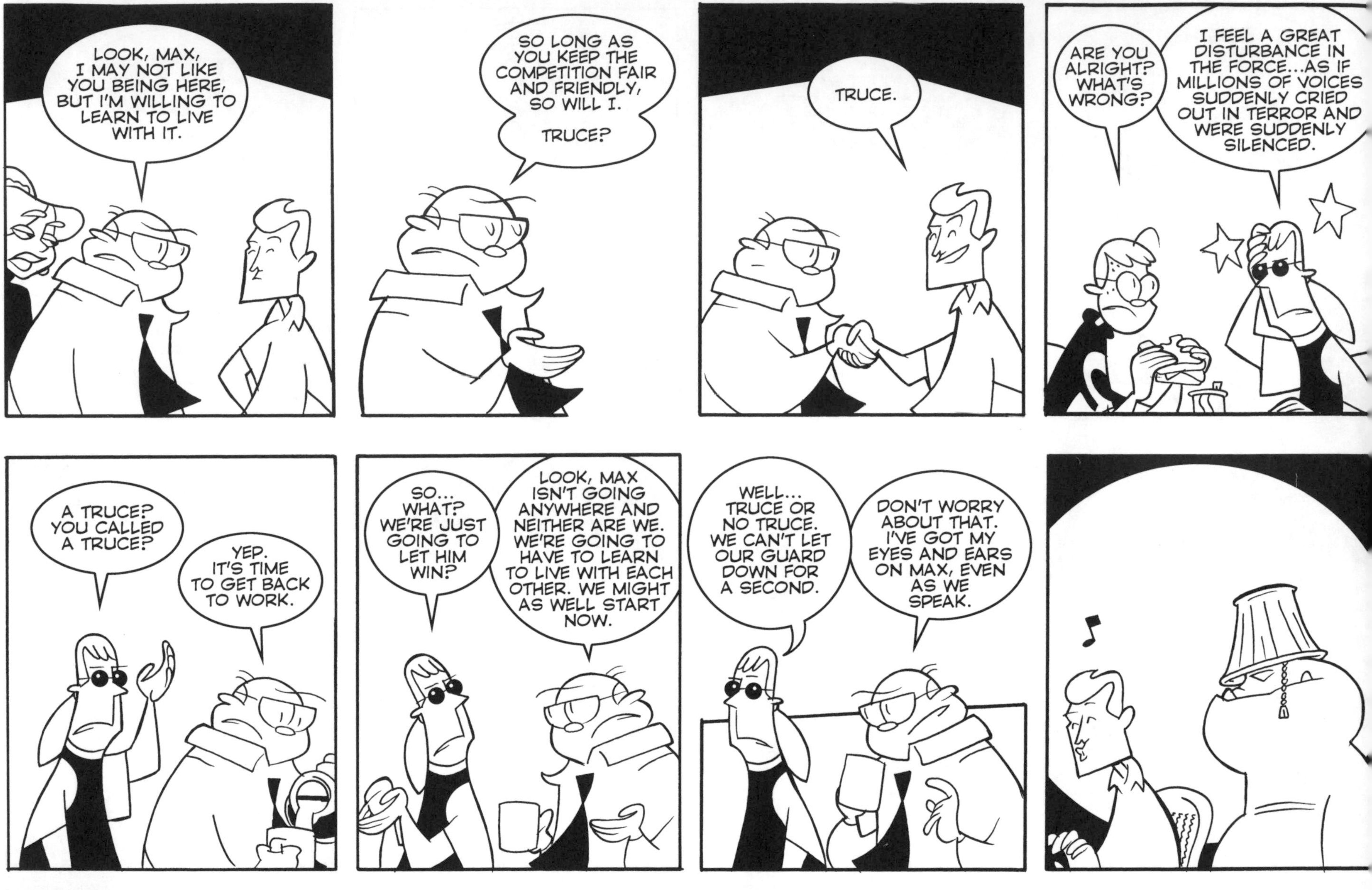

LOOK, MAX, I MAY NOT LIKE YOU BEING HERE, BUT I'M WILLING TO LEARN TO LIVE WITH IT.
SO LONG AS YOU KEEP THE COMPETITION FAIR AND FRIENDLY, SO WILL I.
TRUCE?
TRUCE.
ARE YOU ALRIGHT? WHAT'S WRONG?
I FEEL A GREAT DISTURBANCE IN THE FORCE...AS IF MILLIONS OF VOICES SUDDENLY CRIED OUT IN TERROR AND WERE SUDDENLY SILENCED.
A TRUCE? YOU CALLED A TRUCE?
YEP. IT'S TIME TO GET BACK TO WORK.
SO... WHAT? WE'RE JUST GOING TO LET HIM WIN?
LOOK, MAX ISN'T GOING ANYWHERE AND NEITHER ARE WE. WE'RE GOING TO HAVE TO LEARN TO LIVE WITH EACH OTHER. WE MIGHT AS WELL START NOW.
WELL... TRUCE OR NO TRUCE. WE CAN'T LET OUR GUARD DOWN FOR A SECOND.
DON'T WORRY ABOUT THAT. I'VE GOT MY EYES AND EARS ON MAX, EVEN AS WE SPEAK.

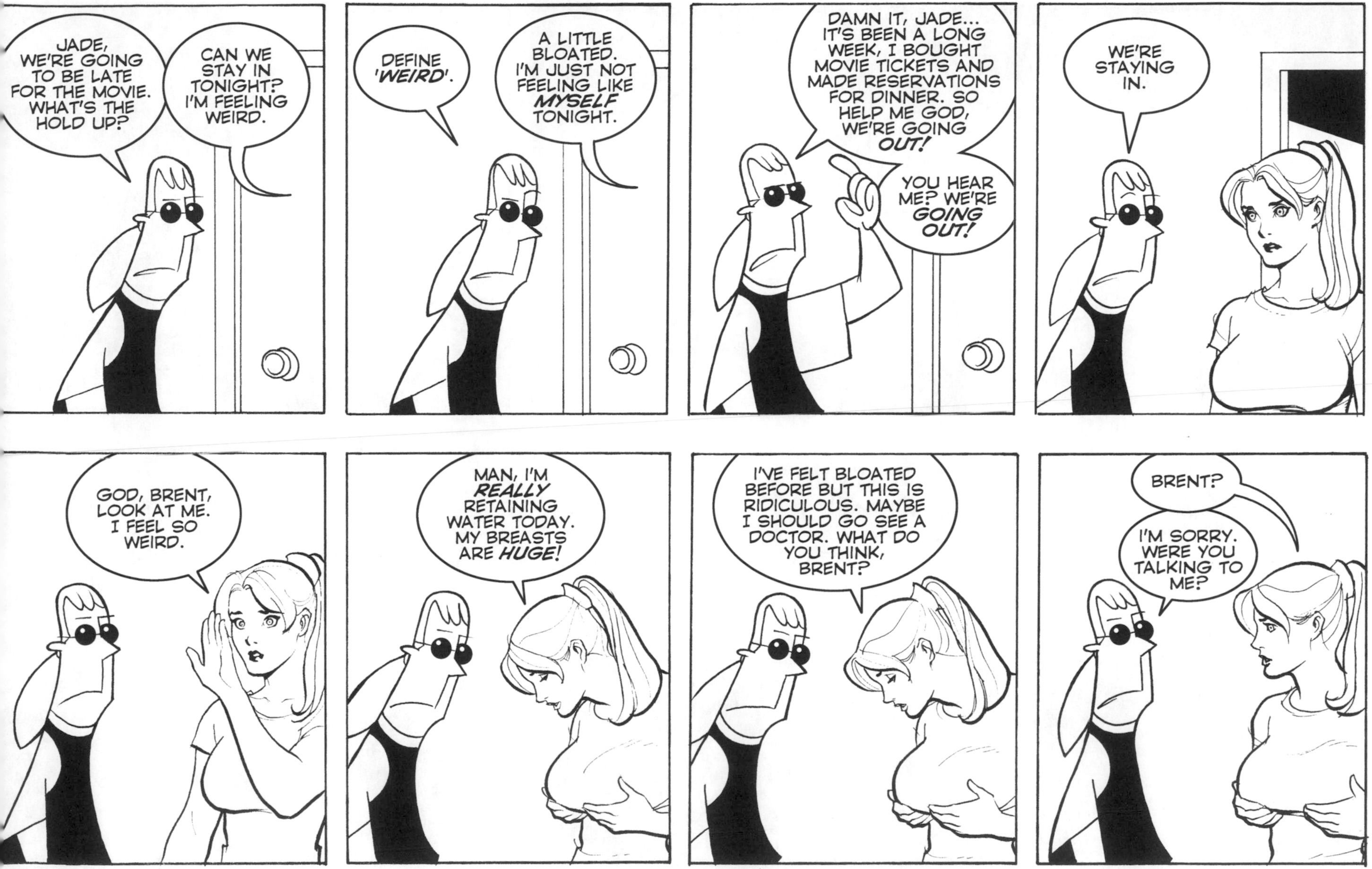
JADE, WE'RE GOING TO BE LATE FOR THE MOVIE. WHAT'S THE HOLD UP?
CAN WE STAY IN TONIGHT? I'M FEELING WEIRD.
DEFINE '*WEIRD*'.
A LITTLE BLOATED. I'M JUST NOT FEELING LIKE *MYSELF* TONIGHT.
DAMN IT, JADE... IT'S BEEN A LONG WEEK, I BOUGHT MOVIE TICKETS AND MADE RESERVATIONS FOR DINNER. SO HELP ME GOD, WE'RE GOING *OUT!*
YOU HEAR ME? WE'RE *GOING OUT!*
WE'RE STAYING IN.
GOD, BRENT, LOOK AT ME. I FEEL SO WEIRD.
MAN, I'M *REALLY* RETAINING WATER TODAY. MY BREASTS ARE *HUGE!*
I'VE FELT BLOATED BEFORE BUT THIS IS RIDICULOUS. MAYBE I SHOULD GO SEE A DOCTOR. WHAT DO YOU THINK, BRENT?
BRENT?
I'M SORRY. WERE YOU TALKING TO ME?

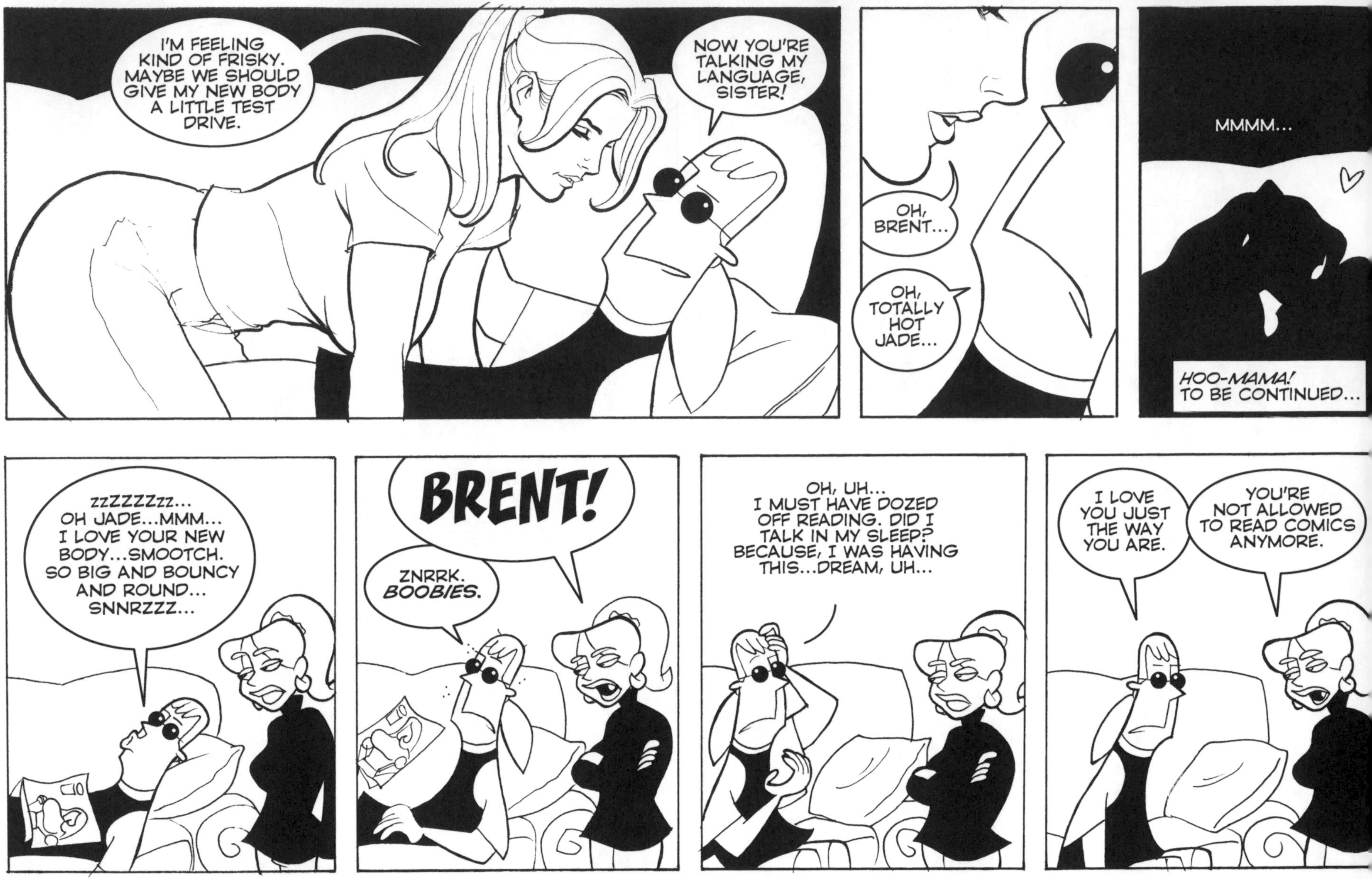
I'M FEELING KIND OF FRISKY. MAYBE WE SHOULD GIVE MY NEW BODY A LITTLE TEST DRIVE.
NOW YOU'RE TALKING MY LANGUAGE, SISTER!
OH, BRENT...
OH, TOTALLY HOT JADE...
MMMM...
HOO-MAMA! TO BE CONTINUED...
zzZZZZzz... OH JADE...MMM... I LOVE YOUR NEW BODY...SMOOTCH. SO BIG AND BOUNCY AND ROUND... SNNRZZZ...
BRENT!
ZNRRK. BOOBIES.
OH, UH... I MUST HAVE DOZED OFF READING. DID I TALK IN MY SLEEP? BECAUSE, I WAS HAVING THIS...DREAM, UH...
I LOVE YOU JUST THE WAY YOU ARE.
YOU'RE NOT ALLOWED TO READ COMICS ANYMORE.

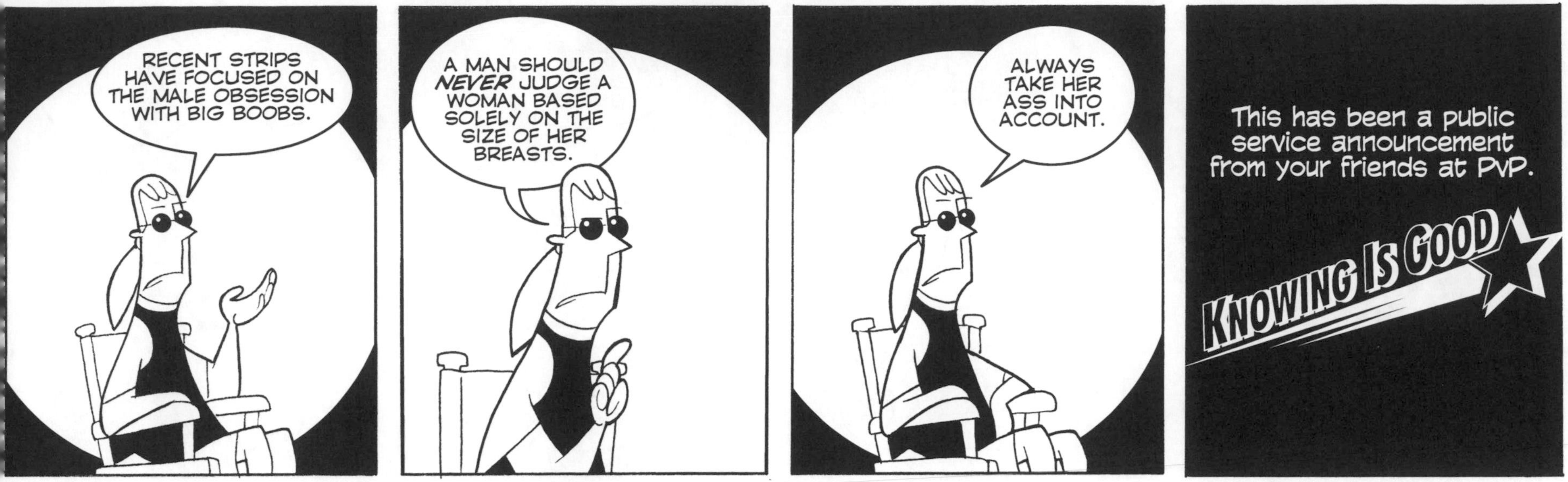
RECENT STRIPS HAVE FOCUSED ON THE MALE OBSESSION WITH BIG BOOBS.
A MAN SHOULD *NEVER* JUDGE A WOMAN BASED SOLELY ON THE SIZE OF HER BREASTS.
ALWAYS TAKE HER ASS INTO ACCOUNT.
This has been a public service announcement from your friends at PvP.
KNOWING IS GOOD

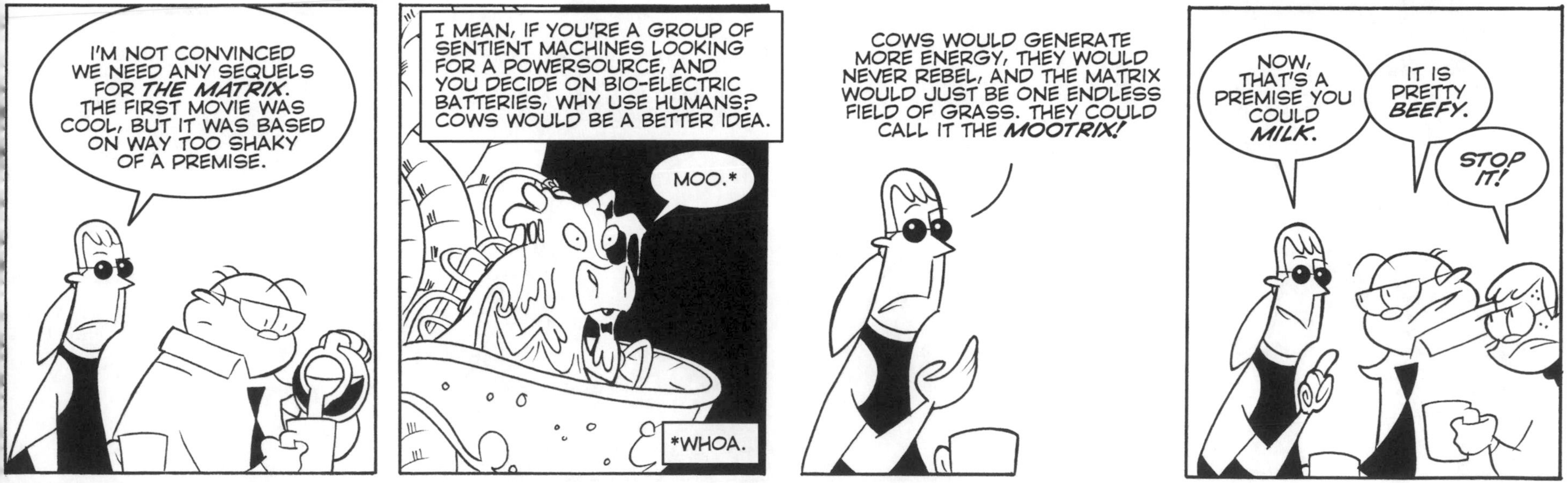
I'M NOT CONVINCED WE NEED ANY SEQUELS FOR *THE MATRIX*. THE FIRST MOVIE WAS COOL, BUT IT WAS BASED ON WAY TOO SHAKY OF A PREMISE.
I MEAN, IF YOU'RE A GROUP OF SENTIENT MACHINES LOOKING FOR A POWERSOURCE, AND YOU DECIDE ON BIO-ELECTRIC BATTERIES, WHY USE HUMANS? COWS WOULD BE A BETTER IDEA.
MOO.*
*WHOA.
COWS WOULD GENERATE MORE ENERGY, THEY WOULD NEVER REBEL, AND THE MATRIX WOULD JUST BE ONE ENDLESS FIELD OF GRASS. THEY COULD CALL IT THE *MOOTRIX!*
NOW, THAT'S A PREMISE YOU COULD *MILK*.
IT IS PRETTY *BEEFY*.
STOP IT!

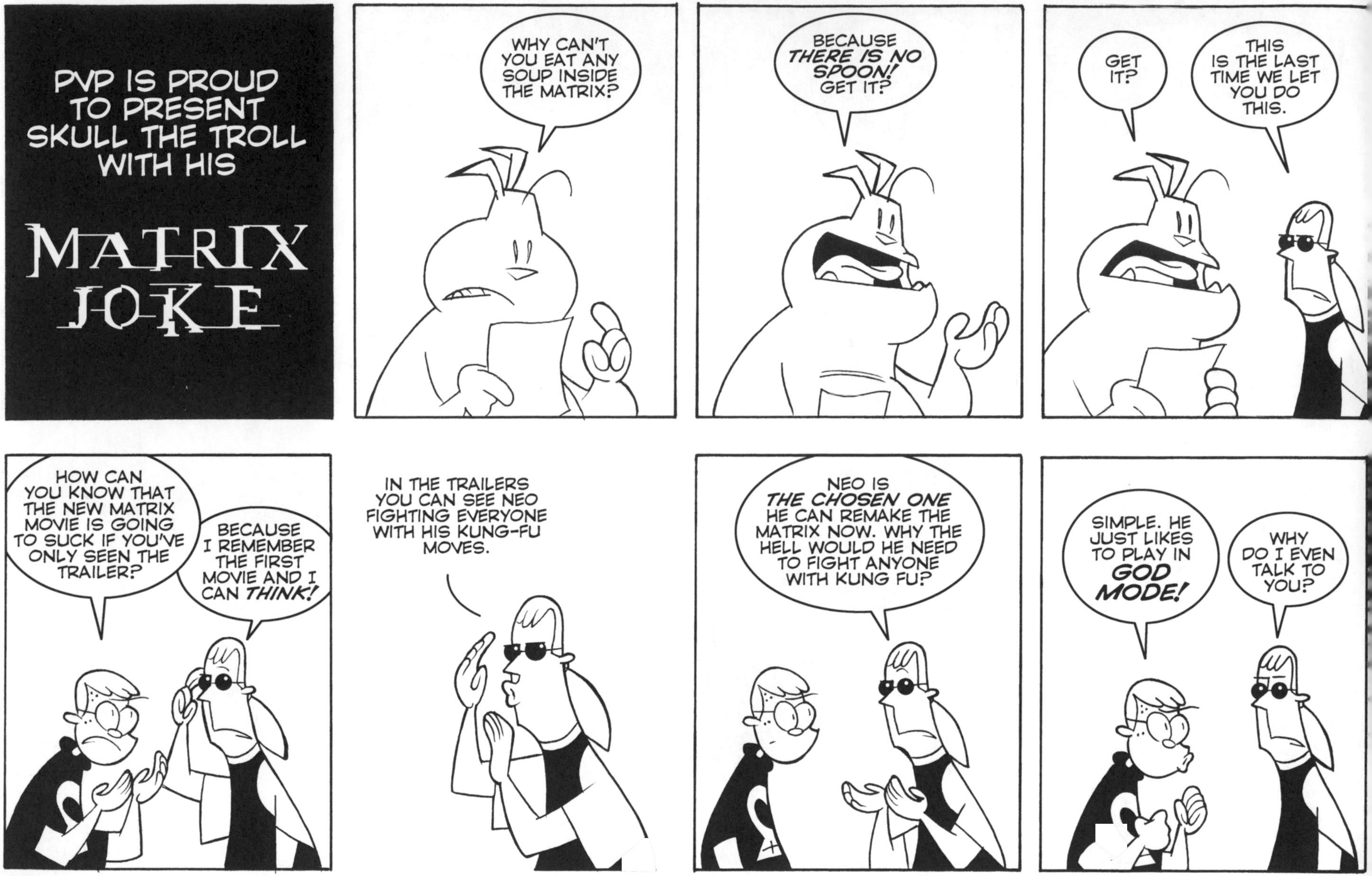
PVP IS PROUD TO PRESENT SKULL THE TROLL WITH HIS
MATRIX JOKE
WHY CAN'T YOU EAT ANY SOUP INSIDE THE MATRIX?
BECAUSE THERE IS NO SPOON! GET IT?
GET IT?
THIS IS THE LAST TIME WE LET YOU DO THIS.
HOW CAN YOU KNOW THAT THE NEW MATRIX MOVIE IS GOING TO SUCK IF YOU'VE ONLY SEEN THE TRAILER?
BECAUSE I REMEMBER THE FIRST MOVIE AND I CAN THINK!
IN THE TRAILERS YOU CAN SEE NEO FIGHTING EVERYONE WITH HIS KUNG-FU MOVES.
NEO IS THE CHOSEN ONE HE CAN REMAKE THE MATRIX NOW. WHY THE HELL WOULD HE NEED TO FIGHT ANYONE WITH KUNG FU?
SIMPLE. HE JUST LIKES TO PLAY IN GOD MODE!
WHY DO I EVEN TALK TO YOU?

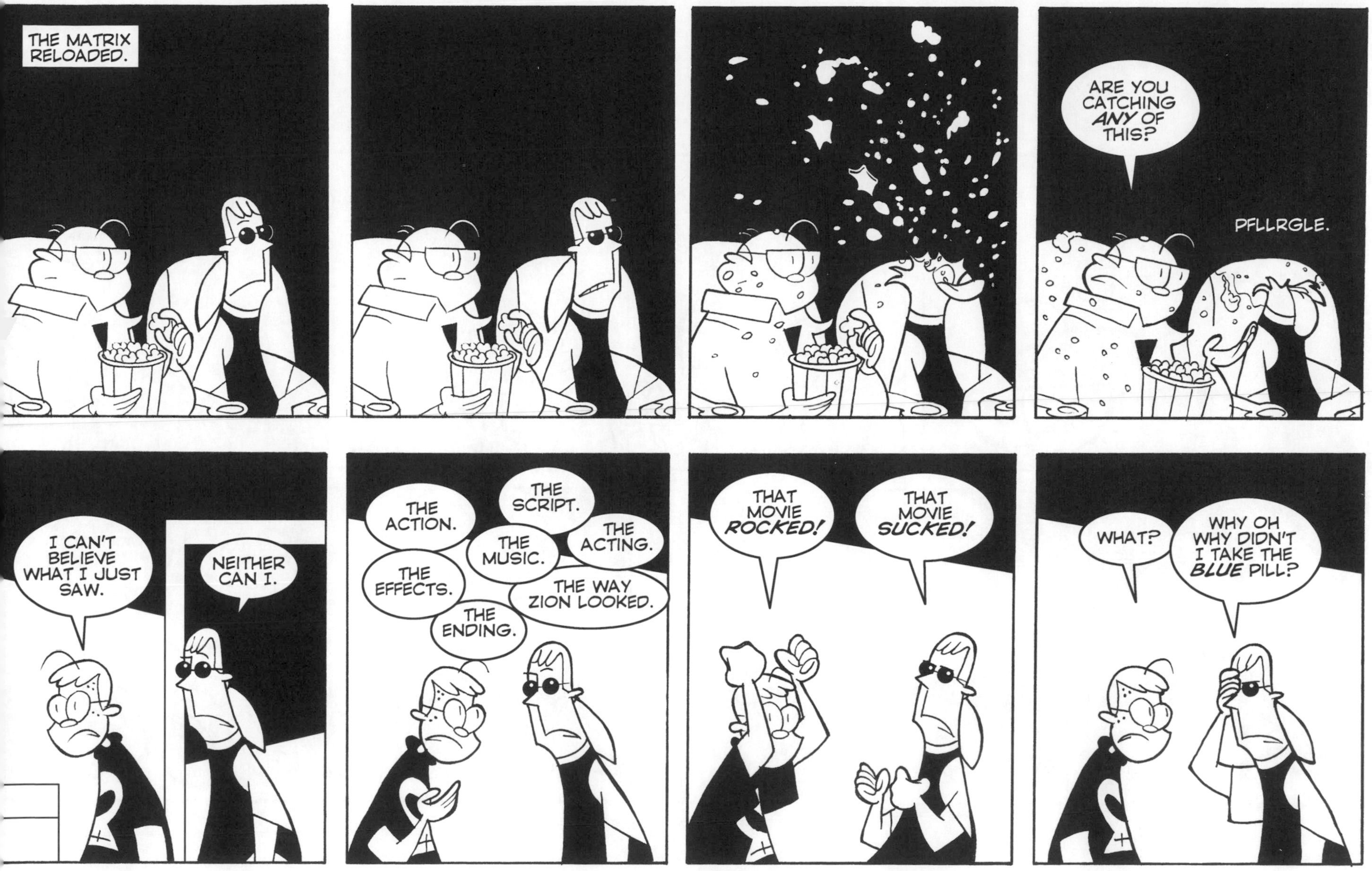
THE MATRIX RELOADED.
ARE YOU CATCHING *ANY* OF THIS?
PFLLRGLE.
I CAN'T BELIEVE WHAT I JUST SAW.
NEITHER CAN I.
THE ACTION.
THE SCRIPT.
THE MUSIC.
THE ACTING.
THE EFFECTS.
THE WAY ZION LOOKED.
THE ENDING.
THAT MOVIE *ROCKED!*
THAT MOVIE *SUCKED!*
WHAT?
WHY OH WHY DIDN'T I TAKE THE *BLUE* PILL?

THE PEN IS MIGHTIER...

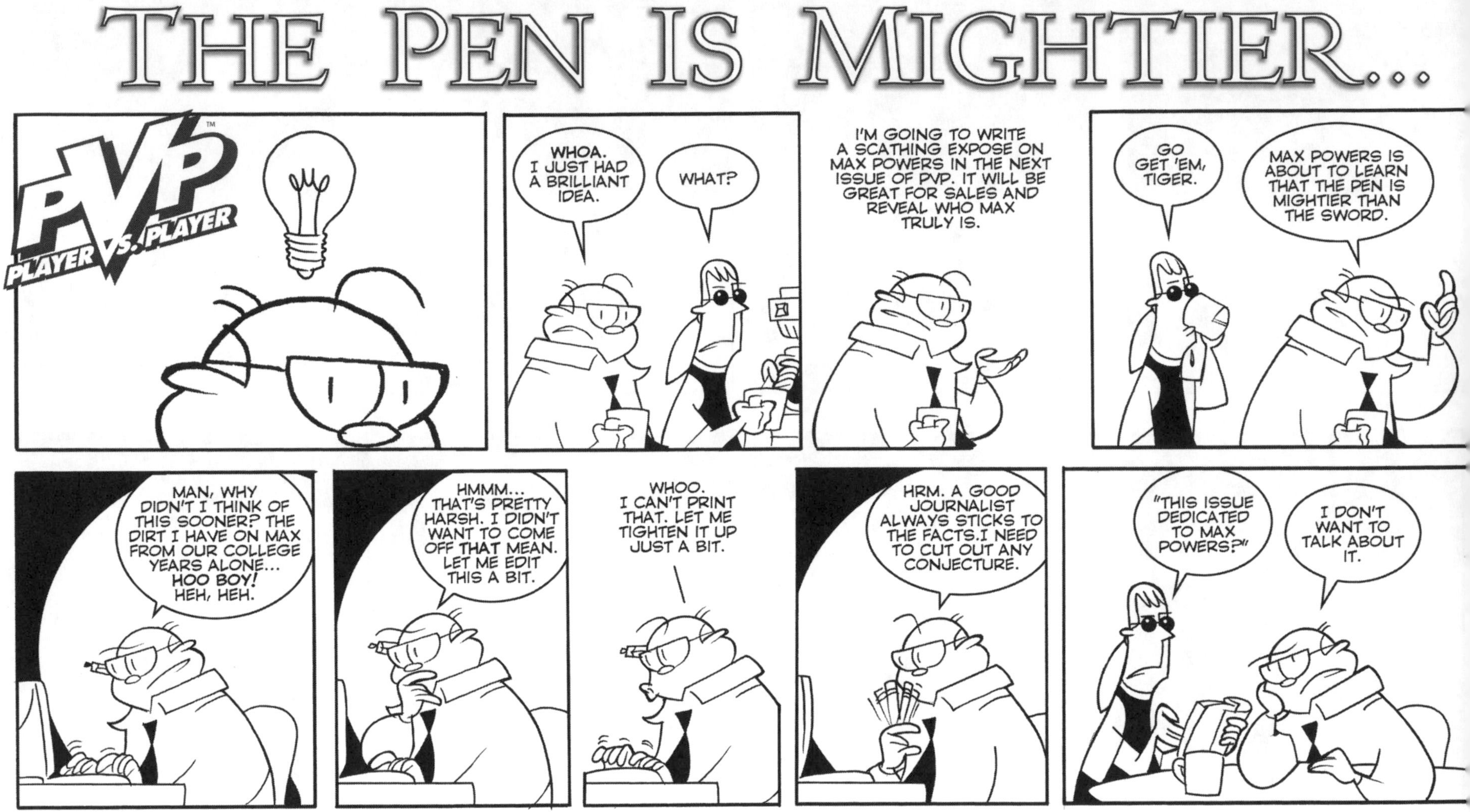

PVP
PLAYER VS. PLAYER
WHOA. I JUST HAD A BRILLIANT IDEA.
WHAT?
I'M GOING TO WRITE A SCATHING EXPOSE ON MAX POWERS IN THE NEXT ISSUE OF PVP. IT WILL BE GREAT FOR SALES AND REVEAL WHO MAX TRULY IS.
GO GET 'EM, TIGER.
MAX POWERS IS ABOUT TO LEARN THAT THE PEN IS MIGHTIER THAN THE SWORD.
MAN, WHY DIDN'T I THINK OF THIS SOONER? THE DIRT I HAVE ON MAX FROM OUR COLLEGE YEARS ALONE... HOO BOY! HEH, HEH.
HMMM... THAT'S PRETTY HARSH. I DIDN'T WANT TO COME OFF THAT MEAN. LET ME EDIT THIS A BIT.
WHOO. I CAN'T PRINT THAT. LET ME TIGHTEN IT UP JUST A BIT.
HRM. A GOOD JOURNALIST ALWAYS STICKS TO THE FACTS. I NEED TO CUT OUT ANY CONJECTURE.
"THIS ISSUE DEDICATED TO MAX POWERS?"
I DON'T WANT TO TALK ABOUT IT.

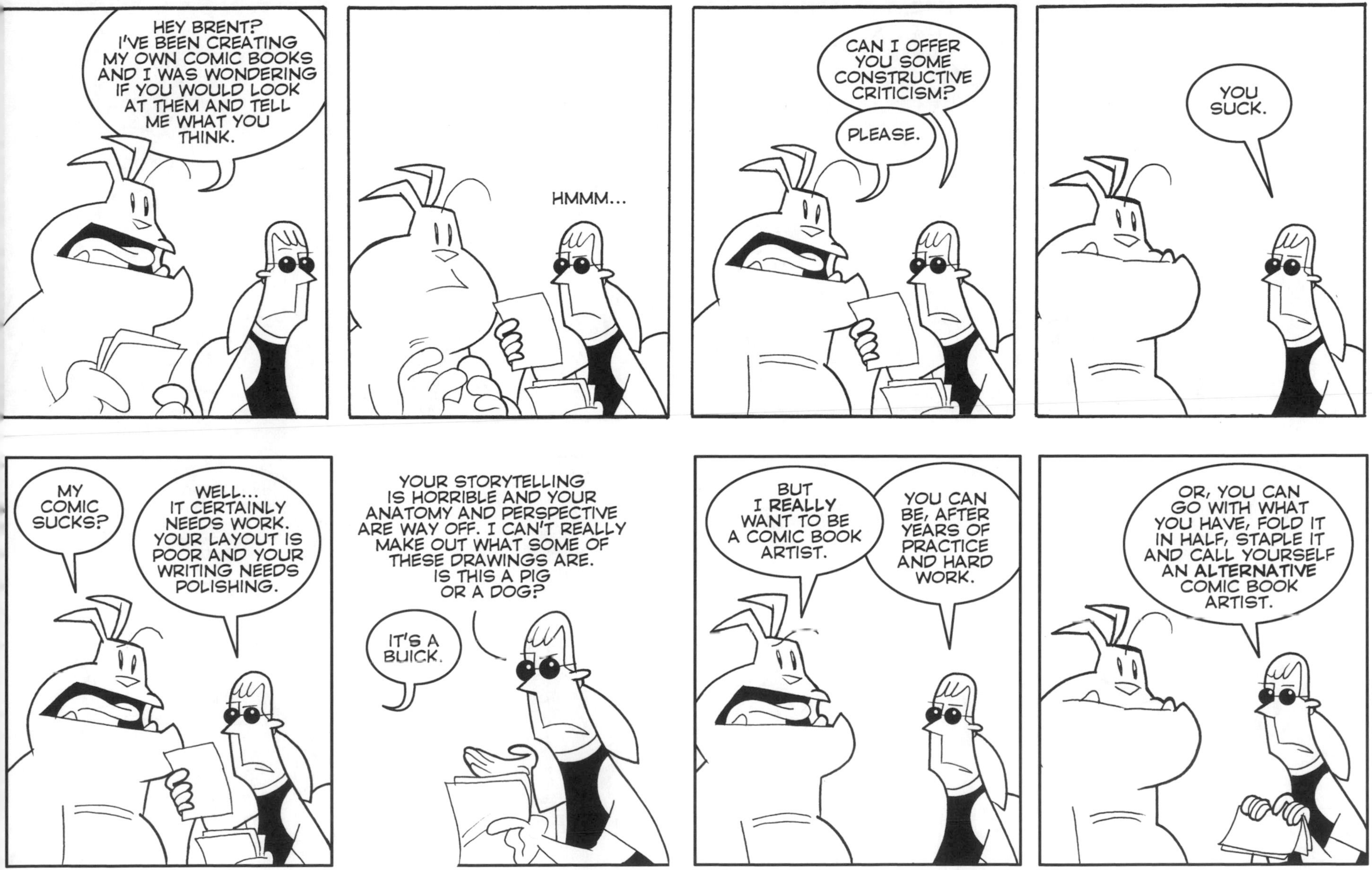
HEY BRENT? I'VE BEEN CREATING MY OWN COMIC BOOKS AND I WAS WONDERING IF YOU WOULD LOOK AT THEM AND TELL ME WHAT YOU THINK.
HMMM...
CAN I OFFER YOU SOME CONSTRUCTIVE CRITICISM?
PLEASE.
YOU SUCK.
MY COMIC SUCKS?
WELL... IT CERTAINLY NEEDS WORK. YOUR LAYOUT IS POOR AND YOUR WRITING NEEDS POLISHING.
YOUR STORYTELLING IS HORRIBLE AND YOUR ANATOMY AND PERSPECTIVE ARE WAY OFF. I CAN'T REALLY MAKE OUT WHAT SOME OF THESE DRAWINGS ARE. IS THIS A PIG OR A DOG?
IT'S A BUICK.
BUT I **REALLY** WANT TO BE A COMIC BOOK ARTIST.
YOU CAN BE, AFTER YEARS OF PRACTICE AND HARD WORK.
OR, YOU CAN GO WITH WHAT YOU HAVE, FOLD IT IN HALF, STAPLE IT AND CALL YOURSELF AN **ALTERNATIVE** COMIC BOOK ARTIST.

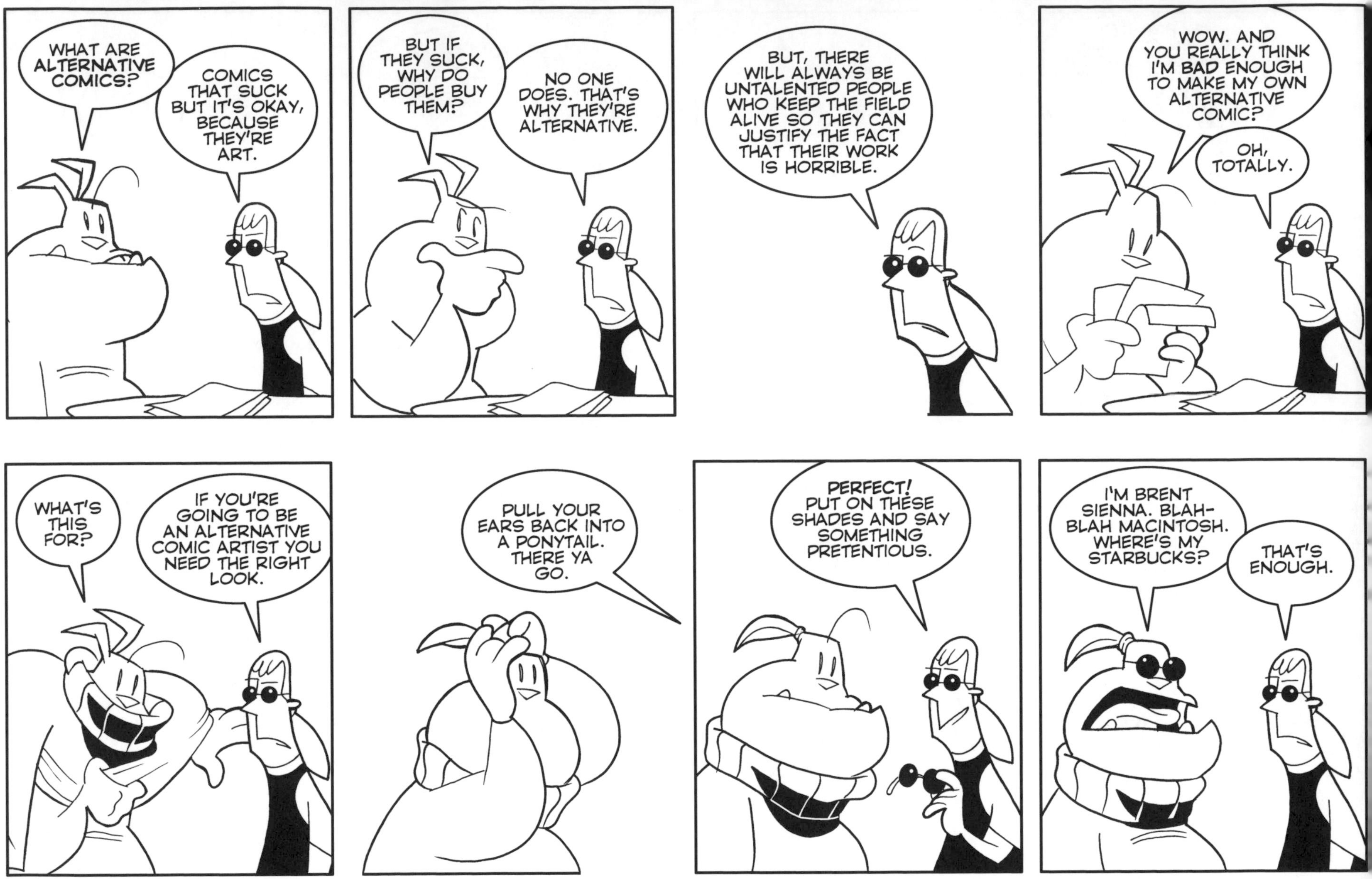
WHAT ARE ALTERNATIVE COMICS?
COMICS THAT SUCK BUT IT'S OKAY, BECAUSE THEY'RE ART.
BUT IF THEY SUCK, WHY DO PEOPLE BUY THEM?
NO ONE DOES. THAT'S WHY THEY'RE ALTERNATIVE.
BUT, THERE WILL ALWAYS BE UNTALENTED PEOPLE WHO KEEP THE FIELD ALIVE SO THEY CAN JUSTIFY THE FACT THAT THEIR WORK IS HORRIBLE.
WOW. AND YOU REALLY THINK I'M BAD ENOUGH TO MAKE MY OWN ALTERNATIVE COMIC?
OH, TOTALLY.
WHAT'S THIS FOR?
IF YOU'RE GOING TO BE AN ALTERNATIVE COMIC ARTIST YOU NEED THE RIGHT LOOK.
PULL YOUR EARS BACK INTO A PONYTAIL. THERE YA GO.
PERFECT! PUT ON THESE SHADES AND SAY SOMETHING PRETENTIOUS.
I'M BRENT SIENNA. BLAH-BLAH MACINTOSH. WHERE'S MY STARBUCKS?
THAT'S ENOUGH.

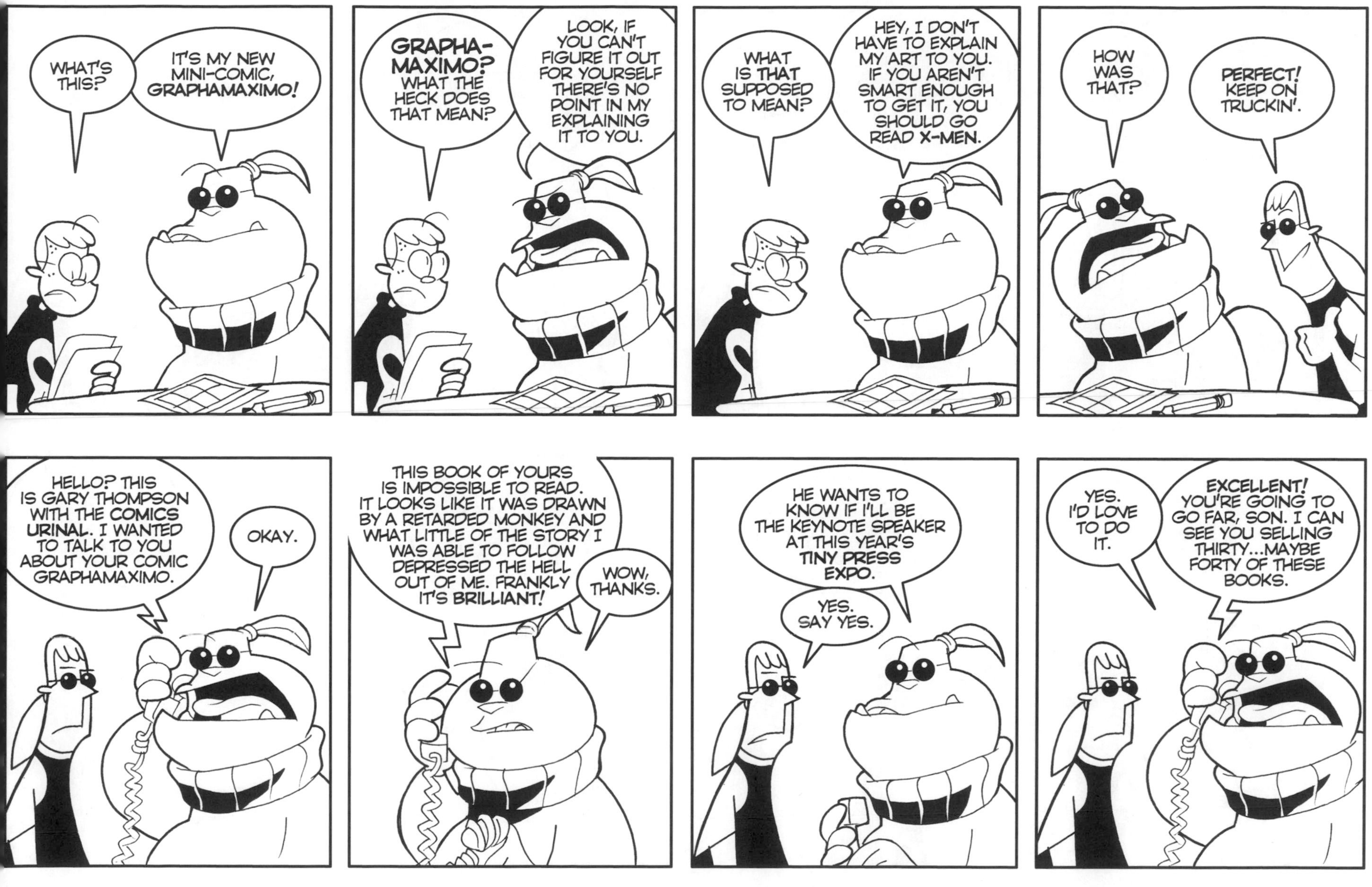
WHAT'S THIS?
IT'S MY NEW MINI-COMIC, GRAPHAMAXIMO!
GRAPHA-MAXIMO? WHAT THE HECK DOES THAT MEAN?
LOOK, IF YOU CAN'T FIGURE IT OUT FOR YOURSELF THERE'S NO POINT IN MY EXPLAINING IT TO YOU.
WHAT IS THAT SUPPOSED TO MEAN?
HEY, I DON'T HAVE TO EXPLAIN MY ART TO YOU. IF YOU AREN'T SMART ENOUGH TO GET IT, YOU SHOULD GO READ X-MEN.
HOW WAS THAT?
PERFECT! KEEP ON TRUCKIN'.
HELLO? THIS IS GARY THOMPSON WITH THE COMICS URINAL. I WANTED TO TALK TO YOU ABOUT YOUR COMIC GRAPHAMAXIMO.
OKAY.
THIS BOOK OF YOURS IS IMPOSSIBLE TO READ. IT LOOKS LIKE IT WAS DRAWN BY A RETARDED MONKEY AND WHAT LITTLE OF THE STORY I WAS ABLE TO FOLLOW DEPRESSED THE HELL OUT OF ME. FRANKLY IT'S BRILLIANT!
WOW, THANKS.
HE WANTS TO KNOW IF I'LL BE THE KEYNOTE SPEAKER AT THIS YEAR'S TINY PRESS EXPO.
YES. SAY YES.
YES. I'D LOVE TO DO IT.
EXCELLENT! YOU'RE GOING TO GO FAR, SON. I CAN SEE YOU SELLING THIRTY...MAYBE FORTY OF THESE BOOKS.

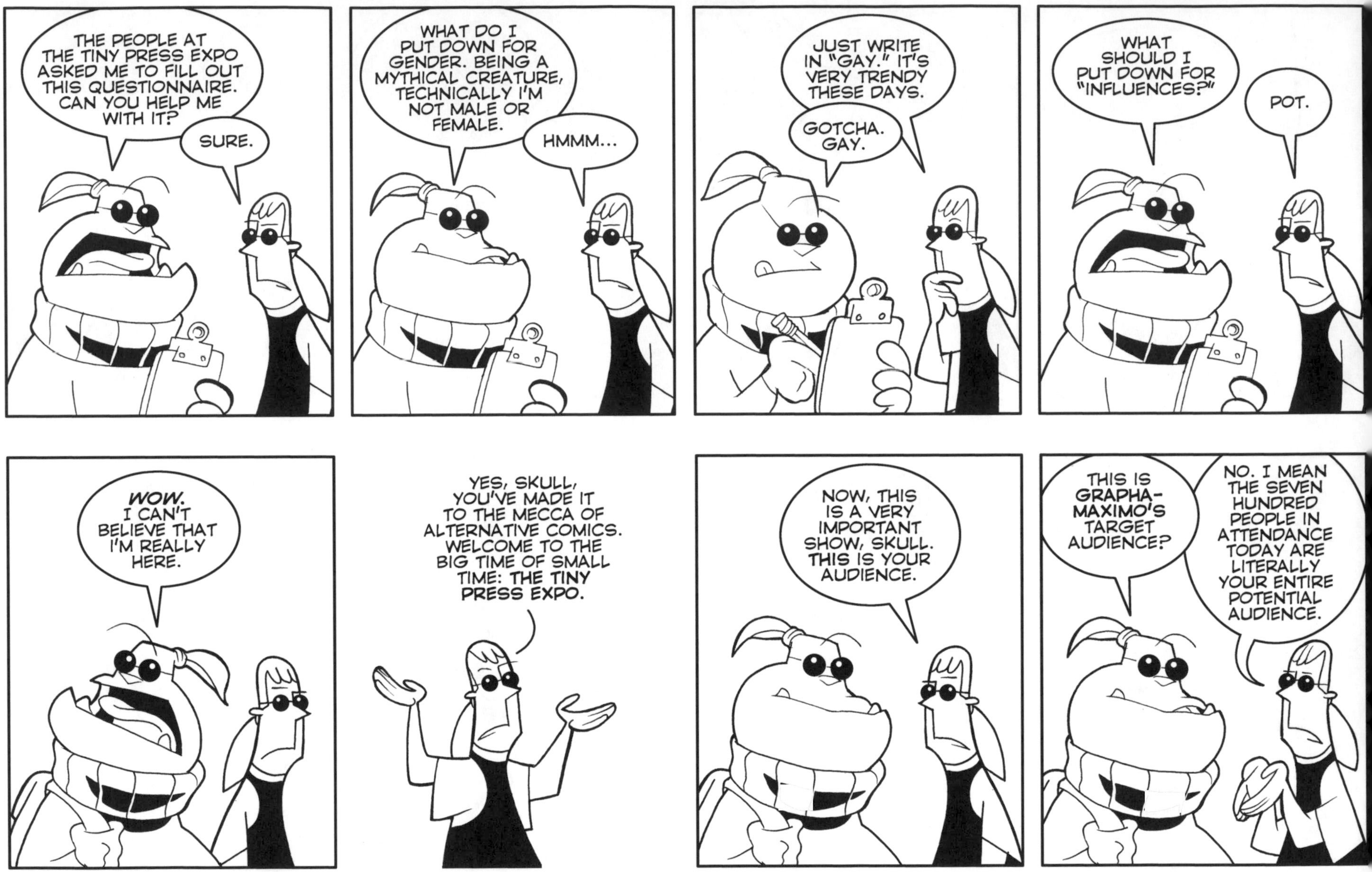
THE PEOPLE AT THE TINY PRESS EXPO ASKED ME TO FILL OUT THIS QUESTIONNAIRE. CAN YOU HELP ME WITH IT?
SURE.
WHAT DO I PUT DOWN FOR GENDER. BEING A MYTHICAL CREATURE, TECHNICALLY I'M NOT MALE OR FEMALE.
HMMM...
JUST WRITE IN "GAY." IT'S VERY TRENDY THESE DAYS.
GOTCHA. GAY.
WHAT SHOULD I PUT DOWN FOR "INFLUENCES?"
POT.
WOW. I CAN'T BELIEVE THAT I'M REALLY HERE.
YES, SKULL, YOU'VE MADE IT TO THE MECCA OF ALTERNATIVE COMICS. WELCOME TO THE BIG TIME OF SMALL TIME: **THE TINY PRESS EXPO.**
NOW, THIS IS A VERY IMPORTANT SHOW, SKULL. **THIS** IS YOUR AUDIENCE.
THIS IS **GRAPHA-MAXIMO'S** TARGET AUDIENCE?
NO. I MEAN THE SEVEN HUNDRED PEOPLE IN ATTENDANCE TODAY ARE LITERALLY YOUR ENTIRE POTENTIAL AUDIENCE.

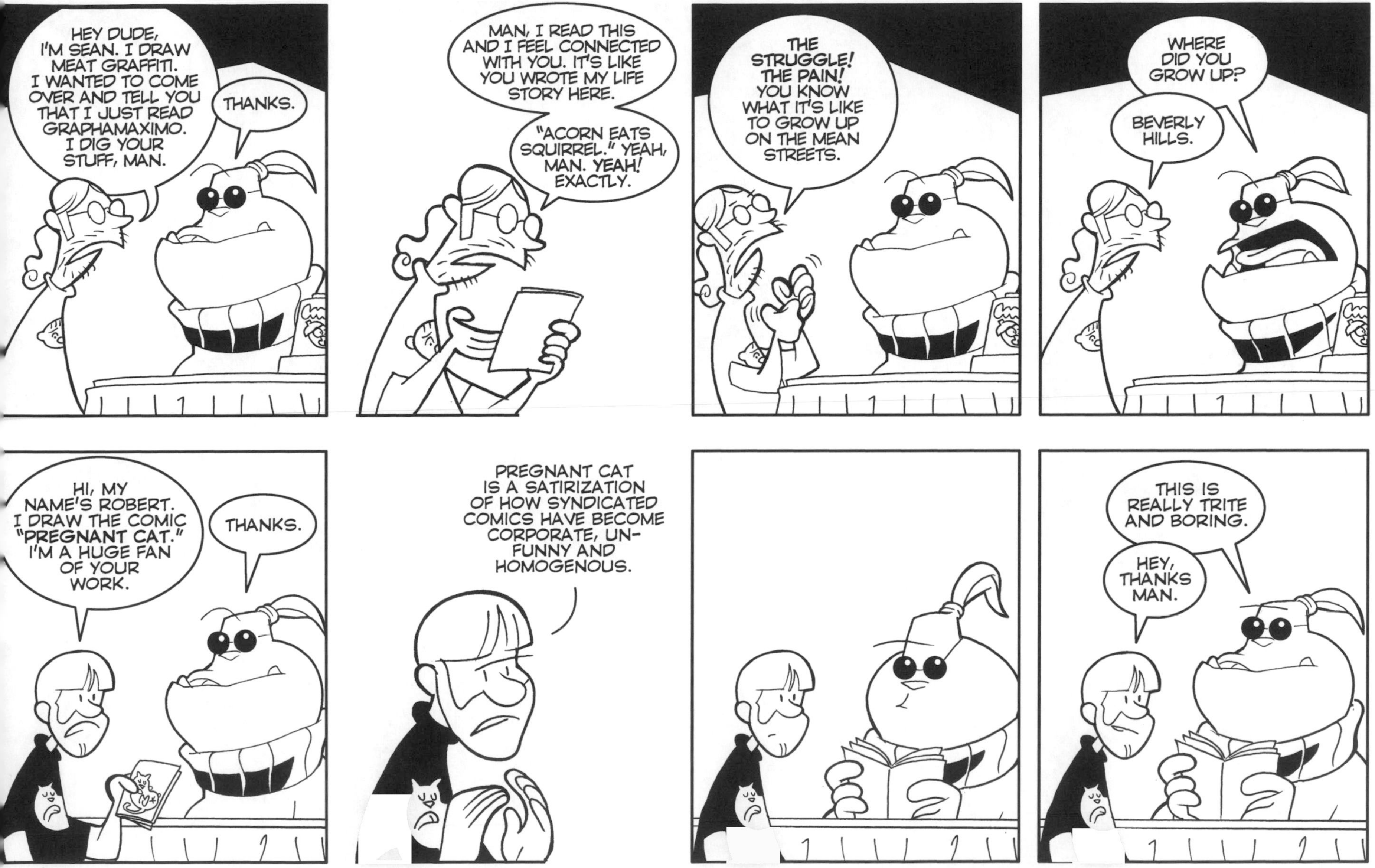
HEY DUDE, I'M SEAN. I DRAW MEAT GRAFFITI. I WANTED TO COME OVER AND TELL YOU THAT I JUST READ GRAPHAMAXIMO. I DIG YOUR STUFF, MAN.
THANKS.
MAN, I READ THIS AND I FEEL CONNECTED WITH YOU. IT'S LIKE YOU WROTE MY LIFE STORY HERE.
"ACORN EATS SQUIRREL." YEAH, MAN. YEAH! EXACTLY.
THE STRUGGLE! THE PAIN! YOU KNOW WHAT IT'S LIKE TO GROW UP ON THE MEAN STREETS.
WHERE DID YOU GROW UP?
BEVERLY HILLS.
HI, MY NAME'S ROBERT. I DRAW THE COMIC "PREGNANT CAT." I'M A HUGE FAN OF YOUR WORK.
THANKS.
PREGNANT CAT IS A SATIRIZATION OF HOW SYNDICATED COMICS HAVE BECOME CORPORATE, UN-FUNNY AND HOMOGENOUS.
THIS IS REALLY TRITE AND BORING.
HEY, THANKS MAN.

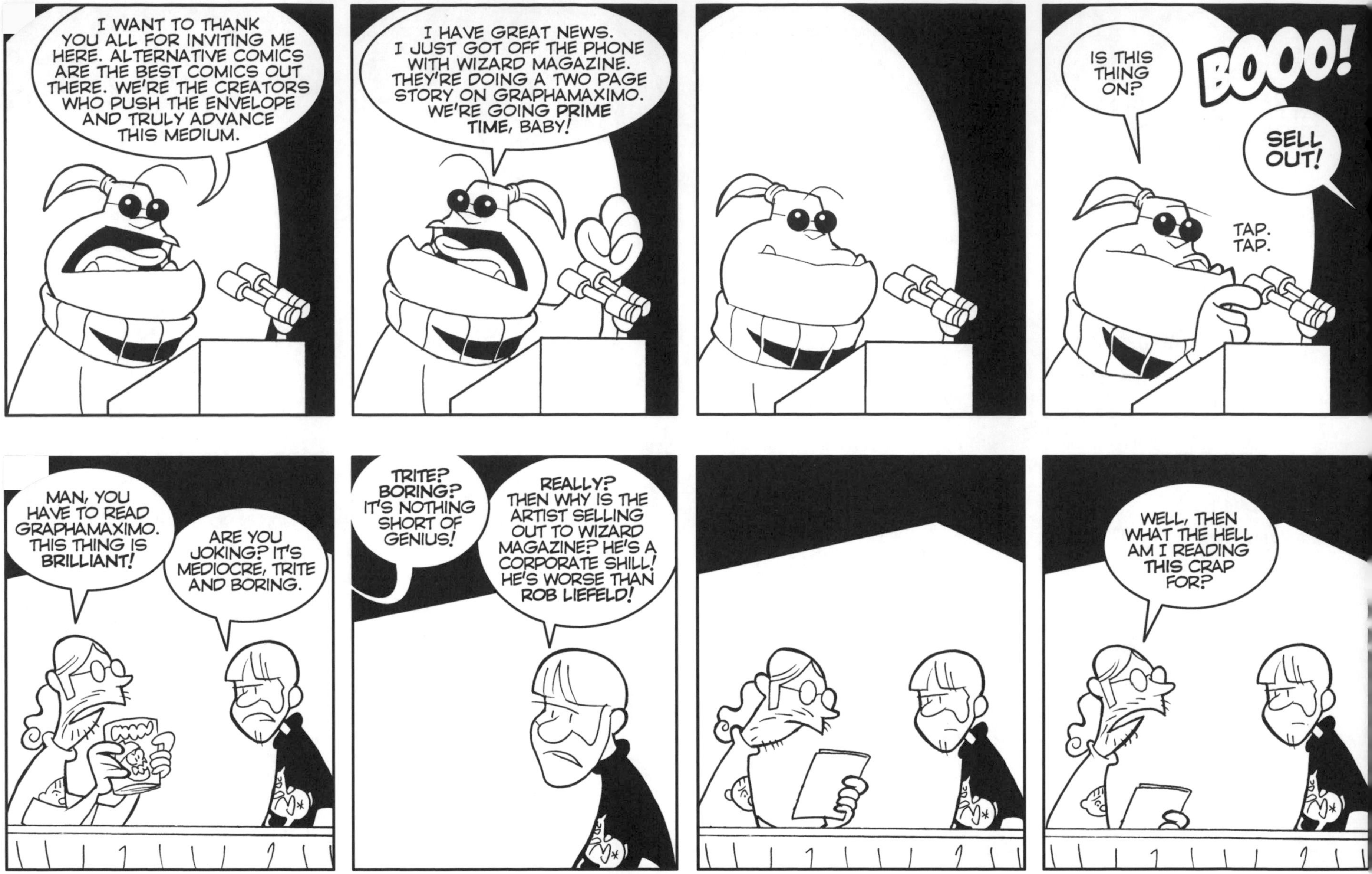
I WANT TO THANK YOU ALL FOR INVITING ME HERE. ALTERNATIVE COMICS ARE THE BEST COMICS OUT THERE. WE'RE THE CREATORS WHO PUSH THE ENVELOPE AND TRULY ADVANCE THIS MEDIUM.
I HAVE GREAT NEWS. I JUST GOT OFF THE PHONE WITH WIZARD MAGAZINE. THEY'RE DOING A TWO PAGE STORY ON GRAPHAMAXIMO. WE'RE GOING PRIME TIME, BABY!
IS THIS THING ON?
BOOO!
SELL OUT!
TAP. TAP.
MAN, YOU HAVE TO READ GRAPHAMAXIMO. THIS THING IS BRILLIANT!
ARE YOU JOKING? IT'S MEDIOCRE, TRITE AND BORING.
TRITE? BORING? IT'S NOTHING SHORT OF GENIUS!
REALLY? THEN WHY IS THE ARTIST SELLING OUT TO WIZARD MAGAZINE? HE'S A CORPORATE SHILL! HE'S WORSE THAN ROB LIEFELD!
WELL, THEN WHAT THE HELL AM I READING THIS CRAP FOR?

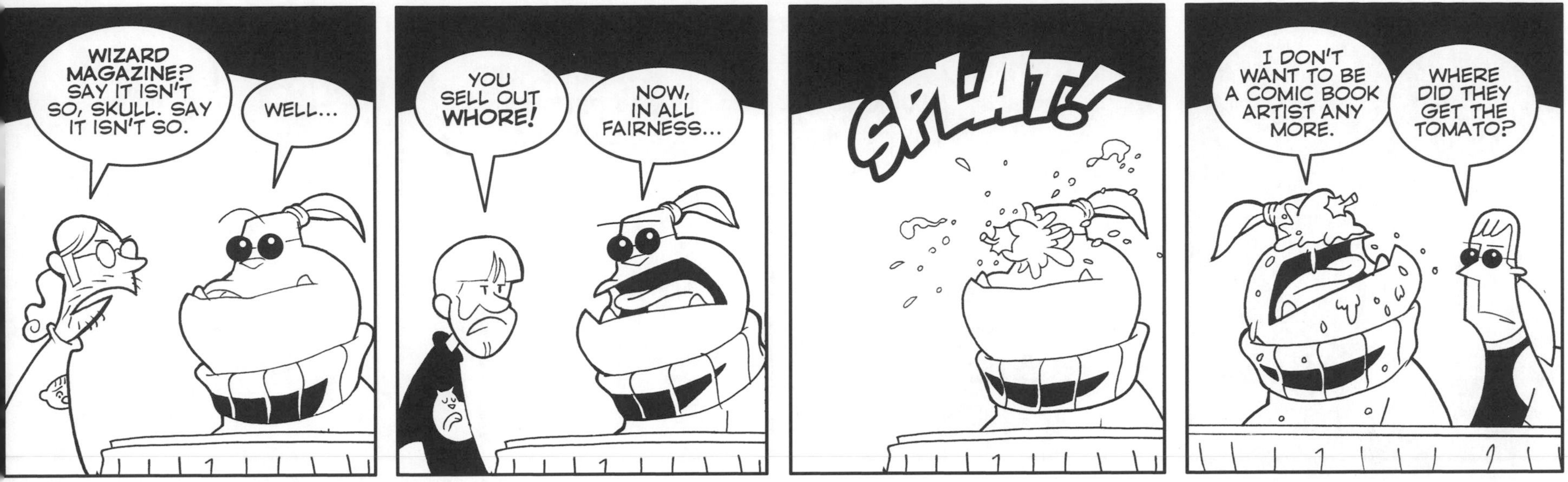
WIZARD MAGAZINE? SAY IT ISN'T SO, SKULL. SAY IT ISN'T SO.
WELL...
YOU SELL OUT **WHORE!**
NOW, IN ALL FAIRNESS...
SPLAT!
I DON'T WANT TO BE A COMIC BOOK ARTIST ANY MORE.
WHERE DID THEY GET THE TOMATO?

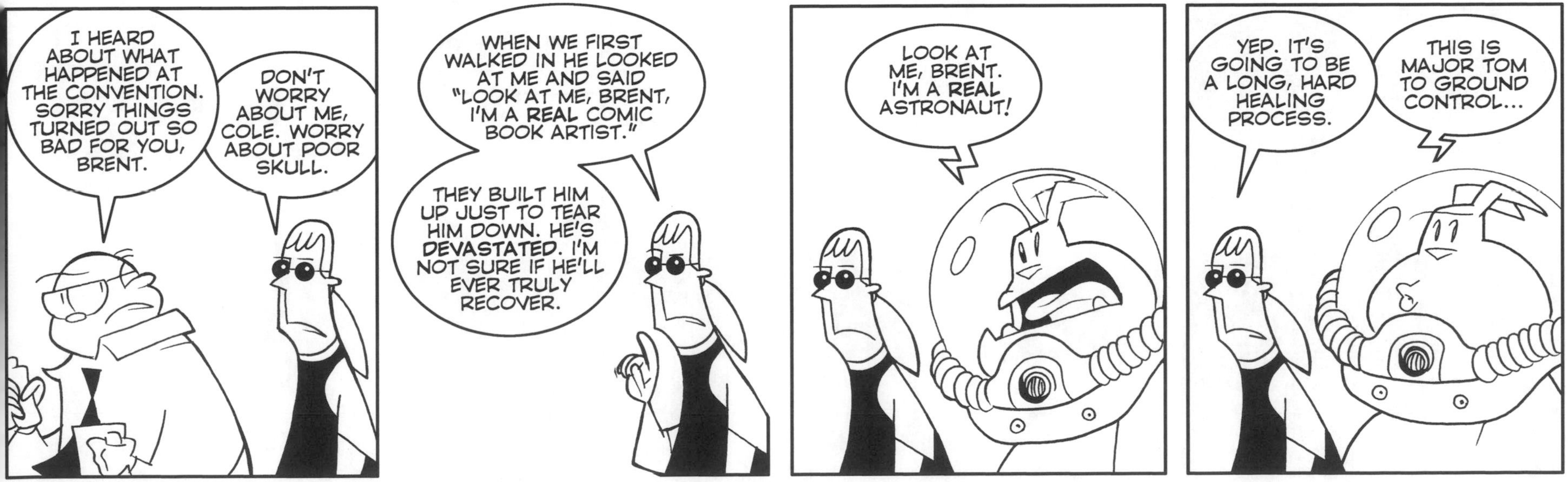
I HEARD ABOUT WHAT HAPPENED AT THE CONVENTION. SORRY THINGS TURNED OUT SO BAD FOR YOU, BRENT.
DON'T WORRY ABOUT ME, COLE. WORRY ABOUT POOR SKULL.
WHEN WE FIRST WALKED IN HE LOOKED AT ME AND SAID "LOOK AT ME, BRENT, I'M A **REAL** COMIC BOOK ARTIST."
THEY BUILT HIM UP JUST TO TEAR HIM DOWN. HE'S **DEVASTATED**. I'M NOT SURE IF HE'LL EVER TRULY RECOVER.
LOOK AT ME, BRENT. I'M A **REAL** ASTRONAUT!
YEP. IT'S GOING TO BE A LONG, HARD HEALING PROCESS.
THIS IS MAJOR TOM TO GROUND CONTROL...

Due to the amount of controversy surrounding his recent strips, and fearing for his safety, Scott Kurtz has been taken to an undisclosed location until things blow over.

In the meantime, PvP has been replaced with the alternative comic **PIRATE VS. NINJA**

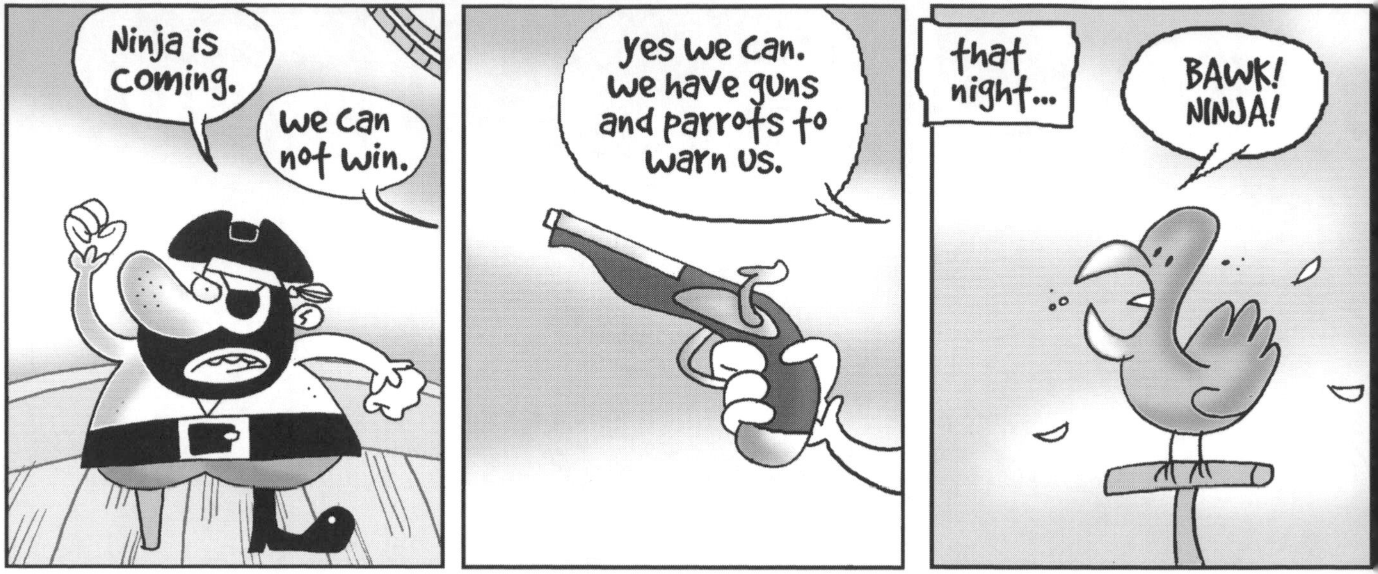

Ninja is coming.
we can not win.
yes we can. we have guns and parrots to warn us.
that night...
BAWK! NINJA!

Due to people flipping-out over his comments, cartoonist Scott Kurtz has retreated to his well-fortified summer cottage to reflect.

meanwhile, we continue the epic conflict that is:

PIRATE VERSUS NINJA

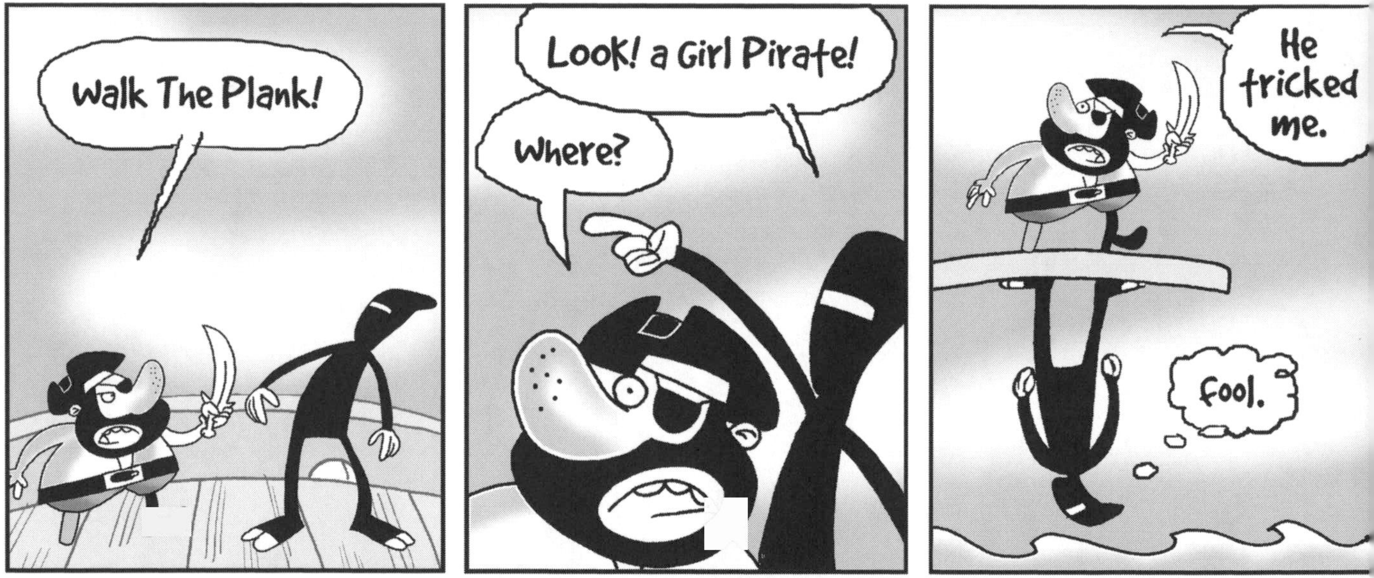

Walk The Plank!
Look! a Girl Pirate!
Where?
He tricked me.
fool.

Due to the negative response his recent work has generated, Scott Kurtz has retreated to a hidden bunker or cave (possibly a day spa) until things can cool down.

Meanwhile, PvPonline.com continues its presentation of **PIRATE VERSUS NINJA**

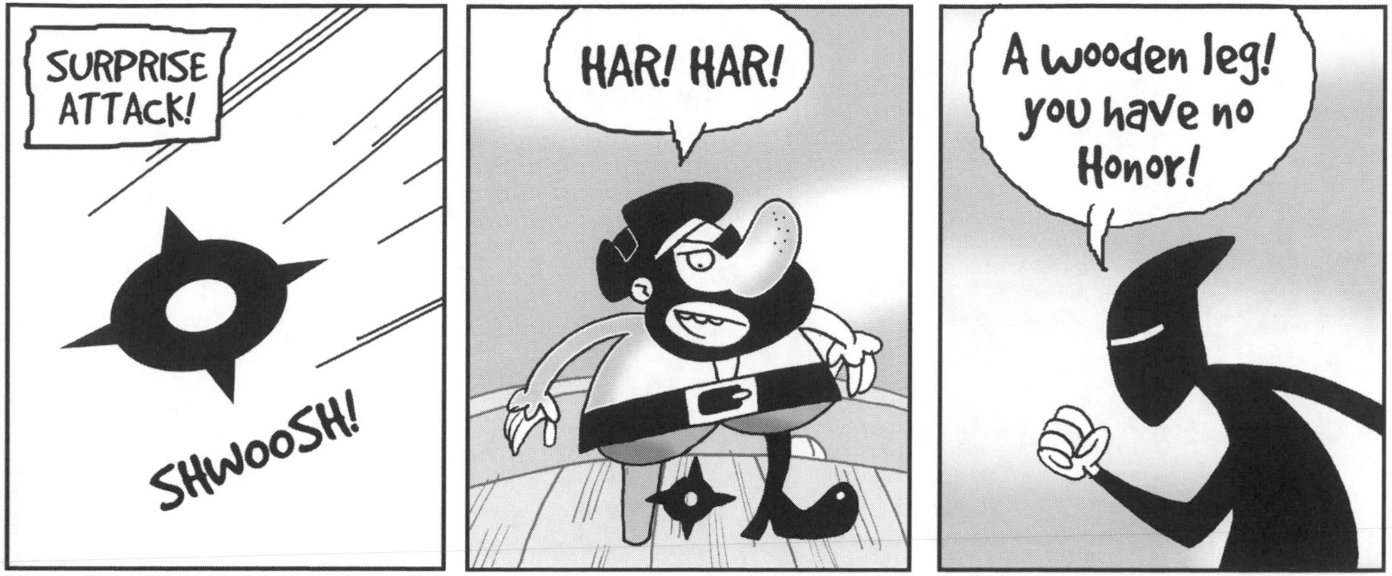
SURPRISE ATTACK!
SHWOOSH!
HAR! HAR!
A wooden leg! you have no Honor!

Last week, Scott Kurtz upset many in the comic book community by shooting off his mouth... AGAIN. This week he's consulting with his publicist on how to reinvent himself.

Meanwhile, we inch closer to the exciting conclusion of the epic: **PIRATE VERSUS NINJA**

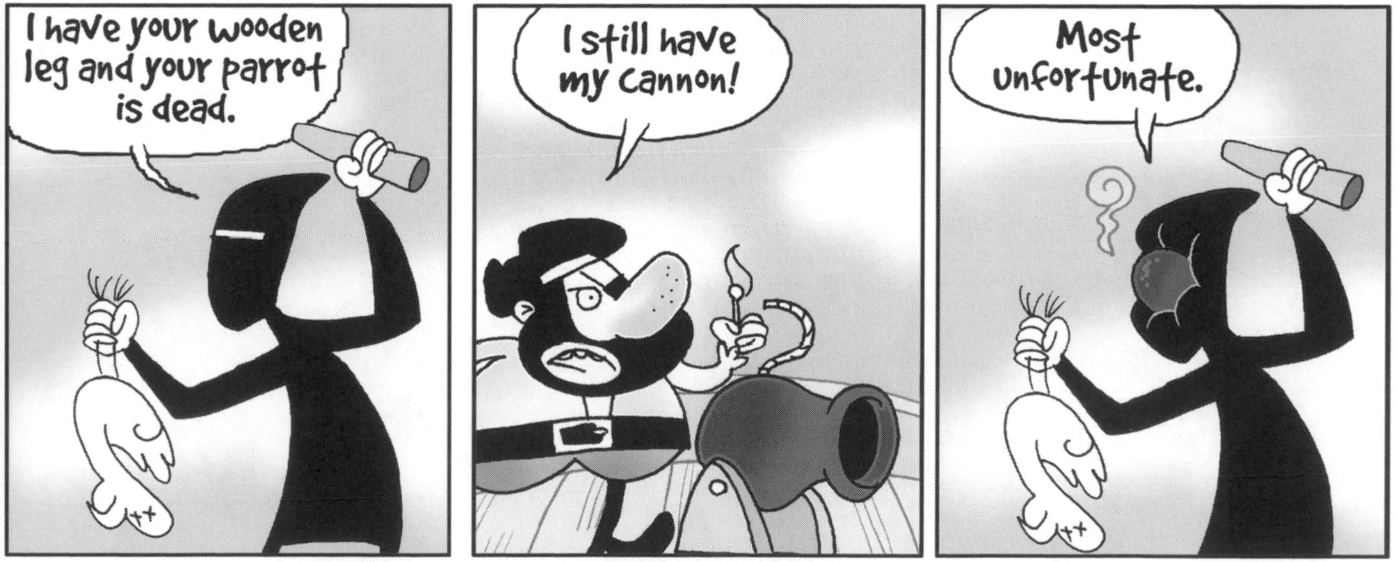
I have your wooden leg and your parrot is dead.
I still have my cannon!
Most unfortunate.

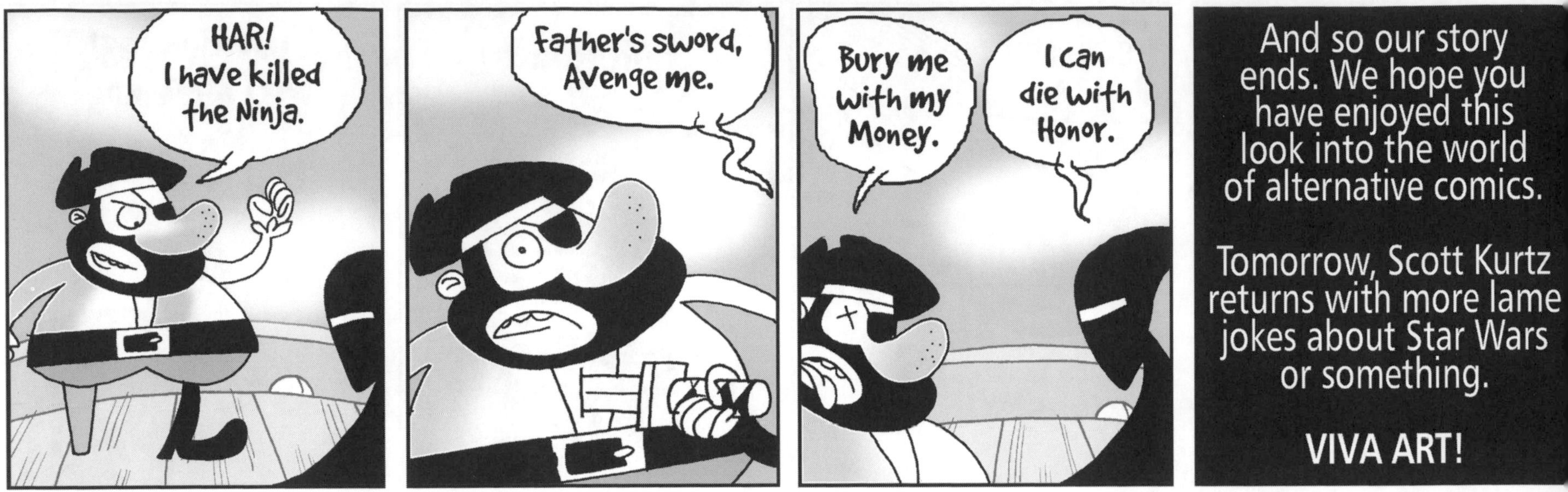
HAR! I have killed the Ninja.
Father's sword, Avenge me.
Bury me with my Money.
I can die with Honor.
And so our story ends. We hope you have enjoyed this look into the world of alternative comics.
Tomorrow, Scott Kurtz returns with more lame jokes about Star Wars or something.
VIVA ART!

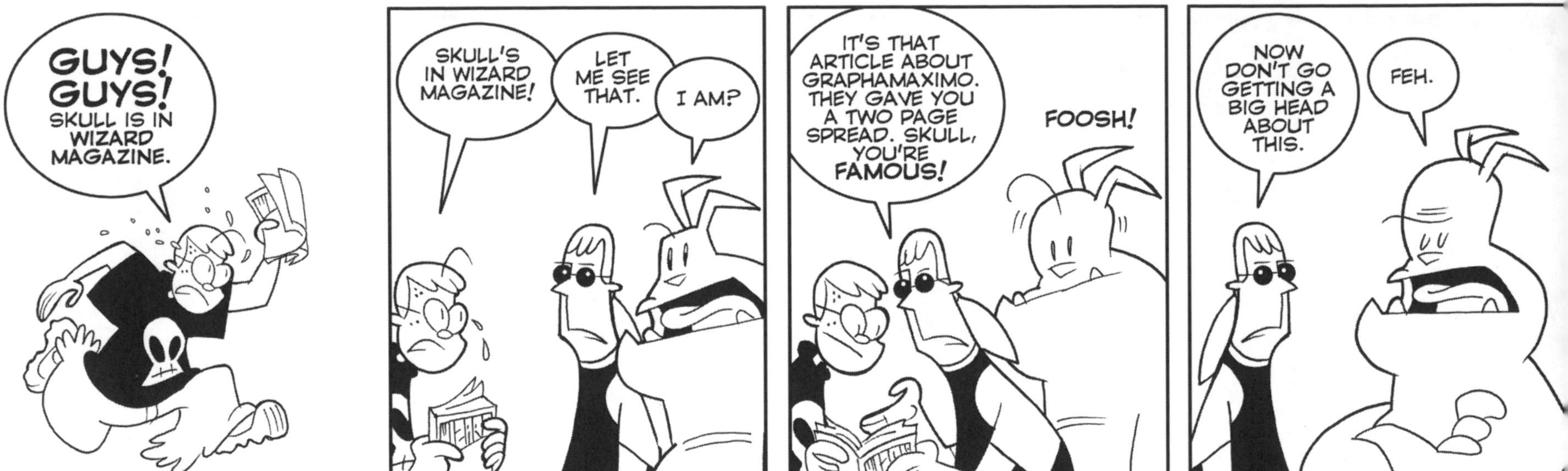
GUYS! GUYS! SKULL IS IN WIZARD MAGAZINE.
SKULL'S IN WIZARD MAGAZINE!
LET ME SEE THAT.
I AM?
IT'S THAT ARTICLE ABOUT GRAPHAMAXIMO. THEY GAVE YOU A TWO PAGE SPREAD. SKULL, YOU'RE FAMOUS!
FOOSH!
NOW DON'T GO GETTING A BIG HEAD ABOUT THIS.
FEH.

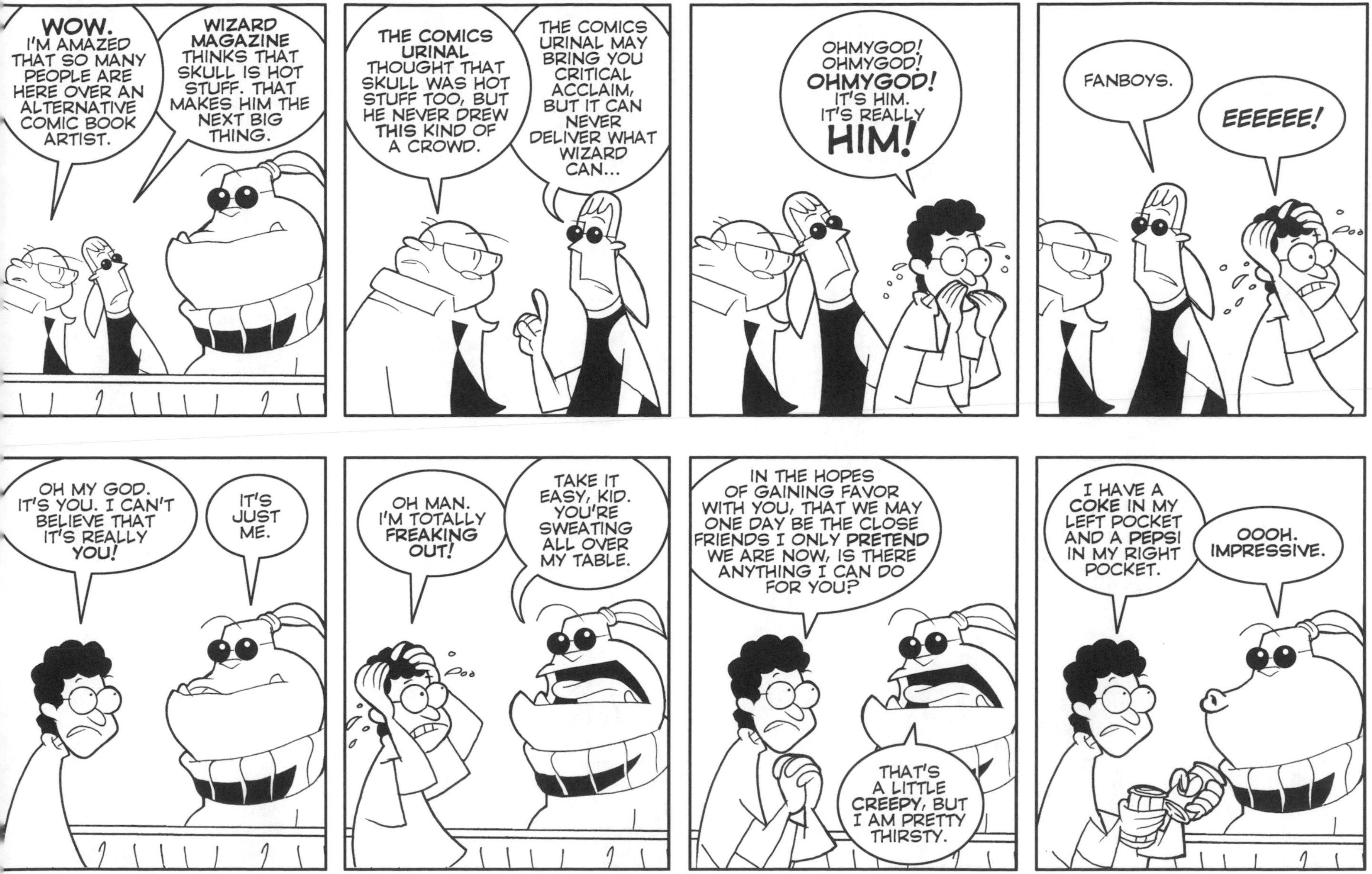

WOW. I'M AMAZED THAT SO MANY PEOPLE ARE HERE OVER AN ALTERNATIVE COMIC BOOK ARTIST.
WIZARD MAGAZINE THINKS THAT SKULL IS HOT STUFF. THAT MAKES HIM THE NEXT BIG THING.
THE COMICS URINAL THOUGHT THAT SKULL WAS HOT STUFF TOO, BUT HE NEVER DREW THIS KIND OF A CROWD.
THE COMICS URINAL MAY BRING YOU CRITICAL ACCLAIM, BUT IT CAN NEVER DELIVER WHAT WIZARD CAN...
OHMYGOD! OHMYGOD! OHMYGOD! IT'S HIM. IT'S REALLY HIM!
FANBOYS.
EEEEEE!
OH MY GOD. IT'S YOU. I CAN'T BELIEVE THAT IT'S REALLY YOU!
IT'S JUST ME.
OH MAN. I'M TOTALLY FREAKING OUT!
TAKE IT EASY, KID. YOU'RE SWEATING ALL OVER MY TABLE.
IN THE HOPES OF GAINING FAVOR WITH YOU, THAT WE MAY ONE DAY BE THE CLOSE FRIENDS I ONLY PRETEND WE ARE NOW, IS THERE ANYTHING I CAN DO FOR YOU?
THAT'S A LITTLE CREEPY, BUT I AM PRETTY THIRSTY.
I HAVE A COKE IN MY LEFT POCKET AND A PEPSI IN MY RIGHT POCKET.
OOOH. IMPRESSIVE.

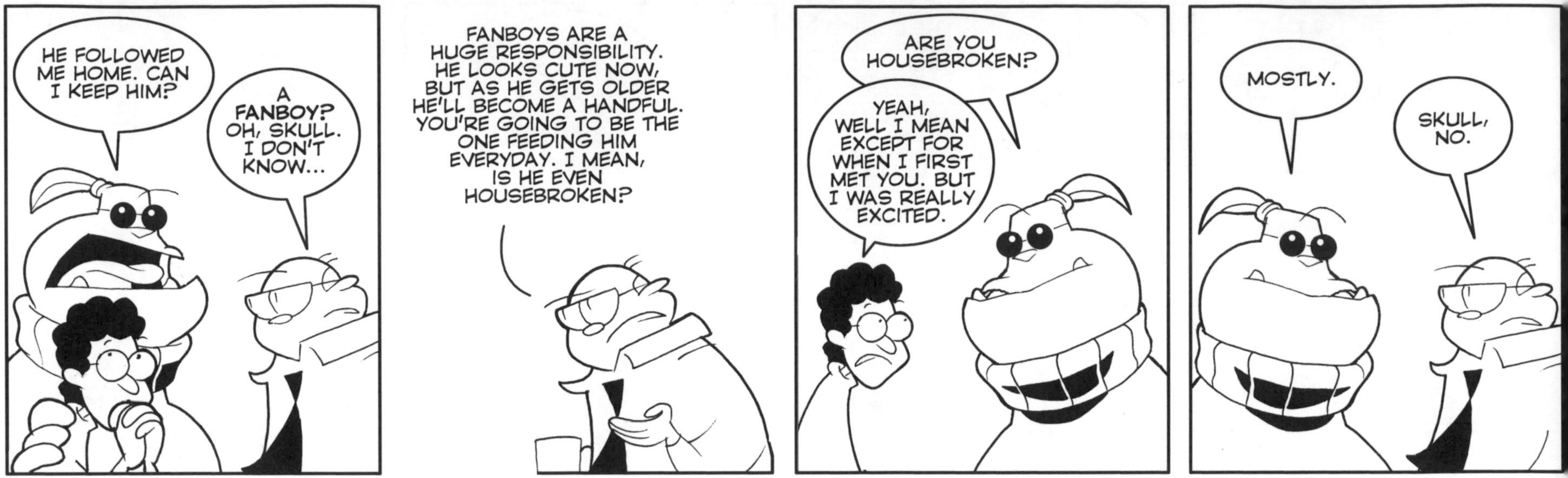
HE FOLLOWED ME HOME. CAN I KEEP HIM?
A FANBOY? OH, SKULL. I DON'T KNOW...
FANBOYS ARE A HUGE RESPONSIBILITY. HE LOOKS CUTE NOW, BUT AS HE GETS OLDER HE'LL BECOME A HANDFUL. YOU'RE GOING TO BE THE ONE FEEDING HIM EVERYDAY. I MEAN, IS HE EVEN HOUSEBROKEN?
ARE YOU HOUSEBROKEN?
YEAH, WELL I MEAN EXCEPT FOR WHEN I FIRST MET YOU. BUT I WAS REALLY EXCITED.
MOSTLY.
SKULL, NO.

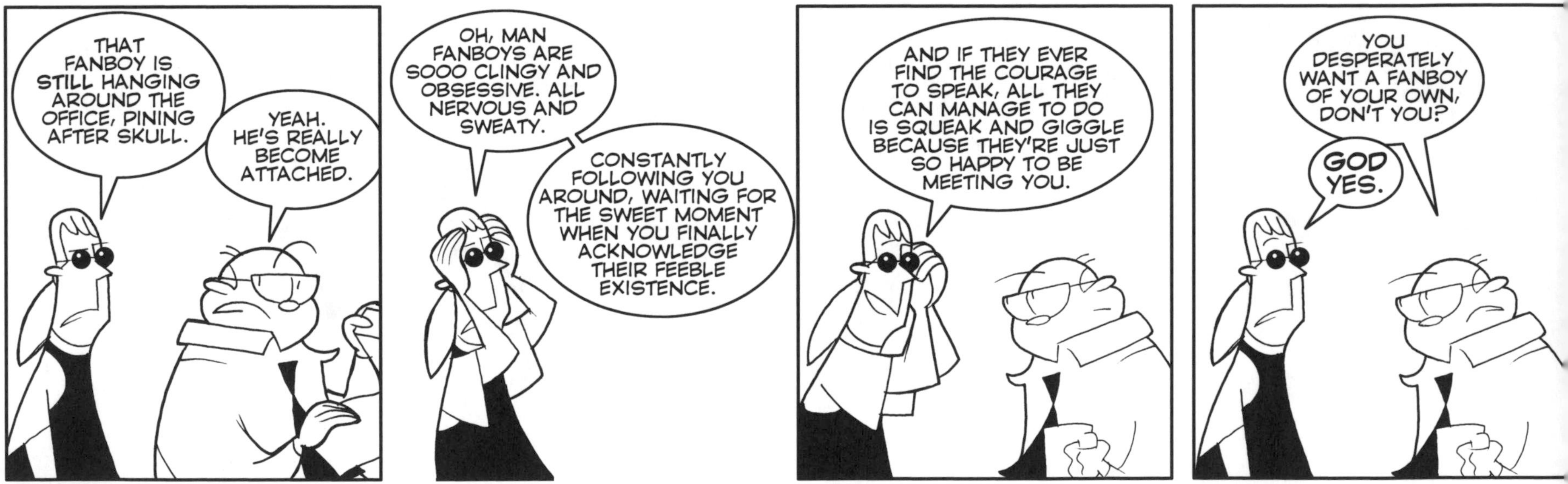
THAT FANBOY IS STILL HANGING AROUND THE OFFICE, PINING AFTER SKULL.
YEAH. HE'S REALLY BECOME ATTACHED.
OH, MAN FANBOYS ARE SOOO CLINGY AND OBSESSIVE. ALL NERVOUS AND SWEATY.
CONSTANTLY FOLLOWING YOU AROUND, WAITING FOR THE SWEET MOMENT WHEN YOU FINALLY ACKNOWLEDGE THEIR FEEBLE EXISTENCE.
AND IF THEY EVER FIND THE COURAGE TO SPEAK, ALL THEY CAN MANAGE TO DO IS SQUEAK AND GIGGLE BECAUSE THEY'RE JUST SO HAPPY TO BE MEETING YOU.
YOU DESPERATELY WANT A FANBOY OF YOUR OWN, DON'T YOU?
GOD YES.

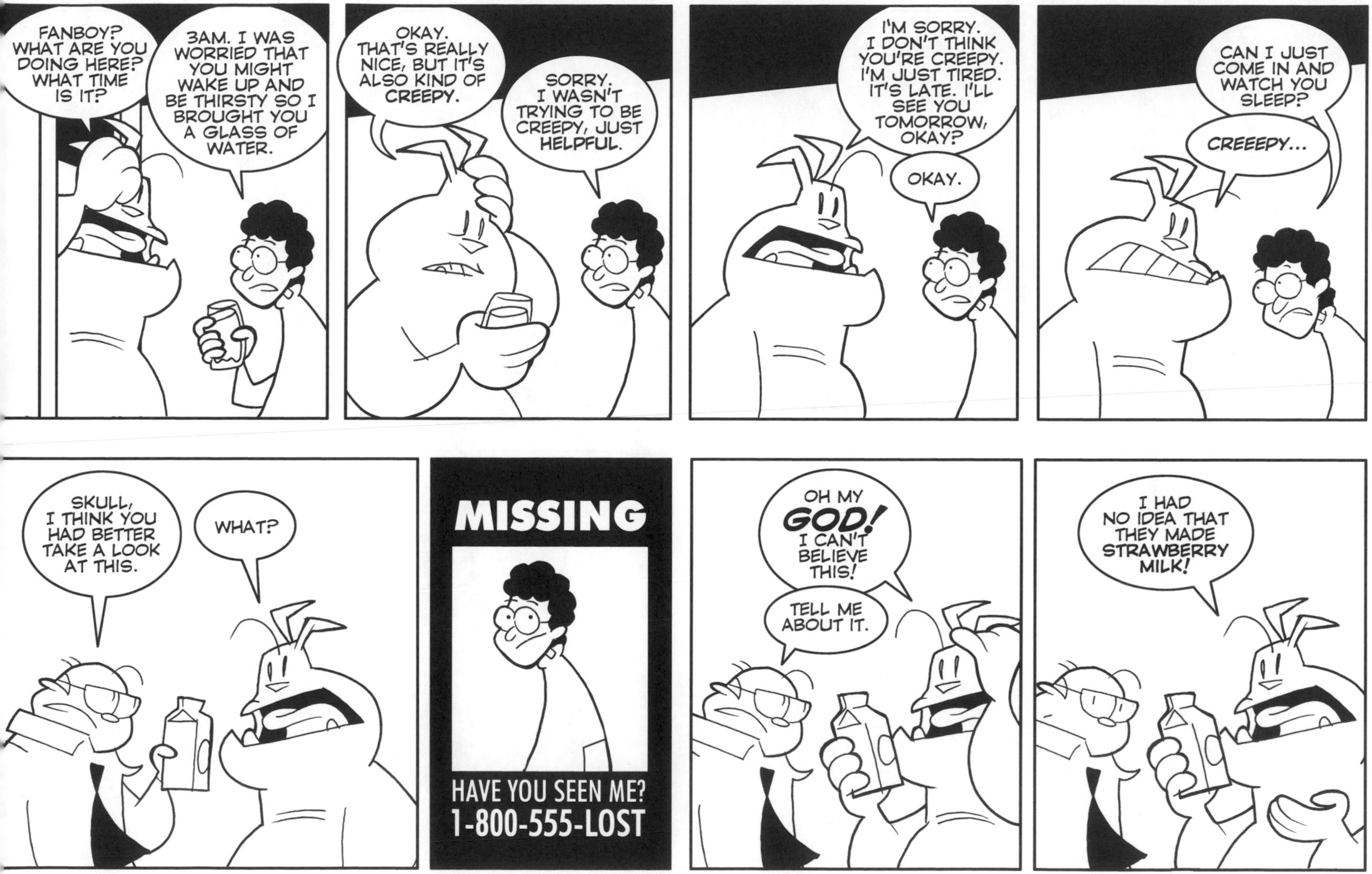
FANBOY? WHAT ARE YOU DOING HERE? WHAT TIME IS IT?
3AM. I WAS WORRIED THAT YOU MIGHT WAKE UP AND BE THIRSTY SO I BROUGHT YOU A GLASS OF WATER.
OKAY. THAT'S REALLY NICE, BUT IT'S ALSO KIND OF CREEPY.
SORRY. I WASN'T TRYING TO BE CREEPY, JUST HELPFUL.
I'M SORRY. I DON'T THINK YOU'RE CREEPY. I'M JUST TIRED. IT'S LATE. I'LL SEE YOU TOMORROW, OKAY?
OKAY.
CAN I JUST COME IN AND WATCH YOU SLEEP?
CREEEPY...
SKULL, I THINK YOU HAD BETTER TAKE A LOOK AT THIS.
WHAT?
MISSING
HAVE YOU SEEN ME?
1-800-555-LOST
OH MY GOD! I CAN'T BELIEVE THIS!
TELL ME ABOUT IT.
I HAD NO IDEA THAT THEY MADE STRAWBERRY MILK!

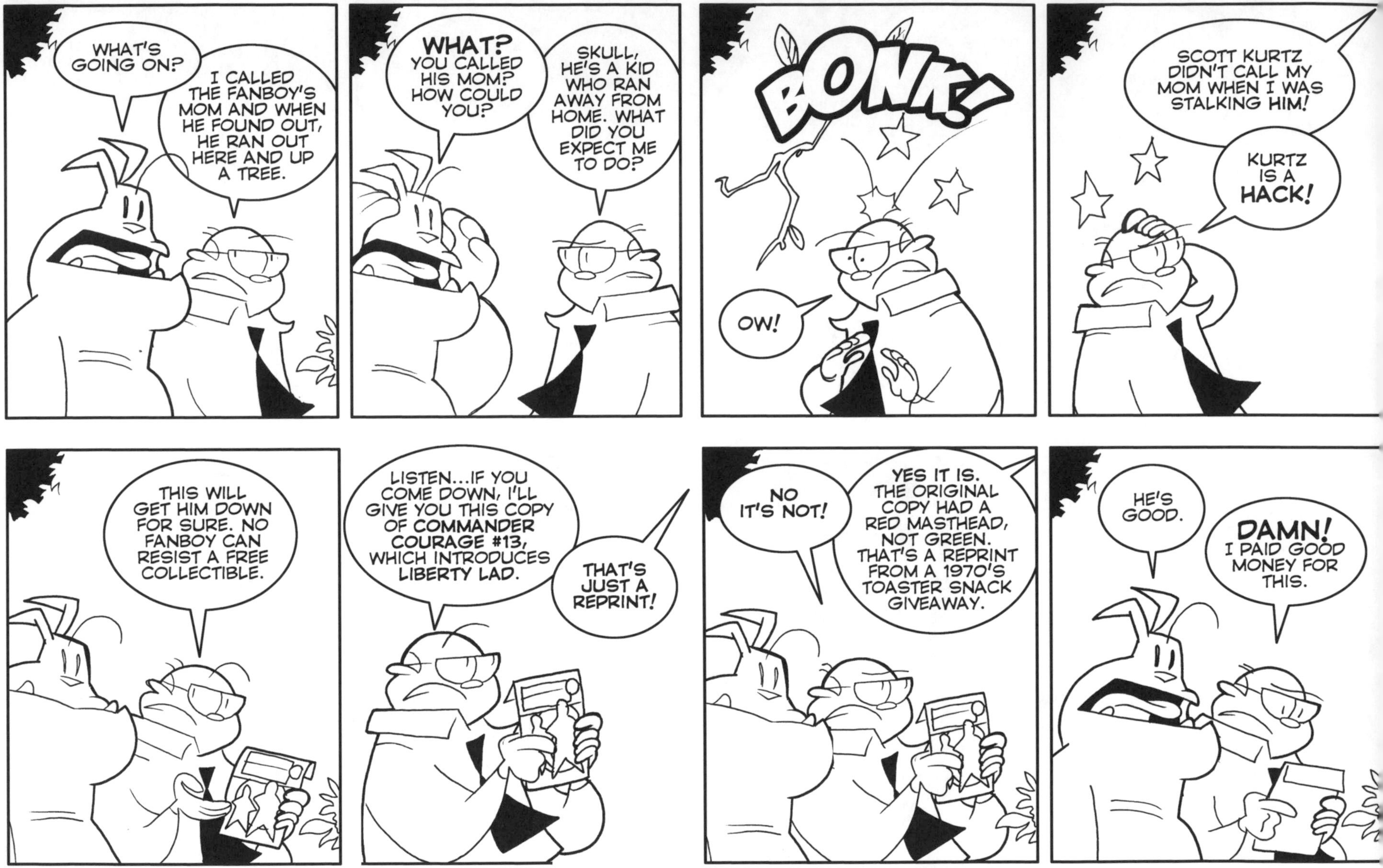
WHAT'S GOING ON?
I CALLED THE FANBOY'S MOM AND WHEN HE FOUND OUT, HE RAN OUT HERE AND UP A TREE.
WHAT? YOU CALLED HIS MOM? HOW COULD YOU?
SKULL, HE'S A KID WHO RAN AWAY FROM HOME. WHAT DID YOU EXPECT ME TO DO?
BONK!
OW!
SCOTT KURTZ DIDN'T CALL MY MOM WHEN I WAS STALKING HIM!
KURTZ IS A HACK!
THIS WILL GET HIM DOWN FOR SURE. NO FANBOY CAN RESIST A FREE COLLECTIBLE.
LISTEN...IF YOU COME DOWN, I'LL GIVE YOU THIS COPY OF COMMANDER COURAGE #13, WHICH INTRODUCES LIBERTY LAD.
THAT'S JUST A REPRINT!
NO IT'S NOT!
YES IT IS. THE ORIGINAL COPY HAD A RED MASTHEAD, NOT GREEN. THAT'S A REPRINT FROM A 1970'S TOASTER SNACK GIVEAWAY.
HE'S GOOD.
DAMN! I PAID GOOD MONEY FOR THIS.

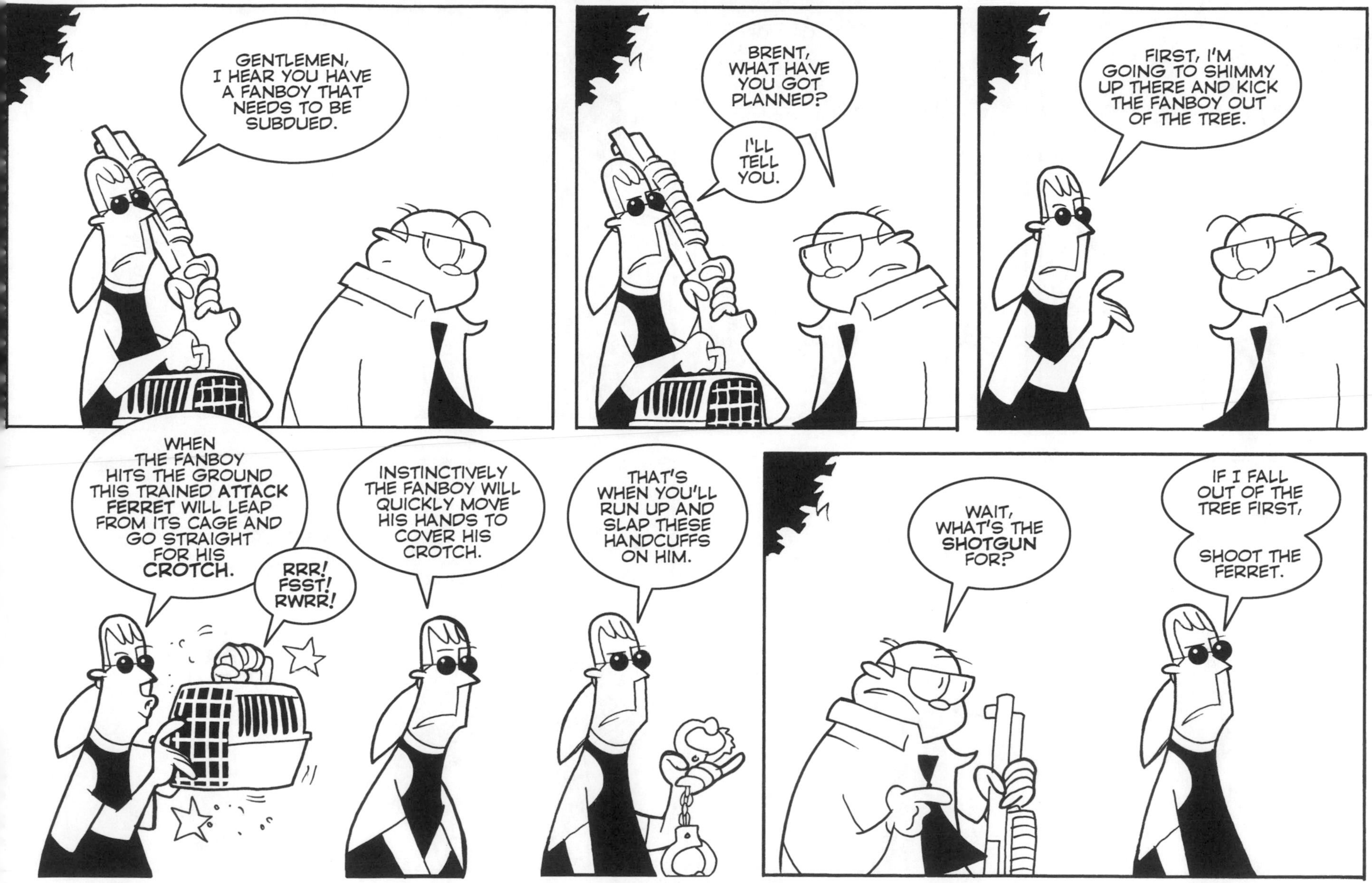
GENTLEMEN, I HEAR YOU HAVE A FANBOY THAT NEEDS TO BE SUBDUED.
BRENT, WHAT HAVE YOU GOT PLANNED?
I'LL TELL YOU.
FIRST, I'M GOING TO SHIMMY UP THERE AND KICK THE FANBOY OUT OF THE TREE.
WHEN THE FANBOY HITS THE GROUND THIS TRAINED ATTACK FERRET WILL LEAP FROM ITS CAGE AND GO STRAIGHT FOR HIS CROTCH.
RRR! FSST! RWRR!
INSTINCTIVELY THE FANBOY WILL QUICKLY MOVE HIS HANDS TO COVER HIS CROTCH.
THAT'S WHEN YOU'LL RUN UP AND SLAP THESE HANDCUFFS ON HIM.
WAIT, WHAT'S THE SHOTGUN FOR?
IF I FALL OUT OF THE TREE FIRST,
SHOOT THE FERRET.

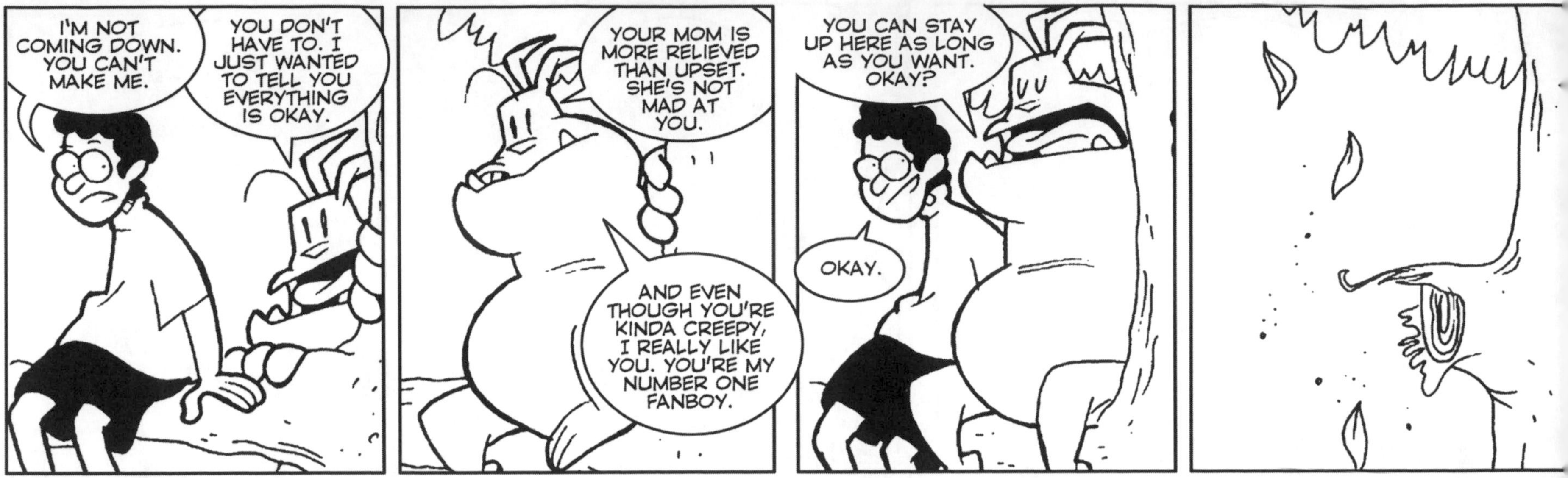
I'M NOT COMING DOWN. YOU CAN'T MAKE ME.
YOU DON'T HAVE TO. I JUST WANTED TO TELL YOU EVERYTHING IS OKAY.
YOUR MOM IS MORE RELIEVED THAN UPSET. SHE'S NOT MAD AT YOU.
AND EVEN THOUGH YOU'RE KINDA CREEPY, I REALLY LIKE YOU. YOU'RE MY NUMBER ONE FANBOY.
YOU CAN STAY UP HERE AS LONG AS YOU WANT. OKAY?
OKAY.

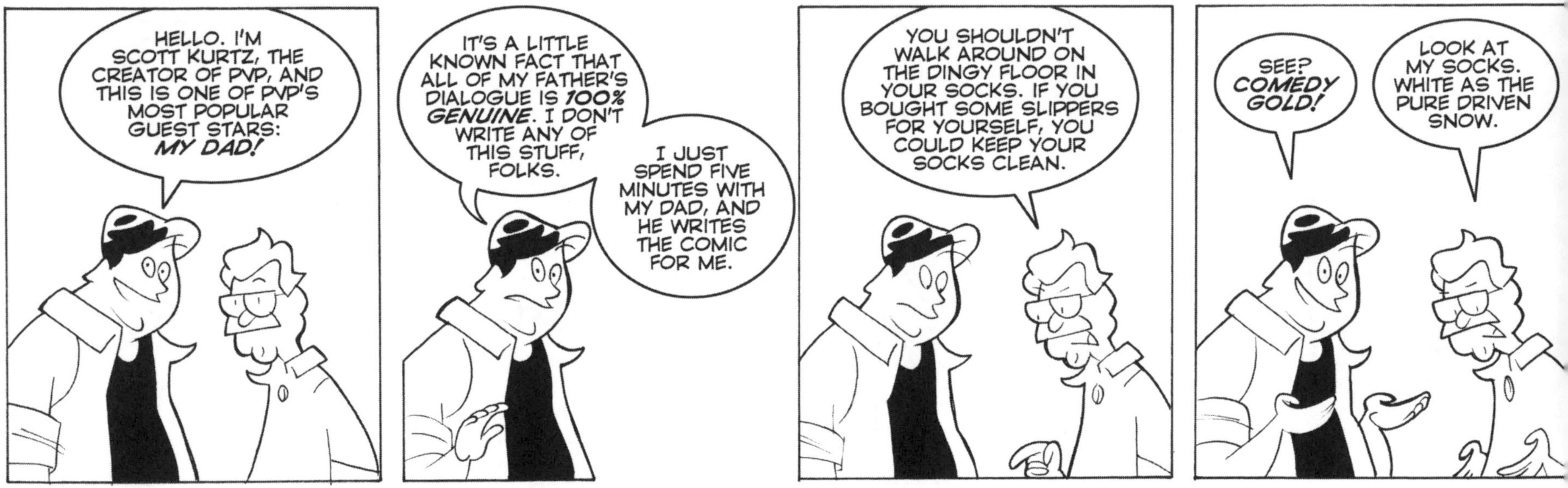
HELLO. I'M SCOTT KURTZ, THE CREATOR OF PVP, AND THIS IS ONE OF PVP'S MOST POPULAR GUEST STARS: ***MY DAD!***
IT'S A LITTLE KNOWN FACT THAT ALL OF MY FATHER'S DIALOGUE IS ***100% GENUINE***. I DON'T WRITE ANY OF THIS STUFF, FOLKS.
I JUST SPEND FIVE MINUTES WITH MY DAD, AND HE WRITES THE COMIC FOR ME.
YOU SHOULDN'T WALK AROUND ON THE DINGY FLOOR IN YOUR SOCKS. IF YOU BOUGHT SOME SLIPPERS FOR YOURSELF, YOU COULD KEEP YOUR SOCKS CLEAN.
SEE? ***COMEDY GOLD!***
LOOK AT MY SOCKS. WHITE AS THE PURE DRIVEN SNOW.

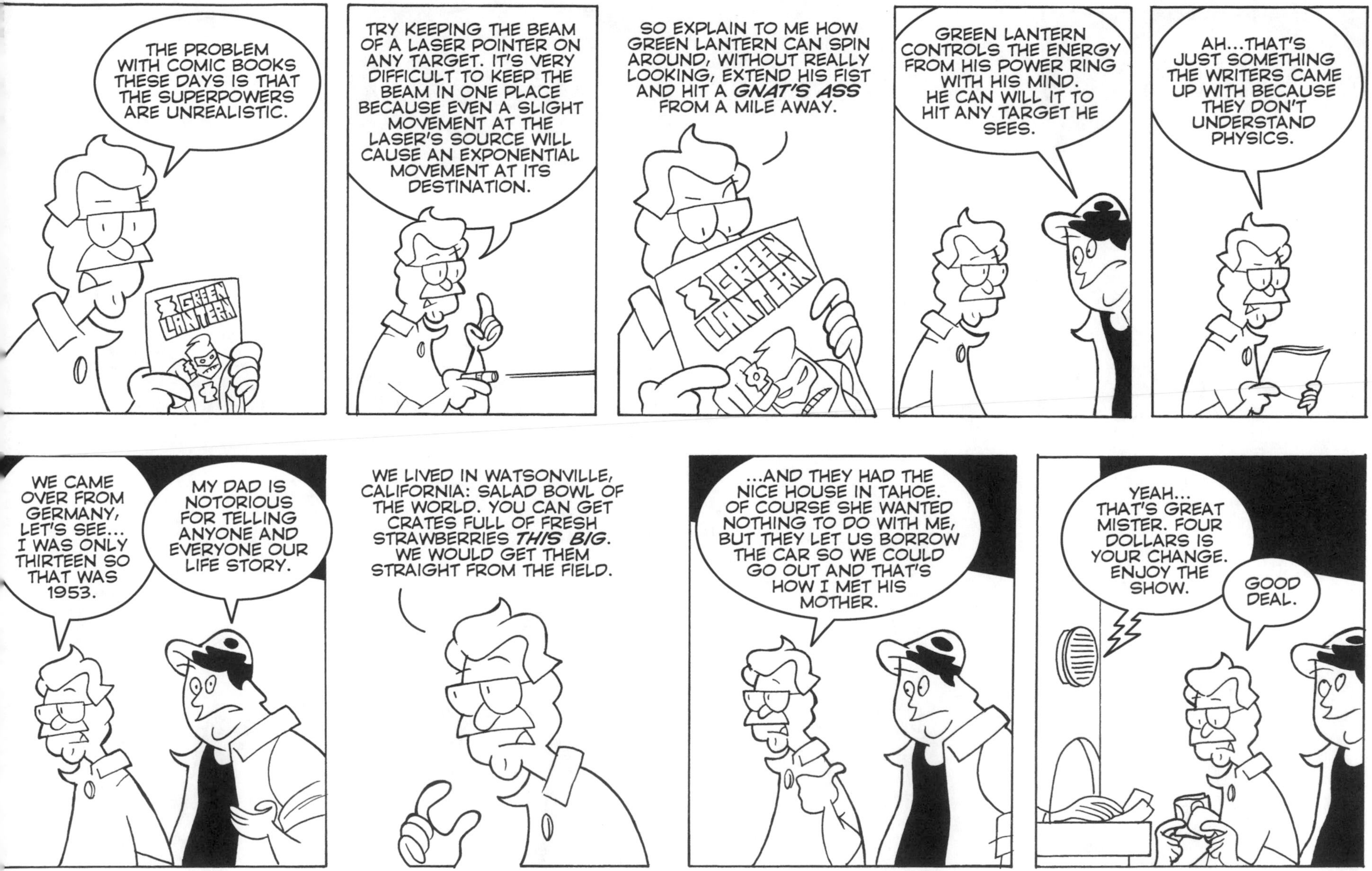
THE PROBLEM WITH COMIC BOOKS THESE DAYS IS THAT THE SUPERPOWERS ARE UNREALISTIC.
GREEN LANTERN
TRY KEEPING THE BEAM OF A LASER POINTER ON ANY TARGET. IT'S VERY DIFFICULT TO KEEP THE BEAM IN ONE PLACE BECAUSE EVEN A SLIGHT MOVEMENT AT THE LASER'S SOURCE WILL CAUSE AN EXPONENTIAL MOVEMENT AT ITS DESTINATION.
SO EXPLAIN TO ME HOW GREEN LANTERN CAN SPIN AROUND, WITHOUT REALLY LOOKING, EXTEND HIS FIST AND HIT A *GNAT'S ASS* FROM A MILE AWAY.
GREEN LANTERN
GREEN LANTERN CONTROLS THE ENERGY FROM HIS POWER RING WITH HIS MIND. HE CAN WILL IT TO HIT ANY TARGET HE SEES.
AH...THAT'S JUST SOMETHING THE WRITERS CAME UP WITH BECAUSE THEY DON'T UNDERSTAND PHYSICS.
WE CAME OVER FROM GERMANY, LET'S SEE... I WAS ONLY THIRTEEN SO THAT WAS 1953.
MY DAD IS NOTORIOUS FOR TELLING ANYONE AND EVERYONE OUR LIFE STORY.
WE LIVED IN WATSONVILLE, CALIFORNIA: SALAD BOWL OF THE WORLD. YOU CAN GET CRATES FULL OF FRESH STRAWBERRIES *THIS BIG*. WE WOULD GET THEM STRAIGHT FROM THE FIELD.
...AND THEY HAD THE NICE HOUSE IN TAHOE. OF COURSE SHE WANTED NOTHING TO DO WITH ME, BUT THEY LET US BORROW THE CAR SO WE COULD GO OUT AND THAT'S HOW I MET HIS MOTHER.
YEAH... THAT'S GREAT MISTER. FOUR DOLLARS IS YOUR CHANGE. ENJOY THE SHOW.
GOOD DEAL.

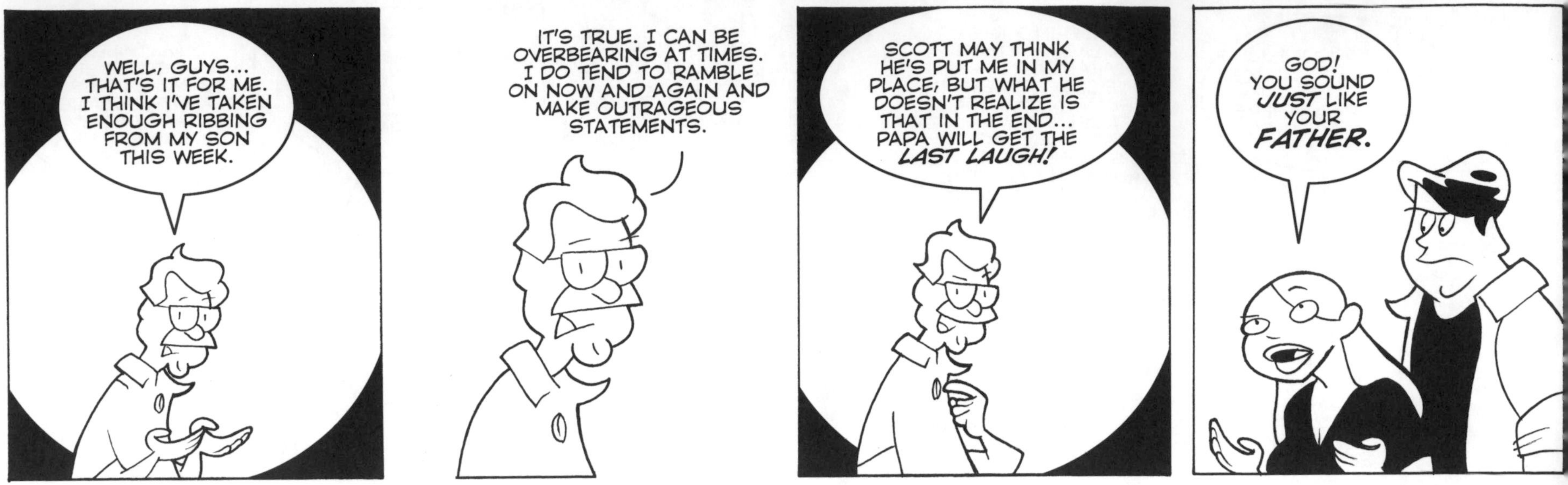
WELL, GUYS... THAT'S IT FOR ME. I THINK I'VE TAKEN ENOUGH RIBBING FROM MY SON THIS WEEK.
IT'S TRUE. I CAN BE OVERBEARING AT TIMES. I DO TEND TO RAMBLE ON NOW AND AGAIN AND MAKE OUTRAGEOUS STATEMENTS.
SCOTT MAY THINK HE'S PUT ME IN MY PLACE, BUT WHAT HE DOESN'T REALIZE IS THAT IN THE END... PAPA WILL GET THE *LAST LAUGH!*
GOD! YOU SOUND *JUST* LIKE YOUR *FATHER.*

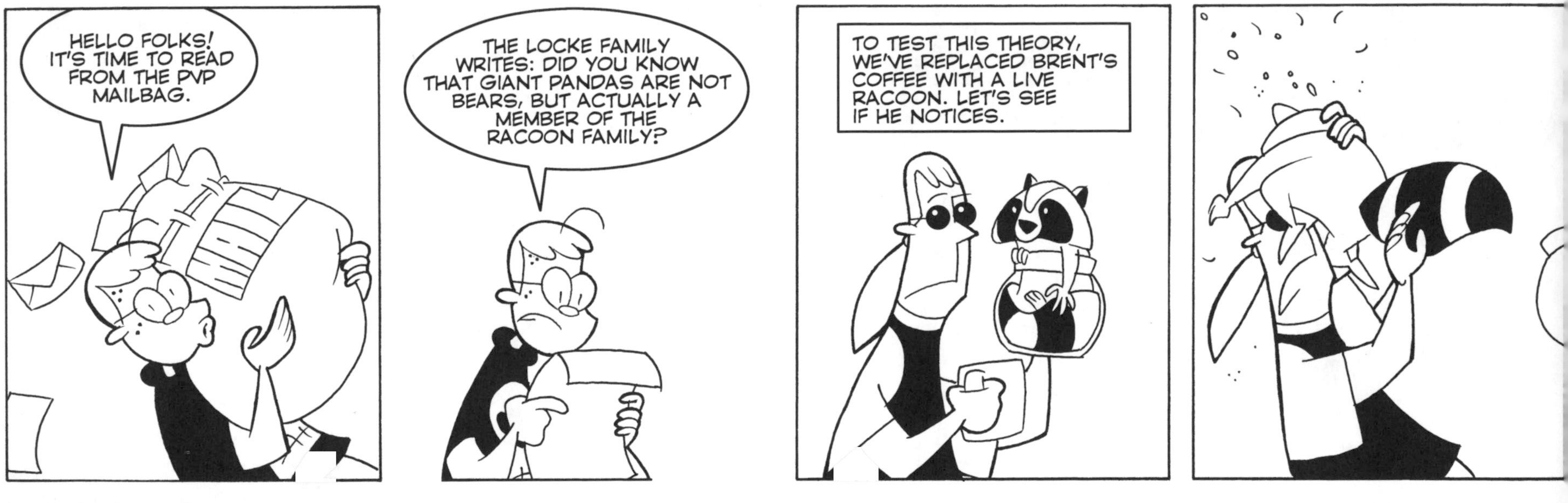
HELLO FOLKS! IT'S TIME TO READ FROM THE PVP MAILBAG.
THE LOCKE FAMILY WRITES: DID YOU KNOW THAT GIANT PANDAS ARE NOT BEARS, BUT ACTUALLY A MEMBER OF THE RACOON FAMILY?
TO TEST THIS THEORY, WE'VE REPLACED BRENT'S COFFEE WITH A LIVE RACOON. LET'S SEE IF HE NOTICES.

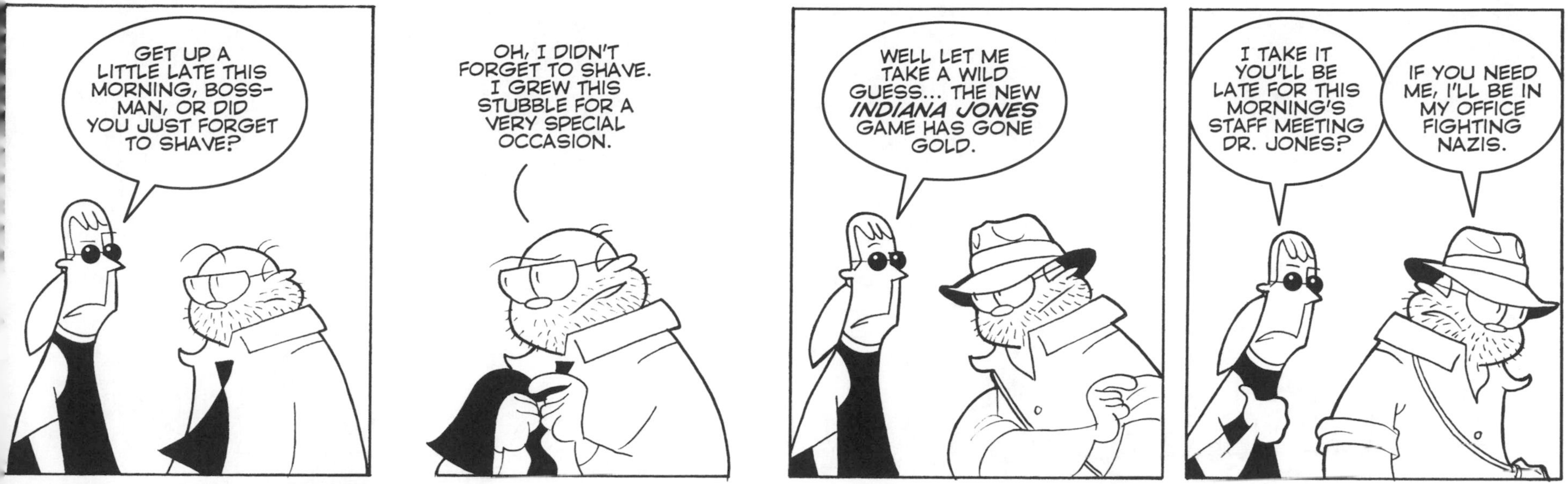
GET UP A LITTLE LATE THIS MORNING, BOSS-MAN, OR DID YOU JUST FORGET TO SHAVE?
OH, I DIDN'T FORGET TO SHAVE. I GREW THIS STUBBLE FOR A VERY SPECIAL OCCASION.
WELL LET ME TAKE A WILD GUESS... THE NEW *INDIANA JONES* GAME HAS GONE GOLD.
I TAKE IT YOU'LL BE LATE FOR THIS MORNING'S STAFF MEETING DR. JONES?
IF YOU NEED ME, I'LL BE IN MY OFFICE FIGHTING NAZIS.

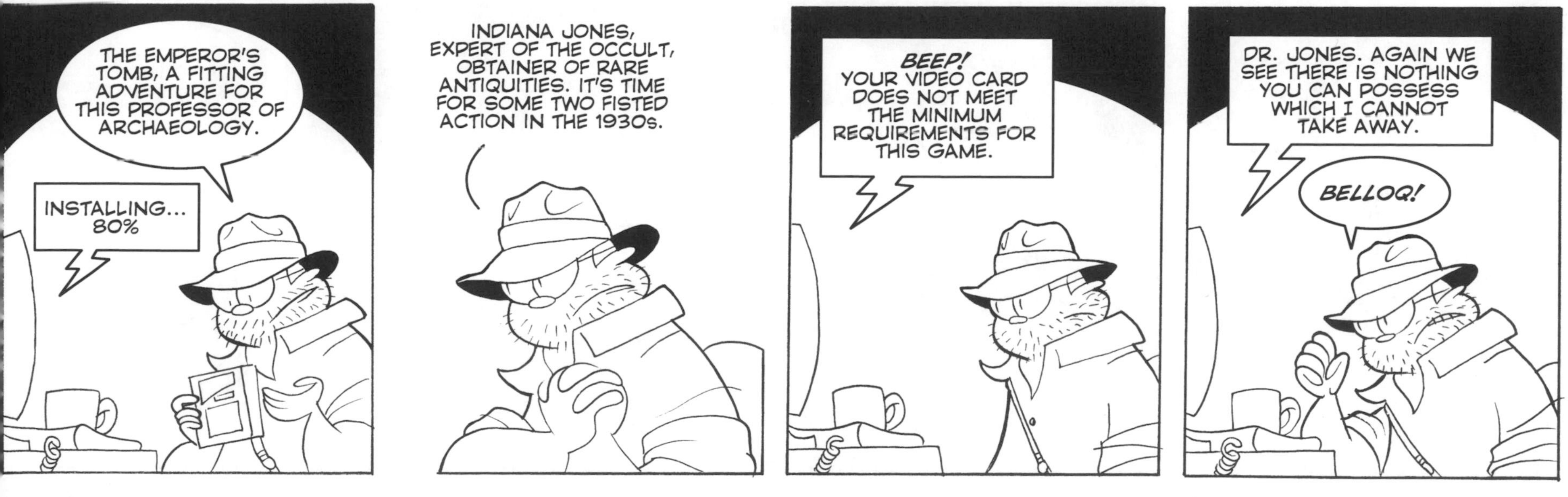
THE EMPEROR'S TOMB, A FITTING ADVENTURE FOR THIS PROFESSOR OF ARCHAEOLOGY.
INSTALLING... 80%
INDIANA JONES, EXPERT OF THE OCCULT, OBTAINER OF RARE ANTIQUITIES. IT'S TIME FOR SOME TWO FISTED ACTION IN THE 1930s.
BEEP! YOUR VIDEO CARD DOES NOT MEET THE MINIMUM REQUIREMENTS FOR THIS GAME.
DR. JONES. AGAIN WE SEE THERE IS NOTHING YOU CAN POSSESS WHICH I CANNOT TAKE AWAY.
BELLOQ!

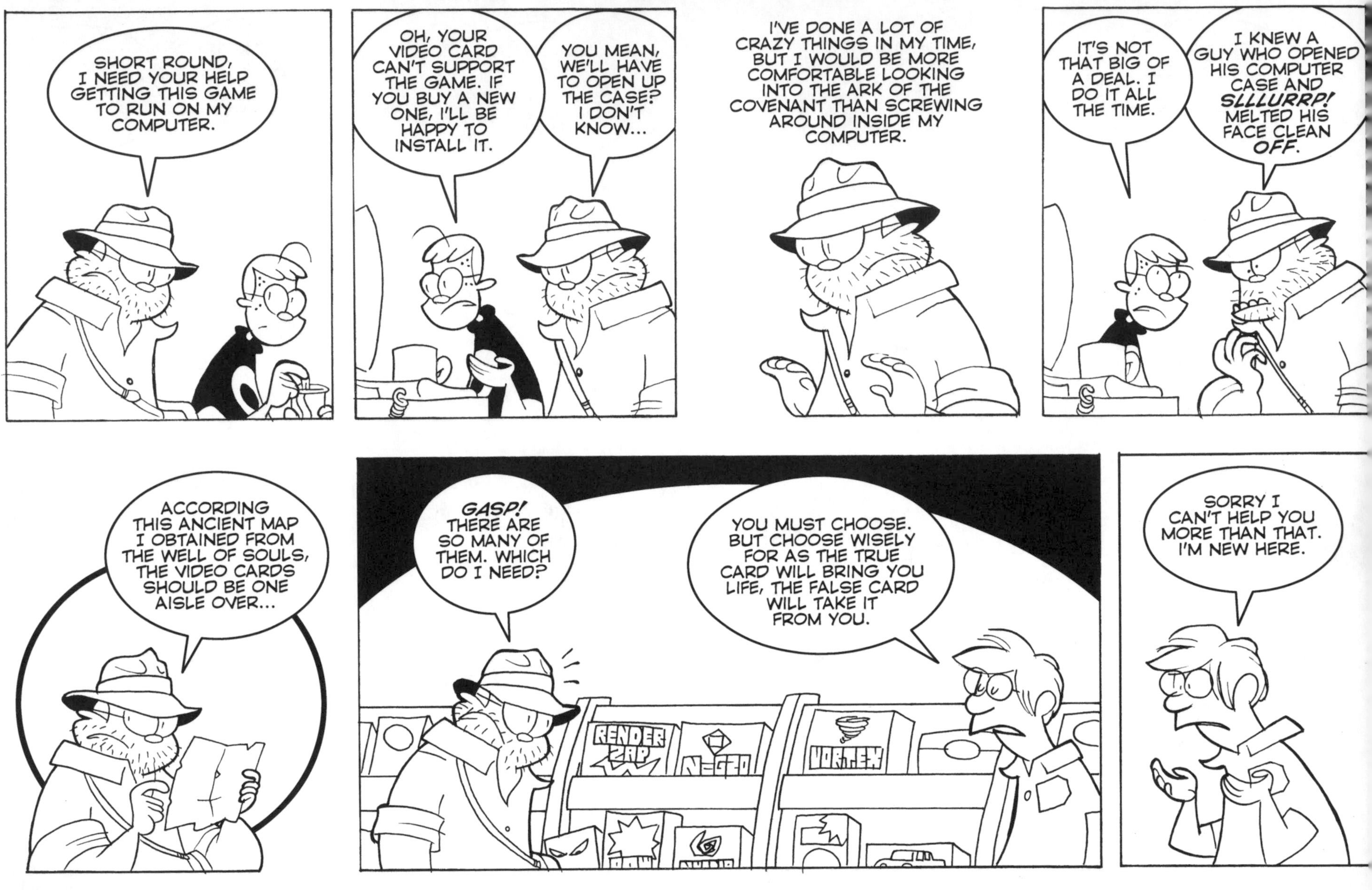
SHORT ROUND, I NEED YOUR HELP GETTING THIS GAME TO RUN ON MY COMPUTER.
OH, YOUR VIDEO CARD CAN'T SUPPORT THE GAME. IF YOU BUY A NEW ONE, I'LL BE HAPPY TO INSTALL IT.
YOU MEAN, WE'LL HAVE TO OPEN UP THE CASE? I DON'T KNOW...
I'VE DONE A LOT OF CRAZY THINGS IN MY TIME, BUT I WOULD BE MORE COMFORTABLE LOOKING INTO THE ARK OF THE COVENANT THAN SCREWING AROUND INSIDE MY COMPUTER.
IT'S NOT THAT BIG OF A DEAL. I DO IT ALL THE TIME.
I KNEW A GUY WHO OPENED HIS COMPUTER CASE AND ***SLLLURRP!*** MELTED HIS FACE CLEAN ***OFF***.
ACCORDING THIS ANCIENT MAP I OBTAINED FROM THE WELL OF SOULS, THE VIDEO CARDS SHOULD BE ONE AISLE OVER...
GASP! THERE ARE SO MANY OF THEM. WHICH DO I NEED?
YOU MUST CHOOSE. BUT CHOOSE WISELY FOR AS THE TRUE CARD WILL BRING YOU LIFE, THE FALSE CARD WILL TAKE IT FROM YOU.
RENDER ZAP
VORTEX
SORRY I CAN'T HELP YOU MORE THAN THAT. I'M NEW HERE.

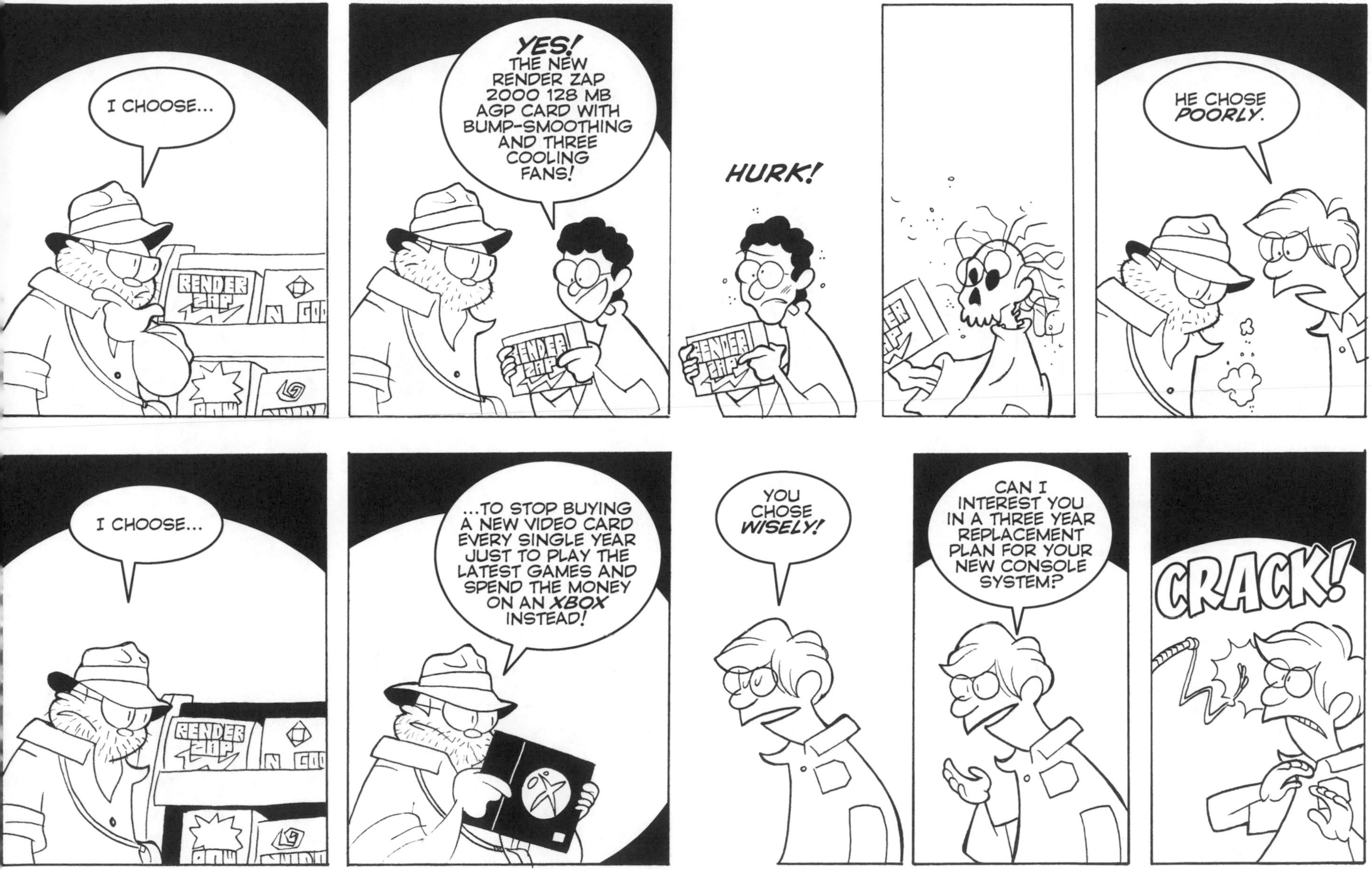
I CHOOSE...
YES! THE NEW RENDER ZAP 2000 128 MB AGP CARD WITH BUMP-SMOOTHING AND THREE COOLING FANS!
HURK!
HE CHOSE POORLY.
I CHOOSE...
...TO STOP BUYING A NEW VIDEO CARD EVERY SINGLE YEAR JUST TO PLAY THE LATEST GAMES AND SPEND THE MONEY ON AN XBOX INSTEAD!
YOU CHOSE WISELY!
CAN I INTEREST YOU IN A THREE YEAR REPLACEMENT PLAN FOR YOUR NEW CONSOLE SYSTEM?
CRACK!

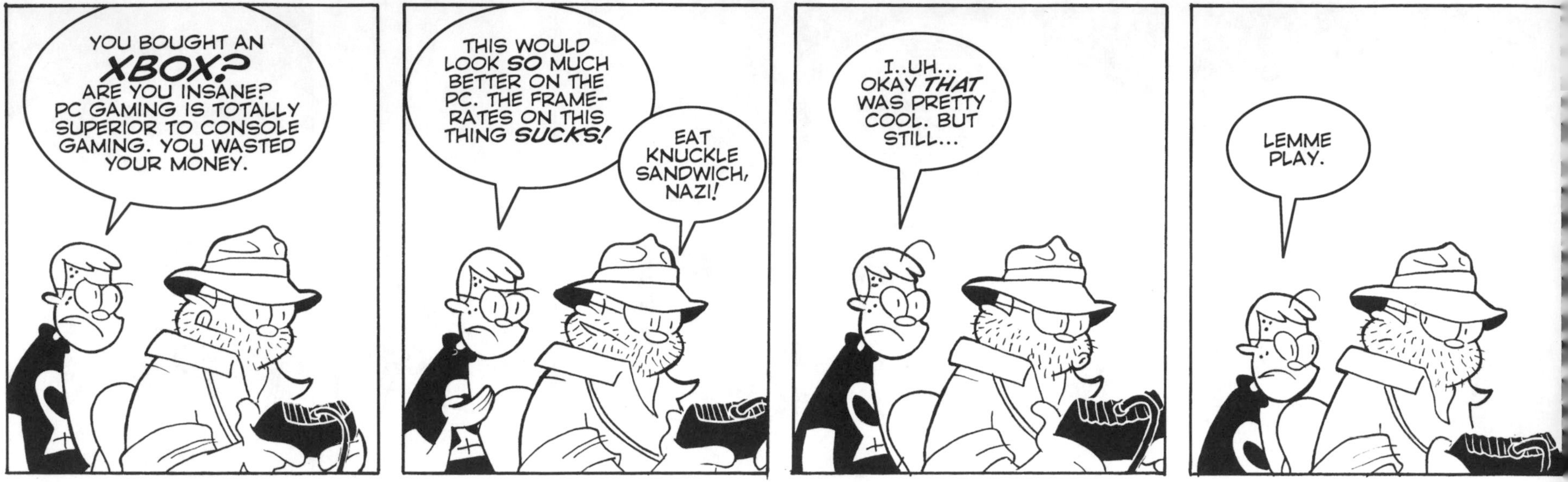
YOU BOUGHT AN XBOX? ARE YOU INSANE? PC GAMING IS TOTALLY SUPERIOR TO CONSOLE GAMING. YOU WASTED YOUR MONEY.
THIS WOULD LOOK SO MUCH BETTER ON THE PC. THE FRAME-RATES ON THIS THING SUCKS!
EAT KNUCKLE SANDWICH, NAZI!
I..UH... OKAY THAT WAS PRETTY COOL. BUT STILL...
LEMME PLAY.

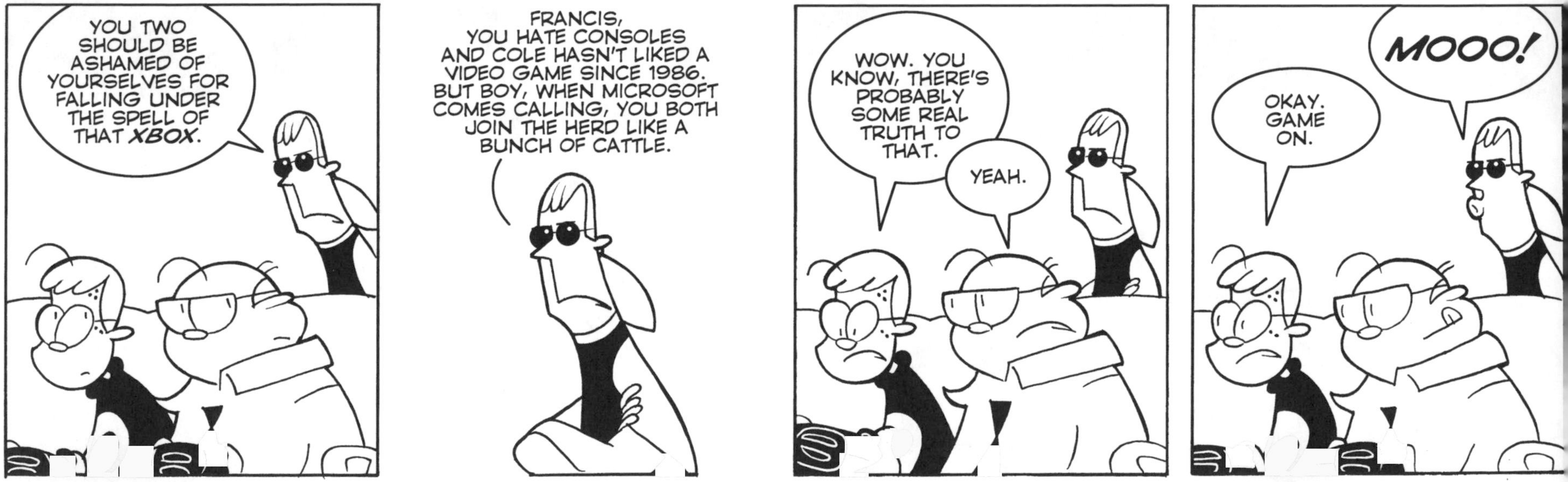
YOU TWO SHOULD BE ASHAMED OF YOURSELVES FOR FALLING UNDER THE SPELL OF THAT XBOX.
FRANCIS, YOU HATE CONSOLES AND COLE HASN'T LIKED A VIDEO GAME SINCE 1986. BUT BOY, WHEN MICROSOFT COMES CALLING, YOU BOTH JOIN THE HERD LIKE A BUNCH OF CATTLE.
WOW. YOU KNOW, THERE'S PROBABLY SOME REAL TRUTH TO THAT.
YEAH.
OKAY. GAME ON.
MOOO!

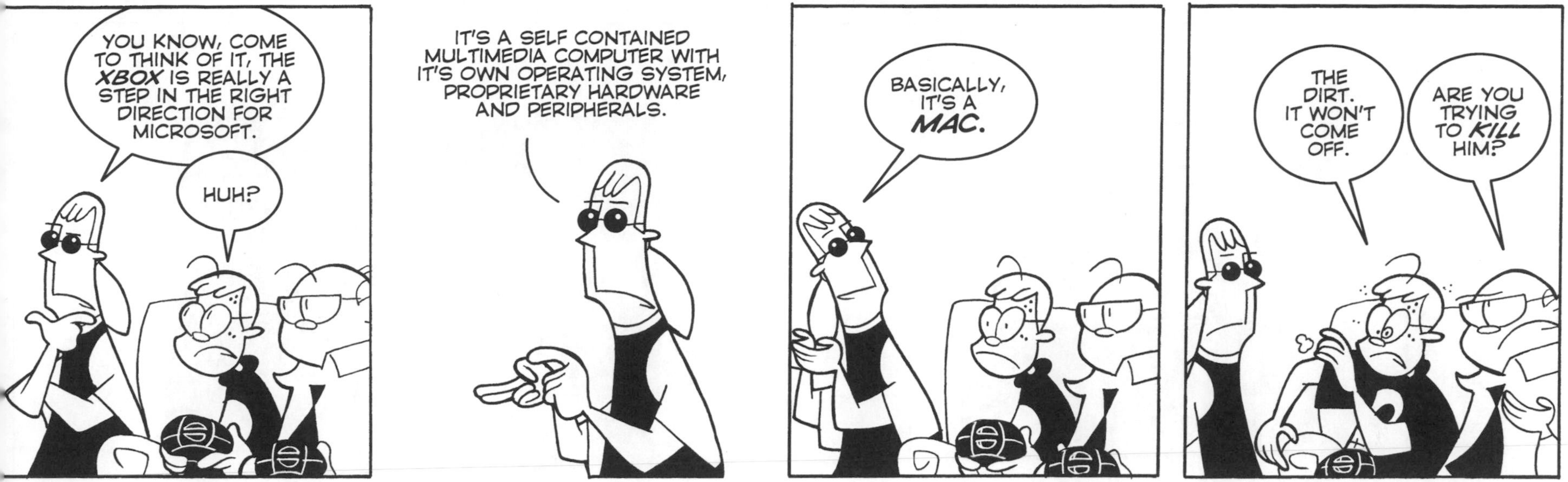
YOU KNOW, COME TO THINK OF IT, THE XBOX IS REALLY A STEP IN THE RIGHT DIRECTION FOR MICROSOFT.
HUH?
IT'S A SELF CONTAINED MULTIMEDIA COMPUTER WITH IT'S OWN OPERATING SYSTEM, PROPRIETARY HARDWARE AND PERIPHERALS.
BASICALLY, IT'S A MAC.
THE DIRT. IT WON'T COME OFF.
ARE YOU TRYING TO KILL HIM?

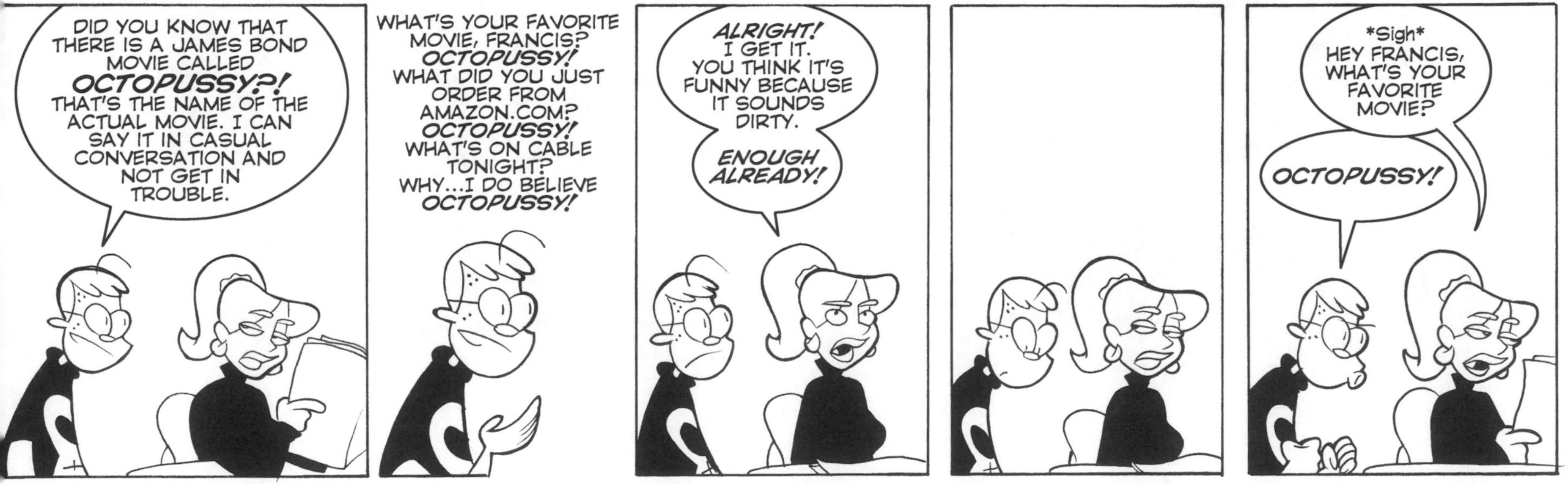
DID YOU KNOW THAT THERE IS A JAMES BOND MOVIE CALLED OCTOPUSSY?! THAT'S THE NAME OF THE ACTUAL MOVIE. I CAN SAY IT IN CASUAL CONVERSATION AND NOT GET IN TROUBLE.
WHAT'S YOUR FAVORITE MOVIE, FRANCIS? OCTOPUSSY! WHAT DID YOU JUST ORDER FROM AMAZON.COM? OCTOPUSSY! WHAT'S ON CABLE TONIGHT? WHY...I DO BELIEVE OCTOPUSSY!
ALRIGHT! I GET IT. YOU THINK IT'S FUNNY BECAUSE IT SOUNDS DIRTY.
ENOUGH ALREADY!
Sigh HEY FRANCIS, WHAT'S YOUR FAVORITE MOVIE?
OCTOPUSSY!

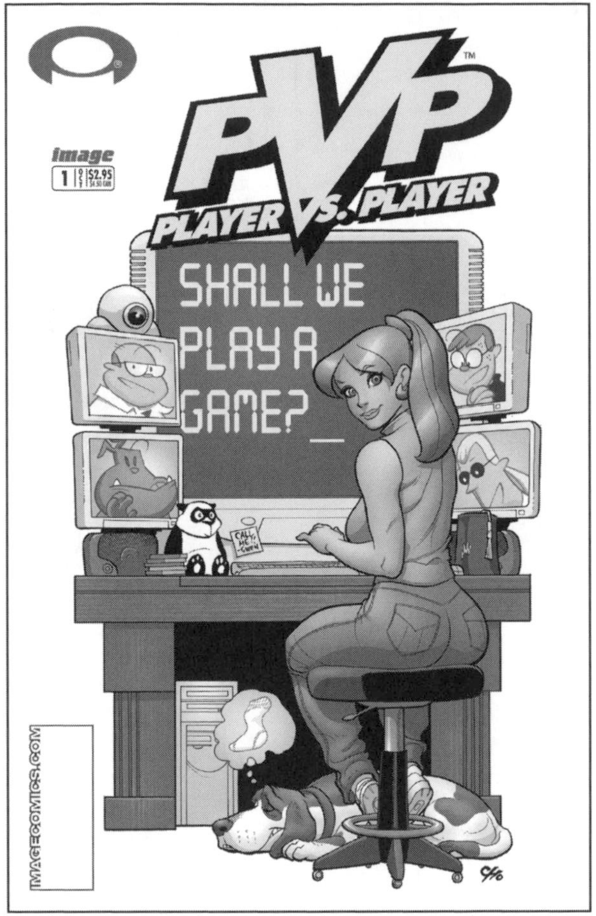
image
1
$2.95
PVP
PLAYER VS. PLAYER
SHALL WE PLAY A GAME?_
IMAGECOMICS.COM

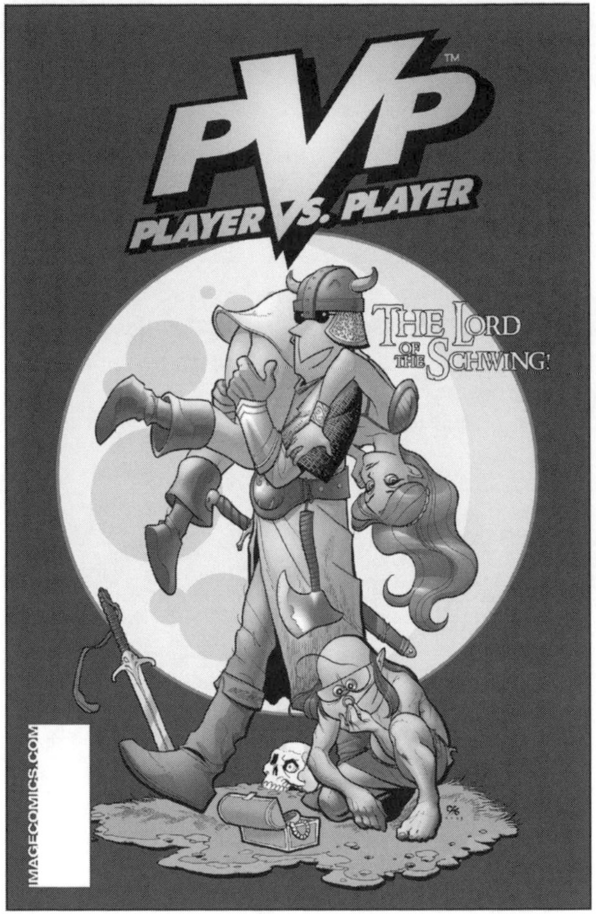
PVP
PLAYER VS. PLAYER
THE LORD OF THE SCHWING!
IMAGECOMICS.COM

Frank Cho (of Liberty Meadows fame) was kind enough to illustrate the first two covers of PvP.

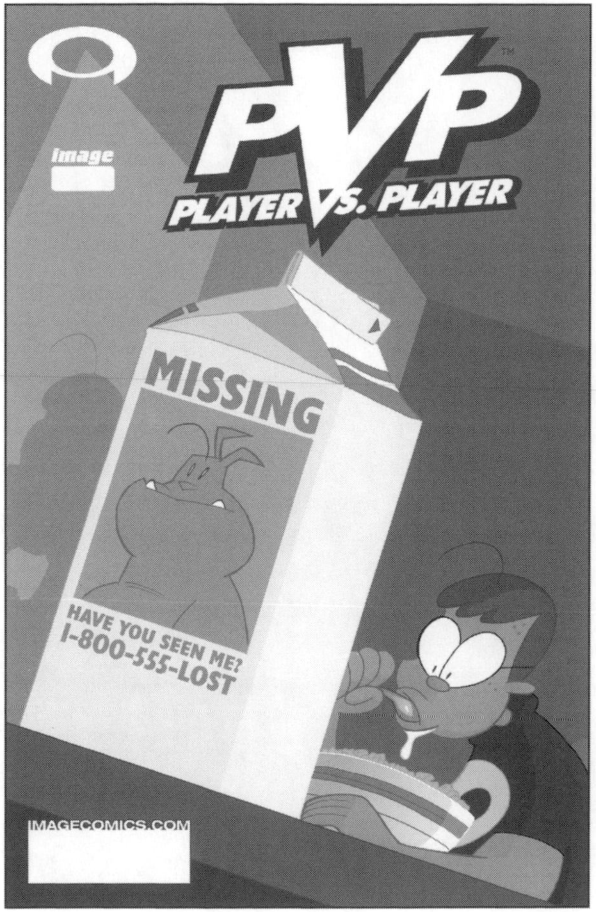
PVP
PLAYER VS. PLAYER
image
MISSING
HAVE YOU SEEN ME?
1-800-555-LOST
IMAGECOMICS.COM

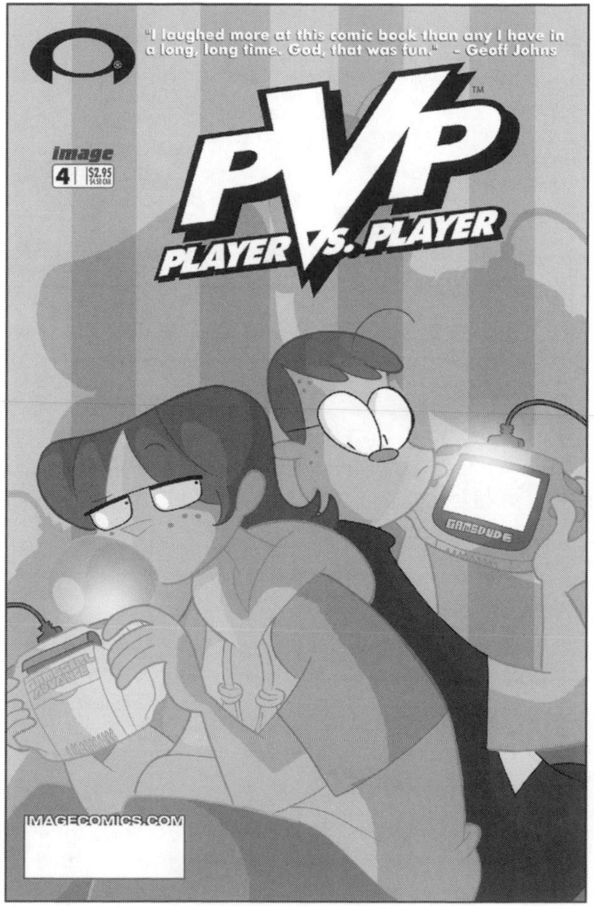
"I laughed more at this comic book than any I have in a long, long time. God, that was fun." - Geoff Johns
PVP
PLAYER VS. PLAYER
image
4
$2.95
GAMEDUDE
IMAGECOMICS.COM

IMAGE COMICS GROUP
image
PVP
PLAYER VS. PLAYER
CAUGHT IN THE CLUTCHES OF: MAX POWERS
IMAGECOMICS.COM

image
PVP
PLAYER VS. PLAYER
IMAGECOMICS.COM
KOCHALKA

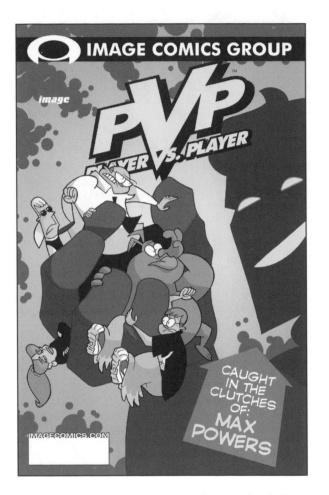

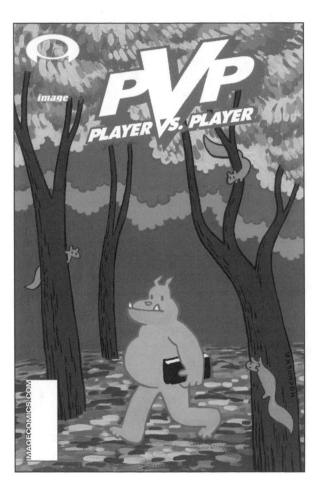

Issue six featured a fully painted cover by indie artist James Kochalka

MORE GREAT BOOKS FROM IMAGE COMICS

For a comic shop near you carrying graphic novels from Image Comics, please call toll free: 1-888-COMIC-BOOK

AGE OF BRONZE
VOL. 1: A THOUSAND SHIPS TP
ISBN# 1582402000
$19.95
VOL. 2: SACRIFICE HC
ISBN# 1582403600
$29.95

THE AMAZING JOY BUZZARDS, VOL. 1 TP
ISBN# 1582404984
$11.95

THE BLACK FOREST
VOL. 1 GN
ISBN# 1582403503
$9.95
VOL. 2: CASTLE OF SHADOWS GN
ISBN# 1582405611
$6.99

DAWN
VOL. 1: LUCIFER'S HALO NEW ED TP
ISBN# 1582405689
$17.99
VOL. 1: LUCIFER'S HALO
SUPPLEMENTAL BOOK TP
ISBN# 1582405697
$12.99

DEATH, JR TP
ISBN# 1582405263
$14.99

EARTHBOY JACOBUS GN
ISBN# 1582404925
$17.95

FLIGHT
VOL. 1 GN
ISBN# 1582403816
$19.95
VOL. 2 GN
ISBN# 1582404771
$24.95

GIRLS, VOL 1: CONCEPTION TP
ISBN# 1582405298
$14.99

GRRL SCOUTS
VOL. 1 TP
ISBN# 1582403163
$12.95
VOL. 2: WORK SUCKS TP
ISBN# 1582403430
$12.95

GUN FU, VOL 1 TP
ISBN# 1582405212
$14.95

HAWAIIAN DICK, VOL. 1:
BYRD OF PARADISE TP
ISBN# 1582403171
$14.95

KANE
VOL. 1:
GREETINGS FROM NEW EDEN TP
ISBN# 1582403406
$11.95
VOL. 2: RABBIT HUNT TP
ISBN# 1582403554
$12.95
VOL. 3: HISTORIES TP
ISBN# 1582403821
$12.95

VOL. 4: THIRTY NINTH TP
ISBN# 1582404682
$16.95
VOL. 5: UNTOUCHABLE RICO COSTAS &
OTHER STORIES TP
ISBN# 1582405514
$13.99

LAZARUS CHURCHYARD:
THE FINAL CUT GN
ISBN# 1582401802
$14.95

PvP
THE DORK AGES TP
ISBN# 1582403457
$11.95
VOL. 1: PVP AT LARGE TP
ISBN# 1582403740
$11.95
VOL. 2: PVP RELOADED TP
ISBN# 158240433X
$11.95
VOL. 3: PVP RIDES AGAIN TP
ISBN# 1582405530
$11.99

REX MUNDI
VOL. 1: THE GUARDIAN OF THE TEMPLE TP
ISBN# 158240268X
$14.95
VOL. 2:THE RIVER UNDERGROUND TP
ISBN# 1582404798
$14.95

RIDE, VOL. 1 TP
ISBN# 1582405220
$9.99

RONIN HOOD OF THE 47 SAMURAI
ISBN# 1582405557
$9.99

SEA OF RED, VOL. 1:
NO GRAVE BUT THE SEA TP
ISBN# 1582405379
$8.95

SPAWN
SPAWN COLLECTION, VOL. 1 TP
ISBN# 1582405638
$19.95
SPAWN MANGA, VOL. 1 TP
ISBN# 1582405719
$9.99

TOMMYSAURUS REX GN
ISBN# 1582403953
$11.95

ULTRA: SEVEN DAYS TP
ISBN# 1582404836
$17.95

THE WALKING DEAD
VOL. 1: DAYS GONE BYE TP
ISBN# 1582403589
$12.95
VOL. 2: MILES BEHIND US TP
ISBN# 1582404135
$12.95
VOL. 3: SAFETY BEHIND BARS TP
ISBN# 1582404879
$12.95
VOL. 4: THE HEART'S DESIRE TP
ISBN# 1582405301
$12.99